Losing the Plot

Losing the Plot

FILM AND FEELING
IN THE MODERN NOVEL

Pardis Dabashi

THE UNIVERSITY OF CHICAGO PRESS
CHICAGO AND LONDON

The University of Chicago Press, Chicago 60637
The University of Chicago Press, Ltd., London
© 2023 by The University of Chicago
All rights reserved. No part of this book may be used or reproduced in any manner whatsoever without written permission, except in the case of brief quotations in critical articles and reviews. For more information, contact the University of Chicago Press, 1427 East 60th St., Chicago, IL 60637.
Published 2023
Printed and bound by CPI Group (UK) Ltd, Croydon, CR0 4YY

32 31 30 29 28 27 26 25 24 23   1 2 3 4 5
ISBN-13: 978-0-226-82924-1 (cloth)
ISBN-13: 978-0-226-82925-8 (paper)
ISBN-13: 978-0-226-82926-5 (e-book)
DOI: https://doi.org/10.7208/chicago/9780226829265.001.0001

The University of Chicago Press gratefully acknowledges the generous support of Bryn Mawr College toward the publication of this book.

Library of Congress Cataloging-in-Publication Data

Names: Dabashi, Pardis, author.
Title: Losing the plot : film and feeling in the modern novel / Pardis Dabashi.
Description: Chicago : The University of Chicago Press, 2023. | Includes bibliographical references and index.
Identifiers: LCCN 2023012215 | ISBN 9780226829241 (cloth) | ISBN 9780226829258 (paperback) | ISBN 9780226829265 (ebook)
Subjects: LCSH: Larsen, Nella. Quicksand. | Barnes, Djuna. Nightwood. | Dietrich, Marlene. | Faulkner, William, 1897–1962. Sound and the fury. | Ophuls, Max, 1902–1957—Criticism and interpretation. | Camille (Motion picture : 1936) | Madame de . . . (Motion picture) | Motion pictures and literature—United States. | American literature—20th century—History and criticism. | Plots (Drama, novel, etc.) | Motion pictures—History.
Classification: LCC PN1995.3 .D23 2023 | DDC 813/.509—dc23/eng/20230505
LC record available at https://lccn.loc.gov/2023012215

♾ This paper meets the requirements of ANSI/NISO Z39.48-1992 (Permanence of Paper).

*To Ali Alemohammad (1922–1992),
who started it all.*

Those who believe in the unseen . . .

—Qur'an 2:3

الَّذِينَ يُؤْمِنُونَ بِالْغَيْبِ

—سورة البقرة : ٣

Contents

INTRODUCTION:
THE ARTS OF INCONSEQUENCE 1

1: NELLA LARSEN AND GRETA GARBO:
ON (IN)CONSEQUENCE 43

PREMIÈRE ENTR'ACTE 85

2: DJUNA BARNES AND MARLENE DIETRICH:
ON THE SECURITY OF TORMENT 89

DEUXIÈME ENTR'ACTE 127

3: WILLIAM FAULKNER AND EARLY FILM:
ON THE LIMITS OF THE PRESENT 131

CODA:
MAX OPHULS: ON LOVE AND FINITUDE 177

Acknowledgments 231
Notes 235
Index 271

INTRODUCTION

The Arts of Inconsequence

> *There the flawed became whole, the blind sighted, and the lame and halt threw away their crutches. There death was dead, and people made every gesture in a cloud of music. There the black-and-white images came together, making a magnificent whole—all projected through the ray of light from above and behind.*
>
> TONI MORRISON, *The Bluest Eye*

On multiple occasions in 1935, Emily Coleman's letters to close friend and fellow writer Djuna Barnes were permeated with enormous self-consciousness. Coleman was unofficially editing Barnes's novel-in-progress, *Nightwood*, and helping to place it at Faber and Faber. But she was also herself completing a book; and though she wanted very much for Barnes to read it, she was scared of what Barnes would think of it. What Coleman was absolutely certain would displease Barnes was that her novel had a plot. "My book is a story, Djuna," she writes on May 2, "That's what I'm afraid you won't like. I like to tell a story. I just can't help it. I can't write anything without a dramatic plot."[1] And on August 1, she again writes, "I am very anxious for you to see this book—but Djuna, it has a PLOT." A "natural plot, which just came to hand," she continues, rationalizing her aesthetic choice, "starting with facts, and then it just unrolled, and char-acter is created. Which I believe to be essential, if you are going to show anything through passion. Because passion does not exist without char-acter, in my humble opinion. These 2 facts (plot & character) I am afraid are going to put you off the book, with your ideas on the same, and then I shall be brokenhearted."[2] And finally, on October 27, her preemptive self-protection reaches a fever pitch: "Please SAY EXACTLY WHAT YOU THINK. Otherwise I will not send it [to you]. Especially say what you do not like."[3]

Coleman's book would unfortunately never go on to be published. But the intensity of her nervousness in showing a plotted novel to her "hellraising Djuna,"[4] whose own novel would be championed by T. S. Eliot and eventually cement Barnes's place within the high-modernist literary canon, exposes effectively the stigma attached to plot in modernism. Coleman's sheepishness about plot is evidenced in the way that she minimizes her statements by making them personal to her, adding an "I believe" or an "in my humble opinion" to otherwise Aristotelian claims concerning the interdependence of action and character that largely govern realist fiction. And as if to exonerate herself, she pervades her explanation—for she is indeed explaining herself—with a language of automaticity: "I just can't help it"; "a natural plot, which just came to hand, starting with facts, and then it just unrolled." It's not my fault, Djuna, please don't judge me; plot just sort of happened.

Coleman's embarrassment in front of her cool modernist friend for writing a plot and believing in its value as a formal vehicle for character and passion is consistent with one of the articles of literary-critical faith this book wishes to defamiliarize so as to complicate: that a definitive feature of modernist fiction and an index of its emphatic departure from realism was its devaluation, if not abandonment, of plot. There are a number of very good reasons why this assumption has become so familiar as often to warrant merely cursory mention if not tacit presupposition, not the least of which is that early celebrations of modernism helped to generate it. As early as the 1930s, the negative force of modernist aesthetics was thought to be bound up in its abandonment of plot as plot was mobilized in the nineteenth-century novel. In the writings of Theodor Adorno, for example, one of the twentieth century's harshest critics of narrative unity, what affords modernism its critical purchase is its ability to reflect in its fragmented form the internal contradictions of capitalist modernity and its entanglements with fascistic thought.[5] Bertolt Brecht's theorization and practical development of the alienation effect (*Verfremdungseffect*) in modern theater, meanwhile, was a similar attempt to interrogate the stupefying effects he believed were elicited by plot and its invitation to narrative immersion associated with the bourgeois interests of the dramatic theater.[6] And for early critics such as Edmund Wilson and eventually Joseph Frank, modernism's devaluation of plot in favor of formal experiments with the discontinuities of time, space, and style—modernism's "spatial form," as Frank put it—makes it what Wilson called in *Axel's Castle* "a self-conscious and very important literary movement."[7] And although critical, rather than celebratory, Georg Lukács's Marxist reading of the "ideology of modernism" assumes that modernism turns away from action and structures of causality by amplifying what he considers the politically impoverished "descriptive method" of naturalists such as Émile Zola and Gustave Flaubert.[8]

And this early belief that modernism's critical and aesthetic élan extends from its rejection of plot as the most constrictive inheritance of the nineteenth-century novel draws further authority from modernist authors' own denunciations of plot. In her essay, "Modern Fiction," for instance, Virginia Woolf writes that the realist author seems "constrained, not by his own free will but by some powerful and unscrupulous tyrant who has him in thrall to provide a plot." "Is life like this?" she asks. Far from it. Woolf calls for a fiction not "in thrall" to the artificial contrivances of narrative but one that would track the labyrinthine pathways of human consciousness and experience as they are lived, a literature that attests to what she famously calls the "incessant shower of innumerable atoms." She thus proposes that modern authors "record the atoms as they fall upon the mind in the order in which they fall," that they "trace the pattern, however disconnected and incoherent in appearance, which each sight or incident scores upon the consciousness."[9] Henry James, meanwhile, in the 1907 preface to the New York edition of *Roderick Hudson*, anticipates Woolf's remarks about the plotlessness of life, writing that because "really, universally, relations stop nowhere," it is the "exquisite problem of the artist" to "draw, by a geometry of his own, the circle within which they shall *appear* to do so."[10] And despite its shrill misogyny, Filippo Tommaso Marinetti's *The Futurist Manifesto* articulates an integral element of modernism's alleged impatience with the immersive pleasures of storytelling when it says, "Literature has up to now magnified pensive immobility, ecstasy and slumber. We want to exalt movements of aggression, feverish sleeplessness, the double march, the perilous leap, the slap and the blow of the fist."[11]

But Barnes's response to Coleman does not support the view that plot in modernism is an object of unequivocal disdain (let alone the target of a blow with the fist) or that it is completely divorced from the realities of lived time. As a result, her response goes some way toward introducing the central argument of this book. "I am happy you are so glad about your book, and so pleased with it," she writes back on August 19, 1935. "I can't wait to get my hands on it. I do not recall," she continues, "ever having said I disliked plot . . . but that I simply could do nothing about it, tho I did say that I did not think that life (which is not a work of art, God knows) has little or none."[12] The double (if not quadruple) negative in this final clause obstructs Barnes's meaning—a moment in her otherwise clearly written letters that resembles her obscure literary prose. But what she is saying, counterintuitively as a modernist, is that life *does* have some measure of plot, that she does not actually disdain plot in the way that Coleman fears, and finally, that—like Coleman—she feels powerless over it: "I simply could do nothing about it." What emerges here is a vision of plot not as the work of a tyrant, an artificial ruse, or a constriction that the writer, in order to be modern, must cast aside so as to do the supposedly real, more serious work of capturing life "as it is." Instead, what emerges in Barnes's remarks is a vision of plot as a powerful force with which she does not quite know how to contend and a vision of life as itself permeated, however minimally, by the contours of narrative. For Barnes, plot has a hold on us; and perhaps that is because, contra Woolf's and James's remarks, it is indeed not entirely unlike life.[13]

Taking a page from Barnes and Coleman's exchange, *Losing the Plot* contends with the fortitude of plot as a formal operation, plot's power to work on us even against our will or better judgment. That fortitude was for Samuel Taylor Coleridge what made reading novels akin to being in a dream state, robbed of volition; it is precisely what has historically rationalized the critical dismissal of plot, especially among modernist theorists, as the feature within the temporal arts—that "low atavist form," as E. M. Forster puts it—to be gotten past so as to discern what its pleasures conceal.[14] But this study lingers with that fortitude, taking it seriously as an index of existential—rather than just readerly—desire, *despite* what those pleasures conceal. Plots have a hold on us not only because they make us want to read or watch further. Rather, they make us want to read or watch further because, as Walter Benjamin famously claims, they give us a temporary fictional vehicle through which to imagine our own lives as being cradled by a secure narrative architecture.[15] Within the history of modernist studies, plot in the nineteenth-century novel tends to have a reputation for being the aesthetic proxy for forms of social control and ideologically pernicious constraint. And the function of plot's immersive pleasures, most notably in the work of Roland Barthes and eventually D. A. Miller, is thought to be the camouflaging and thus naturalizing of that ideological project, the process through which plot, in Miller's words, brings deviant formal contingencies "into line."[16] Modernism's refusal to allow readers to get immersed in the story of, say, Leopold Bloom or Clarissa Dalloway in quite the same way one would that of Honoré de Balzac's Rastignac or Charles Dickens's Pip thus extends from the modernist impulse to disrupt readerly complacency by exposing the discursivity of literary worlds, denaturalizing their ideological work by showing their textual seams. In the process, they not only depict a modern world bereft of theological design, collective sources of normative value, and formal reconciliation—the persistence, as Adorno would have it, of nonidentity—but they also attempt to disrupt the process by which plot, perhaps better than any other formal vehicle, can subtly inculcate in its readers or viewers normative expectations for how to be.

And undoubtedly to the disappointment of some, this book will not actually claim the contrary. *Losing the Plot* will not recuperate nineteenth-century plot—romance, domestic, and bildungsroman plots in particular—as formal operations *not* bent toward the prescription and institutionalization of normative life. It will largely adhere to the view of these plots as productive of various forms of political, social, and ideological constraint. And this is not because those plots are not themselves far more complex and replete with self-reflective complications than what we might call the "complicity" model of plot historically prevalent among students of modernism would seem to accommodate.[17] *Losing the Plot* relies on the complicity model of bourgeois plot for the simple but important reason that this is how it gets depicted in the modernist period not only by its early theorists but also, as this book will examine, the novels of modernist authors themselves. There is a reason, for instance, that Coleman was convinced Barnes would not like her book on the grounds that it tells a coherent story about coherent characters. As Barnes's unofficial editor of *Nightwood* during its early stages of development, Coleman was intimately familiar with Barnes's radical experiments with narrative form. She knew and often struggled with how central it was to the force of Barnes's aesthetic intervention to flout the formal mandates of storytelling precisely because those mandates, as they are pit in *Nightwood*, correspond to the heteronormative concepts of character and temporal continuity that were central to domestic fiction and as such were inhospitable to the affective intensities and marginal social positionalities that Barnes was committed to exploring aesthetically.

What *Losing the Plot* does claim, however, is that despite the emphatic and often polemical claims against plot in early twentieth-century literary and critical discourse, the modernist novels this book examines do not retreat from plot with any measure of polemical *certainty*. To the contrary, if an art form can be said to have an attitude, these major works of modernist fiction betray profound *ambivalence* vis-à-vis the devaluation of plot in favor of what Anna Kornbluh, by way of Giorgio Agamben, might call a "destituent" aesthetics that values disassemblage over assemblage.[18] These novels both theorize plot's teleological ordering as coextensive with forms of social, psychic, and political unfreedom and at the same time express deep longing for the existential supports that they understand those forms to provide. This book thus argues that plot emerges in the work of Barnes, Nella Larsen, and William Faulkner as an aesthetic constraint rife with existential allure. *Losing the Plot* examines what happens to modernist literary form when it does two contradictory things simultaneously: when it critiques plot's complicity while also expressing the intractable existential temptations of that complicity. When it sees plot as a point of foreclosure to opportunities for more emancipated modes of being and nevertheless still says, "I just can't help it" and "I can't wait to get my hands on it." In so doing, these novelists express profound ambivalence vis-à-vis their own negative commitments.

But an important caveat presents itself, which is that modernism does not entirely jettison plot to begin with. Thus, to claim that modernists were ambivalent about rejecting a formal feature that no one thinks they actually fully rejected anyway might strike us as counterintuitive. The so-called mythical method, for instance, names the persistence of the epic plot in modernism (best emblematized in *Ulysses*) as a form of making meaning where modernity seems to have stripped meaning away. Indeed, in some cases, such as in F. Scott Fitzgerald, Joseph Conrad, D. H. Lawrence, Ernest Hemingway, and Franz Kafka (even Marcel Proust, some Gertrude Stein, and Henry James), modernist novels tell outright stories—of turning, for instance, into a bug, of becoming fascinated with a peculiar neighbor and his lifestyle, of the romantic and economic trajectories of three working-class women, of a middle-aged man tasked with bringing home the wayward son of his fiancée.

Nor does modernism fully jettison what below I will insist is a central feature of plot: structures of causality. Gregor transforms into an enormous cockroach, Kurtz arrives in the Congo, Swann meets Odette, and so on. The world is not the same after these events have taken place; they effect an irreversible change in what follows from them. Clarissa Dalloway decides to buy the flowers herself, Isabel Archer suddenly recognizes the significance of her experiences, Gabriel Conroy is stunned by the arresting sight of his wife at the top of a flight of stairs. Modernism carefully explores the nature of events, of action, as well as the complex, obscured, or even latent forms of causality associated with human psychology. And the colossal transitions of history are everywhere registered in the degenerating aristocratic worlds of Barnes, Proust, James, and Joseph Roth; the Jim Crow US of Nella Larsen, Jean Toomer, and Zora Neale Hurston; the traumatized post–World War I Britain of Woolf and Forster; and the New South of Faulkner. Things happen in modernism.

And even when a plot feels especially remote, some form of order, design, or curation persists. *To the Lighthouse*, *The Making of Americans*, even *Finnegans Wake* and *The Unnameable*, are broken up into sections, *Cane* into stories and poems, *Mrs. Dalloway* into hours, *The Man without Quali-*

ties into volumes, *Absalom, Absalom!* into nine massive and unwieldy chapters. Even Lukács's charge that Quentin Compson's stream of consciousness narration exhibits the "bad infinity" that modernism lets loose by diving into the unrestrained territory of the mind rather than remaining fixed to the material life of human action is an exaggeration. Quentin's thoughts are guided by a set of personal and historical anxieties; they are, in ways I describe in chapter 3, tragically, obsessively bounded. While many modernist novels do refuse to tell a coherent story, we would be very hard pressed to find one that fully abandons any ordering structures—the "figures in the carpet," as James would have it—that would make sense of experience if not give it closural form. The Manichean vehemence with which early commentators insisted on modernism's abandonment of plot does not quite correspond to the facts on the ground; it bears the marks of those championing or denouncing the unfamiliar features of a young movement. Even Woolf's remark concerning the "tyranny" of plot is made in the context of an explicitly polemical essay that only partially reflects her own fiction. Modernism has its own injunction to make sense of nonsense, to shore modernity's fragments against its ruin. And to that end, it does not so much lose the plot, we might say, as transform its formal terms to fit different social and historical circumstances.

Sometimes that adaptation takes the form of composing coherent, largely realist plots that otherwise accentuate the limits of human perspective, the materiality and contingency of language, the particularities, if not failures, of subject formation in capitalist, especially urban, modernity. At other times it takes the form of fashioning structural substitutes to take the place of nineteenth-century plot—such as the epiphany, epic schemas, sections, days, hours, or page breaks—that, though perhaps loosening the boundaries integral to much realist narrative structure, nevertheless lend the text some form of order that keeps human experience from seeming an undifferentiated, torrential onslaught of sensorial data and keeps the novel from devolving into a pile of words, if not letters, held together by no frame other than the book binding.[19] And though it may, in its more experimental moments, even reject structures of causality, modernist novels often substitute causality for relations of correlation, constellation, or parataxis. In order to avoid the familiar kinetics of plot as it was dominantly represented in nineteenth-century fiction, as Jacques Rancière has argued, modernism forged alternative ways of connecting one moment to another.[20]

But it is the central contention of this book that for the writers I examine—Nella Larsen, Djuna Barnes, and William Faulkner—those critiques are not undisturbed and those structural substitutes themselves prove inadequate. Indeed, what these writers' novels show ambivalence about letting go of is neither plot nor causality as such. Rather, what becomes an object of complicated longing in the novels under examination here is what those critiques and compensatory relational structures—correlation, constellation, parataxis, and so forth—do not provide despite their attempts to analogously order human experience and consciousness. Those critiques and structural alternatives deliberately do not provide—and often try intentionally to subvert—the psychic and social promises particular to the romance, domestic, and bildungsroman plots of bourgeois realism, the temporary but no less powerful ease, comfort, and satisfaction associated not just with the consumption of realist plots but also with their *existential* promises: imagining one's own life as formally secured within and socially sanctioned by the regime of normative fantasy.

Variously constellational, correlational, or paratactical structures—as they were fashioned by modernists including but not limited to Larsen, Barnes, and Faulkner—were fashioned precisely in order to denaturalize so as to critique the philosophical, social, and political assumptions modernists saw as underpinning the structures of causality in bourgeois realism. The turn toward relations of constellation and away from teleological causality was tantamount to an attempt to expose the ideological dangers of realist aesthetics' acute ability to prescribe and institutionalize conceptual and embodied staples of normative life, namely, possessive liberal individualism, heterosexual marriage, and a progressive and teleological view of history. It is this normative valence—the special ability of plot, as it was perfected in the nineteenth-century bourgeois novel, to prescribe what Lauren Berlant, Michael Warner, and others might describe as "the normal"—that modernism's formal alternatives to bourgeois realism set out to avoid and that the novels I examine nevertheless mourn.

The point is not that modernism releases itself from the shackles of a normativity intractably embedded within realist form and realist plot in particular. Modernism, as we have seen, is not so new and different as that; neither is realism so conservative and monolithic as that. The point, rather, is a media-historical one, broadly speaking, and a film-historical one more specifically. By the time these modernist writers are producing their novels, those nineteenth-century plots are getting mediated through, if not transported to, one of the most popular, commercially successful, and ideologically conservative cultural forms of the twentieth century: the classical Hollywood cinema. *Losing the Plot* argues that it is in the face of that cultural relocation—watching Hollywood films do the cultural, formal, and psychic work of the bourgeois novel, even amplifying its normative promises (or threats)—that modernist novelists come to recognize the psychic and social cost of their critical skepticism of bourgeois plot. That is, the novel recognizes what it loses in the process of refashioning its formal terms from those of the Aristotelian unity central to bourgeois realism to an aesthetics that takes the fragment as its fundamental modality. The writers I examine come to *miss* the normative securities promised by bourgeois plot—not what plot necessarily actually did in nineteenth-century realism but what it came to *feel* like it did once it was redirected through the channel of the silver screen and the shibboleth of Hollywood fantasy, what the realist novel seemed to be able to promise when perceived through the retrospective glow of the Hollywood ending.

Indeed, modernism's ambivalence toward the felt mandate to retreat from plot and how that ambivalence shapes the form of these novels becomes clear once we understand the formal developments of the novel not as endogenous but as an expression of the novel's relationality to other forms, its awareness of and responsiveness to other technologies of representation. This study conceives of the novel not as an isolated art form but as a participant, an agent, in a modern media ecology, a complexly layered ecosystem of cultural technologies that includes literature, painting, sculpture, theater, photography, and film.[21] Modernist literary form is, as Cara L. Lewis puts it, a "dynamic form" created by modernism's intrinsic "intermediality."[22]

But only a select few of the media within the modern media ecology rely on or have intimate histories with *plot*. If we are interested in talking about plot as it gets negotiated in modern aesthetic media, then we find ourselves concentrating primarily on the narrative arts: the novel, theater, and film. And in terms of the strength of their reliance on plot, the two most powerful media among these three were the novel and film. Just as literary modernism was decentering plot in favor of aesthetic experiments with contingency, fragmentation, the aleatory, and the nonclosural, film was becoming, slowly and unevenly, a narrative medium from one primarily geared toward the recording of everyday occurrences. Indeed, at the turn of the century, when Euro-American modernism had started to distance itself from the nineteenth-century novel, film was developing techniques of editing, cinematography, mise-en-scène, and eventually sound that came to dominate narrative feature filmmaking through the studio era and beyond, stitching stories together—many of them drawn from nineteenth-century fiction—from what had previously been the flux of visual data that film was uniquely capable of recording.[23] Film was moving from what Tom Gunning calls the "cinema of attractions," a cinema based in visual shock and spectacle predicated on formal discontinuity and nonimmersive reception practices, to the early narrative cinema of approximately 1903–13, often called the "transitional period," and eventually to the classical narrative cinema most hegemonically represented in Hollywood film.

To be sure, as scholars of the new film history have argued, we should avoid at all costs lending too neat a narrative arch to this formal and institutional process of development, an arch bent toward anything resembling a teleological journey from primitivity to sophistication, embryo to actualization. Whatever we call film at a given point in time is not the product of a linear genealogy in the Nietzschean sense but one iteration among the multiply layered and mutually networked iterations that constitute what, borrowing from Michel Foucault, Thomas Elsaessear calls "film history as media archaeology."[24] Accordingly, the narrative traditions of the theater were integral to film's formal and institutional development. Not only were early films often adapted to the screen from the stage but also the popular theater supplied motion pictures what Judith Mayne aptly calls a "ready-made audience."[25] Early theorizations of the cinema indeed evince just how closely audiences associated motion pictures with theater plays. In *The Art of the Moving Picture* (1915), for instance, Vachel Lindsay claims that theater and film "are still roughly classed together by the public. The elect cannot teach the public what the drama is till they show them precisely what the photoplay is not."[26]

But as highly attended and culturally significant as theater was, it was no match for film in terms of its capacity for distribution and dissemination. By virtue of its technological reproducibility and cheaper cost, the narrative cinema was simply more accessible than its theatrical counterpart. Indeed, there is an importantly brute sense in which, as Mayne, David Bordwell, and others have argued, popular film, through a process of gradual, uneven, and nonlinear development, became the twentieth century's most widely distributed and culturally influential medium of middle-class storytelling, arguably replacing the nineteenth-century novel as the vehicle for the articulation of middle-class ideals.[27] If the film industry wanted to survive economically once the cinematograph's initial novelty wore off, it had to rescue the medium from what had become its stigma as working-class, immigrant entertainment based in visual shock and spectacle. And thus, in a relatively short amount of time and through formal and institutional processes that film historians have illuminated, motion pictures became the twentieth century's version of the nineteenth-century novel in terms of its *normative* social function. In order to flourish rather than founder economically (speaking of ecology), film needed to become white, proper, middle class.[28] "What were the novels of Dickens for his contemporaries, for his readers?" writes Sergei Eisenstein famously;

"There is one answer: they bore the same relation to them that the film bears to the same strata in our time. They compelled the reader to live with the same passions."[29] As modernism was losing the plot, plot was becoming, for the film industry, something like an illegitimate child from another medium or mediums, but one that it could not shake, that is, if it wanted to make money.

And make money it did, a lot of it. And this had at least in part to do with the other reason for its ecological strength: its unrivaled powers of narrative immersion and audience identification. Once film had become a narratively sophisticated medium in the late 1910s—and certainly by the 1920s onward—it had developed a capacity to engulf its audiences within fictional worlds whose illusion of reality was more acute than any previous medium. Walter Benjamin captures this well when he writes in the "Work of Art" essay, "The painter maintains in his work a natural distance from reality, whereas the cinematographer penetrates deeply into its tissue." Film thus provides an "equipment-free aspect of reality" and "does so precisely on the basis of the most intensive interpenetration of reality with equipment."[30] And for Benjamin, it is film editing that yields this illusion of a formal totality so convincing in its fictive wholeness that it looks like our world. Whereas "the painter's is a total image," that of the cinematographer is "piecemeal, its manifold parts being assembled according to a new law. Hence, the presentation of reality in film," he writes, "is incomparably the more significant for people of today." Movies look like life, our lives, and the way that they (at least analogue films) do that is by stitching images of the actual world together so seamlessly that it appears that they have not been stitched together at all.

The powers and pleasures of cinema's immersive effects are charted across the work of theorists with otherwise vastly different commitments. Though they may have disagreed about fundamental aspects of the medium, later theorists, such as Jean-Pierre Oudart, Jean-Louis Baudry, Daniel Dayan, and Christian Metz, shared a concern with the sense of unity and closure afforded by classical film's technological self-effacement. These theorists took that self-effacement as a primary basis for critiquing the ideological power of the fantasies of Hollywood narrative, lulling its viewers, as it so easily can, into a state of impassive reception and—crucially—identification. Filmic suture, understood as the constitution of the viewing subject through techniques of style and editing, reaches its apex of narrative sophistication and self-effacement in the continuity system of the classical Hollywood cinema in the period approximately between the late 1920s and the 1960s. Techniques such as shot-reverse shot editing, cutting on action, eyeline matches, and so on, work to create a vision of the world on screen as spatially and temporally stable, continuous, total. And these techniques generate a point of view, naturalized as a transcendent subject who identifies if not with the protagonist, then with the camera itself. In short, film's power to penetrate reality so deeply with technology that it looks like the technology has disappeared transforms the empirical spectator sitting in a seat at the movie theater into a transcendent viewer inside the fictional world itself.

The commercial cinema thus imbues the narrative desire so expertly generated by the nineteenth-century novel with an unprecedented degree of identificatory investment. The "cinema," Metz writes, "is now copying (semiologically), continuing (historically), and replacing (sociologically . . .)" the "classical nineteenth century novel with its plot and characters."[31] If the bourgeois novel, as Benjamin argues, produces in the reader a sense of surrogate curiosity, the desire to read about the fate of others so as to gain some indirect access to knowledge of our own fate, the power of cinematic suture to make the world on screen look exactly like ours amplifies the "what happens next?" of readerly desire with the even greater vicarious intensity of "what will happen to *me*?"

Understanding what happened to plot in modernism thus involves understanding what happened to it in the cinema, not only the most popular cultural form of the twentieth century but one with which all the writers I examine had very intimate experiences and with whose formal and ideological operations their fiction is in conversation. *Losing the Plot* shows that while these writers were withdrawing from plot as the unwanted inheritance of the nineteenth-century novel, they were also seeing legacies of it in the commercial narrative cinema—through which plot *returns* to the novel in deeply ambivalent form. Plot, this book argues, was transformed from the nineteenth- to the twentieth-century novel via the movies.

In order to demonstrate the consequences of classical Hollywood cinema for the narrative form of the novels I examine as well as, ultimately, the oppositional stance expressed in that form, *Losing the Plot* examines the vital role of popular film in the lives of Larsen, Barnes, and Faulkner. For these writers, going to the movies—not the avant-garde cinema, but the classical Hollywood cinema and its narrative precursors—were rituals of distraction and self-soothing during periods of extreme personal distress and by extension, important elements in the formation of an aesthetic sensibility. For instance, while suffering from depression, substance abuse, the aftershock of a plagiarism scandal, and the discovery of her husband's affair with a white woman, Nella Larsen was watching Greta Garbo films. William Faulkner, while growing up in Oxford, Mississippi, and trying to determine the professional, psychic, and sexual trajectory of his life in the face of unrelenting course-changing disruptions, was steeped in the culture of early narrative film and its development toward classical Hollywood style. And during the same years that Barnes was working on *Nightwood* before sending it off to Eliot for review, she was nursing a broken heart over her lover, Thelma Wood, with whom she had had an eight-year relationship that Barnes ended because of Wood's infidelities. She was also watching Marlene Dietrich films.

Our abiding New Critical tendency to eschew author biography as an axis of literary-critical inquiry might encourage us to view these as merely curious anecdotes. But those working at the intersection of modernist literature and film history know that the field has historically been plagued by the methodological problem of how to track the relationship between film and literature without relying on too loose theoretical arguments "by analogy," as David Trotter puts it (one typical line being that montage as it was championed in early, especially Soviet avant-garde cinema is "like" modernist fragmentation). The field's answer to that problem has been to turn to the historical (the historicist) with the intention of grounding interdisciplinary inquiry not in what had come to read like imprecise observations of intermedial correspondences but in the examination of what films modernist writers "might conceivably have seen."[32]

Later in this introduction I will discuss the methodological problems that arise when we take the principle of probable spectatorship as our guiding rubric, problems primarily having to do with what many consider the radical affective privacy of the experience of watching movies and, as we will see especially in the case of Larsen, the critical lacunae that emerge when to work from extant archival evidence means to disrupt neat chronological inquiry. Here I will simply mention that in this book I take the disciplinary provocation to turn to the biographical seriously, especially because the study of plot inherently invites it. "Ultimately at stake in the structural identity" of the "narrative function as well as in that of the truth claim of every narrative work," Paul Ricoeur argues, "is the temporal character of human experience."[33] It is because of the structural correspondence between human experience and narrative forms—the latter being a projection of the former, in the tradition of hermeneutics—that the concern with narrative structure and narrativity more generally have been integral both to philosophical inquiry into the nature of lived time (such as in the work of Martin Heidegger, Jean-Paul Sartre, and Galen Strawson) and literary and film theory (such as in Walter Benjamin, André Bazin, Peter Brooks, Frank Kermode, Paul Ricoeur, and Pier Paolo Pasolini). Plot, which, following Brooks, I understand as the organizing and directing force that drives narrative forward (and thus distinct from narrative tout court) is the formal device par excellence of the projection of the desire for human experience to achieve narrative unity: the desire for life to mimic art. And not, we will see in the case of these novels, just any kind of unity but formal unities promised to be attended by specific social and psychic arrangements. In a nutshell, I take the concept of "human experience" central to hermeneutic, philosophical, film-theoretical, and literary-theoretical investigations of narrativity out of abstraction by grounding it in key disciplinary concerns governing recent media historiography of literary modernism. How did Larsen—not an abstract "one"— experience the desire for her life to achieve narrative unity? What about Barnes? Faulkner? How did the films they actually, or conceivably, saw pique those desires, and how did those structures of feeling permeate the structures of their fiction? That we can't fully know the answers to these questions and thus must to a certain extent guess will be taken up later in this introduction. *Losing the Plot* does embark on that partially speculative task, however, treating these modernists' spectatorial experiences as clues for what may have moved them in crucial ways that in turn make their characters move—and desire—in particular ways.

Plot and its various manipulations in the films these writers were watching not as critics, but as consumers—melodramas, for instance, romance dramas, and early execution films—provide precisely the psychic palliation these modernists had set out, for different reasons, to critique about nineteenth-century realism. Plot in the film narratives they were watching corresponded to the development of the autonomous subject over time and their integration into bourgeois liberal society; it corresponded, too, to the bourgeois normative ideals of heterosexual coupledom and futurity; and it corresponded, finally, to a linear, continuous, and progressive view of time and history. And crucially, the deviations from these norms that the films do entertain, especially as those deviations manifest themselves in the excesses of style associated with celebrity, either are resolved by way of the happy ending (which, as James MacDowell has argued, need only involve the restoration of the "final couple," dead or alive) or are rendered an object of audience desire through the hypnotizing residue of star performance.[34] And it is because of these correspondences—what Mayne identifies as the shared formal, social, and ideological work of classic literary realism and classical film narrative[35]—that modernism has historically been thought to define its experiments against the culture industry. In displacing story for style—in writing, as Flaubert famously put it, a literature "about nothing"—modernist novelists have historically been thought to refuse capitulation to the aesthetic, philosophical, and political underpinnings of not just literary realism but also the Hollywood cinema in particular.

But this book discovers that while modernist novels ranging from *Nightwood* and *Quicksand* to *The Sound and the Fury* and *As I Lay Dying* may celebrate narrative failure as what Gregory Castle calls one of the "critical triumphs" of modernist aesthetics,[36] these authors' encounters with classical Hollywood film—which featured amplified versions of the narrative pleasures they were supposed to have rejected in nineteenth-century fiction—allow us to see these novels' deeply vexed attitude toward that precise project of writing "about nothing." While formally nonrealist, these novels nevertheless center characters—such as Helga Crane, Nora Flood, the Doctor Matthew O'Connor, and Quentin Compson—who try to bend the form of the novels they inhabit so as to recover what I argue is the primary organizing feature of plot: structures of *consequence*. I will explain what I mean by this.

WHAT IS PLOT?

In this book, I adhere to a kinetic, interpretive, and normative conception of plot. Plot tracks and contains movement; in containing it, it makes that movement mean something, something that either implicitly or explicitly establishes norms. I draw this definition primarily from Peter Brooks's classic study on the topic, *Reading for the Plot*, which, in combining Barthesian structuralism and the psychoanalytic formalism of desire revises the somewhat static vision of plot that emerges in Aristotle's *Poetics*, Russian formalism, and French narratology. Brooks argues that what we call plot is the result of the delicate calibration of what in *S/Z* Barthes calls the "hermeneutic code" (the code of interpretation) to the "proairetic code" (the code of action). The hermeneutic code is the interpretive force that casts narrative meaning on proairetic data; it is what allows us to understand the narrative import of—to make sense of—the events that are taking place as they are taking place. Thus, for Brooks, plot is, importantly, a dynamic force, at once propelled forward by the momentum of interpretation and discovery—a momentum mirrored in our own "narrative desire" to know what happens next—and backward by the power of retrospective signification.[37] These movements—captured, too, in James Phelan's use of the word *progression* effectively to mean plot[38]—is predicated on what Gérard Genette calls the principle of "deferred significance" determining narrativity, what in relation to *The Sound and the Fury* I call the "hermeneutic poverty" of proairetic data in the present and the interpretive work that time accomplishes. Plot relies on the ability of time to resolve, either fully or partially, the semantic indeterminacy of the present. French narratology referred to the retrospective ordering operation of plot as *discours* and the events themselves as *histoire*; Russian formalists referred to these as *sjuzhet* and *fabula*. By way of Barthes and Freud, Brooks makes the simple but important point that whatever we want to call them, the relation of these two entities, or forces, is kinetic, a dynamism captured well in Ian Watt's discussion of "delayed decoding" in Joseph Conrad whereby Marlow comes to understand what is happening to him only after first experiencing it in the form of inchoate impressions.[39]

What I would like to emphasize in this book is that precisely in being a dynamic force, plot tracks change. And not just change of any kind: important change. For this reason, I find Tzvetan Todorov's discussion of narrative equilibration especially helpful. "The minimal complete plot," he writes in *The Poetics of Prose*, "consists in the passage from one equilibrium to another. An 'ideal' narrative begins with a stable situation which is disturbed by some power or force. There results a state of disequilibrium," and "by the action of a force directed in the opposite direction, the equilibrium is re-established; the second equilibrium is similar to the first, but the two are never identical."[40] Girl walks down a city street bouncing a ball = first equilibrium. An ambulance truck drives by and suddenly turns on its siren = disturbing force. Girl gets startled and loses control of the ball + ball rolls into the street = disequilibrium. Girl chases after the ball, weaving between cars = attempt to reestablish equilibrium. Girl grabs the ball, successfully dodging cars + girl resumes her walk, this time with her ball tucked under her arm = second equilibrium. This rudimentary formulation allows us to see an integral element of Todorov's theory of plot that is central to the argument of my book: the primacy of what I am calling *consequence* and *consequentiality* in plot.

Consequence refers both to causality (the consequence of shutting the door is that the door is shut) and significance (the consequence of the girl momentarily losing her ball is that she is now more careful with it). I use the term *significance* here to mean an important occurrence, similar to how Genette means the word *singulative* in *Narrative Discourse* to refer to an event that is distinct in nature, impact, and frequency from the habitual "iterative" events that constitute a narrative world's initial equilibrium.[41] Indeed, one of the distinguishing features of the singulative event is that it happens once, disturbing the flow of iterative events, which happen repetitively. Stendhal's Julien Sorel, for instance, might have met a number of women, but it was his encounter with Madame de Rênal that changed the course of his life; Tolstoy's Anna Karenina might have innocently flirted with this or that man, but it was in meeting Vronksy that her world began to unravel. The singulative event, or what in this book I refer to as the *consequential* event, marks a moment or moments of especially formative causality, a moment or moments that make experience formally *matter*. For Aristotle, there was indeed only one such consequential event: a reversal and recognition. Oedipus finds out that his wife is also his mother, and that knowledge leads to the transformation of his good fortune to bad fortune.[42] In modern aesthetics, that consequentiality is typically distributed across a number of smaller instances. Rastignac, for example, moves to Paris from the provinces (first consequential event), meets Père Goriot (second), falls in with the milieu of Goriot's daughters (third), and so on. And as I will discuss in chapters 1 and 2, the bildungsroman and domestic fiction are perhaps especially representative of the quieter, more gradual kinds of formativity we see in nineteenth-century literary plots.

One way of understanding the modernist novel's turn away from teleological and closural plot is that modernists voided consequentiality, invalidating its formal capacity to establish significant causality. The formal flatness of Flaubert's *Sentimental Education*, for instance—the sense that so much happens and nothing comes of it—reflected his and his French literary contemporaries' belief that revolution had itself been voided of consequence. Despite the series of revolutions that took place in France during the long nineteenth century (1789, 1830, 1848), all they did was reproduce different versions of an essentially enduring antidemocratic authoritarianism in different forms and under different political regimes. Karl Marx's *Eighteenth Brumaire*, as Peter Nicholls has pointed out, expresses well that disillusionment with the impotence of time and history to generate novelty: for Marx, as for Flaubert, modernity had proved itself to be a "history without events; a course of development only driven forward by the calendar, and made wearisome by the constant repetition of the same tensions and relaxations." Thus, "history has been painted grey on grey."[43]

The genealogy of Euro-American modernism, in other words, originated with and continued to be permeated by the sense that modern life is constituted by a regime of inconsequentiality, an iterativity only exacerbated by the repetitive temporalities of the production line, the constant, but nonteleological changes governing the world of fashion and advertisement, the swarming masses of the modern city, and the emergence of a concept of the human psyche as bound to the recursive temporalities of trauma and the unconscious rather than the efficacy of experience. Modern life seemed to nullify the notion of time as formative in any other way than as a Tayloristic measure of productivity. Hence, such novels as Franz Kafka's *The Trial*, where experience yields nightmarish disorientation rather than knowledge, or Gertrude Stein's *Three Lives*, where the aesthetic approximation of what Stein called the "continuous present" yields a vision of life as a mass of iterative instants productive, ultimately and simply, of death.[44]

But these examples show, too, the dialectical quality of the modernist turn to the inconsequential. Just as modernism's rejection of telos extended from disillusionment and irony, in many instances it simultaneously expressed a denunciation of the relations of instrumentality governing capitalist production, the logic of use central to capitalism's functioning. The modernist resistance to narrative sensemaking thus emerges, too, as a critique of capitalist relations, a refusal, to put it simply, to use narrative data in the way that capitalism uses nature and people. The aesthetics of contingency, the nonclosural, even the nonsensical, is an expression, too, of modernism's resistance to narrative instrumentalism. Modernist fragmentation is thus an insistence on what Adorno called, by way of Hegel, the "negation" of formal reconciliation, a formal gesture of nonclosure that corresponded to or was underpinned by an oppositional gesture—a "No!" to capitalism, to bourgeois culture, to concepts of unified selfhood, ownership, and use central to Enlightenment modernity.

And the criticality of modernist negation comes even more fully into view when we remember the kinds of social, moral, and political constraint that consequential plot also represented. Thus, the reason I like the term *consequence*, rather than *sequence* or even *singularity/singulative*, is that in addition to capturing the ability of plot to confer significance on sequential forms, it also captures the normative valences of sequential narrativity, which modernists viewed as central to the social project of the nineteenth-century novel. *Consequence* expresses the normative stakes that modernists saw at play in the fulfillment of certain narrative outcomes. The death of Bertha Mason in *Jane Eyre*, for instance, is the consequence of her throwing herself off the roof of Rochester's home. But this instance of narrative causality is also underpinned by a normative project: Bertha Mason must be ejected from the novel in order for Jane and Rochester to be able to marry and in so doing give the project of British colonialism for which Bertha Mason is a synecdoche the appearance of moral rectitude. The term *consequence* thus gets at how plot is both a kinetic form and an exclusionary one.

Here it would be important to remember the oft-noted spatial valences of the term *plot*—as in a plot of land—to see how plot offers a set of formal boundaries that correspond to normative ones: in order for a plot to take place, it must tell this and not that, it must happen here and not there. And from the perspective of its modernist critics, plot's constitutively exclusionary work in the nineteenth-century novel corresponded to the social, moral, and political constraints that modernists wished to subject to critical scrutiny if not reject outright. The fact that James Joyce takes us into the bathroom with Bloom while he is defecating and reading the newspaper, for example, extends from Joyce's refusal to exclude information, to expand the spatial and thematic boundaries of Victorian plot to include bathrooms and the things we do in them; in the process, he flouts Victorian norms of social decorum and moral rectitude implicitly bound up in the plot of, say, *Middlemarch* or *Oliver Twist*. And Stein's interstitial aesthetics, wherein her characters emerge as masses of minute verbal brushstrokes, is an implicit critique of nineteenth-century realist representations of the self, whose coherent rendering through a more modest "discursive economy," to borrow Deidre Lynch's useful term, corresponds to what Stein saw as their governance by the norms of heterosexual futurity of which she was distinctly critical.[45] The erosion of consequence in modernist aesthetics, then, expresses a critique of what consequence—structures of formative and significant causality—comes to mean socially, philosophically, and politically to modernists regarding the nineteenth-century novel. It is a critique of the Enlightenment subject; of the rationalization of time, experience, and human life under capitalism; and of the social relations and moral systems underpinning what Michael Sayeau calls the "evental structures" of realist narrative.[46] No wonder Coleman was scared to show Barnes her book.

But we need to refine these definitions to account for the abovementioned point that modernism's retreat from plot was not total. The modes of "linkage" governing premodernist fiction, Jacques Rancière tells us, demarcated the causes and effects of actions undertaken by special (politically powerful) persons who choose to act and rightly expect their actions to have ramifications—demarcations that lent clarity and intelligibility to the story being told.[47] Though we often think of modern fiction as widening the sphere of those who can act, its central concern is actually to show that the powers of "delimitation" internal to the formal structures of Aristotelian fictional rationality—which include action, but also events, locations, character, and so on—are no longer available after the advent of the modern, social-scientific understanding of human life as a historical sequence of factual occurrences bent not toward narrative intelligibility but toward infinite succession.[48] The "modern literary revolution," for Rancière, is the sublimation of these two epistemes of how we think human experience to be organized—as plotted and as infinitely sequential—into a single art form that rather than take causal relations for granted makes causality its central problem.

Modern fiction either "invents, as needed, new genres to retrace the boundary" between narratable and unnarratable events (the consequential and the inconsequential) "or else to duly note its erasure."[49] If the fictions of Aristotelian rationality rely on certain boundaries—between fiction and the ordinary, between important and unimportant persons—then modern literature faces a problem of delimitation. Either it generates new kinds of boundaries—delimits in other ways than by creating clearly individuated actions, events, and characters organized by structures of causality—or it thematizes the fact that there are no such boundaries left with which to craft fiction that looks anything like it used to. Boundaries in modernist fiction get blurred: characters aren't as distinct from one another as they used to be; locations aren't as intelligibly unique from one another; and the relational structures suturing events to each other either do not abide by principles of causality or, if they do, we are provided a vantage from which to discern and critique their artificiality.

And Rancière considers this to be a good thing. With the collapse of what had been the intractably hierarchical political terms of the representational regime (emblematized, for Rancière, in the French monarchy) comes an abolition, too, of the aesthetic hierarchies attending that regime. Hence Rancière's faith in what he periodically calls the "democratic" effect of modern aesthetics, the flux of details—of modernist *écriture*—that undermines causal relations by drowning them in too much information. But the influx of modernist textuality does not inundate the space of fiction gratuitously; it destroys its infrastructure in order to clear space for imagining more emancipated, less subordinated modes of being.[50] Therefore the modernist relational structure par excellence, for Rancière (as for Adorno), is parataxis. To erode plot by flooding its causal architecture with the theoretical infinitude of the paratactical is to signal a new aesthetic episteme that disrespects the hierarchical structure of representational aesthetics, which subordinate parts to the whole. It forges new relations between fiction and that which is outside of it, new subjects, psychic structures, and social formations.

But for whom is this good? How are paratactical relations experienced? A more probing way to put it: what does ineffectuality feel like? Might it not feel a bit like quicksand? Note that this is not the same as asking what the political import of crafting such an aesthetics is (or theorizing it, for that matter). When Charles Tansley, for instance, suddenly realizes, "it was this: it was this:—she [Mrs. Ramsay] was the most beautiful person he had ever seen," it is a punctuated moment of recognition and psychic difference that, rather than catalyze a love story between Mrs. Ramsay and Charles Tansley, only ephemerally breaches the surface of *To the Lighthouse* before vanishing within the novel's stream of similarly structured psychic pauses.[51] It is exemplary of Woolf's more general critique of the romance plots of Victorian fiction that were integral to the naturalization of gendered domestic life and the colonial ideology of British nationhood. That the Samsa parents turn their attention to Gregor's sister's "young body" almost immediately after Gregor has died from their neglect and exploitation suggests that Gregor's story is not unique but one in a chain of similar occurrences yet to come, occurrences that Kafka recognizes as endemic to rationalized life in capitalist modernity. And so on. Modernism's turn to paratactical relations was a choreographed affront—on the part of *modernists*—to the causal structures of premodernist aesthetics, which they saw as being attended by various normative constraints and thus ripe for undermining.

It would be wrong to claim one formal strategy as unifying all of what today we count as modernist aesthetics. Like Dora Zhang in *Strange Likeness*—a book to which my own is very much indebted—I refer to "the modernist novel" throughout this book for ease of communication, fully aware of the diversity of modernist fiction. But I suggest that Larsen, Barnes, and Faulkner are part of a certain strain of literary modernism that stages a palpable desire on the part of modernist *characters* to right the numerical relations between consequential and inconsequential information—to unflood the space of fiction such that its prior causal relations would again become visible and reliable. What these authors' characters seek are the social and psychological effects that representational aesthetics pledged would ensue from properly functioning systems of causality. And they do this (this is key) against the current of what their novels—their authors—are doing.

Crucially, however, these characters do not want to restore to modernist aesthetics the kinds of causality generated by the efficacious human action that Lukács found in realism. For him, plot was central to realism's ability not simply to record the apparent fragmentariness and contingency of surface appearances but to show the dynamic contradictions of history and the truth of social relations actually at work. In retreating from causality, Lukács thought, modernism's "descriptive" method abdicated the novel's power to expose why certain kinds of events happen to certain kinds of people at specific moments (showing chance to be necessity) and to expose the larger social forces that determine individual fates. On this reading, plot is not ideological mystification but the properly narrative means of demystification. And modernism's withdrawal from causality not only renders it incapable of narrating history but also makes it an expression of political nihilism, depicting a world devoid of any possibility of humans effecting change from the status quo.

The characters this book examines do act, or at least they try to. But their actions are not bent toward changing the status quo; they are bent—even more egregiously, from Lukács's perspective—toward mourning, if not reinscribing it. Contra Lukács's claims about modernism, Larsen, Barnes, and Faulkner do show the historical forces that have irrevocably determined the lives of their characters—the decline of the aristocracy in *Nightwood*, the Civil War and the determinism of family blood in Faulkner, the psychic and political damages of the legacy of slavery in Larsen. In this key sense, they do not abandon consequentiality entirely. But from within the fallout of these gross ramifications of history, whose resultant social fragmentations are depicted in the creative destruction of modernist *écriture*, key characters seek out not the relations of causality that promise politically potentialized action but those that promise to secure some of the representational regime's most regressive and politically depotentialized social, psychic, and subjective formations—coherent selfhood, romantic fidelity, an authoritative system of explanation—no matter how false. They seek out specters of "the normal" so as to stabilize themselves, however briefly or delusionally. Lukács believed modernism's withdrawal from plot was evidence of its defeatist concession to the inhumanities of capitalism. *Losing the Plot* disappoints Lukács even further. It locates in modernism a desire for plot not as a way out of the determinisms of history but as a mode of palliative escape from its realities. But that desire for palliation, this book claims, is one of the most human things imaginable, and a recognition of it is a necessary basis for any pursuit of a liberatory politics. *Losing the Plot* charts modernism's aesthetic exploration of this admission and claims that that admission is one of modernism's most profound contributions.

No matter how emancipatory the aesthetic choices of these authors may be, their characters desperately reach for the narrative forms—the structures of consequence—they sense would deliver them from the groundlessness of paratactical experience. That ambivalence, that double feeling of repudiation and longing generated by the modernist novel's encounter with the commercial narrative cinema—the primary inheritor of representational aesthetics in the twentieth century—manifests itself in the novels this book examines in the form of intense and contradictory textual dynamics resulting from a cleavage between the textual excesses of the works themselves and the characters who are subject to those textual excesses.

CHARACTERS IN SEARCH OF AN AUTHOR

Since its professionalization in the modernist period of the early twentieth century, the practice of literary criticism has been largely predicated on a view of literary character as a thoroughgoing product of textuality.[52] Characters are typically considered so ontologically distinct from real people that any suggestion to the contrary evinces one's misunderstanding of how fiction works. To treat characters as if they had breathing life outside—let alone agency over—the texts they inhabit would be the embarrassing or wrongheaded result of what Mieke Bal calls the "realistic fallacy,"[53] the treatment of characters as if they were real people, a behavior we often discourage in our students. James Phelan's and John Frow's influential theories of literary character offer exemplary analyses of the textuality of character as distinct from personhood, thus representing well the dominant text-based vision of character to which literary studies largely adheres.[54] The dominant view is that what we call "Anna Karenina" is a "synthetic" entity born of text, to borrow Phelan's term, whose "mimetic" dimensions are what allow us to recognize her as being *like* a real person. However, according to this rubric, no matter how legible Anna is to us as personlike, to ask, for example, whether she likes kiwis is to forget that her mimetic dimension, albeit expertly wrought, is a function of her status as a synthetic being, and synthetic beings don't like kiwis because they don't have desires of any kind other than those that have been explicitly mentioned, implied, or alluded to in the text. The same logic applies to questions such as "how does Anna like being in *Anna Karenina*?" or "what are Elizabeth Bennet's thoughts about being in *Pride and Prejudice*?" If we treat the distinction between characters and persons as intransigent, these questions are nonsensical.[55]

However, this is not strictly the case when discussing characters in cinema, especially when they are played by stars. The study of stardom operates from the premise that there is always an excess of personhood that leaks, if not floods over the borders of the text a character inhabits. This is because the material from which the character is created is the actor's body, an entity that the viewer knows has life distinct from the character the actor plays. (When the cameras stop rolling, Checker Girl #2 may momentarily disappear, but the actress who plays her may stretch her legs.) When that body is extremely famous—as was the case with Greta Garbo and Marlene Dietrich—the viewer's awareness of that surfeit is especially heightened. That is because over and above the other levels of embodiment that the average actor possesses, the star has what Vivian Sobchack describes as the "Personified body." In addition to their "Prepersonal" (material) and "Personal" (conceptual) bodies, the average actor also portrays an "Impersonal" body, or what we would more colloquially call a "character." In excess of that Impersonal body ("Checker Girl #2"), the star, Sobchack tells us, has a "Personified Body," which is an "amalgam of screen images" and publicity material that over time generates a "metaphorized and reified body of [the star's] overall cinematic accumulation."[56] Thus, when we watch a star playing a character, the star's Personified Body will not only exist in addition to the Impersonal body but will also probably overwhelm it. When we watch Garbo playing Marguerite Gautier in *Camille* (George Cukor, 1936), we are aware that this is Garbo the eternal fixture who looms over the character in the script.

It has been observed that there are literary "stars," characters who appear in multiple works and therefore generate an extratextual residue akin to this "amalgam" or "accumulation" characteristic of film stars. Eugène de Rastignac, for instance, populates different pockets of Balzac's *Comédie humaine*, or several of Faulkner's characters do the same in the fictional Yoknapatawpha County. In reappearing periodically, these characters generate an illusion of existence outside the bounds of the texts they inhabit. For instance, when we encounter Rastignac in *Lost Illusions* after having read *Père Goriot*, we might start imagining what he had been up to between "then" and "now." Even though we know full well that he was "up to" nothing at all because he doesn't exist in the physical world—and, moreover, that "then" and "now" are functions of the fictionalization of time rather than references to its reality—Balzac nevertheless makes available the line of inquiry, regardless of how self-consciously fictive. The efficacy of Balzac's world building in the *Comédie humaine* indeed depends in large part on how recurring characters' extratextual existence—a figment entirely of our imagination—suggests the reality of the world we're reading about, that it, too, exists somewhere outside the pages, and that Balzac is merely giving us access to it. It is part of the self-conscious game of make-believe that realist literature asks us to play.

But literary characters' extratextual presence will always remain analogical, rather than identical, to that of film stars. Greta Garbo *is* "up to" something in the time between her appearance in *The Painted Veil* (Richard Boleslawski, 1934) and *Camille*, between *The Kiss* (Jacques Feder, 1929) and *Anna Christie* (Clarence Brown, 1930). Garbo was famously reclusive, so it was rarely clear of what activities those intervals consisted; but that her body (Prepersonal and Personal, if you'd like) occupies real spacetime is never in question, nor is it a self-conscious game of make-believe. A full examination of the similarities and distinctions between literary and cinematic characters warrants its own book-length study. But here I will emphasize the most important distinction for our purposes, which is not only that the film star's extratextual presence is literal (Garbo eats breakfast, reads the newspaper, etc.) but that her Personified body (the "Swedish Sphinx," "L'énigme," etc.) can be so overpowering as to create an entire system of meaning in excess of the character she plays *while she is playing it*. That surfeit inflects the meanings built into the scripted character. And depending on the content of the role and the content of the Personified body—what the star persona comes to be "known" for, the affects she exudes, and so forth—the relationship between those two systems of meaning can be felicitous, antagonistic, or somewhere in between. This relationship will become especially salient in chapter 3.

The important takeaway here is that in the cinema, and especially when dealing with stars, this relationship is even something to consider at all. It does make sense to ask what Garbo thinks about being in *Camille*, not just in the literal sense (as it happens, the extremely selective Garbo was delighted to work with George Cukor, though she wound up being physically ill throughout the entire shoot). It also makes sense to ask it in a more abstract sense: what is the quality of the relationship between the system of meanings generated by Garbo the Enigma and those internal to the character of Marguerite Gautier as she was adapted by Zoë Akins from Alexandre Dumas fils's source material? These questions do not commit the realistic fallacy; they evince an understanding of how cinematic representation works.

Losing the Plot thus encourages us to recall that the textual ontology of character is not fixed but contingent on factors having partly to do with medium specificity. It draws inspiration from the residue of characters' extratextuality in film so as to lean into rather than away from the realistic fallacy in literature. It does not do so in order to treat these authors' characters as real people. Rather, *Losing the Plot* draws on the wrongness of the realistic fallacy in literary representation because doing so allows us to recognize how these literary characters' desires differ, often radically, from what the novels they inhabit are doing formally—that their actions and psychic habits often work in contradiction to the novels' form, trying to get it to do something different, something that would make them *feel better* than what their fictional conditions of possibility have made available to them. In the moment of literary history where the textuality of literary characters is often considered to be most conspicuous, we find them in fact trying to overcome their status as text: to become real and thus agential, "up to" something other than what their authors are. Tuning into the meaningful difference between what these characters want and what their novels are asking them to do, not do, be, or not be would be only slightly to amplify the connotation subtly permeating Alex Woloch's description of the "distributional matrix" of fictional character, that fictional forms have agency. "The discrete representation of any specific individual" in nineteenth-century fiction, Woloch writes, "is intertwined with the narrative's continual apportioning of attention to different characters who jostle for limited space within the same fictive universe."[57]

While the characters I examine do not jostle for space, they do jostle for structures of causality that would give them what they want. So many characters in search of an author, these characters reach, sometimes destructively, always unsuccessfully, for scaffolds of meaningful and formative narrative causality that would render their experiences productive of coherent selfhood, romantic fidelity, and a structure of *reasons* to explain personal suffering, structures that the textual excesses of modernist *écriture* have otherwise dissolved. They jostle for consequentiality—not against other characters but against their own novels, which have given them a life defined by suffering, and against their authors, whose omniscient presence has dissipated into the specious self-effacement of modernist impersonality. This search and the forms it takes are thrown into relief once seen in the light of their successful achievement in the popular movies these writers were watching. These literary characters attempt to wrangle the textual excesses of the modernist novel into a successful bildungsroman plot (as in Larsen), a successful romance plot (as in Barnes), or a plot that would at the very least provide palliative etiologies that would mitigate the unmanageability of the present (as in Faulkner). And they do so in the way Garbo's films make of her characters' disparate parts a coherent whole despite all the material circumstances that would realistically foreclose it, the way Dietrich's films make rejecting the terms of the heteronormative romance plot look like the easiest thing in the world, and in the way the early execution genre, for all its rudimentary brutality, can nevertheless tell us where we were, where we're going, and why.

BAD MODERNISTS

At the center of this argument is an alternative way of understanding modernist cinematic spectatorship. *Losing the Plot* is not a typical study of literary modernism's relation to popular visual culture in that it does not posit negativity and critique as the primary mode of modernist engagement with the culture industry. Recent film histories of literary modernism broaden their purview to include a diversity of mass-cultural texts, which had previously been disregarded by the field in favor of avant-garde visual culture.[58] And yet these studies still focus on the breakdown of form and the ways that modernist literature sees itself in popular culture's fissures and lapses.[59] Even when turning their attention to popular film, in other words, film histories of literary modernism have yet to fully come out from underneath the weight of Andreas Huyssen's formidable "great divide" argument, which posited modernism as predicated on the rejection of the *massness* of mass culture, precisely its profound conventionality.[60] In our current accounts, what modernism doesn't see at the movies is a world truly different from itself. Instead what it finds are the formal breakages in popular visual culture that belie its mass appeal.

As illuminating as these accounts are, they evince what Natalia Cecire has recently called attention to as the tendency in literary studies to view experimentalism (manifest most obviously in an overt attention to form, breakages, rupture, etc.) as somehow inherently good—that if it is broken, then it is better, more critical and sophisticated, than if it is still whole—a critique in line with Toril Moi's recent work on the aversion in literary studies, especially modernist studies, to taking content ("the actual words" characters say) seriously as a fund of a work's criticality.[61] Accordingly, current film histories of literary modernism seem to operate from the assumption that in order for popular movies to be worthy of study in conjunction with modernism, then we need to prove that those movies are also ridden with ruptures, traces of an unknowing (or even knowing) experimentalism. This is no doubt one of the reasons why even when older film histories of literary modernism would discuss popular film they would focus mostly on slapstick comedy, a genre based so much in the disruption of narrative continuity that it was often championed by avant-garde filmmakers or, as in the case of René Clair, overlapped with avant-garde filmmaking.[62]

Similarly, within the context of film studies, the abiding criticism of David Bordwell, Janet Staiger, and Kristin Thompson's 1985 *The Classical Hollywood Cinema*, which attempted to identify the stylistic, narrative, and ideological codes organizing commercial narrative films from the advent of sound in the late 1920s through the 1960s, has largely been erected on the grounds of what Miriam Hansen calls its excessively "totalizing" view of the classical period. Bordwell, Staiger, and Thompson's book, Hansen argues in her famous essay "The Mass Production of the Senses: Classical Cinema as Vernacular Modernism," offers not only too "universalist" a concept of the classical period, which she and other critics have rightly insisted was more generically, formally, and ideologically heterogeneous than *The Classical Hollywood Cinema* would seem to allow; but that, by virtue of that heterogeneity, it was more critical because more modernist.[63] The image of the classical Hollywood period that emerges from *The Classical Hollywood Cinema* is indeed an economically and ideologically interested mode of aesthetic production bent toward the construction and affirmation of white middle-class values. It is an uncritical cinema, to put it too crudely, that subsumes any transgressive fissures that periodically violate the norms of its aesthetic mode back into its formal system.[64]

To be clear, Hansen's and other critics' impulse to complicate the picture that emerges in *The Classical Hollywood Cinema* is, I think, correct.[65] However, Hansen's move to rescue the classical Hollywood cinema from charges of exhaustive complicity by claiming it as a "vernacular modernism" is indicative of the normativizing gesture that Cecire ascribes to the category of experimentalism. It is as if, were we to be able to prove that this popular art form often considered the epitome of bourgeois complicity is actually modernist—if it is not the Ideology Machine we tend to think it is but rather a complex vehicle for social and collective experiences that in the multiplicity of its situations of spectatorship and global distribution subvert that ideological coercion—then we can justify studying it and in institutional contexts that might otherwise shun it. That may be so; but this move might also mean that we would no longer have to contend with how powerful that coercion is, how well it does its job.

Classical Hollywood's "vernacular modernism," Hansen argues, lay in its ability to "articulat[e] and mediat[e] the experience of modernity" and in the process to generate "a discursive form in which individual experience could be articulated and find recognition by both subject and other, including strangers."[66] But at least one issue presents itself. There is nothing either especially modernist about aesthetically articulating the experience of modernity or about creating a cultural source of collective normativity and recognition. The realist novel, too, performed that cultural and normative work. This was Raymond Williams's point, for instance, when he drew the important distinction between the modernists and a writer such as Dickens. Dickens, too, was registering the conditions of the modern industrial metropolis, but it was the modernists who would go on to register those conditions at the level of form in a sustained and assaulting way. Where a writer such as Dickens (or, say, Balzac) uses the novel to lend narrative shape to a world thrown into structural upheaval by modern industrial capitalism, containing the intensities and experiential unfamiliarities of modern life by subjecting them to the formal contours of linear chronology and narrative design, the modernists would shatter the form of the novel, precisely, as Adorno also argues, to reflect rather than to contain those intensities and unfamiliarities.[67] And as Sergei Eisenstein argued, although Dickens's use of literary "montage" anticipated D. W. Griffith's, and Griffith, in turn, influenced Eisenstein's own avant-garde montage, there is indisputably something cohesive about Dickens's and Griffith's storytelling.[68] However much, through our own critical activity, we are able to draw out moments of formal discontinuity that disrupt the teleological flow of narrative, thus exposing its internal political contradictions, if not its hidden violence, the overall effect of these narratives is that they *hold together*. Reading Dickens is not like reading Gertrude Stein. Watching Griffith—for all the baffling insanity of his politics—is not like watching Dziga Vertov.

But that cohesiveness does not make it somehow less worthy of critical analysis. Or rather, the critical desire to locate fissures and self-critique in that cohesiveness does not manage away its formidable ideological power. Indeed, art forms based on assemblage rather than disassemblage are not of necessity less epistemologically and critically valuable than fragmented ones, as Cecire, Kornbluh, and Moi have suggested in their respective ways. But—and this is the simple point that I'd like to emphasize in this book—cohesive storytelling in classical Hollywood cinema *is* extraordinarily powerful if for no other reason, as Mayne has argued, than that it often deals in fantasy. "The reconciliations posited by narrative," she writes, "are more appropriately described as fantasies—fantasies in which the terms reconciled are often irreconcilable in everyday existence."[69] It is not that classical Hollywood films—in particular the romance dramas, melodramas, and other narrative films this book examines—are telling stories with no holes in them. It is that through the operations of lighting, music, editing, cinematography, and, often, the right star and story, these films make the holes that they do have and that they do sometimes show seem entirely unimportant—inconsequential. "There the flawed became whole, the blind sighted, and the lame and halt threw away their crutches," Toni Morrison writes in *The Bluest Eye*, the novel I quote in my opening epigraph and that arguably best captures the brutal power of classical Hollywood cinematic images to tell its audiences what is right and what isn't, what is beautiful and what isn't. "There death was dead," she continues, "and people made every gesture in a cloud of music. There the black-and-white images came together and made a magnificent whole—all projected," she writes, anticipating Christian Metz's psychoanalytic theorizations of the cinematic apparatus, "through the ray of light from above and behind."[70] It is the extraordinary force of the classical Hollywood film to tell you what you should want, who you should be, what you should look like, whom you should hate—its power to turn its seeming descriptions into normative prescriptions—that, as Lauren Berlant spent so much of their career showing us, made it one of the most ruthless producers of cruel optimism.[71] "That the movie star is an 'escape' personality," James Baldwin writes in *The Devil Finds Work*, having anticipated, too, Berlant's remarks on the cruelty of that attachment, "indicates one of the irreducible dangers to which the moviegoer is exposed: the danger of surrendering to the corroboration of one's fantasies as they are thrown back from the screen."[72] The classical Hollywood movie tells us what to fantasize about; then it makes those fantasies *feel* attainable—if we just looked and acted in a certain way, if just certain things were to happen to us and in the right order.

What if modernists did not overcome this danger entirely? What if they were not too critical for it, too cool for it? Or what if that criticality was imperfect, ambivalent, did not preclude its own failures? What if sometimes, in the privacy of their own minds, in their letters, in their red velvet seats, they were . . . bad modernists? I use the term *bad modernist* periodically throughout this book but in a way slightly different from the way its originators, Douglas Mao and Rebecca Walkowitz, use the term.[73] I use it to refer to the imperfect, ambivalent, and often failed performances of the affront associated with modernist negation, or in some cases, antinormativity—failed not in the institutional sense that Mao and Walkowitz mean it but in the embodied sense of not living up, in one's everyday life, to an ideal of negativity or antinormativity, not being able to be bad without being racked by the temptation to be good. Or when one's private desires are simply not as bad as they should be, given what one knows to be true. When one cannot say "No!" without wanting to feel the warmth of what is renounced in the name of better politics—the warmth not of esteem per se but of normative subjectivity, normative ways of being.

Ambivalence, when understood in the context of politics, testifies, as Clare Hemmings explains, to the aspects of experience that complicate straightforward celebrations of negativity and antinormativity. Considering ambivalence allows us to consider, too, "what is lost in a politics of certainty" and in so doing to acknowledge the daily textures of human experience and feeling that make *doing* negativity and antinormativity hard, however emancipatory it may be.[74] *Bad* is thus a word we might use to describe the "ugly feelings," as Sianne Ngai might put it, that often keep us from fully renouncing the psychic, social, and political structures invested in our unfreedom and of which we are otherwise deeply critical.[75] Or when our desires look an awful lot like unfreedom to those we consider our allies and whose community we seek and need.

PAULINE AND JAMES

It is telling that the writers I have so far mentioned as being especially good at talking about the dangerous fantasies of wholeness offered by classical film narrative are not straight white men or women. Morrison's *The Bluest Eye* charts the ugly feelings that can arise, especially in minoritized subjects, from the forms of immersive and identificatory spectatorship the classical cinema invites. Pauline Breedlove, the mother of Morrison's protagonist Pecola, goes to the movies as a mode of periodic escape from an unhappy marriage, poverty, and a sense of isolation from a Black community after having moved to Ohio from Kentucky. Through Pauline's "education at the movies," she "was introduced" to "romantic love" and "physical beauty," the "most destructive ideas in the history of human thought. Both originated in envy, thrived in insecurity, and ended in disillusion." Although a "simple pleasure," the narrator continues, "she learned all there was to love and all there was to hate." "*The onliest time I be happy seem like was when I was in the picture show*," Pauline herself says, "*the screen would light up, and I'd move right on in them pictures. White men taking such good care of they women, and they all dressed up in big clean houses with the bathtubs right in the same room with the toilet. Them pictures gave me a lot of pleasure, but it made coming home hard, and looking at* [my husband] *Cholly hard*."[76] The "picture show," in *The Bluest Eye*, is a factory of temporary palliatives that generates internalized racism, the ugly feeling of "self-contempt" most obviously exemplified in Pauline's attempt to style her hair like Jean Harlow: "*It looked just like her. Well, almost just like.*"[77] In the context of Black film historiography, groundbreaking scholarship by Jacqueline Najuma Stewart, Anna Everett, and Charlene Regester has illuminated modes of Black spectatorship based not in the escapism epitomized in Pauline's moviegoing practices but in what Stewart, referring to early twentieth-century Black film culture in Chicago, calls a "reconstructive" practice wherein "African Americans used the cinema as a literal and symbolic space in which to rebuild their individual and collective identities in a modern, urban environment."[78] This is a fundamentally critical mode of spectatorship—akin to what bell hooks might call "oppositional," or Manthia Diawara "resistant"[79]—and in *not* practicing it, Pauline is also unable to access the forms of self- and communal affirmation that Stewart describes and that *The Bluest Eye* implicitly suggests would go some way toward healing Pauline's psychic wounds.

James Baldwin, on the other hand, does practice that critical spectatorship, most famously in the passage from *The Devil Finds Work* where he describes his formative encounter, as a child, with the image of Bette Davis. "So, here, now, was Bette Davis," he writes, "on that Saturday afternoon, in close-up, over a champagne glass, pop-eyes popping. I was astounded.... For, here, before me, after all, was a *movie star*: *white*: and if she was white and a movie star, she was *rich*: and she was *ugly*." "I was held," he continues, "by the tense intelligence of the forehead, the disaster of the lips: and when she moved, she moved just like a n——."[80]

This passage plays a central role in José Esteban Muñoz's explication of his concept of "disidentification." And that is because through his critical engagement with images of white hegemony, Baldwin is able to lay the foundation for a politics of resistance. Baldwin's experience with the image of Davis is exemplary of disidentification for Muñoz because he mobilizes the image despite its hegemony. "A black and queer belle-lettres queen such as Baldwin," Muñoz writes, "finds something useful in the image; a certain survival strategy is made possible via this visual disidentification with Bette Davis and her freakish beauty." As a young Black boy, Baldwin, otherwise not represented in hegemonic culture or represented in disparaging or incorrect ways, "transforms the raw material of identification (the linear match that leads toward interpellation) while simultaneously positioning himself within and outside the image of the movie star."[81] Whereas Baldwin keeps one foot "outside" the Hollywood image, as it were, a distantiation that affords him critical purchase, Pauline moves *"right on in them pictures"* and is thus led down the destructive path of interpellation.

But let us note how Baldwin's critical mastery of his disidentification with Bette Davis is accentuated by the emphatic retrospective quality of his theorization of it. "I had not yet heard Bessie Smith's *'why they call this place the Sing Sing? / Come stand here by this rock pile, and listen to these hammers ring,'* and it would be seven years before I would begin working on the railroad. It was to take a longer time than that before I would cry; a longer time than that before I would cry in anyone's arms; and a long long long long time before I would begin to realize what I myself was doing with my enormous eyes—or vice versa. This had nothing to do with Davis, the actress," he concludes, "or with all those hang-ups I didn't yet know I had: I had discovered that my infirmity might not be my doom; my infirmity, or infirmities, might be forged into weapons."[82]

There is an extremity to Baldwin's depiction of the pastness of the Davis encounter. The repeated iterations of the word *long*, together with the variety of future and past perfect tenses, places strong emphasis on the radical antecedence of that moment, which although formative—he learned something important—needed time in order to emerge, formally, as such. It is a profoundly novelistic moment of narration, an act of Dickensian narrativization of childhood experience that, although Baldwin had more explicitly explored it in his semiautobiographical bildungsroman *Go Tell It on the Mountain* (1953), here emerges in concentrated form as an expression of the epistemic mastery afforded by retrospection. By the time he is writing *The Devil Finds Work*, Baldwin thoroughly understands what happened to him that day in that movie theater, he knows what it meant for the subsequent course of his life, and he describes it in no uncertain terms;

he plots it out as would an omniscient narrator. And the eloquence of that narration, though typical of all his work, here is especially expressive of the extent of his self-knowledge. And that eloquent retrospective signification, typical of realist narration, is of a piece with the fact that a politics emerged from that moment. The retrospective narration emphasizes, indeed, how he uses the encounter, "transforms" it, in Muñoz's words, into a politics of resistance. Baldwin thus implicitly shows the *process* through which the flimsy uncertainties and ambivalence of the present—the "ineloquent" intensity, as Berlant would call it, of "change" as it is "lived on the body before anything is understood"[83]—settle into a pristine retrospective prose that admits of no uncertainty. He didn't know what it meant then, but he knows now, and thus can tell it how it needs to be told.

Pauline's narration, meanwhile, shows a messier, more ambivalent situation, one that I would insist is not entirely uncritical because it is not unknowing. Pauline is often considered a quintessential example of a naive spectator, taken in by the ideological operations of the classical Hollywood cinema. She "submerges herself," in Stewart's words, "in white screen fantasies in order to be transported away from her lonely, modest existence."[84] But the phrase "in order to" in Stewart's claim is important. Pauline may be getting immersed in the pleasures of the movies, but she knows that she's doing it; she is indeed submerging *herself*. It is an analgesic she seeks out deliberately, the way Jean Epstein describes going to the movies as getting a "dose":[85] "*Every time I got,*" she says, "*I went. I'd go early, before the show started. They'd cut off the lights and everything be black. Then the screen would light up and I'd move right on into them pictures.*" The pictures do not pull Pauline into them, Pauline moves herself into the pictures in a knowing ritual of cinephilic self-soothing. "*There I was,*" she says, even making a dark joke at her own expense after dressing up like Jean Harlow and eating a piece of candy that pulls out one of her teeth, "*five months pregnant, trying to look like Jean Harlow, and a front tooth gone.*"[86]

Most importantly, the movie theater is the place she goes in order to fulfill the part of her that wants—that needs—order, the same part of her that "liked," as a child, to "arrange things," to "line things up in rows" and "organize" whatever "plurality" she encountered into "neat lines, according to their size, shape, or gradations of color." Pauline's life is cracked apart by the displacements of labor migration, domestic abuse, poverty, and racism, and in response to this, she seeks out the movies. And that is because, in their uncanny ability to reconcile the irreconcilable, to make order from disorder, the movies "put," as Pauline herself has always tried desperately to put, "all of the pieces together"; they "make coherence where before there had been none."[87] Pauline is engaging in the obsessive, addictive, affectively complex repetitions of the cinephile, not the one associated with the cinematic elitisms of postwar France but the one, recently theorized by Sarah Keller, based in various—and often anxious—expressions of a love haunted by loss, "an insatiable need for repeated encounters with the object of desire."[88] Cinephilia, writes Keller by way of Nico Baumbach, draws on the "tensions between passivity and consciousness about the object of one's love."[89] Indeed, Pauline is interpellated; but she knows she is interpellated; which means that she is not entirely interpellated. She's not a great modernist, but she's not a terrible one, either.

This comparison between Baldwin and Pauline allows me to make two points that are central to the function of moviegoing in the lives of Larsen, Barnes, and Faulkner and the forms of ambivalence that it generates in their novels. The first point is that Pauline's narration testifies to the Berlantian observation that experience in time does not make itself available to the eloquent theorizations on display in Baldwin's passage on Davis. Life as it is lived, in Pauline's rendering, looks something more like how Woolf describes it, a site of formal and psychic fragmentation resistant to closed expressions of thought and art. The second point, however, is that unlike how Woolf describes the fragmentation of "life as it is"—a description largely detached from historical specificity and thus naturalized as simply true—that formal and psychic fragmentation is not necessarily a good thing. On the contrary, what comes through more clearly in Pauline's narration than in Baldwin's, and what I discuss throughout all my chapters, is how fragmentation is often a source of enormous suffering. Pauline's life—unlike the floating "life" Woolf names in "Modern Fiction"—is shattered to pieces; she wants and needs stabilizing solidities, the "order," as Kornbluh calls it, "of forms."[90] The movies offer her that solidity, its "magnificent whole[s]" providing her what Deidre Lynch would call a "coping mechanism" with which to manage—indeed, temporarily manage away—the fragmented unmanageability of her life.[91] Fragmentation, for Pauline, is something to be endured, not celebrated polemically as a fact of modernity but suffered through until the next time she can pretend it isn't there.[92]

The point here is not to name Baldwin's retrospective mastery as a falsehood and to cast Pauline's as somehow more authentic. It is to suggest that Baldwin's retrospective mastery showcases the critical affordances of distance, the fact that certainty about what things have meant, what we believe to be right, and our ability to act in accordance with those beliefs tend to be the product of a removal from the vulnerability of those events as we live them in real time. Baldwin's knowing look back, its acumen accentuated by the fact that this is a late Baldwin who had spent decades as a prominent public intellectual telling us stories about his life, shows a sophisticated order rescued from the disorder that must have been swarming the young Baldwin's mind as he was actually sitting in that theater—an *in*eloquent vulnerability that perhaps looked something like John's in *Go Tell It on the Mountain*, when overcome with emotions he doesn't know how to handle, he stands with "bowed" head, "teeth on edge," little "fists clenched against the windowpane"—as if pressed up against a screen—crying, "What shall I do? What shall I do?"[93] The ambivalence permeating John's moment of crisis settles, in the Davis scene, into a reassuring certainty. It is an older Baldwin who can assure the younger that all this terror will mean something important someday, that all that fragmentation he endured will settle eventually into a sharp critical tool.

Pauline's narration, meanwhile, effects a position more proximate to experience; she is not in it as she narrates, but close enough such that Morrison shows her *somewhat* narrativizing it, lending her experiences the slight contours of a narrative event here, a soft turning point there. She makes observations such as "*Everything went then. Look like I just didn't care no more after that*," or "*I don't know what all happened. Everything changed*," or "*That was the lonesomest time of my life*," or "*When I first seed Cholly . . . it was like all the bits of color from that time down home when all us chil'ren went berry picking after a funeral . . . and they mashed up and stained my hips.*"[94] Pauline's narration suggests that though life may be resistant to closed expressions of thought, unavailable for sophisticated theorization, it is often available for open expressions of thought, for provisional, imperfect, and partial theorization. "Relations," to borrow Henry James's term again, may "stop nowhere" from the point of view of outer space, but from our own points of view, as we live, Pauline's narration suggests, we are always narrativizing, always conferring significance, establishing correspondences, revising meanings. We see our lives, in short, as a story in progress, always anticipating the "tock," as Frank Kermode would have it, after the initial "tick."[95] And as such, *The Bluest Eye* (Morrison's first novel) suggests that as we live, we occupy a space at the threshold of criticality and uncriticality. And perhaps what is most coercive about the classical Hollywood cinema, Morrison suggests, is that it is especially good at taking advantage of our desire for hermeneutic plenitude, taking advantage of the ambivalence of the present and for making wholeness not just look but *feel* possible by appealing not to thought but to desire. And when the hermeneutic poverty of one's present, as in the case of Pauline—and Larsen, Barnes, and

Faulkner—feels especially threatening, even the specious order of violent wholes, what Sarah Ahmed might call the "promise of happiness," comes to seem a mode of deliverance, at least for now.

The model of cinematic spectatorship that emerges in the work of the writers I examine here is predicated on a knowing participation in acts of temporary distraction, not quite what contemporary television studies scholars would call "binge-watching" but its precursor in what Kracauer referred to as the "cult of distraction," whereby modern subjects turn to the movies as a way to avoid the psychic challenges wrought by modernity.[96] It is a term that attempts to name a culture of avoidance by way of the cinematic image, a temporary psychic retreat "that allows forgetting," as early film critic Milena Jesenská put it. It is a giving oneself over to the cinema "in order to better endure life." The cinema, Jesenská writes, describing this culture and mode of engagement, is "easier to bear, because in the face of our deformed lives, we are powerless."[97]

Indeed, what might irk us about this line of inquiry, and perhaps one of the reasons we have not yet explored it in film histories of literary modernism, is that modes of spectatorship such as identification, narrative immersion, longing, distraction, and wish fulfillment do not typically form the basis of an oppositional art or mode of cultural engagement that we like to see in our modernists, perhaps especially the minoritarian ones. Escapism and identification are typically thought to belong to the realm of interpellation and hegemony of which writers such as Larsen, Barnes, and to a lesser extent Faulkner have all in their own respect been considered deeply critical. But Berlant teaches us, in Ngai's words, to "refus[e] to be contemptuous of people's desire for the normal, even or especially as that desire complicatedly persists" after "fantasmatic clarities about the conditions for enduring collectivity, historical continuity, and infrastructural stability have melted away."[98] If we dismiss that complicated desire, we lose the opportunity to confront and understand the forms of psychic security to which we remain affectively—and understandably—beholden. *Losing the Plot*, too, refuses to be contemptuous of the desire for normalcy as it expresses itself both in the desire for the formal security of plot and in the ritual of escapism. Understood broadly as an attenuation of the self, escapism warrants critical examination if for no other reason than that it indexes a desire momentarily not to be oneself, momentarily not to endure what one typically has to endure. It is its own survival strategy, but one quite different from what Muñoz describes in *Disidentifications*, less negative, more ambivalent, less clearly bent toward building tools for political resistance and more toward making it to the end of the day. Ambivalence, as Kobena Mercer argues, permeates the "identifications we actually inhabit in living with difference." As such, Kyle Kaplan insists, ambivalent identifications "neither easily satisfy liberatory projects" nor "lead to political aloofness."[99] They point, rather, to a thinking through, moving through, working through what one thinks and feels, even as those feelings and thoughts are at odds with what one otherwise believes to be politically right.

WHO ARE YOU AND WHAT DID YOU SEE?

The study of cinematic reception has been just as plagued by questions surrounding the affordances and limitations of writing about what you know and who you are personally as have broader debates concerning subject-based epistemology. The affective experience of the reception of film texts is often considered so private and particular to each individual that scholarship on what a person or groups of people were feeling when they encountered a certain cinematic image have been founded on tireless methodological self-reflection. The simple question of film programming, "What did you see?" is haunted by the far thornier one of response, "What did you *see* in what you saw?" Despite the paratextual evidence we might be able to marshal—reviews, ticket sales, newspaper articles, and so on—there is an intractable unknowability that characterizes the cinematic reception of others: "In an important sense," Annette Kuhn writes, "we hardly know these people at all."[100]

The issue here concerns proof. How do we know what another person thought—or even more difficult, felt—about a film they saw? Thus working from what modernists "might conceivably have seen" solves certain problems but nevertheless confronts us with the primary methodological problem that has historically beset the study of affects of film reception: the risk of overgeneralizing from one's particular affective experience or having one's particular affective experience fall into perilously meaningless particularity. Discussions of cinephilia, for example, always come up against the limits of theorizability, not only because loving something in a complicated, obsessive, or even destructive way is hard to put into words (a matter I discuss at length in my coda) but because one's own personal experience seems the most reliable way to talk about reception, and as such, it risks bearing "the taint with which subjectivity, individuality, and contingency have been charged in intellectual fields."[101] Christian Keathley famously considers personal anecdotes of cinephilic encounters, however uncomfortable to relay in an academic setting, a crucial part of the process of generating an organic historiography of film reception. Eugenie Brinkema, meanwhile, solves what she sees as the overreliance of affect theories of film reception on the subjective experience of the theorist by studying what she considers the objective form that affects take, the movements and shapes defining the expression of affect in film that are available to most, if not all careful viewers.[102] In film histories of literary modernism, this methodological problem has often been solved by recourse to firsthand accounts written by modernist writers. For example, Woolf's 1926 essay "The Cinema" has held pride of place in the film historiography of literary modernism because it is a quintessentially obedient piece of evidence. It provides Woolf's firsthand account of her experience watching films, which scholars then use to analyze her fiction.[103] On this model, the proof is in the archival pudding. Easy peasy; no need to disclose potentially embarrassing personal anecdotes that would compromise the critical authority of the theorist.

But this approach has at least two perils. The first is that it privileges the presence of archival evidence, and therefore what is considered historically rigorous scholarship on the film history of literary modernism is in danger of being limited to the study of writers whose encounters with the cinema are institutionally supported by the racialized processes of exclusion that have historically determined patterns of archivization. For example, it is only because of Larsen's first biographer, Thadious Davis, that we know Larsen watched Garbo's *Camille* multiple times and that it was one of her favorite films. Davis learned this through interviews with one of Larsen's friends from the 1930s.[104] But there is not a shred of evidence in her meager archives that would tell us what she thought about Garbo. To be clear: archival absences should not be fetishized as the doomed fate of minoritarian culture makers.[105] Djuna Barnes's archive, for instance, is positively overflowing. But as tends to be the case with many minoritarian academic fields—such as subaltern studies, which had to overcome archival absence in order to forward scholarly inquiry—Black historiography has demanded informed conjecture on the part of the scholar so as not to take the absence of archival evidence as the termination point of critical investigation.[106] Black historiography, writes Saidiya Hartman, demands a recuperative, sensuous, and affective "specula[tion] about what might have been."[107] The influence that the speculative archival work of these scholars, particularly Hartman and Allyson Nadia Field, has had on my approach will no doubt be most evident in chapter 1, in which I examine the fiction of Larsen in conjunction with the films of Greta Garbo. But in a sense it is everywhere in this book—as I believe it is everywhere in any form of aesthetic criticism.[108]

The second is that speculation about what another person was thinking and feeling is risky, the primary risk being that one could simply be wrong.

For evidence, *Losing the Plot* draws primarily on the novels these writers wrote, putting them into conversation with the films and film cultures in which I have discovered them to have been immersed during periods of extreme personal despair. I perform film and literary textual analysis alongside biographical research into the lives and moviegoing practices of these writers, treating them as empirical beings, humans who needed consolation or other kinds of satisfaction and got it, in complicated forms, from the place we seem to want to think they did not. When possible, I have drawn on archival material, including film programming and contemporary reviews, to flesh out my claims. But regardless of the degree of available evidence, by virtue of discussing the affects of film reception of other people, I perform, of necessity, a speculative critical practice, and I do so fully aware of all of its potential hazards. Indeed, I do not speculate as to what Larsen, Barnes, and Faulkner may have felt when at the movies—or as to the affects produced by Max Ophuls's films—because I am certain that I am right. I do so because I would prefer to incur the risk of being wrong and in the process of being wrong open up new lines of inquiry rather than continue to tread the same and therefore safer academic waters. It turned out that Coleman was wrong about what Barnes thought of plot; but in being wrong, she invited Barnes to tell her something intriguingly counterintuitive that allows us to see her work differently.

To that end, the first two chapters study the fiction of Larsen and Barnes alongside the films of Greta Garbo and Marlene Dietrich, which they were watching while moving through periods of alcoholism, depression, and heartbreak brought on by divorce, separation, and in the case of Larsen, reclusion and a plagiarism scandal. I show how these moviegoing practices illuminate a central governing ambivalence at the heart of their novels, which is the desire for the very plots—of self-becoming and romantic love—that Larsen and Barnes otherwise critique as psychically damaging fictions that have historically been either inhospitable to minoritarian subjectivity or thought anathema to its "authentic" expressions. In chapter 3, I then see what happens when we extend the rubrics of ambivalence developed in the first two chapters to the work of majoritarian subjectivity by studying Faulkner's work in conjunction with the culture of early narrative cinema in which he was immersed while struggling to determine the narrative course of his life and facing multiple obstacles. I chart the implications of those discoveries for his later work writing for classical Hollywood. The cinema of Max Ophuls's late French period then supplies me with the end of my story, a turn to what many consider cinema's own properly modernist moment in the midcentury.

CHAPTER OVERVIEWS

In chapter 1, reading the novels of Nella Larsen in conjunction with the films of Greta Garbo, I show how Garbo's films—many of which feature her as a woman whose identity is plagued by a problematic twoness—both expose the constructedness of white racial identity and naturalize it through techniques of costume design, lighting, and cinematography, making whiteness appear coextensive with the fantasy of narrative unity. The chapter focuses on a reading of Larsen's semiautobiographical bildungsroman *Quicksand* in conjunction with one of her favorite films: George Cukor's MGM box office hit *Camille*. *Camille* integrates its protagonist, a consumptive courtesan played by Garbo, into a plot of bourgeois social arrival by rendering moot the material circumstances that would realistically foreclose that outcome. Drawing on the speculative archival practices of contemporary film and literary studies as well as what David Eng calls the "affective" archival practices within queer studies, I argue that reading *Quicksand* in light of *Camille*—placing this later moment of Larsen's life in stereoscopic relation to an earlier one—allows us to see that *Quicksand* stages a biracial woman's repeated attempts to plot a *consequential* experience, experience that coordinates cause to effect in such a way that would produce a coherent self precisely in the way that *Camille* does.

Djuna Barnes, meanwhile, was watching Marlene Dietrich's collaborations with filmmaker Josef von Sternberg while nursing a broken heart over her lover Thelma Wood and composing *Nightwood*, the novel that elegizes that heartbreak. Chapter 2 brings Barnes's actual writings about Dietrich, which I have discovered in Barnes's archive, to bear on *Nightwood*, whose central character, Robin Vote, is Wood's literary avatar. Barnes was fascinated with Dietrich's silences, the queer icon's emotional minimalism embodied in such films as *Morocco* and *Shanghai Express*, that made her characters appear uninvested in the outcome of the heterosexual love plot. Barnes, I argue, wanted to be like Dietrich—who, like Wood, embodied her queer negativity with ease, quietly subverting the love plots that von Sternberg's films already treated ironically. Due to what Mari Ruti calls the "fetishization of negativity" within queer theory, Barnes scholarship tends to downplay the fact that Barnes wanted to be with Wood in what S. Pearl Brilmyer, Filippo Trentin, and Zairong Xiang call that "least queer of all relational forms"[109]—a monogamous couple. Grappling with this inconvenient fact, I read *Nightwood* from the perspective of Nora Flood, who in her clamor to build a structure of narrative causality from *Nightwood*'s morass of modernist textuality—to create with Robin a love plot on the model of domestic fiction such that she would be her only lover—is not antithetical to *Nightwood*'s queer modernist project, as is typically assumed, but expressive of *Nightwood*'s and Barnes's own ambivalent feelings about queer antinormativity.

Chapter 3 examines how early film and its cultures of exhibition are integral to an understanding of how William Faulkner's earlier modernist novels interrogate the narrative poverty of lived experience in time. Archival research of film programming and exhibition venues in Oxford, Mississippi, during the late nineteenth and early twentieth centuries reveals that while growing up and struggling to determine the professional and sexual trajectory of his life, Faulkner was steeped in the culture of early film as it developed, unevenly and gradually, from a primarily documentary medium to a narrative one—from the "cinema of attractions," as Gunning has famously called it, to what is often referred to as the "transitional" cinema of approximately 1903–13 and eventually the classical Hollywood cinema. Through a network of references to that formal and institutional history, *The Sound and the Fury* and *As I Lay Dying* show plot to be a paranoid form of sensemaking. But it is one that Faulkner's characters nevertheless reach for in the form of imperfect but palliative formal structures—such as blame assignment and narratives of victimization—that mitigate their dread as they navigate a modern world seemingly abandoned by any author and thus bereft of palliative etiologies.

The book ends by considering the cinema of German-French filmmaker Max Ophuls, whose late masterpiece *The Earrings of Madame de . . .* (1953) suggests that even knowledge of the violence underpinning that most ideologically powerful of all plots—the love story—is not enough to dispel entirely our desire for its fulfillment. Through a cinematography of depth and natural space often considered anathema to Ophulsian artifice, *Madame de . . .* depicts a love affair between the aristocrat Louise de . . . and the Baron Donati that has the power to generate world-shaking narrative consequences. The formative force of that love—as distinct from the tautological formalisms of desire circulating inconsequentially within the film's gorgeous but asphyxiating interiors—undermines the structures of colonial violence supporting French aristocratic prosperity and possessive liberal individualism. But it is also predicated on the refusal of the lovers' union. Through a manipulation of haptic aurality—allowing us to hear the sounds of Louise's body as it longs and eventually dies for Donati—the film elicits in us a kind of identification based not in escapism but in an arresting recognition of our own mortality and thus our own longing, too, to be with the beloved, just as we know, with equal force, the political cost.

I have argued elsewhere that we tend to perform certainty in our critical claims when they are put to paper or computer screen; rhetorics of certainty are part of our argumentative conventions, part and parcel of forwarding our disciplines.[110] But when we talk to one another in our everyday lives—over coffee, over dinner, at the movies, on the couch watching Netflix—we tend to do so far less often. We often find ourselves wondering whether we've gotten something right, thinking about alternative possibilities for how to articulate a thought we thought we had arrived at with certainty. We think through, move through, thought. Thought, like life, is not plotted, but it is also not unplotted. One book cannot enumerate the full range of instances in which the encounter with the classical Hollywood cinema and its narrative precursors render plot an object of ambivalence in the modernist novel. What it can do, however, is provide a set of potent examples in which the cinema does appear to do that. Thus this book, I hope, will bring us up against the limits of our often unconsciously held assumptions about what happens to plot in modernism, what modernism's attitudes toward its own negative commitments were, what modernists saw when they went to the movies, and what we see when we do too.

ONE

Nella Larsen and Greta Garbo
On (In)Consequence

You know, that unexpected situation of kind of wanting to be the heroine and yet wanting to kill the heroine, at the same time. And that kind of dilemma, that push and pull, is sort of the basis, the underlying turbulence that I bring to each of the pieces that I make.

Visual artist Kara Walker on watching Scarlett O'Hara
in *Gone with the Wind*, 2003

By the mid-1930s, Nella Larsen had begun to vanish from the scene. Her career had started off with tremendous vitality, her literature championed by prominent figures of the Harlem Renaissance, including not just close friend Carl Van Vechten but also W. E. B. Du Bois, whose vehement support helped catapult her into literary fame. And as late as March 1930, Larsen was awarded a fellowship from the prestigious Guggenheim Foundation, an important biographical detail that challenges the common narrative that Larsen's career plummeted after the plagiarism scandal surrounding her short story "Sanctuary." However, by the mid-1930s, she was struggling with depression and substance abuse. Not only had it become very difficult for her to place her work but in 1933, her husband Elmer Imes, a physicist and member of the Black aristocracy, left her for a white woman Larsen knew him to be having an affair with since at least 1930—Ethel Bedient Gilbert, the director of publicity and finance at Fisk University, where Imes worked as chair of the physics department. The accumulation of challenges plunged her into despair and reclusion for years, during which time she also cut ties with most if not all of her friends, including Van Vechten and Dorothy Peterson, with whom she had been very close for almost two decades.

In the midst of all this, Larsen was going to the movies, and she liked one particular film more than most. Apparently, Larsen went multiple times to see George Cukor's MGM box office hit *Camille* (1936): it was, according to her biographers, one of her "favorites."[1] Based on Alexandre Dumas fils's novel *The Lady of the Camellias* (1848) and his own 1852 stage adaptation, *Camille* tells the story of a love affair between the young bourgeois Armand Duval (Robert Taylor) and the consumptive courtesan Marguerite Gautier (Greta Garbo)—an affair that results in the lovers' despair and Marguerite's death. It is a film about a woman who drags herself out of rural poverty through high-end prostitution, supporting her extravagant urban life through sexual liaisons with the aristocracy and haute bourgeoisie of mid-nineteenth-century Paris. Marguerite eventually dies of consumption, not having been able to marry and live with her true lover, Armand, a petit bourgeois whose family forces them to separate so as to protect his professional and social prospects. It is a film, in short, about passing—about the attempt to shroud one's origins with the trappings of a different life, a different look, and what happens when that attempt fails. But whereas Dumas's novel makes the consequences of that failure brutally apparent, unforgiving in the finality with which it shows the lovers' union to be a social and economic impossibility, Cukor's film manages those consequences away with all the magical insouciance suggested in Toni Morrison's epigraph opening the introduction to this book. Hollywood, as Morrison suggests, is where the blind regain their sight, where the lame throw aside their crutches; it is, as James Baldwin writes, where one's fantasies are corroborated and dangerously so precisely because we are invited to escape into the very skin of the star. Again and again, as Larsen was struggling through the most demoralizing period of her life, she went to see Garbo at the Capitol Theatre on Broadway and 51st Street. There, she would have repeatedly witnessed the image of Taylor clutching Garbo to him as she dies in his arms, morally redeemed and flouting, with every inch of her glamorous face, the grotesque horror of the original novel.

Larsen's fascination with *Camille* has been biographically noted but critically unexamined. Far from merely a curious anecdote, it affords important insight into her fiction, especially her semiautobiographical bildungsroman *Quicksand* (1928). It also offers a way to reassess and revise one of the principal critical commitments of modernist aesthetics regarding the relation of time and events to the construction of the self. Reading *Quicksand* in light of Larsen's repeated viewings of *Camille*—positioning this later moment of her life in stereoscopic relation to a previous one—allows us to see *Quicksand* differently, not as a rejection of the bildungsroman but as an extended attempt to deliver on the social and psychic promises generated by that genre's fundamental feature in its nineteenth-century form: plot. It demonstrates how the functions and affordances of plot as they emerged in classical Hollywood films were profoundly alluring even within a modernist literary framework assumed to have grown overwhelmingly suspicious of plot—especially plots pressed in service of narratives of personal development.

The "generic failure" marking the trajectory of the modernist bildungsroman is often seen as "a successful resistance to the institutionalization of self-cultivation," an emancipation from what Fredric Jameson calls the "regime of the *récit*."[2] "What we perceive to be the failures of Bildung in modernist Bildungsromane," Gregory Castle writes, "can thus be read as critical triumphs."[3]

However, we should interrogate, rather than take for granted, the distinction between aesthetic and critical triumph on the one hand and the lived realities of personal failure on the other.[4] For what if the failure to become an autonomous subject feels extraordinarily painful, the social and psychic consequences of that failure barely endurable? What if that "critical triumph" is an index of an enormous amount of personal and communal suffering? If one of the things that plot does best is to generate characters out of textual matter—to make mimetic beings out of synthetic ones, to borrow James Phelan's terms[5]—then what, we should ask, would it be like not to be provided the shelter of that formal architecture? There is a substantive distinction between the aesthetic performance of that shattering and the feeling, in one's living and breathing existence, of being shattered.

Asking this question means engaging to some degree in what Mieke Bal calls the "realistic fallacy," the act of treating characters as if they were real people.[6] The job of the modernist critic is more often than not to ask, after Roland Barthes, "Who speaks?" Indeed, because of what Toril Moi has recently reminded us is literary criticism's genealogical entanglements with modernist formalism—the foregrounding of style over content, form over story[7]—we tend to ask far more seldomly, "What must the living do when the author absents themselves?" To insist that there are bodies to be taken seriously behind the literary discourse that creates them is, after all, not so different from what many theorists have insisted on in the context of Black studies and others in queer studies: that the theoretical discourse of fragmentation, negativity, decenteredness, difference, otherness, and so forth, is at best limited because of its tendency to devolve into unthought academic dogma and is at worst deaf to the lived precarities of subjects for whom some form of affirmative wholeness—some solid ground—would be woefully desirable if not a welcome respite from a life of enforced precarity.[8] It is this general inattentiveness to the distinction between aesthetic achievement and individual pain that has played a significant part in modernist studies' difficulty engaging, in a systematic and meaningful way, with Black studies in particular.

In their 2013 special issue of *Modernism/modernity*, Adam McKible and Suzanne W. Churchill set out to address the problem of what Houston Baker in 1987 called the "'old lacunae' of critical practices that occlude and obscure the connections between the field(s) of study that are called—quite imperfectly—the 'Harlem Renaissance' and 'modernism.'"[9] The tenacity of this intrafield separation has yielded what Michael Bibby reveals to be a strikingly low percentage of panels and presentations dedicated to Black modernists at the annual conferences of the Modernist Studies Association and articles dedicated to Black writers in *Modernism/modernity*—the two preeminent arteries of modernist scholarship.[10] In the time since the publication of McKible and Churchill's special issue, modernist scholars have been rushing to redress this biting diagnosis.[11] But despite its inclusionist aims, the new modernist studies—both as an intellectual project and as a professional institution—has struggled not only to account sustainedly for Black cultural production but also to be systemically permeated by critical sensibilities that do not take for granted the fundamental aesthetic premises of modernist art as desirable modes of being and moving through the world.

That struggle remains alive, and I suggest that it has to do at least in part with modernist studies' abiding—albeit often implicit, if not unconscious—valuation of states of social and subjective fragmentation. Within discourses of minoritarian subjectivity, including Black studies but also queer theory and postcolonial studies, such states are treated with ambivalence, considered both the site of a unique criticality—as in Du Boisian "double consciousness" and Saidian "contrapuntal" subjectivity—but also traumatic dissociation, as in Frantz Fanon's "neurosis."[12] What Bibby calls the "racial formation of modernist studies," which is a white racial formation, has to do with the fact that despite the inclusionary aims of the new modernist studies, the field is only recently starting to incorporate into the fabric of its critical ethos an acknowledgment that subjective fragmentation means something entirely different for persons subject to psychic and historical genealogies of racial subjugation, racialized histories of enforced labor, sexual violence, deracination, and exile than it does for someone like Ezra Pound, T. S. Eliot, Gertrude Stein, Jean-Luc Godard, or Alain Resnais.[13] Fragmentation, in many discourses of minoritized subjectivity, is an index of traumatic loss, a state that one finds "strategies," to borrow Muñoz's term, to repair rather than leave open bleeding.[14]

By thinking through the distinction between aesthetic achievement and individual pain—the impulse to shatter in art and the desire for stability in life—as that distinction emerges in *Quicksand*, this chapter will also go some way toward addressing this disciplinary issue. The primary formal site of that tension is plot, for it is plot's ability to provide lived experience a set of formal boundaries, to form what otherwise threatens formlessness, that makes it both an aesthetic restriction and an existential refuge. Plot thus emerges in *Quicksand* as the object not just of critical contestation but also of longing.

Larsen's interest in *Camille* helps illuminate that tension. Taking into account the role that *Camille* may have played in Larsen's life—including as a possible source of self-soothing during a time of extreme personal distress—affords us a perspective from which to see *Quicksand* as having a far more complex, if vexed, relation to plot than rejection or liberation.

Quicksand, I will show, is a formal meditation on *inconsequence*, what happens when the formal logic of causality malfunctions, when plot doesn't congeal and thus experience doesn't seem to matter, formally or socially. No matter what Larsen's protagonist Helga Crane does, no matter where she goes, she is unable to fully become herself in the way that she wishes, to gain the sense of completion she desires from the very beginning of the novel. *Camille*, meanwhile, representative of a broader tendency in 1930s Hollywood melodramas, flaunts its capacity to bend consequences to its liking: simultaneously to generate the forms of coherent selfhood afforded by the proper functioning of narrative causality and to make irrelevant the material circumstances that would realistically disable such a narrative and subjective formation from taking place—reconciling, as Judith Mayne would put it, terms "irreconcilable in everyday experience."[15] Larsen's repeated visits to *Camille*—a film that through plot restores its protagonist to a narrative of social arrival from which the original novel had banished her—suggest her fascination, if unsettled and ambivalent, with Hollywood cinema's reliance on the primacy of plot. It suggests a conflicted form of affective investment in plot on the part of a writer otherwise committed to subverting it on social, political, and aesthetic grounds. And this aesthetic crisis—that is, the longing for what plot promises to provide, despite all that it takes away—is illuminated once we understand the way classical Hollywood film generated the illusions of social belonging and psychic unity that were historically the generic dominion of the nineteenth-century bildungsroman.

In my introduction I mentioned that the call for film historians of literary modernism to work from what films modernist writers may have actually seen generates methodological problems having to do with archival absences, the privacy of spectatorship, and historical chronology. While the former two problems (which I see as generative rather than prohibitive) animate all of my chapters, it is the latter—historical chronology—which is most evident in the case of Larsen. I am not making the anachronistic claim that Larsen's viewings of *Camille* influenced *Quicksand*. Rather, I want to suggest that Larsen's first novel reads differently—is thrown into relief differently—once one knows that its author, though she was reclusive, suffering depression, and struggling with substance abuse, repeatedly went to see a film that rescues its protagonist from the forms of social ostracization and psychic strain that beset her own Helga Crane. I substitute a stereoscopic theory of history for one of chronological influence, orienting critical inquiry in terms that create a three-dimensional space, a plot, of historical and formal traces rather than a series of consecutive events. As such, I draw on the work of Alix Beeston, Wai Chee Dimock, David Eng, Allyson Nadia Field, Saidiya Hartman, Julie Beth Napolin, and Jacqueline Najuma Stewart, who, taken together, have theorized modes of criticism based in a conception of history as malleable, sensuous, and affective rather than synchronous, empirical, and chronological.[16] I share these scholars' belief that much is lost if we limit our understanding of history to a series of discrete and chronological events we know happened with Cartesian certainty and the work of criticism to the obedient charting of this history. This conventional view of historiographical criticism has indeed governed what Joseph North calls the "historicist/contextualist" paradigm dominant in contemporary literary studies, and certainly the film historiography of literary modernism, which, since the publication of David Trotter's *Cinema and Modernism* (2007) and Laura Marcus's *The Tenth Muse* (2007), has been especially vehement about the need to radically historicize the film-literature relationship.[17]

But Dimock and Napolin show that texts have a life of their own, "resonating" across time and space, changing, sounding, and looking different once put into contact with cultural and critical acts beyond their immediate historical context. The labor of criticism on this model is to capture the text's multiple and centrifugal movements when apprehended from varying and asynchronic viewpoints—what Beeston, by way of Susan Stanford Friedman, calls the work of "critical superimposition"—rather than to try to "lock" the text in its immediate context."[18] Other scholars, meanwhile, recuperate glimpses of experience and cultural production that have escaped our attention by virtue of the racialized processes of exclusion in conventional historiography. The critical account of marginalized lives, Hartman shows, demands historiographical methods that decenter the empirical, since historians of minoritarian groups are "forced to grapple with the power and authority of the archive and the limits it sets on what can be known, whose perspective matters, and who is endowed with the gravity and authority of historical actor."[19] Historiography demands informed conjecture, a recuperative, sensuous, and affective "specula[tion] about what might have been."[20]

It is with this project in mind that we may take Larsen's viewings of *Camille* as an integral coordinate in what Dimock would call the "resonant universe" or what Eng would call the hidden "affective history" of not just Larsen herself but also of her fiction.[21] As will become clear, one of the primary axes linking Helga Crane to Greta Garbo is the representational problem of dimensionality, the illusion of volume that motivates both visual verisimilitude in the popular cinema and the psychic depth of the classical bildungsroman's protagonists. Modeling this concern with depth and dimensionality, this chapter reconstructs that resonant universe or affective history by opening up a three-dimensional historiographical architecture—plotting out a space—within which Larsen's literature and Garbo's films can rotate around and reflect evanescently against one another, in turn shifting all their appearances.

Larsen's 1929 novel *Passing* is a nearer historical antecedent to *Camille*. And as we will see, Larsen's interest in Garbo—whose own racial performance is itself often inflected with the logic of twoness—will have implications for *Passing* in ways that will add further texture to our understanding of *Quicksand*. Hutchinson speculates that Larsen was drawn to *Camille* because the rise and fall of Marguerite Gautier into and out of Parisian high society mimicked her own trajectory through Harlem's cultural elite.[22] But there are more complex connections between Larsen's semiautobiographical novel and Cukor's film—and between Larsen's fictions of passing and Garbo's racial performances—than thematic resemblance. A closer and more sustained look at Garbo's work—or, more accurately, a closer and more sustained look at Garbo and how in her films the visual logic of passing gets invoked and its anxieties subsequently quelled—yields more critically provocative possibilities for why Larsen may have been drawn to Garbo than simply resemblance between her own life and Cukor's film. The sparseness and evasiveness of Larsen's epistolary activity by 1936 provide no firsthand account of her impressions of *Camille*. However, in line with Hartman's and Field's insistence that we not allow the "extant" to overdetermine the limits of historiographical inquiry—and with Stewart's claim that much of our "reconstructive work" concerning early twentieth-century Black spectatorship "must be performed creatively"[23]—we can speculate as to what drew her to it, given the meditation, at the center of *Quicksand*, on the kind of self-possessing bourgeois personality the modernist bildungsroman would not permit itself to produce. Larsen would have been primed to detect the way *Camille* relies on staple techniques of classical Hollywood melodrama—a genre of cultural production for which plot was gospel—to resolve the formal and subjective crises that animate *The Lady of the Camellias* and that *Quicksand* systematically stages and laments.

Cukor had probably not read *Quicksand*; he was known to read white male modernists. Zoë Akins, however, *Camille*'s primary screenwriter, very well may have, considering her more capacious literary curiosity and the success of Larsen's novel.[24] But most strikingly, an early draft of *Camille*'s opening intertitles in Akins's archives reads as follows:

> 1[8]47—... In Paris... In the half-world where the prettiest creature was queen of the moment, great men forgot their troubles; and the pretty creatures themselves, living on the quicksands of popularity, brightened their wit with champagne and their eyes with tears. For them romance was a flower without perfume, as perhaps Marguerite Gautier realized when she chose for her badge the scentless camellia. Never without these rare and expensive flowers which were ruined by a single touch, she was known, respected and fought over in a circle which has no exact counterpart with its sharp lines of demarcation in the world today. But in Marguerite's time, the girl who had suffered one familiar improper touch was like a camellia ruined forever as an ornament of good society; and the man who was seen at her side when she ventured beyond her half-world, was almost equally doomed. To link his life with a woman of Marguerite Gautier's experience was to sacrifice his future and his position in the world. But true love has never been discreet.[25]

The fragility of twoness, the threat of discovery, and the social perils of contamination—the "ruin" of one "improper," "single touch," the doom of one drop—were evidently very much at the forefront of Akins's mind when she was adapting the script from Dumas source material, itself written by a writer whose part-Haitian ancestry made him all too familiar with what it means to belong to a "half-world." Indeed, the shadow text behind the language of a compromised virginity—apart from that of a conquered land, a colonized land—is one of a compromised racial purity, a whiteness destroyed and its destruction contagious. Larsen would not have seen this entire text. It was no doubt deemed too long and perhaps, from the point of view of the Hayes Office, too explicit in its invocation of lost sexual virtue. But what did remain of Akins's original draft in the *Camille* that Larsen saw is not insignificant: it refers not only to the "code" of "discretion" that governs this "half-world" but also, and perhaps most importantly, singles out Marguerite specifically—rather than her cohort of "pretty creatures"—as one "who lived on the quicksands of popularity."

Traveling back to nineteenth-century France by way of 1930s Hollywood, this chapter takes up Dimock's call for the "dislocat[ion]" of literary texts from their particular moment in order to see them productively "fall apart" into "new and strange" figurations of meaning.[26] Knowing Larsen would go on, just eight years later, to grow fascinated by *Camille* allows us to see *Quicksand* in just such a new and strange light. In the retrospective glow of Garbo's image, plot in *Quicksand* emerges not as a site of certain negation or resistance but of mourning. The novel mourns the unavailability of plot's formal securities to its protagonist Helga Crane—and, perhaps proleptically, to Larsen herself.

A THING WITHOUT THOUGHT

The nineteenth-century novel generated aesthetic equivalents for the modern autonomous individual by charting a protagonist's moral and social development. "The history of the novel and the history of the modern subject," Nancy Armstrong writes, "are quite literally, one and the same."[27] For the individual to secure interiority and an intelligible place in bourgeois liberal society, Armstrong notes, she must experience dissatisfaction, a discrepancy between her wants and her reality. Be it Armstrong's "dissatisfaction," Peter Brooks's "desire," or Franco Moretti's "determination," theorizations of the novel acknowledge that *acquisition* is central to the genre. In the classical bildungsroman, in particular, the protagonist acquires personality as they acquire experience. There is thus a fundamental interdependence, in the genre, of plot and selfhood. Yet the novel's labor is also, as Moretti notes, to reconcile the protagonist's personal trajectory to the moral, political, and socioeconomic exigencies of the modern liberal state—namely, the "right to property and personal autonomy."[28] In the novel, to be an individual is also to have the right to own *things*.

But *Quicksand* is fundamentally about the inability of experience to generate selfhood, of causes to generate effects.[29] And as we will eventually see, that failure is partly the result of what Larsen depicts as the inefficacy of possession. The novel tells the story of Helga Crane, a woman who, like Larsen herself, was born to a working-class Danish woman (not insignificantly, Garbo belonged to the Swedish working class) and a West Indian Black father. Now orphaned, however, Helga works as a teacher at a boarding school in the South named Naxos, thought to be a fictional version of Booker T. Washington's Tuskegee Institute, a school for Black students where Larsen momentarily worked in 1915. Sickened by the school's stifling commitment to Black respectability politics steeped in what Helga considers an aspiration to middle-class whiteness, she embarks on a series of geographical displacements—from Naxos to Chicago to Harlem to Copenhagen to stay with members of her extended Danish family, back to Harlem and finally to Alabama—each of which she makes with characteristic suddenness and with the always unmet hope of acquiring a sense of belonging and wholeness. After having witnessed this drama of what Jennifer L. Fleissner might call the "malady of the will,"[30] we see Helga, in the book's final pages, dreaming of her next departure, this time from her rural Southern life with her husband Reverend Pleasant Green, having had three children, seen the death of a fourth, and with the fifth gestating in her womb.

Few in modern literature are more seduced by *things* than Helga Crane. "Always she had wanted, not money," Larsen writes, "but the things which money could give, leisure, attention, beautiful surroundings. Things. Things. Things." From the beginning of the novel, Helga surrounds herself with material markers of the bourgeoisie. Her room at Naxos is strewn with colorful, eye-catching clothing that is both the cause and symbol of her inability to fit in at the school. She is drawn to Anne's home in Harlem for its surplus of decorative objects. And when she establishes a stable middle-class life in Alabama with Reverend Green, she articulates her happiness in terms of the ability to possess: "To be mistress in one's own house, to have a garden, and chickens, and a pig; to have a husband," she thinks, "here she had found, she was sure, the intangible thing for which, indefinitely, always she had craved. It had received embodiment." This pervasive language of ownership suggests that Helga has finally found the bourgeois normative domesticity that corresponds to corporeal embodiment. She has, in short, landed in a situation productive of the possessive liberal individualism she realizes she may have wanted all along, exemplifying the novel's generic doctrine that to have is to be. Yet even attaining the liberal bourgeois ideal leaves her restless and discontent. The novel ends with Helga lacking, still, "confidence in the fullness of her life"[31] and transforming ultimately into something on the order of a birthing machine. The final, harrowing line of the novel tells us that her fifth child is gestating in her womb as she comes in and out of consciousness, contemplating her next decision to leave her life with the Reverend, which she has come to hate as much as all of her previous lives. Not fully a mimetic being, Helga's status as a character is irrevocably haunted by its synthetic axis. She is, Larsen never allows us to forget, made.

For Walter Benjamin, the ritual of turning to novels is itself a life-giving form of acquisition. "The reader of the novel," he writes in "The Storyteller," "seizes upon his material more jealously than anyone else. He is ready to make it completely his own—to devour it, as it were.... He swallows up the material as the fire devours logs in the fireplace."[32] By "virtue of the flame which consumes [the characters' fate]," he continues, it "yields us the warmth which we never draw from our own fate. What draws the reader to the novel is the hope of warming his shivering life with a death he reads about." Novels, then, provide the reader a kind of warmth not unlike what one feels at the hearth.

But the reader is absorbed by *Quicksand* in a different way than by the novels to which Benjamin implicitly refers. Those novels—the Balzacian, Dickensian ones—show the piecing together of a person through experiences that the novelist shapes into events. The retrospective ordering operation of plot gathers together the otherwise inchoate present, "stick[ing]," to borrow Virginia Woolf's phrase from *To the Lighthouse*, "the odds and ends" of experience to the "magnet" of narrative events. Those lives— Rastignac, Pip, Sorel, Bennet—breathe warmth into ours because they allow us to imagine for the duration of our reading that our own lives are composed of such restful summits, "swept ... clean" into a novelistic life.[33] As we watch the subjectivity of another individual form over time and through experience, our own starts to fill out and become whole.

But Helga does not fill out. Barely in command of her words and actions, she seems motivated by a biomechanics beyond her control.[34] Words "tumble" from her "quivering petulant lips"; she impulsively gives a "table support a violent kick"; "automatically her fingers adjust" the pillows on her bed; and she is often surprised by her own reactions to decisions she has made impetuously.[35] Although Helga's psychic inscrutability has been the topic of scholarly debate since the rediscovery of Larsen's fiction in the mid-1980s, scholars have largely eschewed the media-ecological underpinnings of that inscrutability. But Larsen's "textual tableaux," Cherene Sherrard-Johnson writes, "contain passages or frames so visually evocative that they demand a visually informed consideration" that might put figures like Helga Crane within the broader field of artistic production during the early twentieth century.[36] Indeed, making sense of Larsen's fascination with *Camille* demands that we grow sensitive to the ways *Quicksand* itself is thinking through problems of medium, enfolding Helga's crisis of selfhood into vital media-ecological questions about the bildungsroman in modernity. Vibrant, yet internally void, colorful, yet sheer, Helga is less a character than she is a moving picture.

Her room at Naxos is a field of light and shadow. "It was a comfortable room," Larsen writes, "flooded with Southern sun in the day, but shadowy just then with the drawn curtains and single shaded light. Large, too," she continues, "So large that the spot where Helga sat was a small oasis in a desert of darkness. And eerily quiet. But that was what she liked after her taxing day's work." Relaxing in the spotlight cast by a "single reading lamp," Helga reaches for a book to quell the anger she routinely feels toward her colleagues. But soon she throws her book aside and "pin[s] a scrap of paper about the bulb under the lamp's shade, for . . . she wanted an even more soothing darkness."[37] It has been noted that Helga "perceives reality in terms of color . . . tone, and hue."[38] But here, it is precisely the darkness of the room that offers her shelter from Naxos's scopic regime. In total darkness, she sits "motionless," finding tranquility at long last. She finally does "stir," but "uncertainly . . . with an overpowering desire for action of some sort," only for "a second she hesitated, then rose abruptly."[39] Helga's sudden spasms and jolts work to establish her as not so much a human being as an image, flickering in the darkness, starting into animation and then vanishing again into obscurity. Helga seeks comfort in the darkness not because she wishes to be dark, though she will for a brief period think that such cultural darkening would cure her of her restlessness. She seeks a more soothing darkness because there she can be most herself. Helga, after all, *is* chiaroscuro—she is both white and Black, a state to which she attributes her struggle to belong. But in the darkness of her camera obscura she can come to life, just as the cinematic image becomes fully visible only after the houselights are down. Helga rejects the book, instead finding comfort in a habitat evocative of a movie theater.

Cut to 1936, where Helga's dark room finds its specular reflection in Marguerite's bed chamber in *Camille*. Garbo was known for a singularly ethereal, otherworldly—"divinely untouchable"[40]—quality in her performances, the best-known examples of which are arguably her role as the titular monarch in *Queen Christina* (1933) and the despairing ballerina in *Grand Hotel* (1932). But by the time Garbo was playing Marguerite Gautier, her signature "languidness," as one critic puts it in a 1927 *New York Times* review, transforms into a droopy, diaphanous, even weak physicality, exacerbated, no doubt by the fact that she was ill while shooting.[41] Almost always on the verge of collapse, Marguerite must count on the persons and things around her to hold her up. She is immaterial—there, but just barely. The film delivers Marguerite's vulnerability at the level of the image itself. When Marguerite's friend Gaston arrives at her deathbed, the film associates her physical weakness with Garbo's status as a cinematic image. The scene opens with Gaston in long shot walking into her room from the background, toward the camera. The bottom left half of the frame, which cuts off at the threshold of Marguerite's deathbed chamber, is flickering

FIGURE 1. Gaston walks into Marguerite's room in *Camille* (George Cukor, 1936).

from the shadows cast by the flames in the fireplace positioned just outside the frame (fig. 1).

The camera stays on Gaston as he walks toward the flickering half of the frame; it then tracks left to capture Gaston confronting Marguerite sleeping, gaunt and lifeless. The camera stops just at the moment when it shows Marguerite left of center lying in bed, Gaston in profile right of center, and the right side of the frame flickering from the shadows from the fire (fig. 2). In maintaining the flickering shadows within the frame, the film associates Marguerite's ailing health with the image itself, whose flickering suggests a struggling, precarious visibility. It is as if Gaston is not watching Marguerite ill in bed but witnessing the projector of the film itself malfunctioning, the arc lamp inside it flashing and sputtering. The stillness of the shot, moreover, invokes a photograph, collapsing Marguerite into a two-dimensional image and validating Michelle Henning's critical intuition to contextualize Garbo's photographic iconography within the 1920s and 1930s fascination with the death mask.[42] Indeed, the film reminds us that we are not in fact looking at Marguerite in bed but at a cinematic projection of Garbo, whose performance of Marguerite's weakness suggests the insubstantiality of the cinematic image itself. Marguerite is not on the brink of dying; Garbo's image is in danger of disappearing.

Larsen, too, underscores Helga's embeddedness within an optics of

FIGURE 2. Gaston approaches Marguerite's deathbed in *Camille*.

two-dimensionality. She calls atypically ample attention to Helga's body in terms of its volume in space. More specifically, the prose introducing Helga establishes her as not so much a mimetic literary configuration but a synthetic, flattened image unable to become fully three-dimensional. Antonia Lant characterizes the cinema as "an utterly flat medium of presentation, insubstantial, without texture or material, and yet evoking, in a wafer, a fuller illusion of the physicality and exactness of human beings than any prior art."[43] The "perceptual wealth" of the cinematic image, as Christian Metz has famously put it, its illusion of material abundance, is fundamentally at odds with its actual immateriality.[44] Not only does the screen lack volume but the image itself is even more sparse, ostensibly self-generating but irrevocably dependent on another surface for its existence. Larsen's characterization of Helga captures this duality—what Michel Chion would call the "false depth"[45]—of the image, its status as both excessively there and stubbornly not. "A slight girl of twenty-two years, with narrow, sloping shoulders and delicate but well-turned arms and legs, she had, none the less, an air of radiant, careless health. In vivid green and gold negligee and glistening brocaded mules, deep sunk in the big high-backed chair, against whose dark tapestry her sharply cut face, with skin like yellow satin, was distinctly outlined."[46]

The passage yields a complex, if not inconceivable dimensionality. Though Larsen's sentences affect rhythmic ease, a closer look at them exposes logical difficulty. The rhetorical principle of Helga's description is subtle but persisting contradiction, the self-refuting qualification of initial assertions ("none the less"). Her body is "narrow" and "sloping," but the phrase "well-turned" suggests that her limbs are shapely, voluptuous. She is delicate, but radiant, self-effacing in her sloping shoulders but well proportioned in her arms and legs. She is at once richly variegated and silhouetted against the background tapestry. Helga is chromatically brilliant, full, and round—a depth mimicked in her sunken posture in the chair—but her "sharply cut," "outlined" face nevertheless collapses her into two dimensions, endowing her with what Laura E. Tanner has rightly described as "corporeal intangibility."[47] Her figure pops into relief, but the passage also deprives her of such volume, pressing her into a smooth surface. Her skin, moreover, is not like human skin; it is like fabric—satin, which does not have the textured, organic graininess of raw silk but the glossy slipperiness of a manufactured sheet, a screen. That metonymic kinship sliding between Helga's skin, textiles, and the screen gets repeated throughout the novel when, on two different occasions, Larsen describes the clothing Helga drapes around her body as "filmy."[48]

Helga's filminess, however, ultimately heralds her social death, cementing the incapacity of *Quicksand* to narrate her into a self-possessing autonomous individual. By invoking the dimensional poverty of the cinematic image, *Quicksand* expresses its own unwillingness to deliver on the bildungsroman's generic promise to yield a coherent, "deep" subject. Helga's religious conversion is Larsen's last effort to provide the narrative structure necessary for the achievement of personality, and when that fails, it is as if the text admits defeat, permeating Helga's final moments of maternal gestation with evocations of mechanical reproduction.

Narratologists discuss conversion in terms of the "turning point." Turning points, as Angsar Nünning and Kai Marcel Sicks have argued, are retrospective formations that lend order to otherwise undifferentiated time.[49] The bildungsroman has a vexed relationship to turning points, since, as Moretti has shown, as a genre, it sets itself against other, conclusive, and formally neat forms of causality. In Jane Austen, for instance, it is the causal chain of numerous conversations that generates change over time; each conversation—say, between Elizabeth and Darcy, or Marianne and Elinor Dashwood—contributes to the eventual narrative outcome. The formal virtue of conversation, for Moretti, is its nebulosity, the difficulty with which one can conclusively determine its precise part in the causal chain of events. Contrary to the amorphous novelistic conversation, the trial, Moretti explains, is decisive—such as Tamino's rite in Mozart's *The Magic Flute*, which "breaks [his] life into two parts." Before "a prince in exile—

after, the true heir of his father, the King." The starkness of the rite's ability to differentiate before and after is symptomatic of the fact that at stake in a text such as *The Magic Flute* is not the formation of personality but the vindication of values to which those characters, more archetypal than they are modeled on personhood, are ultimately subordinate (e.g., honor, loyalty, wisdom, and so on). Trial in the bildungsroman, he continues, "is instead an opportunity: not an obstacle to be overcome while remaining 'intact,' but something that must be incorporated, for only by stringing together 'experiences' does one build a personality."[50] Because the project of the bildungsroman is to chart the development of personality through experience—the emergence of character as a consequence of doing several things in gradual succession—it depends on an incremental, rather than immediate and drastic, causality.

While it lasts, Helga's religious conversion has more in common structurally with the trial or the rite than it does with conversation or opportunity. Her encounter with the holy rollers brings her to her knees, begging for God's mercy, and fills her suddenly with "a supreme aspiration toward the regaining of simple happiness . . . unburdened by the complexities of the lives she had known." The next day, she "feel[s] . . . utterly different from dreadful yesterday."[51] Conversion starkly discerns before from after: one is reborn pious. What is suggestive about Larsen's recourse to conversion as the last significant event in *Quicksand* is that its temporality is incommensurate with the project of the bildungsroman. It provokes a form of causality too disruptive—given expression in the "thunderclap of joy" erupting around Helga at the moment she yields to a higher power[52]—to be compatible with the gradual, accumulative nature of novelistic events. In staging a conversion, *Quicksand* is getting desperate to secure narrative teleology, to effect plot progression consequential of a coherent self.

Helga's conversion, however, is merely a structurally dramatic version of all her previous movements through time. *Quicksand* begins in that hallmark of the nineteenth-century bildungsroman, the educational institution. But whereas in *Jane Eyre* the departure from the schoolhouse marks entry into the spatial expanses of formative experience,[53] *Quicksand* does not endow that departure with semantic privilege. Instead, Helga finds a version of Naxos wherever she goes—in Harlem, it is the rigidity of a high Black culture saturated with the discourse of racial uplift; in Copenhagen, the cultural ignorance of the Danes; with the Reverend Pleasant Green, the gendered confines of pious motherhood. Departures and arrivals, which in the nineteenth-century bildungsroman were the thematic meat on the skeleton of narrative time, in *Quicksand* have lost narrative consequence beyond the mere fact of their execution. Helga has treated each of these displacements as if she were being reborn, and so the novel has from its very beginning been alienated from its own generic temporality; hence its constant invocations of other media—not just film but also vaudeville, theater, and painting. And in her quasi-suicidal stupor in the final pages, when even her conversion has failed to generate her selfhood, and having just produced her fourth child, Helga detaches from the world, retreating into the privacy of her own solitary consciousness. In the "kind darkness" of her own mind, she

> could watch the figures of the past drift by. There was her mother . . . who appeared as she had always remembered her, unbelievably beautiful, young, and remote. Robert Anderson, questioning, purposely detached, affecting, as she realized now, her life in a remarkably cruel degree; for at last she understood clearly how deeply, how passionately, she must have loved him. Anne, lovely, secure, wise, selfish. Axel Olsen, conceited, worldly, spoiled. Audrey Denney, placid, taking quietly and without fuss the things which she wanted. James Vayle, snobbish, smug, servile. Mrs. Hayes-Rore, important, kind, determined. The Dahls, rich, correct, climbing. Flashingly, fragmentarily, other long-forgotten figures, women in gay fashionable frocks and men in formal black and white, glided by in bright rooms to distant, vaguely familiar music.[54]

Despite the passage's invocation of what might seem like the optics, even spatialization, of film, Larsen probably would not have been invoking the retrospective montage sequences of cinema. Montage sequences that compress narrative time did appear in such earlier films as Abel Gance's *La roue* (1923) and Fritz Lang's *Metropolis* (1927). However, they did not start to become a common cinematic convention until after *Quicksand* was published, with films such as *The Dance of Life* (1929) and *Say It with Songs* (1929). Rather than a "cinematic" passage in a vague sense of the term, Helga's is emphatically novelistic in the vigor with which it organizes past experience into comprehensible nodes on a map. In fact, there is something too comprehensible about this retrospective sweep, an uncomfortable extremity, even artlessness, with which it assigns a neat cluster of adjectives to each character. The Dahls are "rich, correct," and "climbing"; Mrs. Hayes-Rore is "important, kind, determined"; James Vayle is "snobbish, smug, servile"; Axel Olsen is "conceited, worldly, spoiled." The immoderate symmetry of these descriptions, the bluntness with which they predicate their subjects, rather than exhibiting the epistemic privilege inherent to retrospective narration, betrays self-doubt in its very rush to name. That is, Larsen stages the passage to appear as a formal climax, in that it ostensibly marks a moment of uncharacteristic clarity for Helga, who is otherwise remarkably estranged from her own experience. But Larsen also renders it fundamentally precarious, just barely managing to assert its retrospective mastery. Larsen conveys that precarity most distinctly, perhaps, in the moment where Helga's mind settles on Anderson. "At last," she thinks, she "understood clearly how deeply, how passionately, she must have loved him." Instead of using the preterit tense—"she loved him"—which would have signified exhaustive knowledge of what was the case, Larsen chooses the more epistemically modest modal formulation—"must have loved him"—revealing the extent to which not just Helga, but also the novel, in its free-indirect-discursive fusion with her, remains opaque, uncollected.

This passage is therefore motivated by, but failing to deliver on, plot's fundamental project in the bildungsroman: to organize and name the past in service of creating a coherent self. Larsen's elision of the preterit tense—a tense that, as Jameson argues, is the grammatical cornerstone of formal realism[55]—performs what Castle would call a generic failure. It is an acknowledgment of the inability of the modern bildungsroman to perform the epistemic responsibility enacted in its grammar, to exhibit its comprehensive knowledge of the past, and to present the relevant pieces of it with certainty.

But it is not merely a defiant act of modernist negation. Larsen does not let us sit comfortably with the critical triumph that such a generic failure might index. To the contrary, she makes evident the extent to which that triumph arrives at the expense of Helga's psychic and epistemic well-being. Helga has been through so much and still does not *quite* know what has happened to her, still does not *quite* know who she is.

Her failure to come to life in a literary sense—to become unproblematically mimetic rather than hauntingly synthetic—is indeed a critical triumph on Larsen's part, a mirror held up to a social world and literary tradition hostile to the subject formation of biracial women. Larsen registers with equal force, however, the extent to which that performance is the result of Helga's profound suffering and that were Helga to have it her own way, *it would not be so*.[56]

In the final paragraphs of the novel, the free indirect discourse that had frequently permeated the novel's prose becomes constant, collapsing the distinction between Helga and the narrative machinery of her story. "Just then. Later. When she got up. By and by. She must rest," the prose reads with unprecedented terseness. "Get strong. Sleep. Then, afterwards, she could work out some arrangement. So she dozed and dreamed in snatches of sleeping and waking, letting time run on. Away." The distinction here between Helga and *Quicksand* has become so thin, if not moot, that it is as if Helga is now trying to take over the novel itself, to wrest the architecture of narrative meaning that has narrated her into the ground and to plot out her own subject formation, since her author won't. But the novel ends by cleaving that authority away from her. "Hardly had she left her bed and become able to walk again without pain . . . when she began to have her fifth child."[57] The diction of the final clause is strikingly, strategically, vague. Is the novel really locating the precise beginning of the fifth child's gestation? This sort of intrusion not into the mind but the body of the protagonist—her womb, no less—is unprecedented in this novel, reaching into uncharted territory. *Quicksand* has otherwise been markedly unable to locate the source of Helga's actions, to account for the psychic origins of her decisions, let alone her physical movements. But here, for the first and only time in the novel, Larsen makes *Quicksand*'s powers of penetration tremendously acute, allowing the novel finally to pierce to Helga's very center. The effect of the narration's pervasion of Helga's body, though, is not to psychologize her, to render her deep. Rather, Helga's serial, unwanted pregnancies at the end of the novel suggest her exhaustive depsychologization, her psychic interiority having been replaced with the synthetic insides of biomechanical reproduction.

Helga does not become a coherent subject no matter how much plot Larsen throws at her. Instead, a tropology of the reproduction of an insubstantial projected image encroaches on the novel's formal and figurative landscape. The final several chapters pull out exaggerated and overdetermined versions of the bildungsroman's generic stops—narrative event as conversion, deferred significance as aesthetically clumsy retrospection—in a clamor to produce a teleological chain of causation that would generate, from Helga's disparate psychological parts, a coherent novelistic personality. In staging the failure of that project—and foregrounding Helga's desperate desire for its success—Larsen asks whether the memory of the heat emanating from those novelistic hearths feels all the warmer for being so far away.

TWO-FACED WOMAN

The set of visual contradictions we saw Larsen deploy in her introductory description of Helga Crane—Helga is this but "none the less" that—are expressions of a broader interest in the motif of cognitive dissonance in narratives of passing. Observers of the passer are often depicted as not sure of or perplexed by what they see. That "inscrutability," as Gabrielle McIntire calls it, is caused by the disruption of expectation by evidence, an incompatibility between what one sees and what one anticipates.[58]

Passers elicit confusion. "I am perfectly mystified by Miss Leroy," says Dr. Gresham, for instance, of the titular biracial protagonist of Frances Harper's *Iola Leroy* (1892), whose skin is so white as to cause her friend Tom Anderson to wonder that she ever used her hands for forced labor.[59] Clotel's "appearance" in William Wells Brown's *Clotel; or, the President's Daughter* (1853)—described "as white as most of those who were waiting with a wish to become her purchasers; her features as finely defined as any of her sex of pure Anglo-Saxon"—creates "a deep sensation amongst the crowd," a confused shock reflected in the considerable time it takes for them to start to bid on her.[60] The light-skinned Angela Murray of Jessie Fauset's *Plum Bun* (1928), moreover, is persistently met with "astonishment," "bewilderment," and "amazement" when her Black ancestry is revealed to those who hadn't known of it.[61]

Such a lapse of understanding permeates the encounter between Clare Kendry and her childhood friend, fellow biracial woman, Irene Redfield, on the top floor of the Drayton hotel in Chicago in Larsen's novel *Passing*. Spotting Clare from a distance, Irene "studie[s]" her "for some clue as to her identity," trying to determine what she is seeing. "Who could she be?" Irene ponders while staring at Clare with an intensity of concentration that Deborah McDowell has canonically read as imbued with queer desire.[62] Then, drawing a "quick sharp breath" from "so great" an "astonishment that she had started to rise," Irene finds herself "awfully surprise[d]" to discover that it is actually her old friend.[63] Indeed, if racial identification is typically thought to rely on the legibility of the skin—what a person looks like is what that person is—racial passing deals in an inscrutability at the level of dermal evidence. The passer is simultaneously "hypervisible" and visually perplexing: one knows *that* one is seeing someone, but one also doesn't quite know *whom* one is seeing.[64] In Adrian Piper's words, "the person you appear to be" is incommensurate with "the person you are . . . revealed to be."[65] Passing poses a hermeneutic challenge to the epistemology of sight typically governing racial identification.[66] It invites an especially searching and problematically curious form of spectatorship, guesswork full of baggage. As Ralina L. Joseph puts it, a "what are you?"[67]

The chromatic indeterminacy and cognitive dissonance central to the hermeneutics of passing are central, as well, albeit in refracted form, to many of Garbo's films. To be clear: Garbo is not passing in her films in the sense that characters such as Clotel, Iola Leroy, Angela Murray, or Claire Kendry are (or could). To the contrary, Garbo's whiteness is uncontestable. Toni Morrison's choice to have Mr. Henry give Claudia MacTeer the pet name "Greta Garbo" in *The Bluest Eye* (1970) indeed speaks to just how potently, if not paradigmatically, Garbo contributed to the regime of white beauty that scholars such as Richard Dyer and Daniel Bernardi have argued was a primary ideological project underlying classical Hollywood style and narrative.[68] But insofar as the exemplarity with which her whiteness upholds what Bernardi calls "the pale formation" that early and classical Hollywood film helped render hegemonic, it is also worth interrogating.[69]

Garbo's hyperwhiteness was constructed and exaggerated by the aesthetic apparatus of Hollywood production. In order to make sure that Garbo was living up to the expectation of Scandinavians as "paradigmatic Aryan whites," MGM enhanced her whiteness, as it were, through various cosmetic strategies.[70] Not only did she use makeup with silver tones—a common technique to generate a glow to the skin in front of the camera—but she was also instructed to diet fiercely and received surgeries to narrow her nose, cap her stained and crooked teeth, slope her lips, and adjust her hairline.[71] She did have some creative control over the changing of her name from "Gustafsson" to "Garbo"—the former a common patronym among working-class Swedes, the latter a mashup of two other potential surnames, which she conceived with childhood friend Mimi Pollack in 1923 and that was later approved by her then director and mentor Mauritz Stiller.[72] But the change was just as much a move to de-ethnicize and naturalize her screen image as it was a strategy for creating a memorable star persona. And while before sound film MGM had succeeded in rendering Garbo's whiteness so perfected as to be imperceptible—"invisible," in Dyer's terms—the arrival of sound threatened to make it conspicuous and fallible.[73] Garbo's broken English, thick Swedish accent, and husky voice generated a tremendous amount of what Lunde calls "aural anxiety" among studio executives.[74] They feared that the "perfect, glacial surface and conceptual whiteness" of Garbo's face—the one Roland Barthes famously theorized as lifted above all specificity into the realm of abstract purities—would be stained by the vocal particularities the "talkie revolution" demanded.[75] Fred Niblo, who directed Garbo in two silent films (*The Temptress* [1926] and *The Mysterious Lady* [1928]), once called her "a blonde with a brunette voice."[76] That brunette voice of MGM's most profitable star, whose marketability was predicated on her "originless, ethereal" pallor, threatened to expose her roots.[77]

Niblo's comment indeed suggests nervousness about the power of the vocal chords to condemn the passer to racial and ethnic scrutability. That being said, we should resist the temptation to detect in the ethnically evidentiary nature of Garbo's speech too close a resemblance to the "husky tones" of Clare Kendry's voice and the "trill" of her laugh that go some way toward confirming her racial origins to Irene.[78] A version of that vocal exposure is certainly at play in Garbo's first American feature, *The Torrent*

(1926)—the only film for which her hair was ever dyed brown—where she plays a Spanish peasant named Leonora who leaves her village and becomes a famous singer named "La Brunna." Upon her return to her hometown, friends and family recognize Leonora as La Brunna only once she sings for them—moments that shock her listeners into an aural recognition of her true identity. But whereas La Brunna's vocal tell in *The Torrent* enacts *en abyme* the revelation of Garbo as a new star arriving on the scene of the American entertainment industry, Clare's is the first instance of a long process of exposure that leads to her doom. *The Torrent* was prescient: the concern about Garbo's husky voice was quelled instantly with her very first line in her first talkie, *Anna Christie* (1930). "Gimme a whisky, ginger ale on the side, and don't be stingy, baby," she croaked, delivering on the promise extended by the film's primary marketing slogan ("Garbo talks!") to adoring audiences. The differences between Clare's insides and outsides—between the delicacy of her "ivory skin" and her "husky voice" and "dark, sometimes absolutely black" eyes—ultimately splatter her to pieces on the ground.[79] The incongruity generated by the clash of Garbo's voice and image, meanwhile, only made of her a fascinating and seductive whole. We will return to this distinction between Clare and Garbo in a moment, because it is integral to understanding the ideological work performed by Garbo's whiteness. But for now, it is important to prod further this vision of Garbo, represented both in Niblo's comment and in her breakthrough role in *The Torrent*, as inherently dual, since it permeates several of her subsequent roles and goes some way toward explaining why she may have interested Larsen.

Garbo almost always plays someone with a dual identity, and not just in her early vamp films such as *The Temptress*, *Flesh and the Devil* (1927), and *The Kiss* (1929), where she plays duplicitous adulteresses. Nor just in the canonical sequences of *Queen Christina*, where she passes as a man in order to seek momentary respite from her royal duty. In the intimacy of an inn during a snowstorm, Christina exposes herself as a woman to a Spanish envoy (John Gilbert) who subsequently becomes her lover, only to expose herself again later as the Queen of Sweden. But that characterological duality plays out across almost her entire career. In *Two-Faced Woman* (1941), for instance, she plays a woman pretending to be her own twin sister so as to trick her husband (Melvyn Douglas) into returning to her after having momentarily lost interest. In *Love* (1927), *Anna Karenina* (1935), *The Painted Veil* (1934), and *Wild Orchids* (1929), she plays a woman whose love for a man other than her husband sends her into self-destructive and unresolved crises of identity. And in *The Mysterious Lady* (1928), *Mata Hari* (1931), and Ernst Lubitch's *Ninotchka* (1939) she plays an undercover spy. Garbo, in other words, often plays someone pretending to be someone else, someone whose identity slides persistently between two resting places, always in danger of exposure.

If they are discussed, these slippages of identity are situated within the context of Garbo's queer energies (a discussion fueled by the fact that Queen Christina was famously a lesbian). Many have considered Garbo's notorious impenetrability, including her refusal to take photos or conduct interviews for an ever-frustrated journalistic industry, an extension of the inscrutability of her sexuality. She did have multiple relationships with women as well as men, most famously with Mercedes de Acosta and John Gilbert, and her extreme magnetism on screen, which often made her male counterparts nearly invisible, has long been understood as the effect of a queer intensity that made her fit within the typical Hollywood romance plot only with great difficulty.[80] The erotic and androgynous "potency" of her performances, as Betsy Erkkila notes, coupled with her sense of "emotional removal" from the narrative scenario at hand, gives her screen presence an "otherworldly largesse" that undermines the "petty-bourgeois respectability and happily-ever-after domesticity" of the romance plots MGM demanded of her.[81]

Given the erotics of queer desire that critics have long thought to permeate Irene's and Clare's relationship in *Passing*, the queer reading of Garbo is helpful in understanding what might have drawn Larsen to her. But the set of narrative coordinates I have just mentioned—dual identities, the threat of exposure, the exposure itself and its subsequent social, political, or legal consequences—is also central to the literary tropology of racial passing. Secrecy, detection, and exposure are fundamental to the narrative economy of passing, which is why the literature of passing and detective fiction share an intimate history.[82] The moment of recognition and exposure of Black blood in passing narratives, be it even "one drop," serves as a radical narrative threshold of causality. Such instances of anagnorisis, whereby a hitherto hidden truth is revealed, bring altogether new meaning to Barthes's claim that the hermeneutic force driving narrative forward is the "disclosure" of an "enigma."[83] In the case of *Passing*, that disclosure is hyperdramatized in the scene at the Freelands' party at the end of the novel: Clare's white husband, Bellew, who self-avowedly hates Black people, storms into the party in a rage, having come to discover the so-called truth about Clare, herself the enigma fueling the narrative of *Passing*. He has been confronted with what he sees as the offensive reality that this is who his wife has been all along—a deferred recognition enacted in the diction of his proclamation, "So you're a n——, a damned dirty n——!"[84]

Importantly, from the standpoint of Larsen, the formal economy of duality and exposure is at work not just in the characters Garbo plays but also in Garbo's costume design. Indeed, Larsen would probably have been very attentive to this, given both how centrally Garbo's star status was linked to her collaborations with costume designer Adrian—the "Hollywood Fashion King,"[85] who according to one (exaggerating) critic single-handedly engineered Garbo's greatness[86]—and how crucial the theme of clothing is in her fiction. Clothes, in Larsen, often serve as the battleground on which racial identity gets articulated and contested (e.g., at Naxos Helga's bright-colored clothing is considered shameful; in Denmark it is an axis along which she is racially exoticized by her white friends and family). Moreover, Larsen was herself an expert seamstress, having learned from her mother, who was a professional.[87] She thus would have been primed to notice how a number of Garbo's costumes themselves play on a duality. In *The Kiss*, for instance, that duality is designed at the level of structure. Here Garbo plays a woman—named Irene—put to trial for the murder of her husband (a silk merchant from Lyon) who had caught her kissing another man. Adrian lifts the duplicity of Garbo's character to the level of costuming. Irene wears a dress that appears at first glance to be floor length. When she turns around, however, we see that it is actually (or rather, also) knee length, the cut of the dress dramatically shortened in the front (fig. 3). The

FIGURE 3. Garbo as Irene in *The Kiss* (Clarence Brown, 1929).

FIGURE 4. Garbo turns around in *The Kiss* to reveal the front of her dress, dramatically shorter than the back.

effect is of surprising recognition—*this is what the dress actually is!*—and it is enhanced by the fact that the sequence is uncut, and that cinematographer William Daniels chose to shoot it in a long shot. First, we see Irene facing the fireplace, her back to the camera; then she turns around, still in long shot, exposing the front of the dress (fig. 4). The choice not to cut to her front, but to show its exposure in real time heightens the dramatic intensity of the recognition—a sartorial betrayal that enacts at the level of costuming the narrative of disloyalty at the center of the film. With Irene, what you see is not necessarily what you get.

But that sartorial duality plays out elsewhere and more provocatively at the level of color, especially in Garbo's 1931 MGM film *Mata Hari*, where she plays the famed eponymous Dutch exotic dancer and suspected spy for the Germans during World War I. Of the handful of costumes Adrian designed for the character of Mata, the two that enjoy the most screen time are made of materials structurally predicated on chromatic ambivalence: gold mesh and velvet. The result is twofold. In the case of Mata's gold-mesh gown and leggings, there are moments in the film when we are not entirely sure what color we are seeing (figs. 5, 6). The film's frequent reliance on high-key lighting draws out the iridescence of the material: the mesh appears as neither black nor white; neither is it neither. In Werner Sollors's

FIGURE 5. Garbo in gold-mesh gown and leggings designed by Adrian in *Mata Hari* (George Fitzmaurice, 1931).

FIGURE 6. Garbo in gold-mesh gown and leggings designed by Adrian in *Mata Hari*.

FIGURE 7. Garbo in velvet suit designed by Adrian in *Mata Hari*.

formulation, it is "neither black nor white yet both,"[88] the chiaroscuro of the black-and-white image only enhancing the tonal duality of the fabric. The visual language of Mata's velvet suit, meanwhile, reminds us that the textile has structural potential to be another color. When pushed in one direction, the fibers on the velvet appear as one color and when pushed in the other direction appear as another (fig. 7). The fascinating doubleness of the gold mesh and the warm piebald of the disturbed velvet both speak to Mata's profession. She is a shapeshifter, an undercover spy dwelling in twoness by trade. In *The Kiss*, the structural duplicity of Irene's dress offers a formal analogue to her adulterous pursuits. In *Mata Hari*, the chromatic deceptiveness of Mata's costumes provides a visual rhetoric of disguise.

But the surprises and visual perplexities of Garbo's costumes also invoke what Michael Gillespie calls "film blackness." Rather than a mode of filmmaking with an "indexical tie to the black lifeworld," film blackness, for Gillespie, is a mode of reading for how blackness gets formally negotiated, stylistically encoded, and rhetorically complicated. It is less a body of cinematic work burdened by the responsibilities of a representational political program and more a disposition bent toward the stylistic and critical interrogation of blackness as a set of formal possibilities.[89] The chameleonic scales of Mata's mesh gown, the structural dualities of her velvet suit, and above all how they (don't quite) read, fashion a mute formal language of dermal indeterminacy that does not deliberately play out a drama of racial passing but that generates what Gillespie would call the "signifying menace" of passing, "a threat to the categorial regimes of race and being."[90] It is significant, for instance, that the mesh gown has leggings, that the velvet skirt is tight and accompanied by knee-high boots, and that both costumes have accompanying skull caps—Garbo is almost entirely covered by the material, her skin barely visible. And given the film's orientalist framework—that Mata is a Dutch woman performing exotic dance in beaded costumes that operate as a form of Brownface—we would be remiss were we not to see in her costuming a vestural association of Mata's espionage with the performance of racial difference. Indeed, a similar chromatic diffusion often structures Helga Crane's clothing, especially the "cobwebby black net" dress "touched with orange" that her friend Anne thinks shows too much of Helga's skin.[91]

But *Mata Hari* ultimately reneges on whatever racially subversive work haunts Mata's clothing. In a manner typical to the orientalist fetishism of Art Deco, of whose style Garbo was classical Hollywood's leading icon,[92] Garbo is dabbling in Black/Brown racial performance from the position of utter racial safety, the opening in the back of Mata's velvet suit from which her bare back peeks out—as in the revelation of Marlene Dietrich's searing white head from beneath the gorilla suit in *Blonde Venus*—reassures us: *don't worry, she's white, see?* The extent of that safety is conveyed in the final sequence of the film, where, having been sentenced to execution for espionage, Mata bids farewell to her blinded lover Alexei (Ramon Novarro) and is then escorted to the firing squad. The film's ending invokes the narrative features often accompanying the revelation of Black blood in passing narratives, where the exposure of the so-called racial impostor leads to death (e.g., from suicide, from heartbreak) or dire legal ramifications (e.g., the removal to a different public area, the removal of property, the remanding to slavery). But in ways that will anticipate the ending of *Camille*, *Mata Hari* protects Garbo's image from anything resembling the real social and political consequences invoked in those narratives. The final sequence restores Garbo to extreme pigmentational stability, the vampiric whiteness of her face—what contemporary journalist Sylvia Ullback referred to as Garbo's "pale exoticism"[93]—set off by the unequivocal blackness of her cape (fig. 8). Where before there was the flirtation with doubt, now there is the assertion of absolute certainty, a vestural reinscription of Garbo's whiteness with a vengeance. As Mata walks in profile down the staircase, her shadow walks alongside her against the wall, a second self that lingers in the film's spectral unconscious (fig. 9). But rather than suggesting an enduring malleability of pigment—that race, or skin, can

FIGURE 8. Mata meets the firing squad in *Mata Hari*.

FIGURE 9. Mata walks down the stairs in the prison in *Mata Hari*, her shadow cast against the wall.

be just as misleading as cloth—the shot shows blackness cast out. With nervous, overcompensatory monochrome, *Mata Hari* ends with Garbo's white face whole, hardened, safely separate and impermeable. It suggests that whatever blackness Garbo may try on, she can always take it off and set it to the side, cast it off like a shadow or an inky cloak.

Mata Hari thus offers the photographic negative of Larsen's *Passing* and Mata's fate the light to Clare's shadow fate in that novel. The death of Clare—that other vamp in disguise[94]—is the ultimate consequence of racial exposure, the symbolic cost of her racial and erotic audacity. The violence with which the revelation of Clare's racial identity to her husband "discloses" what Barthes would call the "enigma" implicitly posed by all plotted narrative is indicative of the brutal literalness with which *Passing* negotiates the formal economy of causality. Clare's racial exposure functions structurally like a conversion, a stark and unforgiving threshold between two incompatible modes of existence: an irrevocable passage, as Tzvetan Todorov would have it, into a second equilibrium. To pass and to get caught, in *Passing*, is to face unyielding consequences—to have one's actions *matter* in a way that cannot be taken back. And it is precisely against this sort of mattering—*you lied and now you must pay for it*—that Mata, despite being sentenced to death, is ultimately protected. Alexei's blindness at the end of the film enacts, *en abyme*, the way that *Mata Hari* itself ultimately allows us to look over, to look past, not just Mata's deceit—she is lying to protect Alexei (a white lie); he thinks she is going into surgery and will come back to him—but also her death (fig. 10).

The final sequence of *Mata Hari* flaunts the power of the Hollywood ending to administer *consequentiality*: simultaneously to invest us in some forms of causality—*Mata must die, she is dying for love*—while conjuring away others—*Garbo doesn't die, no; she can't die; she must live.*[95] Just as Alexei's blindness will be cured (his parting words to Mata are that his doctors assure him his sight will return), this alleged death scene is simply the birth of Garbo's most iconic imagery. Clare Kendry disappears from the text of *Passing*, leaving doubt to torment the end of the novel—"What happened next, Irene Redfield never afterwards allowed herself to remember. Never clearly."[96] Garbo's face, meanwhile, however indecipherable it may be—l'énigme, Barthes calls her—replaces doubt with a visual rhetoric of racial certainty that bleeds into our certainty, too, that while Mata may be dying, Garbo lives. Alexei's look beyond the frame carves an ocular pathway past the film and toward Garbo's most famous photograph, taken by Clarence Sinclair Bull for *Mata Hari*, in eternal rigor mortis (fig. 11).[97] An undead and magnificent whole.

FIGURE 10. Alexei, temporarily blind, says goodbye to Mata in *Mata Hari*.

THE LADY OF THE CAMELLIAS

Mata Hari shows the power of the Hollywood ending to manipulate the laws of causality such that some things are made to matter and others not at all. Narrative consequence reigns supreme—the plot has to make sense, it has to assimilate ambiguity to meaning and thus make a whole from fragments.[98] But so, too, does inconsequence: the ending can and must conjure away what doesn't *feel good*, make irrelevant what would feel so much better were it to be in fact irrelevant. "Screenwriters writhe on the horns of the dilemma," David Bordwell writes of the classical Hollywood paradigm, "twisting from advice about the need for unity to the demand that the audience not be depressed."[99] And it is this precise double movement that *Camille* achieves masterfully, and at stake in this instance is the white bourgeois self.

Adapted to the screen by Zoë Akins from a combination of Dumas's *The Lady of the Camellias* and his own 1852 stage adaptation, *Camille* generates the social and psychic promises endemic to the classical bildungsroman, even though Dumas's novel had exposed the hidden violence on which those promises are predicated. While not itself a bildungsroman, *The Lady of the Camellias* subjects the genre's terms to trenchant critique. Armand is a petit bourgeois in postmonarchic France. Unlike the noblemen with

FIGURE 11. Garbo, portrait by Clarence Sinclair Bull for *Mata Hari* (1931).

whom Marguerite usually couples, his socioeconomic success depends on securing social ties he does not yet have. In the novel, Armand's father successfully convinces Marguerite to leave Armand, because, as a courtesan, she endangers Armand's acceptance into Parisian high society. The novel ends with a series of letters from Marguerite to Armand documenting the last two months of her life as she dies alone of consumption. When in the novel Armand returns brokenhearted to his family "to be healed,"[100] we are left with the sense that his father was right and that after a long recovery, Armand will return to Paris and resume the path to social distinction that all young bourgeois should follow. The novel vindicates M. Duval's socioeconomic prudence, making the expulsion of Marguerite seem necessary for the peaceful continuation of Armand's ambition plot. In so doing, it also keeps alive the threat of the dilatory social energies symbolized in Marguerite. The fact that she will be disinterred from the bourgeois section of the cemetery and buried in a mass grave—that her burial plot is itself a cite of unrest—expresses the abiding openness of the novel's own plot, a formal vulnerability that signals its reckoning with the real, material impossibility of Marguerite's and Armand's union without the complete upheaval of the postrevolutionary social and economic order.

Camille makes evident the extent to which Dumas's story is fundamentally about the ability to pass—as wealthy, as white, as wealthy and white. Classical Hollywood melodramas like John M. Stahl's *Imitation of Life* (1934, remade by Douglas Sirk in 1959) and Elia Kazan's *Pinky* (1949) openly explore the racial axis of the melodramatic tropes of secrecy, disclosure, and misrecognition, featuring plots that explicitly concern dramas of racial exposure. *Camille* pushes that axis to the subtext, mediating it through the complex optics of class. In what the opening intertitle calls the Parisian culture of "discretion," the open secrecy of Marguerite's prostitution can remain within the bounds of propriety only insofar as she successfully performs whiteness, and of the right kind. In one scene, we watch as, standing at the mirror in her boudoir, Marguerite puts on her white camellias, surrounded by a frame of white curtains and donning a white dress. The white vestures of high-bourgeois/aristocratic distinction mask the rural poverty we know to be Marguerite's origin: fellow prostitute Olympe warns her that if she isn't careful, she'll end up "back on that farm where you came from, milking cows and cleaning hen houses"; and while on Armand's farm, Marguerite shares milking tips with his servant. The failure of Olympe's class camouflage—the film's other poor white woman in the very same economic struggle—is accentuated by the success of Marguerite's, a distinction expressed, too, in their costuming. Olympe is almost always dressed in black *and* white (stark, unintegrated, jamming two things together),

Marguerite in either black *or* white (elegantly this or that, respectful of differences). And the film's most famous costume is Marguerite's shimmering black net gown that, like her mesh in *Mata Hari*—like Helga's "cobwebby black net touched with orange" in *Quicksand*—masterfully and imperceptibly mixes pigments, indicating subtle disguise (figs. 12, 13). And the racial axes of class passing are not reserved in this film to women. The only reason Marguerite can mistake the bourgeois Armand for the Baron de Varville in the film's opening sequence at the opera—a scene whose narrative motor depends on a drama of misrecognition—is because both men are white.

Garbo's naturalized performance of wealthy whiteness is secured, finally, by *Camille*'s commitment to plotted closure. *Camille* ends in the way that Dumas's stage adaptation ends: with Armand arriving at Marguerite's deathbed chamber, professing his abiding devotion to her (fig. 14). The effect of this choice to close the story—to wrap it around, as it were, such that the relationship between Armand and Marguerite does not hang loose, open and disinterred, but is given moral and aesthetic closure—is that Marguerite is rescued from aesthetic and socioeconomic incoherence. By the end of the film, Marguerite is abject, an outcast the object of charity (Gaston puts money into her purse) and petty theft (Prudence, her former Madame, scavenges it out). But the point—crucially—is that

FIGURE 12. Olympe (*left*) in black-and-white dress in *Camille* (George Cukor, 1936).

FIGURE 13. Garbo as Marguerite in famous shimmer black net gown in *Camille*.

FIGURE 14. Robert Taylor ("The Man with the Perfect Profile"), as Armand, talks to Marguerite in her death chamber in *Camille*.

while it was the fundamental falsity of her class performance that in the novel leads to the lovers' permanent separation, in the film, that falsity simply does not matter. The ending of the film conjures away class, using the stylistic arsenal of classical Hollywood style to perform the seemingly impossible task of rendering moot M. Duval's worries and convincing us that Armand and Marguerite would have lived out the rest of their days in blissful, bourgeois marriage.

By the end of the film, Marguerite and Armand are purely projections of our desire, stripped of indexical ties to socioeconomic reality. Taylor croons to Garbo, "The future is ours. My whole life belongs to you. I'll take you far away from Paris, where there are no unhappy memories for either of us, where the sun will help me take care of you and make you well again. We'll go back to the country," he finishes, "where we were happy all one summer." The lines are banal and thus remarkable not because of their poeticism but because coming from Taylor they are utterly believable. Taylor had become a national celebrity since the year before, when he starred in John M. Stahl's *Magnificent Obsession* (1935), and he would, over the course of the late 1930s come to be called the "Man with the Perfect Profile."[101] And by 1936, Garbo had become more a modern myth than a celebrity, so iconically powerful as to make Taylor terrified to play opposite her. Far from incidental, Taylor's beauty and Garbo's iconic force are essential to delivering on the fantasy that M. Duval's worries are, if not unfounded, then irrelevant. Armand's return closes the plot, allows it to come to fruition by answering the question "will the lovers meet before she dies?" But it also compounds narrative sense with affective sense and in the process flouts common sense. The sheer ideological potency of the image of Garbo and Taylor makes an aesthetic whole out of a socioeconomic impossibility. *This cannot happen, what kind of life would she and Armand live? To which class would they belong, in their world so organized by rank? But it doesn't matter; it must happen. For these two it must.* It is thus that *Camille* conjures, out of thin air—or out of our very own blind and unthinking desires— Marguerite's coherent subjectivity. We are no longer seeing, if we were ever seeing, Marguerite and Armand, but Garbo and Taylor. "The glamorous Garbo—handsome Robert Taylor," reads a contemporary advertisement for *Camille*, which, typical to almost all contemporary accounts of the film, elides the characters in favor of the actors who play them "together in a love story."[102] We do not *want* to believe that the socioeconomic strictures of postmonarchic France would pose any real obstacle to a bourgeois and a courtesan marrying. Especially when that bourgeois and that courtesan are being played by them.

In the novel, Marguerite disrupts Armand's ambition plot by virtue of her inassimilability to the framework of postmonarchic bourgeois social advancement. She also disturbs it because of the radical way Dumas embodies her. Her corpse has "sinuous curves," her dead foot protrudes from her white shroud, and an "odor of infection seep[s]" out of the grave when the digger opens it.[103] Anathema to the fully integrated, self-possessed body as the vessel of individual will that was demanded of and constructed by the nineteenth-century bildungsroman, Marguerite's body is decaying, reduced to rotting material. Her final letters to Armand, which he reads posthumously, chronicle her physical deterioration, during which her body takes on a mind of its own, preceding by approximately eighty years the image of Helga Crane: "I passed into the state of a body without a soul," Marguerite writes, "a thing without thought." "I never stop spitting blood," she writes the day before a friend takes over writing her letters, since she no longer has the strength: she has "lost her voice, then the use of her limbs." "I coughed and spat blood all night. Today I can no longer speak; I can hardly move my arms . . . I am going to die . . . and if, . . ." The letter—like Lisa's to Stefan Brand in Max Ophuls's *Letter from an Unknown Woman* (1948); ". . . if only"—ends with a suspension. "After this word," the narrator continues, "the few characters Marguerite had tried to scrawl were illegible, and it was Julie Duprat who had continued."[104]

Marguerite's illness threatens to decompose the novel itself, to make illegible the cultural technology responsible for generating aesthetic models for the possessive liberal individualism toward which a young man like Armand aspires. The novel expels her, then, not simply because she poses a threat to Armand's social pursuits but also because her consumptive body, paying for her sexual sins, tests the capacity of the novel to integrate its subjects psychically and corporeally. She exposes the extent to which the ambition plot is predicated on the expulsion of bodies that strain the genre's power to generate autonomous individuality possessive of a will and subordinate to the state.

With its final close-up, the film rescues Marguerite's subjectivity from becoming decentralized in this way (fig. 15). The close-up collects Marguerite into a coherent individual who, though dying, would have fulfilled a bourgeois ideal married to Armand in the French countryside. Armand (in profile), seeing that Marguerite is dead, leans her back into the chair as the camera dollies in from a medium to a full close-up of Garbo. Plucking Marguerite/Garbo from where she is to place her where she could be (whiter, wealthier, healthier), the patina of Hollywood style safely seals her off from the complications of class, social expectation, and sickness that have thwarted her and her lover's pursuit of a bourgeois existence, insulating her safely within the container of a gorgeous and liberal white

FIGURE 15. Garbo as Marguerite, dead, in the final close-up of *Camille*.

self. The close-up hypnotically assures us that Marguerite/Garbo and Armand/Taylor would have moved to the countryside and lived out their rural, petit bourgeois life undisturbed and wanting for nothing. The end of *Camille* makes plot consequential in the way that it must be in classical Hollywood—Marguerite cannot spring back to life (as Inger does in Carl Dreyer's *Ordet* (1955), for instance, to reclaim breath and the mercy and omnipotence of God). But its affective force also draws strength from what it abstracts away—Marguerite dies precisely so that class does not have to matter, so that the constraints of money do not have the chance to spoil the affordances of form.

Mata Hari imposed on Garbo the modernist mask. The expressionistic decor and chiaroscuro of the final sequence accentuated the contours of her eternal white shell/face. *Camille*, however, yields something that would have probably meant much more to Larsen in 1936: an imperfect and harmed but nevertheless collected human. The low-key lighting of the final close-up allows us to see traces of the damage Marguerite's illness has wrought on her too-thin frame. The murky gray tones of the low-lit room wash out Marguerite's face, revealing the wrinkle creases of her furrowed brow, indices of her body in pain, just as much as they showcase Garbo's signature long lashes. Her hair is slightly unkempt, frizzled from friction with her deathbed pillow. She is beautiful, but a little bit less so. Mata's final image is the reconciliation of structural doubt into an impeccable whole. Marguerite's is of a personality—no longer a concept, but an instance. Not a synthetic image, but a breathing character, and with white flesh all the more dangerous for giving the impression of attainability. *This. This could be me*, it draws from us. *If it were only me.*

■ ■

Helga Crane watches the racial masquerade in the minstrel performance at the circus in Copenhagen with repulsion and longing; and what were Larsen's thoughts when she would watch and rewatch *Camille*?[105] What was she thinking as she witnessed and rewitnessed the intertitle—the one that did remain and that refers to Marguerite as "a pretty creature who lived on the quicksands of popularity"—passing before her eyes, no doubt prompting her to watch the film in alignment with her first novel? The thinness of Larsen's archival collections leaves us to speculate as to an answer, aided by our knowledge of the circumstances of Larsen's life in 1936. Let us recall that three years earlier, her husband, Elmer Imes, had left her for a white woman—an event from which it took Larsen many years to recover, if ever fully. And though Larsen's literary career had started off with such vitality, by 1936, she couldn't place her work. By the time she was sitting in the Capitol Theatre on 51st Street and Broadway repeatedly viewing *Camille*, she was suffering from depression and substance abuse and had cut ties with close friends in the Harlem cultural world of which she had once been an integral part. Not only had the "Negro vogue" of the Harlem Renaissance ended but she, too, was growing obscure and reclusive—smothered by the "quicksands of popularity."[106]

Whereas, as Hutchinson suggests, Marguerite's passage into and out of Parisian high society mimics Larsen's own trajectory through Harlem's cultural elite, *Camille* ultimately retrieves Marguerite from moral and financial destitution. The film uses classical Hollywood plot and its full stylistic arsenal to recover her from social and economic illegibility, reintegrating her into a narrative of upward mobility and social arrival whose internal contradictions and hidden violence Dumas's novel had made so grotesquely evident. Larsen may thus have found herself struck by the ease with which classical Hollywood makes Marguerite a coherent, fully embodied and self-possessing individual—how through effects of lighting, cinematography, and the right star and story it effortlessly rescues her from the kinds of social marginalization that not just Helga Crane in *Quicksand* but at that point, Larsen, too, was enduring. Larsen may have been struck, indeed, by the illusion the film allows itself to entertain and that she herself in her novel did not: that the social and psychic promises of the bildungsroman plot can be generated and sustained for any and all who hold fast to its tenets. Unlike Marguerite's poverty, Helga's drops of Black blood, like Clare Kendry's, do matter. So much so that the narrative architecture of mattering collapses under their weight.

Helga's lack of a coherent self may at first appear as a function of Larsen's critical rejection of literary tradition. It may appear as Larsen's resistance to wield plot in such a way that would forge a kind of selfhood incompatible with the historical challenges of biracial female subjectivity. But if the serial narrative ruptures of *Quicksand*, which persistently render plot inconsequential—*no matter how much I do, I still do not become, become an I*—are simply a refusal, then what is Helga trying to find in her dark room? And what was Larsen trying to find in that dark theater when she would view and review *Camille*, a film that transports from the nineteenth-century novel precisely the sort of plotted coherence that Dumas's novel called so virulently into question, a film in which plot colludes with, indeed enables, the regime of white beauty to affirm a fantasy of social belonging and subjective coherence? In light of Larsen's fascination with Cukor's film, those narrative ruptures—the way that *Quicksand*'s plot is constituted by a formal iteration, unwilling fully to generate its protagonist—seem to express an intense, albeit ambivalent investment in plot itself. Fueled by critique and permeated by longing, this ambivalence reflects something akin to Berlant's "cruel optimism": a knowing return to an object or scene just as soothing as it is injurious.[107]

Did Larsen look on the final close-up of Garbo's white(ned) face and find herself identifying with her, even if just for a moment, seeing in her what she was, what she could have been, what she would never be? Did she, like Kara Walker said of watching Scarlett O'Hara in *Gone with the Wind*, want to kill Marguerite—to kill her and at the same time to become her? Larsen may indeed have been struck by how glowing and replete Marguerite looks, how the shot endows her with that fullness of life Helga could never attain—what Larsen would never give her and what Larsen herself, in 1936, had lost.

Larsen would eventually come out of hiding. About four years after *Camille* was flashing on the screen of the Capitol, Imes died, and the alimony payments he had been making to her since their separation stopped. Shortly after that, Larsen officially entered the New York City hospital system, where she would resume a successful career as a nurse, the other profession at which she had long excelled, until the early 1960s.[108] But during the acute darkness of those preceding years—a darkness that would return in the last few years before she died in 1964, alone and isolated from friends—Larsen may have been especially attuned to the fact that no matter how flat Garbo's image might be, it nevertheless conveys the convincing impression—and we are so ready to be convinced—of emanating an especially voluminous warmth and promise.

Première Entr'acte

One of the final images in Rebecca Hall's 2021 film adaptation of Nella Larsen's *Passing* is of Irene Redfield (Tessa Thompson) standing at the window out of which her friend Clare Kendry (Ruth Negga) has just fallen to her death. Irene's hand is extended to the side, feeling the space where Clare used to be, reaching for the flesh she would never allow herself to touch for fear of what "wild desires" it might unleash in her, a phrase Clare herself used in a letter to Irene earlier in the film (fig. 16).[1] It is a posture of stunned longing for what has been lost eternally and whose tenderness is accentuated by its placement over a shadow belly. Clare's stomach would have been there. It was just there.

Indeed, the single moment wherein Irene does allow herself to touch Clare in Hall's *Passing* is in the split second before Clare falls out the window. As John Bellew (Alexander Skarsgård) charges toward Clare in a rage, Hall has Irene do something Larsen does not. Whereas Larsen's Irene lays her hand on Clare's arm the moment before she falls—a gesture that will continue to haunt her once Clare is gone ("If she.... could only put from her memory the vision of her hand on Clare's arm!"[2]), Hall's Irene reaches her hand over Clare's stomach, pressing it in a gesture just as much of protection as of ejection. It is neither and both. And as such, it is the most intimate moment we witness between Irene and Clare in Hall's film, not because they are finally touching but because the touching expresses with equal force—and in visual terms more arresting than anywhere else in the film—Irene's desire for and hatred of Clare. Irene's hand at the moment before Clare's death rests where she has wanted it to rest all along, across Clare's body in an ambivalent caress whose intensity of queer love is accentuated by the haptic folds generated by the disturbances in the silk on top of Clare's shifting body and underneath Irene's pushing and pulling hand (fig. 17). (Is the gesture a fantasy of impregnation? If she and Clare had a child, what shade of skin would it have? Irene may have wondered, Clare

FIGURE 16. Irene with her hand reaching out to where Clare used to be before she fell (or jumped or was pushed) out the window, in *Passing* (Rebecca Hall, 2021).

FIGURE 17. Irene's hand on Clare's stomach before she falls out the window in *Passing*.

may have feared.) Standing at the point of oscillation, as Laura Mulvey might have it, between fantasies of omnipotence and passivity[3]—did she do it? did she not do it? she diditdidntdoit—Irene looks away from the screen of the window a stunned nonspectator, refusing identification with her own phantom action. The image of Irene with her arm extended out to nothing is an image of astonished grief. Despite all the ways she had wanted Clare gone, she misses her; she wants her back.

Some version of this double feeling may also have drawn the next author to the image not of Garbo, this time, but of what many considered, though she herself denied, was her competition. Marlene Dietrich—broad shouldered, unapologetic, carnal—was less ethereal than Garbo, the inimitable Enigma, the Swedish Sphinx. Marlene—her stage name a mashup of her original Mary and Magdalene—hailed from *this* world, which is possibly what made the forms of desire she elicited all the more difficult to handle. In fact, as we will see, what Djuna Barnes seems to have found so striking about Dietrich was just how much she resembled her former lover Thelma Wood—a woman with whom Barnes was madly in love but whose infidelities and elusive unavailability drove Barnes to the limits of sanity. When Clare falls out of the window, she is pushed out of the plot, out of the frame, released from the bonds of causality that fastened her, however tortuously, to Irene. Dietrich, too, was good at losing the plot, her inscrutable silences just as much the quintessence of style as they were the testament to her indifference to her lovers on screen. In this, Dietrich was also all too much like Wood, whom Barnes left—pushed out of the picture—because she could no longer endure the pain Wood caused her. But not only would Wood animate *Nightwood* in the form of Robin Vote, but that elegiac novel will also feature characters who—like Irene, like Barnes, and so unlike Dietrich—grope for the absent lover and the plots of tortuous security they promised.

TWO

Djuna Barnes and Marlene Dietrich

On the Security of Torment

> *Suddenly I knew what all my life had been, Matthew, what I hoped Robin was—the secure torment. We can hope for nothing greater, except hope.*
>
> NORA FLOOD, *Nightwood*

In 1929 Djuna Barnes left her lover, Thelma Wood, with whom she had been entangled in a tumultuous love affair for eight years. In 1931 she started work on the novel that would attempt to aestheticize, memorialize, and exorcise that heartbreak. In 1936 it was published. *Nightwood*, one of the most stylistically difficult and narratively contorted novels of the modernist period, does not so much tell a story as it allows narrative energy to accrue around a young woman named Robin Vote, a member of the queer bohemian underworld of 1920s Paris and Berlin, who passes through the lives of the would-be aristocrat Felix Volkbein and the publicity journalist Nora Flood, breaking both of their hearts. In this famously autobiographical novel, Nora is a surrogate for Barnes herself, while Robin is the ghost of Wood, so accurate a ghost, in fact, that Wood was horrified and humiliated at the publication of the novel, though it would go on to secure Barnes's position in the canon of high literary modernism.

This chapter turns to Barnes's *Nightwood* to show the romantic dimensions of the modern novel's longing for the formal solace of plot, however specious such solace might be. At stake in the success or failure of linear plot in *Nightwood* is not the formation of the self, as it was in *Quicksand*, but of amorous attachment. The love plot in nineteenth-century domestic fiction depends on the unification of a single couple, the twinning of novelistic form to the construction of one monogamous romantic structure. That socionarrative operation is politically invested in naturalizing what Adrienne Rich in 1980 famously termed *compulsory heterosexuality*,[1] straightness as a necessary fact of mainstream political life. As a result, linear, closural plot has historically been considered hostile to queer marginality, unaccommodating of the challenge that queer subjectivity, sex, and love poses to the structures of novelistic representation intended to reflect the heteronormative morals of the modern nation-state. Thus, queerness must go underground in the nineteenth-century novel, emerging not in the realm of content and action—not, that is, in plot—but in form. The stylistic swerves marking the work of Henry James, for instance, or the narrative lacunae of Herman Melville, indicate queerness not as representable in story but as suggested through style.[2] If queerness is to thrive in literature, then it must resist adherence to the straightness, literal and figurative, of plot, whose primary structural purpose is, as D. A. Miller argues, to bring deviant formal contingencies "into line."[3] High modernism's commitment to displacing story for style—to undermining, in Virginia Woolf's famous phrase, the "tyranny" of plot—would thus seem to offer an especially valuable opportunity for writing queerness, since it is the fragment, rather than the narrative whole, that would appear more aesthetically hospitable to queer desire, typically conceived as centrifugal rather than centripetal, dilatory rather than teleological.

Nightwood is often held up as a literary cornerstone of queer modernism, proverbial in its rejection of plotted telos in the name of an antiheteronormative modernist *écriture*. Named by Joseph Frank as among the few novels representative of modern "spatial form"—"anti-representational," as Scott Herring argues, and resistant, in the words of Julie Taylor, to the "hermeneutic desire" driving nineteenth-century fiction—*Nightwood* is often thought quintessential in its recourse to the fragmentary as a welcome escape from the formal, social, and sexual constraints of the nineteenth-century novel.[4] But as Katherine A. Fama has pointed out, there are "crises" that "linger" in *Nightwood*, having to do with "the insistent desire for narrated meaning." And Brian Glavey observes that the formal tensions in Barnes's work indicate "the imbrication of an aesthetic of negation and a more reparative formalism." Barnes's work is indeed better described as what Daniella Caselli calls an "aesthetics of uncertainty," exhibiting the absence of assurance vis-à-vis its own political and literary-historical commitments.[5] Extending the aims of that work to a consideration of *Nightwood*'s orientation toward modernist form and its assaults on the love plot in particular, this chapter argues that *Nightwood* has a much more complicated attitude toward losing that plot than negative opposition or Rabelaisian mockery. Centering the perspectives of Felix Volkbein and especially Nora Flood, characters so often considered antithetical to the novel's modernist project, I argue that *Nightwood* is deeply ambivalent about the displacement of plot. On the one hand, its radical stylistic experimentalism suggests that the aesthetic constraints of the nineteenth-century love plot are underpinned by an oppressive and repressive commitment to heteronormativity. On the other, however, the novel is populated by characters who rage against the disembodying contrivances of style and desperately seek out the formal shelter of story. While we are often encouraged to see these characters as mere indicators, by negation, of what Barnesian modernism is not, I argue that they convey an impulse integral to that modernism, an impulse toward the retention of conventional desire and its attendant literary forms. As in *Quicksand*, plot in *Nightwood* emerges as both shackle and temptation because of what it seems to promise: in this case, the love and fidelity of one person.

For *Nightwood* may very well be described in terms of the metaphor Barnes herself conveyed to friend Emily Coleman: a "shattered object" to which there is "more surface than a whole" one.[6] But that metaphor, we must remember, refers to Barnes's broken heart, which she very much wished she did not have to suffer. Barnes left Wood in 1929 because she could no longer endure the pain of Wood's infidelities. She wished to have with Wood what S. Pearl Brilmyer, Filippo Trentin, and Zairong Xiang call that "least queer of all relational forms"—the monogamous couple—and Wood simply would not meet that demand.[7] Barnes wanted monogamy, Phillip Herring writes, when "in the circles she frequented, fidelity was a concept found in dictionaries and practiced in the midwestern towns of her youth."[8] However much our critical desire may be to hold *Nightwood* up as the literary quintessence of queer negativity, a novelistic "No!" to the normative assaults of nineteenth-century form and conventional desire, it is nevertheless the case that while composing it, Barnes was coming to terms with her inability to live up to the antinormative ideals Wood seemed to embody so effortlessly.

She was also, it turns out, watching Marlene Dietrich films. Dietrich had taken the world by storm during precisely the period between the official end of Barnes's relationship with Wood and the publication of *Nightwood*. Plucked from the Berlin theater, Dietrich was Paramount's response to MGM's Greta Garbo, an attempt to rival the Swedish Sphinx with another European beauty, this one less enigmatic and otherworldly than she was elusive and carnal. "Garbo is mental, withdrawn, a celibate," *Motion Picture* magazine put it; "Dietrich is of the earth, embracing, maternal."[9] She was "the new German enchantress," as one reviewer wrote, with the power to "threaten Garbo's throne," in the words of another.[10] Arguably still her most famous films to date, her seven collaborations with Austrian filmmaker Josef von Sternberg—*The Blue Angel* (1930), *Morocco* (1930), *Dishonored* (1931), *Blonde Venus* (1932), *Shanghai Express* (1932), *The Scarlet Empress* (1934), and *The Devil Is a Woman* (1935)—worked to further stylize and culturally cement what went on during the 1940s to more officially become the figure of the femme fatale. Herself bisexual—among her many lovers were Garbo's friends and lovers Mercedes de Acosta and John Gilbert[11]—Dietrich quickly became a queer icon, having brought to the big screen the imagery and attitude of her own background before and during her early film career, which, similar to the setting of *Nightwood*, was the queer subculture thriving in 1920s Paris and Berlin. In signature top hat and tails, sometimes white, sometimes black, depending on the film, Dietrich—much to the chagrin of Garbo diehards—was just as much part of the cultural fabric of modernity as what many continued to consider her Scandinavian competition.

While the relevance of film to Larsen's fiction is still noticeably understudied, this is not so in the case of Barnes. In fact Dietrich in particular has quietly loomed over the study of *Nightwood* since the feminist recovery of Barnes in the 1980s and 1990s by such scholars as Mary Lynn Broe, Jane Marcus, and Nancy Levine. Though not working film historically in a systematic sense, feminist Barnes scholars drew on the image of Dietrich as a way of offering a visually striking cultural analogue to the character of Robin. The image of Robin passed out on a bed in room 29 of the Parisian Hôtel Récamier in white trousers and dancing heels in the section of the novel titled "La somnambule," for instance, reminds Marcus (and Laura Winkiel and Alex Goody more recently) of Dietrich's character Helen Faraday in *Blonde Venus*, who famously wears a white tuxedo while performing a number at a Parisian cabaret.[12] This critical work has been foundational and revelatory; it has also been fleeting. No one has quite known what to *do* with this connection. The Dietrich comparison is mentioned in passing, argued for as a sign of popular-cultural osmosis: Dietrich was around, and so Barnes must have known about her. And this is not wrong—Dietrich *was* around, and Barnes surely knew about her.

In fact Barnes, who was a film and theater journalist as well as a novelist, commented on Dietrich in print, something that this book is the first to consider in the context of the Dietrich-Vote inquiry. In January 1931—the same year that Barnes started work on *Nightwood*—she remarked on Dietrich in a column she regularly contributed to for *Theatre Guild Magazine* titled "Playgoers Almanac." She commented admiringly on Dietrich's recourse to silent expressiveness and emotional minimalism, referring specifically to her performance in the film *Morocco*.[13] In bringing Barnes's published thoughts on Dietrich to bear on *Nightwood*, we will see that the significance of Dietrich's persona in relation to the novel is not so simple as a cultural analogue to one of its characters. Barnes's comments, rather, show her admiration for something in Dietrich that she herself did not possess, or if she did, then it was not characteristic of her own literary style, which was given to linguistic excess, a loquacity so marked that it often shrouds meaning. Turning to the archive thus allows us not only to tighten the somewhat loose juxtapositions characterizing much of the extant mentions of Dietrich in relation to *Nightwood* but to reconfigure the structure of that relationship, which, I argue, was more aspirational than analogic, expressive of difference rather than similarity.

Though Dietrich was a "vivid, fascinating woman, bound to stir up storms of talk," as one reviewer correctly prophesied in *Photoplay*,[14] Dietrich's own quietude and minimalism lent her characters a sense of distance and nonchalance vis-à-vis the stakes underpinning the love plots persistently demanded of her. Often giving the impression of being bored of, tired with, and indifferent to narrative outcomes—the formal mandate to end up with her man—Dietrich's characters are what we might call "good" modernists, subverting the formal constraints of plot and relishing instead the stylistic lyricism of lighting, gesture, and silence. In this, she does very much resemble the character of Robin Vote, whose resistance to narrative containment is related, too, to her notorious silence as well as her indifference toward the normative structures of the love plot. And like Robin, Dietrich's characters' palpable lack of investment in the telos of the love plot is informed by how effortlessly, indeed sleepily, she embodies the swerves and side glances of a queer negativity. But Barnes was watching *Morocco* and other Dietrich-Sternberg films, during a time in her life when she was nursing profound psychic wounds having precisely to do with her inability, or unwillingness, to practice such indifference herself. Barnes—unlike Robin, unlike Dietrich—was not distant, silent, uninvested in narrative outcomes. To the contrary, the source of her heartbreak, which would go on to become the stuff of *Nightwood*, was just how invested and attached she was, how much she wanted, in Heather Love's words, to "play for keeps" with Wood,[15] to have her and Wood inhabit one single, solitary love plot. If only Barnes could be more like Dietrich, if only Nora could be more like Robin, then she might have suffered just a small bit less.

Putting Dietrich's persona into the orbit of *Nightwood* as embodying something that Barnes felt she couldn't encourages us to read the novel not as a self-assured expression of queer negativity, a refusal to adhere to the formal constraints of plot and its attendant normative limitations. It encourages us, rather, to read *Nightwood* as a sustained admission on Barnes's part that no matter how urbane and disinterested one might try to be, how much one might want to live above or outside the formal boundaries of plot and its attendant social and political constraints because such would be the marker of one's modernity, sometimes we want nothing more than the shelter of those constraints, to be cradled by their confinements in what Nora calls a "secure torment."[16] Reading *Nightwood* through the aspirational image of Dietrich allows us to center the perspectives of *Nightwood*'s "bad" modernists, characters in the novel who do *not* inhabit the aesthetic and social terms of modernity with sleepy ease but rather grasp desperately for hermeneutic structures that would recuperate narrative order. Felix tries to locate himself unsuccessfully within the narrative trajectory of a Balzacian novel; Nora clamors to be Robin's sole romantic interest, that struggle offering her a source of meaning in a modern world that has made such desires seem naive. Knowing Barnes's admiration for Dietrich's queer silence allows us not to dismiss this hermeneutic panic—the desire for structures generative of narrative meaning—as an embarrassment to *Nightwood*'s urbane, disinterested modernism. It allows us, instead, to read that panic as integral to *Nightwood*'s response to losing the plot. And while we might be tempted still to dismiss Nora and Felix as outliers to the novel's stylistic intensities, harbingers of an older way of life motivated by residual structures of feeling that Barnes wishes to disavow, we will see that the loquacious Doctor Matthew O'Connor also tries to rescue interpretive structures of narrative meaning. Often figured as exemplary of *Nightwood*'s voluble excesses, representative of the novel's ostensible refusal to tell a coherent story, the Doctor in fact also takes part in this hermeneutic drama, racked as he is with guilt from the knowledge that he took part in thwarting Nora's love story, a formative event of betrayal that he goes to great pains to confess. Admitting to his responsibility, the Doctor offers Nora someone to blame and thus the ability to rely on what *Nightwood* persistently denies us: causes.

STORMS OF TALK

Recounting the plot of *Nightwood* is a strange task. The opacity of its style indeed obscures narrative action and sequence to such a degree that the Doctor's line to Nora—that "Life is not to be told, call it as loud as you like, it will not tell itself"—could be used to describe the novel itself.[17] Here is one way of telling it. At some unspecified time in the late nineteenth century, a young man named Felix is born to a Hungarian noblewoman, Hedvig, and her husband, a Jewish sham aristocrat Guido Volkbein. Hedvig dies during childbirth, and Guido had already died earlier than that, so Felix is left to wander the streets of 1920s Paris, a would-be nobleman in a modern world where such distinctions have long grown tired. Through his eventual acquaintance with the Parisian circus world, Felix falls in love with the elusive Robin Vote; they marry and have a child together, and she subsequently leaves them. Nora, a publicity journalist for the circus, meets Robin in New York City; they are together for an unspecified amount of time, first in Paris, then in New York, where Nora buys them a home. Robin, bored with Nora, wanders. Nora attempts to track her down, but eventually loses her to Jenny Petherbridge, a woman whom Robin has met one night at the opera. Robin and Jenny move to New York. Sometime later, in utter despair, Nora pays a visit to the loquacious, unlicensed gynecologist Doctor Matthew O'Connor, asking him to tell her what he knows of the night, a question that at its heart is a supplication to tell her why Robin left her and what she can do to get her back. Nora's questions provoke from the Doctor prolonged speeches about the nature of the night. The Doctor meets Felix in Paris, and they go out to dinner in the outskirts of the city. Felix admits to the Doctor that he is afraid for his son, Guido II, since he seems unlike other children. Felix, Guido II, and a trapeze artist named Frau Mann move together to Vienna. The Doctor begs Nora to stop writing letters to Robin; Nora tells the Doctor about calamitous scenes from her life with Robin. The Doctor goes to his watering hole, the Café de la Maire du VIe, gets drunk, and gives a speech about how tired he is of everyone asking him to console them. In the novel's famous final pages, Robin (having left Jenny, too) sniffs out Nora's home and on her way there encounters her dog. She gets down on hands and knees and plays with it in what Barnes insisted was not an erotic but merely a playful dance with the creature who is excited and confused by her behavior. The end.

From this description, it is clear why *Nightwood* is often considered a quintessential instance of modernist fragmentation and the rejection of teleological plot, an exercise in "spatial form." Most obviously, the novel consistently drops narrative threads. The constellation of characters that begins the novel, for instance—Hedvig, Guido, and Felix—disappears from the novel's landscape almost entirely by about halfway through it. Felix's dinner with the Doctor in the *bois* emerges as if out of nowhere; one could plausibly remove the section "Where the Tree Falls" in which it appears and nothing narratively essential to the novel would be disturbed. Robin's partnership with Nora proves just as temporary as Robin's previous partnership with Felix and, presumably, with Jenny. And Robin's famous dance with Nora's dog at the end of the novel, which has always perplexed critics, seems to be a rich ironization, as Herring has argued, of the Aristotelian notion of an ending.[18] There is no revelation, nor is there a significant resolution to a central conflict, since *Nightwood* has not in fact featured such a conflict but rather a series of brief and intense points of tension between different characters' desires, namely, Felix's and Nora's desires to be Robin's sole object of romantic interest and Robin's evident desire not to adhere to that demand. It is perhaps because the currents of narrative desire typically attached to the love plot are systematically frustrated in *Nightwood* that the final scene of Robin rambunctiously playing with Nora's dog would seem to offer no climactic relief but rather retreats from us, bearing the marks of what Anne-Lise François would call "recessive action."[19]

By virtue of *Nightwood*'s two primary narrative discontinuities—in the form of Robin's romantic rupture with first Felix and then Nora—*Nightwood* does not so much have a plot as it has several plot *points*. And even more so than in Larsen's *Quicksand*, those points do not quite form a coherent whole; they coagulate, rather, into a cluster of loosely related moments. They gesture to a potentially endless series of events that connect to one another through a principle of adjacency or perhaps contagion (Robin is, after all, referred to as an "infected carrier of the past"), but not consequence.[20]

These narrative discontinuities reflect the novel's investment in charting the spiritually damaged and alienated world of urban interwar Europe, a world coming to terms with the evacuation from everyday life of social, familial, historical, and religious structures of meaning—a novel, par excellence, of Lukácsian "transcendental homelessness." One senses everywhere in *Nightwood* the loss of collective sources of normative value, the Doctor's appeals to "God" betraying spiritual panic in their sheer regularity, and the replacement of a real aristocracy with the "pageantry" of circus performers Felix befriends evidence that genealogy no longer secures social significance the way it did even thirty years earlier.[21] Life, to put it simply, has lost the transcendent meaning it once had, understood no longer as an opportunity to fulfill one's destiny but as the Doctor puts it to Nora, merely "permission to know death."[22]

That state of evacuation or recession of narrative meaning is rendered in *Nightwood* most powerfully through its style. The language of the novel is thick, if not choked, a textual equivalent to the "heavy velvet hangings" Robin pulls away from the window in the Viennese hotel she visits with Felix.[23] But while Robin's gesture lets in the refreshing and "cold" evening "air," the reader of *Nightwood* is given no such clarity. Frequently, we are left to parse what is happening at the level of the fabula, what events are taking place, often because we are not entirely sure what is being said. This has much to do with how Barnes makes it difficult for us to visualize what she describes, refusing to adhere to the Conradian novelistic imperative to make us see.

An extreme example of the obstacle Barnes's style poses to our ability to visualize what the prose describes arrives in the section "Watchman, What of the Night?" when Nora surprises the Doctor by walking into his room unexpectedly.

> The doctor's head, with its over-large black eyes, its full gun-metal cheeks and chin, was framed in the golden semi-circle of a wig with long pendent curls that touched his shoulders, and falling back against the pillow, turned up the shadowy interior of their cylinders. He was heavily rouged and his lashes painted. It flashed into Nora's head: "God, children know something they can't tell; they like Red Riding Hood and the wolf in bed!" But this thought, which was only the sensation of a thought, was of but a second's duration as she opened the door; in the next, the doctor had snatched the wig from his head, and sinking down in the bed drew the sheets up over his breast.[24]

The excess of clauses and counterintuitive diction in the first sentence of the passage—*gun-metal cheeks and chin? I see, a half-grown-in beard*—makes it difficult to understand. Grammatical shifts further disrupt comprehension: Barnes describes not the doctor's reaction per se but that of his head—it is the head's black eyes, cheeks, and chin that the wig frames—but then the subject of the sentence mutates halfway through, from the head to the "pendent curls," then back to the doctor, since "his shoulders" feigns the conclusion of an independent clause and the subsequent beginning of another one. That is, "falling back against the pillow" could be a dependent clause forequalifying the doctor (not his head this time). But upon reading "turned up," we realize that we are still with the curls; it is the curls that are falling, not the doctor or his head. The swift movement of reference begins with the doctor, moves to his head, moves then to the pendent curls, then back to him, but that last movement is a feigned one. Barnes finishes the sentence by referring to "their cylinders." The referent of "their," we momentarily struggle before realizing, is the curls; and the cylinders are *not* related to the gun mentioned in "gun-metal cheeks and chin" but refer instead to the shapes created by the unified curvature of the curls' artificial strands.

This is a prose wildly on display. It forces us to try to visualize in order to understand it, but like Robin, whose "gracious and fading" presence makes conjuring up her image, for Felix, "an extreme act of the will," the prose elides our struggle to bring its images fully into view.[25] As the Doctor pulls the sheet up over his breast—accentuating, rather than quelling, as Taylor has argued, the optics of embarrassment shaping this scene of exposure—so, too, does Barnes's prose make a spectacle of itself precisely through its act of concealment.

The result of these textual effects is that we labor to see what is happening in *Nightwood*. Undermining what Dora Zhang calls "the nineteenth century's compulsive visualizing instinct," Barnes's descriptions force us to push through a thick and intricate boundary of text—what Glavey usefully refers to as "language stressing out."[26] And in the process, we become enormously aware of the words on the page. Barnes puts us radically in touch with what James Phelan would call the "synthetic" aspect of her characters, their status as artifice rather than real persons. One of the talents and aims of nineteenth-century literary realism was to obscure the synthetic nature of its characters by amplifying their "mimetic" quality— their similarity to real people in the world—and *Nightwood* is especially good at pulling back that mimetic veil.[27] Paradoxically, in pulling what Sarah Henstra calls a "rhetorical curtain" over what Barnes describes, giving us more language than we need to understand what is taking place, she exposes the status of her characters as artifice, beings akin to the "living statues" Frau Mann (a trapeze artist the narrator compares to a lozenge and a doll) looks forward to seeing with the Italian Count Onatorio Altamonte.[28] *Nightwood* does not track a continuous love plot either with Felix or Nora at least in part because it also disrupts mimetic immersion in easily intelligible scenes, images, and characters.

WHAT ARE YOU LOOKING AT?

As I've noted, critics have drawn comparisons between Robin and Dietrich, focusing particularly on the image of Robin when we are first introduced to her in the "La somnambule" section of the novel. Lying prostrate on a bed "surrounded by a confusion of potted plants, exotic palms and cut flowers, faintly over-sung by the notes of unseen birds," Robin, dressed in white pants and patent leather dancing heels,[29] exhibits powerful overtones of the character of Helen Faraday (whose stage name in *Blonde Venus* is "Blonde Venus"), and precisely in the ways that scholars have described. The image of a woman in white pants and heels surrounded by various tropical plants does indeed seem to "conflate," as Winkiel puts it, two images from *Blonde Venus*.[30] The first is of Blonde Venus performing a song titled "I Couldn't Be Annoyed" in a white tuxedo at a Paris cabaret before millionaire Nick Townsend (Cary Grant) takes her back to the United

FIGURE 18. Helen Faraday as "Blonde Venus" performing in signature white tuxedo at a Paris Cabaret in *Blonde Venus* (von Sternberg, 1932).

States (fig. 18). The second is the infamous "Hot Voodoo" number much earlier in the film, wherein, apart from a group of Black dancers wearing exaggerated nativist costumes, the stage props for Blonde Venus's performance include a cornucopia of tropical plants, creating a racist-Orientalist backdrop for the moment in her act when she removes a gorilla suit to reveal her platinum blonde hair and florescent white skin.

Moreover, the descriptions of Robin's skin as having "the texture of plant life," that "beneath it one sensed a frame, *broad*, porous and sleep-worn, as if sleep were a decay fishing her beneath the invisible surface" and that around "her head there was an effulgence as of phosphorous glowing about the circumference of a body of water" do indeed powerfully evoke the image of Dietrich.[31] This last quotation in particular invokes the iconic close-ups of Dietrich lit with her and von Sternberg's signature butterfly lighting. And Robin's "hands, long and beautiful" that "lay on either side of her face" mimic almost precisely the pose Dietrich struck in a publicity still for her other 1932 collaboration with von Sternberg, *Shanghai Express*.[32] That image of Dietrich, head clasped in her own hands with long fingers creeping like algae around her face, makes of her a gorgeous and sleepy amphibious creature—"a wild thing caught in a woman's skin," as the

FIGURE 19. Publicity still of Dietrich as "Shanghai Lily" in *Shanghai Express* (von Sternberg, 1932). Courtesy of Wikimedia Commons.

Doctor says of Robin—staring upward from the water's depths through a hazy and glowing beam of light "at once transparent," in James Phillips' apt phrasing, "and opaque" (fig. 19).[33]

But the resonances between *Nightwood* and Dietrich's oeuvre do not stop there. These analogies, albeit potent, remain relatively literal and local; and we need not limit ourselves to those already mentioned. For instance, we could, if we chose, link Robin's marriage to Felix, which surprises even him—"he was taken aback to find himself accepted, as if Robin's life held no volition for refusal"[34]—to the marriage between the German peasant Lily (Dietrich) and the Baron von Merzbach (Lionel Atwill) in Rouben Mamoulian's 1933 *Song of Songs*. Lily, like Robin, accepts the proposal merely by not refusing it, and once married and a baroness, she is miserable and leaves in a literal conflagration of dissent. And compared with the remarkably thin-framed Garbo, Dietrich was often thought of as having "broad" shoulders and a "broad" face, lending her sexuality a masculine edge.[35] Moreover, the language of sleep and somnambulance attached to Robin, not just in this instance but throughout the novel, may very well be another cloaked reference to Dietrich, who was the original star sleepwalker—the "gorgeous girl with the slumberous eyes," as one contemporary advertisement put it.[36] French actor Maurice Chevalier once referred to her, moreover, as a "ravishing" "sleepwalker," and Pare Loretz described her in *Vanity Fair* (disparagingly) as giving in *Blonde Venus* a performance akin to "an exhibition of somnambulance."[37] As if ironizing that reputation, in a scene in Frank Borzage's *Desire* (1936), Dietrich, as jewel thief Madeleine de Beaupré, feigns sleep while Gary Cooper, as naive American Tom Bradley, professes his love to her. In fact, an air of disinterestedness and fatigue permeated so many of Dietrich's performances that Alfred Hitchcock, too, would ironize it in his film *Stage Fright* (1950). There, Dietrich plays stage singer/murderer Charlotte Inwood; her performance of Cole Porter's "The Laziest Gal in Town"—throughout the number, she periodically lies down on chaise lounges placed throughout the stage— would later be parodied by Madeline Kahn singing the number "I'm Tired" as Lily von Shtupp in Mel Brook's *Blazing Saddles* (1974). Robin, too, seems always to have fallen asleep, a sign of her indifference to the advances of especially Felix, as when on their honeymoon in Vienna, he turns to find her "sleeping, one arm fallen over the chair's side," or "dozing" on another occasion with the memoirs of the Marquis de Sade sitting under her fallen hand.[38]

But the aesthetics of Dietrich and von Sternberg share a more general affinity with those of Barnes than merely local references. More striking and provocative than these acute analogies is the more generalized kinship between the strategies of stylistic occlusion that both Barnes and von Sternberg deploy. In Barnes, the viscosity of the prose overdescribes and thus threatens to obscure the characters from view. The effect of that textual thickness is that Barnes transforms the task of the novel from the articulation of plotted action to the revelation of the synthetic dimension of her characters, their status as words on the page, rather than fully mimetic beings in a story. Von Sternberg, similarly, so saturates his shots that we lose track of their narrative purpose. Rather than get enlisted voyeuristically in discerning a story, the viewer's gaze is persistently brought back up to the surface of the image in such a way that accentuates their spectrality.

Far from a "cinematic" style,[39] Barnes's is intensely literary; she forces us to read, read, and reread, yet then to not quite see. Similarly, von Sternberg shows, but often shows too much, and in so doing obstructs narrative comprehension. Von Sternberg became famous relatively quickly in Hollywood for making Dietrich a star, a partial truth that downplayed the agency she did exercise throughout their collaborations but that nevertheless resulted in a proliferation of comparisons to Svengali and Trilby. But from the perspective of the Hollywood studios, which wanted to profit from his films, he also became infamous for making films driven more by stylistic vision than by an investment in narrative. Given to comparing his work to a painter's, von Sternberg was interested above all in the graphic quality of the images he produced. He exerted notoriously obsessive control over the entire process of production, and very little if any of that intensity was directed toward storytelling. It would be an exaggeration to call von Sternberg a full-blown avant-garde director along the lines of some of his contemporaries, such as Sergei Eisenstein (an admirer turned rival)[40] or Luis Buñuel. And his works with Dietrich never approach the level of graphic abstraction of, for instance, Fernard Léger's *Ballet mécanique* (1925) or the ecstatic rejection of narrativity on display in Dziga Vertov's *Man with a Movie Camera* (1929)—although there are moments, especially in *The Scarlet Empress* (1934), as we will see, that flirt with both. Unlike these modernist and avant-garde directors, von Sternberg's films with Dietrich operate within relatively conventional modes of storytelling. And this is evinced not least by the fact that barring *The Blue Angel*, which he made for Hollywood's European competitor at the time Universum-Film Aktiengesellschaft (UFA), he made all of his Dietrich films for Hollywood's Paramount. Having to operate within the conservative aesthetic constraints of the classical continuity system that preserved spatial and temporal relations from shot to shot to maintain clear narrative action—and eventually the priggish constraints of the Hays Code—von Sternberg's style nevertheless stretched those conventions to their limits.[41] For instance, like Max Ophuls (the subject of my coda) but to very different effect, von Sternberg relied heavily on lengthy tracking shots, a technique of camera movement that unlike the pan, which mimics the movement patterns of a human head, moves through space on a dolly, calling attention to the status of the camera as a machine.

But one of the most conspicuous examples of the liberality with which von Sternberg approached the continuity system is his use of prolonged dissolves. As opposed to a cut or a fade out (or in), where one image instantly replaces another or an image fades to black and another fades into view, the dissolve gradually transitions from one shot to the next by momentarily allowing the next image to overlap with the previous one. In the classical Hollywood cinema, the time it takes for the previous image to yield to the next must be brief enough such that the illusion of narrative continuity is preserved and neither the artificiality of the moving image nor, by extension, the editing process is allowed to sink into the viewer's consciousness. There are multiple effects that the dissolve can produce, some of them spooky, as in the famous image of a skull overlapping in a suspended dissolve over the face of Norman Bates in Hitchcock's *Psycho* (1960). But for the most part during the classical Hollywood period, the intended aim of the dissolve was to ease narrative development by providing a barely perceptible transitional lubricant between moments in the plot. A trademark of Sternberg's cinema was to protract the dissolve such that the viewer cannot help but recognize that they are not being given access voyeuristically to a story that already exists in the world among living and breathing people—what Christian Metz canonically considered the primary ideological operation of the classical continuity system.[42] Rather, they are made aware that they are watching a synthetic object in motion, a celluloid film that has been cut and spliced and stitched together. By prolonging the time of the transition and allowing the second image to sit on top of and bleed into the first for several seconds, von Sternberg disrupts narrative continuity and heightens our awareness of the film's artifice. In *Shanghai Express*, for instance, a dissolve marks the transition between a shot of nameless passengers shuffling toward the exit of the train and descending to the platform at the command of Chinese police officers in search of an insurgent on board and one of another stream of passengers also descending the train, led by three main characters—Hui Fei (Anna May Wong) followed by Mrs. Haggerty (Louise Closser Hale) and Sam Salt (Eugene Pallette). The duration of the dissolve from the first image to the next is a full six seconds. For six seconds (a long time in narrative film), we have very little idea of where we are and what is happening.

Von Sternberg's tendency toward visual excess has even more deleterious effects on narrative continuity, however, when it emerges *during* a scene rather than between scenes. He often chokes the frame with objects, bodies, and materials (lace and netting are his signatures), which results in a deluge of graphic intensity that overwhelms character and narrative development. Examples abound throughout his work, some of the most famous perhaps being the shots of carnival celebrations in *The Devil Is a Woman* (1935) (Dietrich's own favorite: "in my view the most beautiful film that was ever made," she said).[43] Streamers, balloons, and confetti litter the frame, often obscuring our view of the characters, whose carnival masks enact *en abyme* the film's own strategies of occlusion.

But the most pronounced instances in which von Sternberg's decadent mise-en-scène, like Barnes's prose style, impedes narrative intelligibility are in *The Scarlet Empress*, a historical drama set in the eighteenth century and loosely based on the story of Catherine the Great's rise to the throne of Russia. Originally an innocent young Prussian noble, Catherine is ordered by her mother and the Empress of Russia to wed the Empress's nephew, the Grand Duke. Catherine, having fallen in love with Count Alexei, the man who has come to escort her to Moscow, is doubly horrified to learn upon meeting the Duke (played menacingly by Sam Jaffe) that he is neurodivergent; a title card refers to him ableistically as the "royal half-wit." Soon thereafter, Catherine learns that despite his advances toward her, Count Alexei is actually entangled romantically with the Empress. Catherine grows nihilistic, sleeping with members of the Russian court and army to amuse herself and seek revenge. Having borne an illegitimate son that the court nevertheless recognizes as the future emperor, Catherine's claim to the throne remains secure until the Empress dies and the Duke sets out to assassinate Catherine. She steals away in the night, gathering supporters (among them Count Alexei and the Russian army) to stage a coup. The Duke is killed, and Catherine and her troops storm the throne room. The film ends with a series of dissolves, including one of Dietrich smiling madly as flags wave and cannons crack, confirming her ascension to power.

Von Sternberg referred to *The Scarlet Empress* as "a relentless excursion into style," and he indeed shows little to no restraint in his aesthetic choices.[44] The atmosphere of the film is nightmarish, replete with expressionistic and surrealistic settings. The film did extremely poorly at the box office precisely because it was, to date, the one in which von Sternberg

FIGURE 20. Inside the church during the marriage scene in *The Scarlet Empress* (von Sternberg, 1934).

threw narrative caution most to the wind. Shots of the wedding ceremony are exemplary in their emphasis on the dark visual lyricism of decor over narrative meaning. Like the protracted dissolves mentioned above, languorous tracking shots inside the church capture so much in the frame that narrative comprehension is subordinated to visual awe (fig. 20). The shot is congested with *things*—candles, banners, lamps, people, crosses, banisters—and in their aggregate, they form a flooded and cacophonous palette. Most strikingly, perhaps, is what the cinematography and lighting do to the space of the shot despite that overwhelming quantity. The space is madly voluminous, flaunting its sheer capacity; but it is also stubbornly, counterintuitively, flat. The "potentiality of perceived depth," as Carole Zucker puts it, "is suppressed by the extreme clutter of the frame."[45] Though in principle we know that the entities swamping the frame occupy multiple planes, there is a remarkable unbrokenness to its ultimate effect, an Escherian impossibility to its dimension that is at once labyrinthine and smooth, mazy and level. The camera, appropriately, tracks "*across* the space rather than into it," as if the camera "*could not* break through the knot of objects and figures."[46] And as if mocking the viewer's struggle to discern the dimensions of the image, Richard Kollorsz's Byzantine paintings of throngs of angels with flat and gray halo disks surrounding their heads stare out from the wall, blending cunningly in with the rest of the decor and reminding us—as does the flickering light in Marguerite's bedchamber scene with Gaston discussed in chapter 1—that we are indeed watching an image, flat and immaterial. There is no difference, in truth, between those Byzantine paintings and the human characters; both are insubstantial. Neither are actually human.

In fact the film exhibits a visual obsession with comparing people to representations of people. Dolls, figurines, and toy soldiers permeate the visual landscape of the film—an especially ominous instance being one in which the Grand Duke, in a room dedicated to storing his toy soldiers, decapitates a doll dressed up like Catherine. And the most prominent feature of the film's decor is a series of enormous humanoid gargoyles famously designed by Swiss sculptor and "long-time Sternberg devotee" Peter Balbusch and created under the director's supervision.[47] The statues are so visually intrusive that they persistently trick the eye; on numerous occasions, the viewer finds themselves realizing that what they thought was a person is in fact a colossal gargoyle. For example, in the scene where Count Alexei walks into a room full of Catherine's attendants asking to meet with Catherine privately, what appears to be two men facing one another in a genuflecting pose of prayer in the foreground of the shot turn out to be statues. And when the imperial priest meets with Catherine to warn her that the Empress's death will destabilize Catherine's claim to the throne, it takes us a moment to realize that it is a row of statues, not actual monks, that hold candles in single file in the background (fig. 21). It is a repetitive visual miscalculation that von Sternberg himself ironizes. In the scene where Catherine storms into a conference the Empress is conducting with a number of courtiers, she turns her head repeatedly side to side as she traverses the room, looking not at the courtiers themselves, but at the gargoyles that tower over them behind their chairs, as if trying to find the right person—or at least *a* person—to address.

Statues litter *Nightwood* too, as in the "living statues" mentioned previously, the "old" weather-beaten "statue in the garden" to which Felix compares Robin, and the "sculptured head" of a man with "shocked protruding eyeballs" and "tragic mouth" that Nora and Robin love so much.[48] And Catherine the Great is even mentioned explicitly in the novel, once among a list of "women in history" whom Robin ponders in church while thinking of the doomed fate of her son, and a second time when the Doctor claims drunkenly that he once bled Catherine with leeches.[49]

But the point here need not be that Barnes was explicitly thinking of *The Scarlet Empress* when composing *Nightwood*. Rather, we might simply observe that by leaning into the materiality of their respective mediums, von

FIGURE 21. Catherine meeting with the imperial priest with a row of statues behind them in *The Scarlet Empress*.

Sternberg and Barnes both show the synthetic seams underpinning their mimetic illusions. Von Sternberg even mocks the voyeurism of narrative cinema in the scene where the Grand Duke and his mistress bore a hole in the Empress's wall with an auger to be able to spy on her. As Catherine helps the Empress prepare for sleep, she gets distracted; the Empress asks her impatiently, "What are you looking at?" Cut to a shot of Catherine staring off-screen, bewildered and turning her head perplexedly side to side, as if the movements will help her discern what she is seeing. Cut then to a horrifying reverse-angle shot of the Grand Duke's auger spinning eerily into the room, straight at the camera and through the eye of a painted angel on the wall, who weeps as she sticks a dagger into her own chest (fig. 22). Catherine's fascinated stare mimics the viewer's own orientation toward the visual perplexities of *The Scarlet Empress*—and the textual ones of *Nightwood*. Appropriately, the film's final sequence is a series of dissolves that, in a parade of translucent sheets, cover Catherine's mad smile with phantom images of church bells clanging and troops storming the streets of Moscow (fig. 23). In other words, the film does not so much end as it simply stops. The Empress's "What are you looking at?" is indeed an apt question for a film so dedicated to undermining the formal authority of plot through an "excursion into style," von Sternberg's characters, like Barnes's, being so many living statues.

FIGURE 22. Reverse-angle shot of the wall; the Duke's augur spins into the room, piercing the eye of a painted angel in *The Scarlet Empress*.

FIGURE 23. Catherine's mad smile at the end of *The Scarlet Empress*.

A GOOD MODERNIST

Dietrich's mad smile at the end of *The Scarlet Empress* suggests the facility, even felicity, that she exhibits vis-à-vis von Sternberg's devaluation of story for the sake of style. Catherine, like so many of Dietrich's other characters, gives the impression of not *wanting* to be constrained by the formal exigencies of plot, happy instead to relish in the lyrical detonations of cinematic style von Sternberg orchestrates. It is perhaps only in the context of discussions of stardom that such an observation, which relies on the conflation of character with actor—character with person—can be made with relative ease. In literary criticism, conflating art with life is often seen as at worst nonsensical and at best the result of a category error, the "realistic fallacy," whereby we treat characters as if they were real people.[50] Charles Grivel argued in 1973 that the literary character "n'est personne [is no one]."[51] And that doctrine, as Toril Moi has recently argued, still dominates contemporary literary criticism. It does not make sense, according to most professional literary-critical accounts, to ask about whether Pip, for instance, "wants" to be in a bildungsroman. Instead, the tacit premise of professional literary criticism is that it is incorrect, even embarrassingly wrongheaded, to talk about literary characters as "wanting" this or that, because the task of the critic is to foreground characters' status as figurations of text.[52] We are taught to ask not what the character wants vis-à-vis the form of the text, since the character and the text are ostensibly indistinct from one another.

In film, however, to conflate, say, the character of Marguerite Gautier with Garbo is to recognize a fundamental feature of cinematic performance. The text constituting character in film is the actor's body; thus, although we do not mistake the actor for the character, that elision is constantly at play in the mind of the viewer. It is a trompe l'oeil intrinsic to cinema, one that constitutes the unique power of its illusion. "The character in a film," as Erwin Panofsky famously put it, "lives and dies with the actor." And that conflation is even more pronounced when the actor playing the part is a star. By virtue of being excessively present as people in our collective consciousness, the star, as Stanley Cavell, Richard Dyer, and Panofsky have argued, merely accentuates the residue of the actor's identity that always remains in excess of the given role they are playing. It is, Panofsky writes, "the entity 'Greta Garbo' incarnate in a figure called Anna Christie or the entity 'Robert Montgomery' incarnate in a murderer who . . . may forever remain anonymous but will never cease to haunt our memories."[53]

To be sure, star personas are just as constructed, Dyer reminds us, as the roles they play; they are images created in the crucible of publicity.[54] But that only amplifies, rather than nullifies, the collapse of person into character that haunts the cinematic role. Stars take roles "onto" themselves, in Cavell's words, precisely because of the potency of their constructed images.[55] And this holds true even when the star persona is one of withdrawal from the public eye. For instance, Garbo's notorious retreat from publicity by refusing interviews and photographs only made her public image—and so, too, her characters—more enigmatic and alluring. In Barnes's own words, "Greta Garbo. Everyone wants to know her, and no one does."[56] And Dietrich, who largely relished fame and did not take the same reclusive stance toward the public, had her own specific affect. As a public figure, her persona ranged from the maternal German hausfrau who brought home-cooked food to her costars;[57] to the wife of fellow German, Rudolf Sieber, and mother to their only child, Maria; to the homewrecker being sued by von Sternberg's wife for one hundred thousand dollars for libel and alienating her husband's affections, which Dietrich always denied.[58] On screen, especially during the time she was making films with von Sternberg, her affect was famously one of distance and distraction. Contemporary reviewers discussed it in terms of a strange calm. "She possesses," writes Sarah Hamilton for a 1931 piece for *Movie Mirror*, "a stout Teutonic calm that's beyond belief. She never gurgles or bubbles. She's seldom animated. She's just calm."[59] Barnes's published comments on Dietrich capture that placidity with especial acuity, focusing specifically on her nonreliance on speech. In January 1931, the same year she started composing *Nightwood*, Barnes writes the following in the mock-almanac style typical to her column "Playgoer's Almanac":

> It is predicted that in the immediate future dialogue will serve merely as an accelerator to action in the moving pictures, a technique employed in the Josef von Sternberg production "Morocco," *starring* Marlene Dietrich. This film has been criticized for this Very Fact, 1 which I find particularly Pleasant, but then I like my human experiences served up with a little *silence* and Restraint. Silence makes experience go further and, when it does die, gives it that dignity of the Thing one has touched but not RAVISHED.[60]

Barnes's assessment of *Morocco*'s reticence is consistent with von Sternberg's more general tendency to rely, when he could, on the expressiveness of images rather than speech. And Dietrich's allure was indeed wrapped up in the embodiment of a sexually powerful restraint.[61] To be sure, Dietrich was deeply vocal, coming onto the cinematic scene from the Berlin cabaret and singing her way into cinematic fame. In *The Blue Angel*, the 1930 film adaptation of Heinrich Mann's 1905 novella *Professor Unrat*, she played the "brazen and vulgar" stage singer Lola Lola opposite Emil Jannings's uptight and naive Professor.[62] *The Blue Angel* was Germany's first feature-length sound film, and it was equipped with multiple stage numbers, including the most famous, "Falling in Love Again." And once Dietrich had become a movie star, she would continue to play roles that required her to sing. As we discussed in chapter 1, the "talkie revolution" in the late 1920s destroyed many careers, most famously John Gilbert's and also eventually Emil Jannings's. We saw that MGM worried (needlessly, it turned out) that Garbo's Swedish-accented, husky moan of a voice would destroy the image of transcendent whiteness achieved in her silent image.[63] But Dietrich faced no such challenges. She was, in Steven Bach's words, "the first international movie star actually *created* by sound."[64]

But *Morocco* brought out another side of Dietrich's persona, one of reticent allure. Von Sternberg always remained a silent filmmaker at heart, a fact captured well by a perceptive contemporary reviewer: "'Morocco,'" the reviewer writes, "is a relatively silent picture with incidental dialogue . . . a film in which thousands of shots are made without a single sound."[65] As such, his work attests to Dietrich's talent for the silent expressiveness Barnes observes.[66] From *Morocco* onward, Dietrich had a sly evasiveness to her, an emotional minimalism that stemmed from her expert reliance on von Sternberg's lighting, rather than facial movements, to bring out what Lutz Koepnick calls the "inner expression[s]" of her face.[67] The "camera," Bach writes, "reads things *into* her," a receptivity of expression exemplified in the close-up of Dietrich as Amy Jolly before performing her first number in *Morocco*. She stares silently into the crowd of men, all of them jeering from disappointment at her tuxedo, save the intrigued Legionnaire Tom Brown, played by Gary Cooper (fig. 24).[68]

But one of the effects of Dietrich's signature "silence and Restraint," in Barnes's words, is that they obstruct narrative teleology in favor of an erotic play of looks. The editing of the first cabaret scene in *Morocco* is indicative of how the stakes of the relationship between Amy and Tom are and remain largely stylistic and affective rather than narrative. There is certainly a story: the singing drifter Amy Jolly travels to Morocco and falls in love with the Foreign Legion soldier Tom Brown. He gets wrongfully accused of sleeping with his commanding officer's wife and gets sent to another town. Before leaving, he proposes to desert the army if Amy will sail with him back to Europe but then loses confidence and leaves her when he realizes she is being pursued by the wealthy La Bessiére (Adolphe

FIGURE 24. Close-up of Dietrich as Amy Jolly, staring silently into the jeering crowd, in *Morocco* (von Sternberg, 1930).

Menjou). She ultimately does marry La Bessiére, but then leaves him for the chance to be with Tom.

One *Variety* article referred disparagingly to the "story" of *Morocco* as "light-weight."[69] And that has largely to do with the fact that the skeletal frame of the story merely offers a pretext for the erotic play between Dietrich and Cooper. Amy and Tom are not bound together hermeneutically; they are not fastened to one another by the causal chains constitutive of the romance plot, as were, for instance, Armand and Marguerite in *Camille*. Rather, what animates the energetic intensity between Dietrich and Cooper is a contactless erotics of distance, the refusal of touch, both editorial and embodied. There are multiple instances of touch throughout the scene, including one of the queerest moments in the classical Hollywood cinema, where Amy famously kisses a woman in the audience on the lips after asking for the flower in her hair. And earlier in the scene, an eager patron manages to place his hand on Amy's arm for a moment before she gently gets up and nudges it away. But not only do Tom and Amy never touch each other during this crucial sequence, they are also editorially set off from one another, never occupying the same frame. Instead, the entire scene is composed of a series of point of view shots edited in shot-reverse shot, such that most of what we see is a series of images of Dietrich and Cooper looking off-screen (e.g., figs. 25, 26).

In a basic sense, they are of course looking at one another; it is the purpose and magic of shot-reverse shot editing according to the 180-degree rule that film renders the drama of mutual gazes visually intelligible. But nevertheless, in their sheer repetition, and cordoned off by the cell of the frame, their looks do not *attach* to anything. Rather, they generate an erotics of unattachment, even detachment: irony figured as a perceptual swerve. What that swerve—the refusal to encase them in the same frame—allows is the interjection of a third, disrupting term, the presence of the spectator (indeed, we might imagine, of Barnes) to consume each star image on its own terms. It is important to note that Cooper was himself becoming known for a "laconic" and feminized receptivity—the "Coop" who didn't say much but whose thoughts the camera drew out, as King Vidor put it famously.[70] Commanding the screen with what Corey Creekmur has termed the spectacle of his "rugged elegance"[71]—contemporary critics often referred to it simply as his "beauty"—Cooper was known to

FIGURE 25. Amy Jolly looking off-screen at Tom Brown in *Morocco*.

FIGURE 26. Tom looking at Amy performing in *Morocco*.

straddle erotic allure with an easy, unbothered masculinity. He was the "pretty cowboy," as Jeffrey A. Brown has suggestively put it.[72] Often that allure, as in this famous scene in *Morocco*, emerged from his comfort with passivity, a "lazy ease" that later in this chapter we'll see comes to be associated, too, with Dietrich's own performances;[73] Dietrich famously throws him her acquired flower, and we cut to him receiving it with titillated repose, twirling it around in his fingers, offering himself up as the thing to be looked at. The lesbian kiss, therefore, suggests the erotic triangulation of looks afforded *us* by the editing—an editing that here is decidedly not only not attached but also not straight. Not just Dietrich but Dietrich and Cooper both are erotic objects here, mirrors of one another.[74] And they need not—especially when considering the bisexuality of both Barnes and Dietrich—be limited to typical pathways of straight or even lesbian desire. By not putting Tom and Amy in the same frame, the film allows the spectator the fantasy of being with them both at the same time. Or, if one likes, one accesses Cooper through Dietrich, (and) or Dietrich through Cooper, in whatever configuration of identification and erotic pleasure one chooses: Dietrich's "fickle, flaunted bisexuality," as Patricia White puts it, is stitched into the editorial grammar of the film.[75]

This evasion of perceptual contact—the fact that Amy and Tom's eyes rarely meet or meet only barely—persists till the very end of the film and has implications for *Morocco*'s ultimate treatment of the love plot. The scene toward the end of *Morocco* where Amy rushes to meet Tom at a bar after thinking he has been injured in battle on the Amalfi Pass ostensibly offers the lovers an opportunity to profess their love for one another and finally reunite in a classical Hollywood ending, providing the audience a narratively and affectively satisfying image, as in *Camille*, of what James MacDowell calls "the final couple."[76] At this point in the film, Amy is engaged to La Bessiére, but there is no narrative reason why she should answer Tom's question "Aren't you gonna marry that rich friend of yours?" with an elongated, ironically mischievous "Of cooourse!" She has shown herself not to care at all for material security and so could very well say to Tom that she loves him, and he, who has moments before been scratching her name into the tabletop with a knife, could tell her the same. But just as their glances yet again evade one another, that narrative opportunity is gratuitously missed, leaving room instead for an extended play of averted gazes (fig. 27). Tom alternately looks down at the table and lowers the bill of his cap so as to avoid Amy's sly stare, and Amy looks at Tom only out of

FIGURE 27. Amy and Tom evading one another's glances in *Morocco*.

the corner of her eye. Instead of offering a crucial link in the chain of narrative causality that would lead to the lover's reunion, the scene remains narratively moot (What has happened in this sequence? Nothing, really.) but stylistically and erotically electrified. Dietrich offers her face, again, to the spectator; and in not meeting her gaze, Tom leaves room, again, for the spectator to occupy the space between them, a space accentuated by that between the stones in the wall behind them—a space, it turns out, referred to in masonry as "the bed joint." Amy and Tom's missed ocular encounters reflect the film's refusal to subordinate its characters fully to the bonds of narrative causality—to attach them to one another, as it were, through the demands of the love plot. Dietrich and Cooper are not bound together by a narrative chain of cause and effect; they hover around one another, and we hover in and between them, in a structure of erotic adjacency.

Appropriately, that missed visual encounter mirrors a very important one of our own: von Sternberg never allows us to see the image of Amy and Tom reunited. She does leave La Bessiére, but only for the chance to *maybe* reunite with Tom. As he walks off into the desert with his regiment to meet his next mission, Amy decides last minute to follow him. She famously throws off her high heels and joins a group of women La Bessiére calls the "rear guard" who follow the soldiers from town to town hoping to possibly catch up with them. The final image of the film—in complete silence save for the sound of the wind blowing in the desert and the faint drumming of the regiment in the far distance—is of Dietrich in extreme long shot, marching into the desert holding not Tom's hand, much less looking into his eyes, but the rope attached to the neck of one of the women's goats. It is a visually striking but narratively befuddling image that presages the one of Robin and Nora's dog at the end of *Nightwood*.

Amy's cool side glances are indicative of how Dietrich's affect imbues her characters with an air of uninvestment in the love plot. As Alice A. Kuzniar has argued, this has largely to do with the queer energy she emanates. "Dietrich," she argues, "acts as if heterosexuality were a huge bore or charade and that she is searching for something else." She "exudes intimations of an other desire" that make her attachments to the male romantic interest seem forced.[77] The intensity of her on-screen chemistry with Cooper somewhat mutes that disinterest, aided no doubt by the fact that they were having an affair during the shoot. But a glaring example of how Dietrich's ironic and distant affect imbues her characters with a sense of indifference to the narrative stakes of the love plot is *Blonde Venus*. *Blonde Venus* tells the story of a woman named Helen Faraday, whose husband, Ned (Herbert Marshall), falls ill of chemical poisoning. To pay for his medical treatments, Helen goes back to her job as a stage performer, adopting the stage name Blonde Venus and striking up an affair with one of her fans, the millionaire Nick Townsend (Grant). Once Ned finds out about Nick, Helen flees with their son Johnny, taking him on the road until the police catch her and take Johnny back home to Ned. Helen at first stays in Europe touring, but Nick eventually finds her and takes her back to the United States to marry her. The night before they are to wed, Nick takes Helen, at her request, to see Johnny. Upon seeing Johnny, Helen is too drawn in by her love for him to leave with Nick, so she decides to stay home with him and Ned. Nick departs; order is restored.

Dietrich's affect, however, renders this narrative closure unconvincing, a difficulty emblematized in the final shot of the film (fig. 28). It is a close-up of Johnny's hand manipulating a musical windup toy with figurines that move along in a circle as the music plays (the figurines and other statues littering *The Scarlet Empress* are foreshadowed here). This gesture of pushing figurines along with gentle authority symbolizes Helen's return at the end of the film to the family she had left behind, a restoration of the familial order that had been overthrown by her departure into the throes of an extramarital affair and the spectacular intensities of the

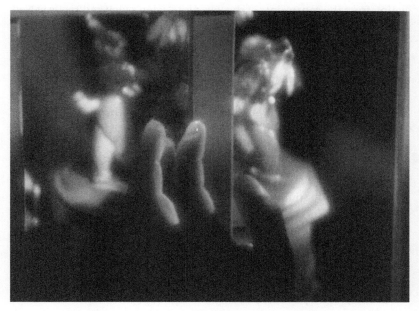

FIGURE 28. Johnny's hand from behind his cradle bars, moving the figures on a toy in the final shot of *Blonde Venus* (von Sternberg, 1932).

nightclubs where she starred. Like the hand taking control of a spinning wheel, Helen's return brings peace back to a domestic life that had been thrown into upheaval.

But the image of a forceful, albeit delicate, maneuvering of a body of cyclically moving figurines is suggestive of the way that that restoration of order is itself a kind of forceful maneuvering. Be the plot points what they may, Dietrich's affect—cool, distant, ironic—makes the reinscription of the bourgeois nuclear family at the end of the film seem entirely "contrived."[78] Dietrich's allure in *Blonde Venus* is indeed so wrapped up in the embodiment of what Barnes calls "restraint" that she seems dissatisfied with the narrative demands that are being placed on her by the plot. She is not angered, but simply indifferent, even vaguely amused. In a painfully awkward two shot toward the end of the film—which suggests compulsory heterosexuality, if not monogamy tout court, as an enclosed cell—Helen casts a patronizing glance at Ned, Ned sheepishly looking back at her. They stand over Johnny's crib, her raised eyebrows and the barely perceptible upward turn of the corners of her lips making it seem as if she is inwardly mocking the very institution of heteronormative domesticity the scene—and the shot composition—ostensibly promotes. As opposed to the averted gazes in Morocco, which suggested a playful and erotic distanciation from the constraints of the love plot, Helen's glower directly at Ned who looks meekly back, suggests how unappealing—indeed, pathetic—the love plot is to her. The superfluity of the male romantic interests in *Blonde Venus* is suggested in a shot toward the end when Ned and Nick wait awkwardly in the living room while Dietrich plays with Johnny in his bedroom. Nick plays uncomfortably with his hat while looking off-screen, Ned sits cast in shadow in the foreground, neither of them knowing quite what to do or say—a nod to the fact that their purpose in the film at this point borders on moot.[79]

Thus, despite the narrative action taking place (in this case, Helen returning to her husband and son), Dietrich's distant, restrained affect allows stylistic residue to spill over the borders of that plot resolution. Dietrich's performative style—knowing, distant, invested elsewhere—suggests that though she will do the love plot if that is what the film is asking of her, she could in truth take or leave whatever love interest is written into the film, that the formal imperatives underpinning the telos of the love plot will always struggle to corral her within its requisite boundaries. Dietrich, like Robin Vote, would prefer to exist outside of plot rather than in it. After all, what we cannot see in the final shot of the film is that while it is Johnny's hand pushing the figurines around like so many characters in a film, it is in fact Dietrich's hand cranking the lever, in control of the narrative operation, but irrevocably outside of it. Dietrich, in short, imbues her characters with an air of distance, inhabiting that irony easily and sleepily, making her involvement with the love interest apparent as a narrative pretext for an excursion into erotic stylistic play. Dietrich's expressive restraint extends from a queer desire that subtends her performance in a disruptive formal swerve emblematized in her glances off-screen.

Barnes's style, meanwhile, is anything but silent and restrained. Robin Vote does indeed resemble Dietrich in her extended silences that baffle and frustrate her loved ones. She barely speaks throughout the entire novel—"she was so silent," Felix thinks—or when she does, it either takes the form of aggressive vocal outbursts, as when she screams drunkenly at Felix to "Go to hell!" or sounds directed obliquely toward absent entities: in Robin's voice one hears the "low drawling 'aside' voice of the actor," Barnes writes, "who, in the soft usury of his speech, withholds a vocabulary until the profitable moment when he shall be facing his audience—in her case a guarded extempore to the body of what would be said at some later period when she would be able to 'see' them."[80] It is only Robin, what Fama refers to as the Doctor's "silent counterpoint," who moves sleepily, absentmindedly, through the novel. And her silence corresponds to her generalized lack of attention to anything in particular, let alone her lovers, whom she treats with what the Doctor refers to as "the great passionate indifference."[81] As in Dietrich's aesthetics of silent inattentiveness, Robin is described as "disinterested" and "noncommittal," expressing a "withdrawal in her movement and a wish to be gone"; Robin's "attention," the narrator observes, "had already been taken by something not yet in history. Always she seemed to be listening to the echo of some foray in the blood that had no known setting."[82] Robin's attention, too, we might say, is directed off-screen.

But other characters, as well as the text of *Nightwood* itself, deal in extreme volubility. As we have seen, Barnes's style relies precisely on overdescription, congesting the page with language. Robin, like Dietrich, thrives in that stylistic excess and the irreverence toward plot that it augers. Dietrich's indifference gestures toward a stylistic refuge from the normative constraints of the Hollywood love plot, directing a pathway out of that narrative architecture and toward an unknown elsewhere freed from the demands of story. Similarly, Robin's refusal to speak and her attendant disinterest in adhering to the telos of the love plot suggests not only that she is at ease in the narrative conditions of a modernist *écriture* but that she somehow emblematizes it. She is, like Dietrich, a *good* modernist. She wanders through space and time seemingly without narrative attachments, inhabiting the textual morass of *Nightwood* with palpable ease.

With no desire for the long-term romantic attachments forged by the love plot, she is in many ways an ideal queer subject in the form imagined by Lee Edelman, her abandonment of Guido II a symbolic, if extreme, gesture of a refusal of heteronormative futurity.[83]

THE NIGHT OF NIGHTS

But other characters, even the Doctor, are not quite as good. They attempt to deliver themselves from that stylistic flux—those structures of adjacency—and to restore plotted sense. They do so by seeking recourse to, if not inventing, structures of causality. Felix and Nora in particular are consumed by what Bonnie Roos, by way of Gordon Teskey, calls "hermeneutic anxiety."[84] They are driven by the desire to know and to understand, an interpretive impulse that critics often read as antithetical to *Nightwood*'s commitment to dismantling the narrative architecture of the nineteenth-century realist novel. They ostensibly provide examples, by negation, of what Herring calls *Nightwood*'s "anti-hermeneutical" recourse to high-modernist textuality.[85] One of the five semic codes Roland Barthes considered to organize all narrative, the hermeneutic code refers to the interpretative force that charges the proairetic code—the code of action—with meaning. As Peter Brooks argues, of the five semic codes, the proairetic and the hermeneutic codes constitute the structural dynamic of plot. The hermeneutic code is the interpretive work that subtends such responses, what allows us to read proairetic information such that it makes sense within a narrative whole. The hermeneutic code relies on and helps build structures of narrative causality. It is the interpretive force that retroactively bridges—makes contact between—what is happening now and what happened before in a narratively meaningful chain of actions and outcomes.

To say that *Nightwood* is antihermeneutical, then, is to say that the novel refuses the interpretive structures integral to plot. And earlier in this chapter, we have said as much. The halting discontinuities that periodically send *Nightwood* in narratively disparate directions would indeed suggest a resistance on Barnes's part to facilitate the hermeneutic bridging of narrative moments dominant in the nineteenth-century novel. As readers, we struggle to reconstruct the causal architecture binding the actions of *Nightwood* together, often giving ourselves over to the flow of language that inundates us and that hangs together in narrative clusters like the trundling train cars of von Sternberg's *Shanghai Express*.

Felix and Nora tend to emerge as scapegoats in the critical work on *Nightwood* in large part because they try to locate themselves within narrative structures of social, sexual, and historical meaning that the novel—and much criticism—ostensibly deems passé. Felix's overvaluation of the ancien régime by way of its lines of European nobility, for instance, is made a mockery of by its false equivalencies in the circus. When Felix arrives in Paris "in search of the particular *Comédie humaine*," he instead "come[s] upon the odd,"[86] having to befriend trapeze artists and quack doctors instead of dukes and earls. The only actual nobles who grace the pages of *Nightwood* either die on the first page (Hedvig) or disappear immediately after being introduced, as in the case of the Count Onatario Altamonte, who enters the café where Felix, the Doctor, and Frau Mann have congregated, orders everyone to "Get out!" and disappears from the novel entirely, save for one brief mention in conversation over dinner between Felix and the Doctor.[87] That *Nightwood* does not comfortably house aristocratic characters suggests that Barnes is loosening the formal terms that supported the social ones the Balzacian novel (to which the *Comédie humaine* is a direct reference) was already calling into question. Lucien de Rubempré and Eugène de Rastignac are pretenders, sham aristocrats like Felix; the structures of social ambition that informed those narrative trajectories, quintessential in their adherence to a hermeneutic narrativity, threw all the more powerfully into relief these characters' social fraudulence while also attempting to compensate for it—to show the available structure of the desire to climb.[88] Even that desire, Barnes suggests, is now a mockery in a modernity shattered by world war, the erosion of Victorian sexual mores, and the age of the mass. The form, too, must now go.

Nora's tireless interviews with the Doctor, moreover, in which she begs him to help her understand—"What am I to do?" she asks him, "What is it? What is it in her that is doing this?"; "What will become of her?"; "What will happen now, to me and to her?"—do indeed index her inability to rest easy in the epistemic obscurity embodied in the Doctor's notion of "the night," that state of "mighty uncertainty" of which Robin, whose life seems "one continual accident," seems the very symbol.[89] Attempting to gather the centrifugal textuality of *Nightwood* into one coherent story, Nora clamors to find hermeneutic structures that would explain the events of her devastation, as if finding out what it is in Robin that makes her abandon those who love her—to make of Robin's actions a coherent narrative—would somehow ease her suffering. To put it simply, and perhaps stupidly, Nora does not want to be in a novel like *Nightwood*, whose very form seems to forget what has come before. She is bad at being modern, at being merely adjacent. She wants causality, consequence. It makes sense, then, that the feature of Robin's personality that hurts Nora the most is her forgetfulness, a baffling amnesia that erases the past and translates into an absence of remorse. "Will Robin *only* regret?" Nora asks the Doctor in exasperated anger. "Perhaps not," she answers herself, "for even her memory wearied her."[90] Robin, like *Nightwood* itself, moves through time with no regard for hermeneutic responsibility, living ecstatically in what Gertrude Stein would call a "continuous present" divorced from diachronic relations to people or narrative time. Robin shows no remorse and in so doing demonstrates her irreverence toward structures of narrative causality.

And our critical desire tends to be to read Barnes as aligned with that project, irreverently kicking out from beneath the history of the novel the hermeneutic structures of causality supporting the love plot. In the process, we often like to think, Barnes has set the novel free from those heteronormative constraints. But what if we were to read this clamor for hermeneutic sense—the desire for the refuge of plot—from the perspective of a writer who did not inhabit queer antinormativity with sleepy ease but who desperately wanted one person and one person only? What if we were to recall that *Nightwood* was written by a writer who wanted monogamy—that "least queer of all relational forms"—with a woman who refused to adhere to that social and ultimately narrative form, a writer who wrote to Coleman that "*No one* could have thrown me into any other arms, not even for the months when I had nothing whatsoever to do with her, not even after we had separated for a number of years."[91] While it lasted, Barnes's relationship with Wood was defined in many ways by conventions of bourgeois domesticity: Barnes was the primary breadwinner, bringing in a steady income from her journalism and other literature, while Wood produced sculptures and silverpoint drawings for little to no money. It was Wood's restless, peripatetic desires that kept the couple from living out what would otherwise have been, had Barnes had her way, a normative relationship defined even by the gendered politics of financial dependence.

Robin's silence—like Dietrich's—is nothing like Barnes's semantic inundations. It recalls Wood: "What gave one the feeling that she lives for sex?" Coleman wrote of Thelma Wood, whom she never liked out of protectiveness of Barnes. "I've never seen a more attractive woman.... She makes one want to make love. But it isn't in obvious ways, that's what is moving. She *seems* to be interested only in what is going on. One feels that underneath that reserve there is a tremendous power.... She hardly open[s] her mouth the whole evening, her reticence and shyness of course adding to the charm of her handsome face and bent-down head." "Next to Thelma (that name!)," Coleman continues, "Djuna appears, to the ordinary eye, unattractive. But she has so much life in her face that the other hasn't got."[92] Thelma's "lifeless," somnambulistic "reticence" was a world away from Barnes, whose fiction is a testament to the loquacity of her heartbreak.

What would it do to our understanding of characters like Felix and Nora—who want nothing less than for narrative order to be restored and thus seem to us passé, even childish—if we were to read them from the perspective of a Barnes who was watching Dietrich so effortlessly subvert the love plot while she herself flailed under her own desperation for its formal confinements? It encourages us not to dismiss these hermeneutic desires as somehow antithetical to Barnes's modernist project but to see them as indexing a longing profoundly rooted in the author herself. Those hermeneutic desires are a meaningful force that bends and influences *Nightwood*'s form, ultimately shifting our understanding of the novel's orientation toward the very conditions of its modernist aesthetics.

For even the Doctor, whose relentless chatter is so often read as metonymic of the linguistic experimentalism of *Nightwood* and thus the ultimate refusal of plotted narrative, is racked with guilt—a structure of feeling that depends on causality. Robin's lack of remorse extends from her refusal to be governed by the emotional tyranny of causes. But the Doctor's regret suggests that despite the apparent affront his ceaseless talk poses to the telos of the novel, he is nevertheless bound internally by a sense of responsibility and thus hermeneutic form. Indeed, what criticism so often overlooks is that "Watchman, What of the Night?" is a scene of confession. In this scene, the doctor performs the process of selection constitutive of all plotted narrative, generating a hierarchy of information out of a textual onslaught. "I'm coming to the night of nights," he tells Nora, after several pages of speaking to her about "the night" as a general concept (e.g., the betrayals we all commit in our dreams, the distinction between French wisdom and American prudishness, the finitude of human life)—"the night you want to know about most of all." And after several more linguistic detours (e.g., consoling her that other women suffer heartbreak as well, recounting an argument he had about where to find the best liqueur in Paris), he finally tells Nora what he has been afraid to tell her: that he was instrumental, one night at the opera, in introducing Robin to Jenny, the woman who would replace her. And thus, he believes himself to be the architect of her heartbreak.

The Doctor's speeches to Nora are often read as quintessentially nonsensical, an extended refusal to provide Nora with hermeneutic satisfaction. Herring, for instance, argues that rather than "filling Nora with information," the Doctor "wipes her interior slate clean." Refusing to participate in the interview in the way that Nora would like, the Doctor, Herring writes, "does not allow her to reach any semblance of epistemological certainty."

"'The story,' like Matthew's investigations of the night, 'do[es] not amount to much.'"[93] But the Doctor's monologues in this particular, crucial case do offer information; they constitute an admission of what he considers a betrayal. He confesses, with agonized shame, that "I saw [Jenny] coming forward . . . saying to me 'Won't you introduce me?' and my knees knocking together; and my heart as heavy as Adam's off ox, because you are a friend of mine and a good poor thing, God knows. . . . I said, 'Certainly, damn it!' and brought them together." "It was me," he continues with pained remorse, "with shoulders under cover . . . the pit of my stomach gone black in the darkness that was eating it away for thinking of you." "What an autopsy I'll make," he cries, "with everything which ways in my bowels!"[94]

The Doctor's tirades are nonsensical only insofar as they are the inarticulate rambling of one who stumbles over words, procrastinates, and hedges when telling a loved one he has done something to bring them pain. The Doctor's speech gives Nora a very important piece of information and in no uncertain terms: *It was I who introduced her to Robin. I am to blame. It is because of me that she left you for her.* The Doctor's confession of culpability—however overstated it may be—is a momentary resurrection of hermeneutic meaning out of the torrent of textuality, a restoration of story from the deluge of the unstoried.[95]

Plot, in *Nightwood*, then, is not done away with easily, silently, sleepily. *Nightwood* recognizes that it is plot—in this novel figured above all as the bonds of causality—that stands a chance of binding us, too, to the ones we love, however naively, however childishly. And in the absence of permanence—for even the Doctor's admission of betrayal does not generate lasting effects, neither on *Nightwood*, whose textual flood continues to rage, nor on Nora, whose demands for answers never cease—even suffering offers a foothold. "The modern child," Felix says, "has nothing left to hold to, or, to put it better, he has nothing left to hold with. We are adhering to life now with our last muscle—the heart."[96] When genealogy, God, the family, no longer mean anything—when "the towers of the church" no longer testify to an existing authority but merely provide "reassuring" fixtures of faint hope, when the power of "the blood" gives way to the freedom of fake names—at least heartbreak and betrayal offer us some assurance that we still mean something to one another, that we can affect one another, matter to each other. "Suddenly I know what all my life had been," Nora tells the Doctor, as if in tacit acknowledgment of this profound concession to the terms of modernity, "what I hoped Robin was—a secure torment. We can hope for nothing greater, except hope."

It would undoubtedly hurt less to be like Marlene, who looks so easy in her distance, cool in her indifference. It would no doubt be more modern to be uninvested like her, to hover teasingly above and around the confines of the love story just enough to take advantage of its lighting. But that, too, like the phantom of bourgeois subjectivity possessing Marguerite Gautier in the final shot of *Camille*, is a fantasy constructed by and for the screen. Stars are paid to make everything look easy, and Marlene made evading the formal grasp of the love plot—constellation rather than causation—look like the easiest thing in the world. She was a very good modernist, the best perhaps. A sly glance to the left or right under half-opened eyes and gone are the hermeneutic bonds tying her to her man, making way for the gorgeous unattachments of style. But that, Barnes may have thought—must have thought—is how it is in the movies, that immaterial realm where anything can happen and we can be whomever we wish. But life is different. "There is no pure sorrow," says the Doctor. "Why? It is bedfellow to lungs, lights, bones, guts and gall!"[97] Barnes was in love with a good modernist, someone who found attachment passé, a bore. She herself was not nearly so good. "I am not a 'modern' after all," she wrote, much later in her life; "Which is strange from one who is considered avant garde."[98] She wanted what was old, embarrassing, and she raged when she couldn't have it. But that attempt to hold with the heart nevertheless allowed her a secure place to stand, with however much torment. At least for a time.

Deuxième Entr'acte

Marlene Dietrich, like Djuna Barnes, lived too long. Her last fiction film was the 1978 flop, *Just a Gigolo*, directed by David Hemmings and starring, apart from Dietrich, Kim Novak, Sydne Rome, and, strikingly, David Bowie. Despite its exciting cast, *Just a Gigolo* was met in Germany, the UK, and the US with scathing reviews, was taken out of circulation quickly, and remained an embarrassment to all involved. It tells the story of a young Prussian aristocrat named Paul von Przygodski (Bowie) whose attempt to fulfill his destiny as a war hero is thwarted when he arrives at the trenches of the Great War on the very day of the Armistice. Crestfallen, he returns to an interwar Berlin he no longer recognizes. He finds his once-great family now poor and socially irrelevant, his home turned into a boarding house, and his mother, who has never had to work, now an attendant at a Turkish bath. Przygodski roams the streets of Berlin in military gear not knowing what to do with himself in a world whose values seem to have irrevocably changed or simply vanished. He wanders from situation to situation, momentarily involving himself with an unhinged German nationalist who obsesses over protecting the German race from foreign elements; moving on, then, to take up work as an advertiser for a liquor company; reconnecting with his childhood friend, Cilly, a cabaret dancer; and even bussing towels at the Turkish bath where his mother works. But having grown intrigued by a prostitute who is one of his family's boarders, Przygodski finally settles on becoming a male escort. He is employed by the Baroness von Semering—played by the seventy-seven-year-old Dietrich—and begins a lucrative career as a gigolo, serving primarily older and wealthy women (among them Helga von Kaiserling, played by Novak). Like Barnes's defunct and wandering aristocrat Felix Volkbein, Paul von Przygodski goes in search of that particular *Comédie humaine* only to come instead upon the odd.

A film remarkably similar to *Nightwood* not just in its thematic content, its resistance to linear plot, and its melancholic tone, *Just a Gigolo* captures, too, the anxiety at the heart of Barnes's novel about the passage of time and the inability of events and human relationships to gain causal traction. It, like *Nightwood*, worries that a world that has been freed from repressive and outdated social mores has also lost meaningful access to structures of significance and consequence of any kind. The world after the Great War, for *Nightwood* as for *Just a Gigolo*, is one in which anything goes and nothing seems to stick. Even an aristocrat can become a gigolo, or, in the case of Felix, can throw in his lot with a trapeze artist, and time will simply continue its indifferent onward march.

Importantly, Dietrich's sly and ironic glances are nowhere to be found in *Just a Gigolo*. In fact in the scene where she sings the titular song to Bowie in an empty café, her signature irony gives way to disarming earnestness and vulnerability. She sings to him not so much as a character but as an aging star, iconic but fading and knowing it. Her song is about the fear of not having mattered.

> Just a gigolo, everywhere I go, people know the part I play.
> Selling every dance, selling each romance, every night some heart betraying.
> There will come a day, youth will go away, and what will they say about me?
> When the end comes I know, they'll say "just a gigolo"
> And life goes on without me.

The performance is startling because it is sincere. The same Dietrich who gave the impression so long ago of not caring a fig about the passage of time, who preferred to relish the synchronic pleasures of style rather than adhere to the diachronic demands of narrative, here emotes unironically about the anxiety of irrelevance, the fear of death. Her eyes, once sleepy and half closed, are here alert, wide open, afraid (fig. 29). *I will die one day and none of it will have mattered. I, once so powerful, will one day be a "just." As will you, young starlet*. It's as if Dietrich is warning the young Bowie, himself an icon of queer androgyny, that though he is now at the height of his career, one day life will go on without him too. Irrelevance is the primary threat plaguing the fate of the star—the horror of no longer mattering that haunts *Just a Gigolo*, but also, more famously, such works as *Sunset Boulevard* (Billy Wilder, 1950), *Whatever Happened to Baby Jane?*

FIGURE 29. Marlene Dietrich in *Just a Gigolo* (David Hemmings, 1978) as the Baroness von Semering, singing to David Bowie as Paul von Przygodski.

(Robert Aldrich, 1962), *All about Eve* (Joseph L. Mankiewicz, 1950), and *A Star is Born* (George Cukor, 1954).

But paradoxically, and perhaps cruelly, the looming horizon of irrelevance is also the very aesthetic principle of glamour, the spectacle of stardom. To threaten the coherence of plot by way of the arresting and distracting/distracted forays of style is to resist the narrative economy of significance, to avow formal irrelevance. It is an excess, in short, of presence. *Look! Marlene Dietrich is singing to David Bowie! Who cares that the scene doesn't do anything for the plot?* Style, which in so many cases serves a purpose—as the gowns of Garbo do, for instance, in *Mata Hari*, where their fascinating scales facilitate espionage—here, makes a mockery of use. And Dietrich's song names this uncomfortable contradiction, suggesting that no matter how glamorous a star may be, a day will most probably come when they will care very deeply about narrative structures of relevance—to have made that "scratch, that undying mark, on the blank face of the oblivion to which we are all doomed," as Judith Sutpen in William Faulkner's *Absalom, Absalom!* puts it.[1] It is telling that in Dietrich's last-ever film, the documentary *Marlene* (Maximilian Schell, 1984), she allowed only her hands to appear on screen, and then only momentarily, for fear that she would expose her no-longer-youthful face. And that she agreed to come out of retirement to appear in *Just a Gigolo* only after the writer Joshua Sinclair had a rose sent to her Paris apartment every single day for two weeks and a bottle of champagne every Saturday. Even Marlene, that is, the quintessence of style on screen, but by then a nearly eighty-year-old person, needed to feel that she was the main love interest. Even she needed to feel that the plot hadn't entirely been lost.

THREE

William Faulkner and Early Film
On the Limits of the Present

> *There is no such thing as was—only is. If was existed, there would be no grief or sorrow.*
>
> WILLIAM FAULKNER

William Faulkner once told critic Malcolm Cowley that *The Sound and the Fury* was like "the first moving picture projector—warped lens, poor light, clumsy gears, and even a bad screen—that had to wait eighteen years for the lens to clear, the light to steady, the gears to mesh and smooth."[1] The eighteen-year period of film history Faulkner uses to describe his first work of modernist fiction spans from 1895 to 1913, from the birth of film to the tail end of what film historians have called the "cinema of narrative integration."[2] When film was first invented, it relied on visual spectacle rather than stories to secure audience interest. Termed by Tom Gunning the "cinema of attractions"—after Sergei Eisenstein's use of the term "attraction" as a form of experience based in shock and excitement[3]—early film did not begin as a narrative medium. At first, the cinematograph was simply a baffling new machine whose mere capacity to capture reality in motion astonished and excited its viewers. Meanwhile, the cinema of narrative integration, spearheaded by D. W. Griffith during his years at Biograph studio, was the first sustained attempt on the part of the budding film industry to curb the semiotic indeterminacy previously plaguing the cinematic image in service of generating comprehensible narratives.[4] Lasting from about 1908 to 1913, it was the period of film history when the cinema could be said to have finally transformed from a primarily documentary medium to one that could and did tell stories with a level of narrative sophistication that would lay the groundwork for the later classical Hollywood cinema. The history of film and its development from a nonnarrative to a narrative medium is integral to understanding the formal experiments of *The Sound and the Fury*.

Faulkner wrote for Hollywood on and off between 1932 and 1954. His contributions to major works of classical Hollywood cinema such as *The Big Sleep* and *To Have and Have Not* have been the subject of much illuminating criticism that has drawn out the complex textual interchanges between his work for the culture industry and the modernist and pulp fiction he was writing during the same years.[5] This chapter attends primarily, however, not to the Faulkner who wrote for the movies but to the one who went to them growing up in Oxford, Mississippi, where a robust early film culture was unsuspectingly thriving. The films that have held pride of place in our limited discussions of Faulkner's moviegoing have been the Western genre and, above all, D. W. Griffith's *The Birth of a Nation*.[6] The former has largely to do with a remark Faulkner's brother, John, made in his biography *My Brother Bill*, that he and William would see Western films together at the Lyric, Oxford's local movie theater. The fact that giants of the Western genre, John Ford and especially Howard Hawks, would champion Faulkner's work in Hollywood has further supported the idea that he was drawn to that genre. And the preoccupation Faulkner scholarship has shown with *The Birth of a Nation* exemplifies what Jane Gaines has rightly called the disproportionately dominant place this "single film" holds in the "historical memory of this period."[7] Just as Gaines displaces *The Birth of a Nation* as the catalyzing event of Black film production, I place Faulkner's early modernist work within a much broader film-cultural context than merely *The Birth of a Nation* or the Western.[8]

Film programming in Oxford's local newspaper, the *Oxford Eagle*—archival research that this book is the first to conduct—indeed shows that an extremely varied body of films across a number of different genres and styles were playing in Oxford in the first three decades of the twentieth century, including Westerns (and yes, *The Birth of a Nation*) but also romance dramas, melodramas, comedies, romantic comedies, war dramas, historical dramas, adventure films, and more. From *Dr. Jekyll and Mr. Hyde* (John S. Robertson, 1920), *The Affairs of Anatol* (Cecile B. Demille, 1921), *The Sheik* (George Melford, 1921), and *The Ten Commandments* (Demille, 1923) to *Always Audacious* (James Cruz, 1920), *Lighthouse by the Sea* (Malcolm St. Clair, 1924), *The Great Divide* (Reginald Barker, 1925), *The Timber Wolf* (W. S. Van Dyke, 1925), and *Soul Mates* (Jack Conway, 1925); from *The Rough Riders* (Victor Fleming, 1927), *The Hidden Way* (Joseph de Grasse, 1925), and *Manhattan Madness* (John McDermott, 1925) to *The Lost World* (Harry O. Hoyt, 1925), *Dark Secrets* (Fleming, 1923), and *Belle of Alaska* (Chester Bennett, 1922), the films shown at the University Theatre at Ole Miss and the Lyric—films of which this list is a mere fraction—suggest that Oxford was a hub of classical Hollywood film exhibition.[9]

That archival research has also unearthed the fact that there was another theater in Oxford that would have been playing films before the opening of the Lyric in 1914. The Lyric, owned by a man named R. X. Williams, eventually managed by F. L. Toole, but managed in its early stages by Faulkner's father, was advertised as The New Opera House. It was probably referred to as such because it seems to have been the new and improved version of an extant Opera House, a theatrical venue that had existed in the main square of Oxford since at least 1885, possibly before.[10] Advertisements for the (Old) Opera House in the *Oxford Eagle* confirm that that venue, which was in essence a vaudeville house, was also playing films, beginning at least as early as the first decade of the twentieth century. Like many transitional venues during this period—which featured musical performances, plays, as well as motion pictures—the Opera House did not advertise specific films it was showing. It simply advertised *that* motion pictures were offered "every night." Archival research thus proves that Faulkner was positively steeped in early film culture as a young man during this crucial period in cinematic history as film was becoming a narrative medium, and growing gradually into the classical Hollywood cinema through a process of uneven development. The fact that the period of film history Faulkner mentions in relation to *The Sound and the Fury* ends precisely the year before the Lyric—or the New Opera House—opened, suggests that he could very well have been implicitly referring to early films he saw as a child and teenager at the original Opera House.

And there is no reason to believe that Faulkner was not attending a host of different genres of classical films in Oxford in his twenties; that the Western genre and *Birth of a Nation* are most comfortably discussed in Faulkner scholarship may say more about the gender politics underpinning that scholarship—as well as the gender politics Faulkner and his brother are willing to have put on the record—than it does about what films Faulkner may actually have seen. Faulkner showed instant technical and narrative acumen when handling his Hollywood scripts.[11] This is no doubt because he probably knew, with studied intimacy, what stories on the narrative screen looked like, stories from which we are wont to think he took ironic distance. In 1947 Faulkner claimed that the "trash and junk writing" he was doing for Hollywood was "corrupting" his own fiction. But *The Sound and the Fury* and *As I Lay Dying*—the two high-modernist novels he wrote before his screenwriting began and while he was being exposed to the development of the narrative cinema—show that corruption to have begun long before that. Both of these novels, to different effects, register the existential urgency expressed in that so-called trash and junk, its palliative promises of narrative unity.

This chapter exposes how in *The Sound and the Fury*, Faulkner's first and most canonical work of modernist fiction, early film and its cultures of exhibition become the figure through which Faulkner articulates modernism's retreat from closural plot. Through a subterranean network of references to the early, prenarrative cinema of attractions and its eventual development toward the narrative and then classical cinema, Faulkner shows emplotment to be not simply artificial but the extension of a pathological will to confer narrative significance on the contingent flow of time and experience.

In embodying early, prenarrative cinematic form—which thrived on an excess of photographic mimesis rather than storied sense—Benjy Compson's section proceeds according to a formal principle of contingency, an aleatory passage from one moment to the next whose resistance to narrative integration reflects Benjy's own nonviolence. Quentin, meanwhile, is anxious to restore narrative order to his world he believes to have been thrown into ideological upheaval by his sister Caddy's pursuit of sexual freedom. He does so by generating a narrative of incest—"to isolate her," he tells his father, "out of the loud world"[12]—whose basis in the exclusion of contingent details Faulkner relates to film's increased reliance on storytelling. And finally, Jason's section no longer interrogates the relationship between contingency and narrative sense. To him, all signifies—all events and details participate in his story of victimhood and persecution. His brutality and greed fully actualize what Faulkner suggests is the violence underpinning plot and the denial of insignificance intrinsic to narrative cinema—the principle of *motivation* fundamental to classical Hollywood's narrative and aesthetic operations.[13] *The Sound and the Fury* suggests that losing the plot for modernism meant losing it *to film*, and Faulkner shows how film's newness allows us to witness with fresh eyes the palliative psychic work accomplished by the formal operations of plot. By way of a systematic engagement with early film history, *The Sound and the Fury* shows plot itself to be a form of paranoid sensemaking, born out of a desire for narrative coherence where that coherence may very well be, and in some cases should be, absent.

Early, prenarrative film comes to represent in *The Sound and the Fury* an unmanageable excess of presence—a relentless onslaught of *is*, as Faulkner puts it in the opening epigraph of this chapter, over which his characters are unable to gain the retrospective foothold of *was*. In *The Sound and the Fury*, that inability generates in its characters unease and panic, ultimately becoming the basis of self-destruction or racist and sexist violence. As a result, this novel provides one of the most powerful arguments against plot in literary history, demonstrating how easily plot, by virtue of its basis in formal constraint, can become the formal vehicle of politically, socially, and physically injurious ideologies. *The Sound and the Fury* lays bare why plot would become the formal axis along which writers such as Barnes and Larsen exercise their modernist negation, revealing the amenability of plot and plotting to an ideology of heteronormative white supremacy hostile to queer and biracial subjectivity.

But Faulkner's next novel, *As I Lay Dying*, shows the desire for plot in a far more sympathetic light. In this novel, the unmanageable excess of presence that *The Sound and the Fury* registers as a formal problem inherent to early film structures the very grammar of the novel. Delivered almost entirely in the present tense, *As I Lay Dying* is populated by characters who, seemingly abandoned by their author, are left to navigate what Gertrude Stein would call the "continuous present" of lived time[14]—a formal dispersion to which the characters must either relinquish mastery or attempt to gain it.

It has been argued that though narrative "seizes life trajectories condemned to stumbling and—by the act of *telling* them—binds those trajectories into retrospective order," Faulkner's work tries to "grasp" at the "unpreparedness" and "cascading trouble" of lived time.[15] But Faulkner's is indeed and emphatically an aesthetics of risk—an aesthetics of the unmanageable—and thus a testimony to what Philip Weinstein describes as Faulkner's self-conscious failure to undermine altogether that "precious ordering" endemic to the very gesture of art.[16] But Faulkner also recognizes in *The Sound and the Fury* and especially *As I Lay Dying*, that in the moment of writing, he is subjecting other beings, his own literary creatures, to that trouble internal to the uncooperative now.

AUTHORS AND THEIR CHARACTERS

To put this point more generally, authors *do* things to their characters. Or, as the case may be, they do not do them, just as parents can shape but also fail or damage their children, abandoning them to forces beyond any control. Thus, one way to begin to focus on this relation between authors and their characters in the context of plot in modernity is via the figure of the child, which has quietly hovered throughout this book, in some moments more conspicuously than others. Helga Crane's four children, as well as the one growing in her womb in the final moments of *Quicksand*, gesture toward the childhood we never witness in Helga herself, despite the centrality of the trials of youth to the genre of the bildungsroman. And while Felix Volkbein's child with Robin Vote, Guido II, is more substantive a presence in *Nightwood* than Helga's children in *Quicksand*, he nevertheless remains spectral, never given a voice, and he ultimately disappears from the narrative landscape of the novel altogether.

The elusiveness of the children in *Quicksand* and *Nightwood* at the level of formal treatment reflects their precarity: in the former, the child is born to a suicidal mother and in the latter to an absent mother and a father whose ability to navigate the modern world is tenuous at best. In *Quicksand*, the precarity of Helga's children is suggestive of Helga's own struggle to "grow up" in the sense in which such a phrase is meant in the context of the bildungsroman. Because plot has proven ineffective in generating a coherent autonomous self from Helga's disparate psychic parts, the character remains despairingly unknowing of herself. And in *Nightwood*, Robin's abandonment of Guido II and Barnes's spare characterization of him indicates the novel's fundamental irreverence toward plot structures that support heteronormative futurity. Guido's eventual disappearance from *Nightwood* is, from one perspective, Barnes's version of Lee Edelman's "Fuck the social order and the Child in whose name [queer people] are collectively terrorized."[17]

However, what this book has emphasized is the need to view these gestures dialectically, as both critical and expressive of longing. Helga may be an instance of "unseasonable youth,"[18] the arrest of her development a sign of the hostility of the bildungsroman genre to her biracial subject position. But it is significant that *she* does not want to be that way. Helga herself, as Rafael Walker has argued, wants very much to become an autonomous subject, to grow into a fully realized, self-possessed person in command of her actions and choices.[19] Her inability to accomplish that aim is a "critical triumph" for Larsen but a source of existential despair for Larsen's character.[20] Similarly, Robin's abandonment of Guido II is a gesture of queer negativity on Barnes's part, but the intensity with which Guido II clings to Felix—"with cold hands and anxious face, he followed his father, trembling"[21]—suggests a state of profound discomfort, a telling absence of what in the previous chapter we referred to as Dietrichian ease. Guido II's feeling, which we might simply call sadness, points to what Heather Love has called the "dark side" of queer marginality, the residue of loss and pain often sidestepped by more "affirmative" accounts of queer representation, which tend to privilege stronger positions such as critique and "strategic response" that offer inroads to "political utility."[22] Indeed, the fact that Guido II doesn't *fit in*—he "was not like other children," "mentally deficient and emotionally excessive, an addict to death; at ten, barely as tall as a child of six, wearing spectacles, stumbling when he tried to run"[23]—suggests that he is representative of queer marginality itself. And his wish to "enter the church"[24] suggests a desire for safety within authorizing structures that would mitigate the suffering brought on by that difference rather than accentuate its politically negative potential. Losing the plot, for Helga and Guido II, means losing access to narrative and psychic structures that would give them a sense of self and belonging however much their authors recognize that safety as temporary, specious, predicated on psychically injurious normative ideologies.

The distinctions drawn here between authors and characters are important however unhabitual they may be in the discipline of literary studies. But understanding literary character alongside the theoretical rubric of star studies, which takes for granted an ever-present performative energy in excess of the film's plot, has allowed us to draw that distinction out and recognize as critically important the fact that in *Quicksand* and *Nightwood*, the difference between what the novel is doing and what the character is feeling or might want for themselves is stark. In both works, what engenders new formal horizons for the author of the novel as a genre is a source of tragedy and panic for the characters. The vexed relationship between children and their parents in these novels is thus an extension, *en abyme*, of that between literary characters and their authors.[25]

In Faulkner the parallel between parents and authors, characters and children, is even more explicit than in Larsen and Barnes. The family—its history, legacy, collapse, and trauma—is central to Faulkner's literary universe in ways that are central, too, to his interrogation of modernism's retreat from plot as the primary set of formal relations holding the novel together. Faulkner kicks out the formal supports of plot from under his characters' feet, as it were, and in so doing, exercises a subtle but irrevocable form of authorial leverage. That leverage finds brutally literal parallels in the relation of parents to children in *The Sound and the Fury* but especially in *As I Lay Dying*, works that thematize the "dependency of children on their parents and the frustration that occurs when that dependency is betrayed."[26] In *The Sound and the Fury*, the Compson brothers, Quentin, Jason, and Benjy, are left with only the memory of their deceased, dyspeptic, and nihilistic father, a living but shrill and useless mother, and a sister whose departure from the home throws their entire sense of order and meaning into irreparable upheaval. And *As I Lay Dying* kills off Addie Bundren, the only competent creator in the lives of the Bundren family, leaving its remaining members to the devices of the incompetent patriarch, Anse Bundren, but also to an existentially and historically incomprehensible present. Situating *As I Lay Dying* within the film-historical context of *The Sound and the Fury* allows us to see that more than any other of Faulkner's novels, *As I Lay Dying* performs an aesthetics of turbulence, just as it stages the repercussions of that aesthetics—just as it ponders what happens to the living when the teller absents himself. To what, it asks, must the living resort?

While certain characters in *As I Lay Dying* navigate that "turbulent present" unproblematically (to borrow from Weinstein), most attempt to deliver themselves from it—either by protracting the present through aesthetic stretches or by forging artificial bonds of culpability where the formal bonds of causation have been denied them, thus creating narrative continuity where it is frustratingly absent. In its various attempts to have present-tense grammar perform retrospective work, *As I Lay Dying* stages a reluctant surrender of preterit, simple-past narration to the turbulence of experience, generating moments in which the body insists on its unaccountable presence to any aesthetic labor that would attempt to abstract it out of existence or in which blame assignment becomes a form of surrogate retrospection, localizing the cause of personal or historical pain to a nameable, albeit inaccurate, source in order to make narrative sense of that pain and thus render it endurable. *The Sound and the Fury* and *As I Lay Dying* are often considered the zenith of Faulkner's modernist project, the author in his quintessentially antirealist mode. But these novels are also profoundly troubled by their own modernist experiments, their fragmentation not emphatic declarations of a liberation from the formal prohibitions of realism but an elegy to the imaginative and contemplative provisions of realist temporality.[27] As if racked with guilt, these novels preoccupy themselves with the possibility that to abandon realist temporality may be to claim one's literary modernity, but it also amounts to a form of authorial cruelty.

Having established the existential promises of narrative unity as a source of vexed desire rather than critical disdain in Faulkner's early modernism, this chapter will end by offering a speculative account of Faulkner in Hollywood less bent on the alignment of his screenwriting with a critical distance from escapist fantasy and more on the expression of a desire for it.

COMPSON FAMILY HOME VIDEO

The Sound and the Fury is a paranoid book. Or at least paranoia is a structure of feeling Faulkner shows to be central among the people navigating the vertiginous historical changes it charts. It is a novel about the decline of the Southern plantocracy, the supplanting of the Old South by the New, and thus the felt encroachment of Northern ways of life—economic, social, sexual—into a South still reeling from its defeat in the Civil War. The economic shifts effected by that defeat, the displacement of an agrarian regime by the labor arrangements of industrial capitalism, were accompanied by social changes offensive to the patriarchal white supremacist Southern gentility such as the fictional Compson family. The intrusion of Northern values was felt not only in the legal emancipation of enslaved men and women but also in the relaxation of expectations surrounding gender performance. Caddy Compson—whose extramarital sexual pursuits and eventual departure from the family home in Jefferson, Mississippi, is the novel's central narrative event—confirms to her family the waning authority of the Southern aristocratic patriarchy largely because she arrogates to herself the right to forge a different kind of life from the one prescribed to her by the Old South. She signifies, as John T. Matthews has argued, the emergence of the New Woman, whose ambition to experience a life emancipated from the Victorian mores of the plantation is just as threatening to the social ideologies of the Southern patriciate as would be the image of her brother Quentin sitting next to a Black man on the train to Cambridge, Massachusetts, where he attends Harvard. Caddy's departure unravels the Compson family, leaving Quentin with no moral center around which to structure his identity and the oldest brother, Jason, mortified at the thought of his family becoming a shameful spectacle of Southern decline. They feel victimized, in short, by Caddy's behavior, and it is thus that Faulkner shows the psychic and narrative dynamics of the Compson family to be imbricated with those of the Old South writ large. Just as the South felt itself destroyed by the North while defending what it held most dear—a narrative of martyrdom and victimization that came to be termed the "Lost Cause"—the Compson family collapses under the pressure of Caddy's lost virginity.

Famous for its extreme fragmentation to the point of incomprehensibility, the first of the novel's four sections, narrated by Benjy Compson, a thirty-three-year-old man with mental disability, offers a counterpoint to that paranoid narrative; it does not integrate its observations into any sort of systematic whole. It is propelled onto the page by an unpredictable and trivial occurrence and proceeds according to chance occurrences in a chain of Benjy's memories. Benjy's caretaker, the young Black boy Luster, loses a coin through a hole in his pocket and thus begins both the search for the money and our initiation into the Compson family history. "'Is you all seen anything of a quarter down here,'" Luster asks some young men in the branch, "'I lost it somewhere. It fell through this here hole in my pocket.'"[28] If the quarter had not fallen through Luster's pocket, the novel would have started some other way; Benjy would not have needed to pass by the golf course—the family pasture the Compsons sold in order to pay for Quentin's Harvard education and Caddy's wedding—in search of the quarter. They would not have heard a golfer cry "caddie," the misinterpretation of which spins Benjy into reverie. Benjy then catches on the fence as he tries to pass through it, which reminds him of an earlier moment with Caddy when he was similarly caught. That memory then becomes the next object of narration, leading to the next, and so on.

Born in 1895, Benjy Compson does indeed perceive and report the world much like what Faulkner referred to as "the first moving picture projector." Also "born" in 1895, the earliest genre of film, now termed the *actuality* and made popular by the Lumière Brothers, recorded unnarrativized visual data. Actualities were above all experiments with the capacity to record. They differed from later narrative and classical Hollywood films in that they captured moments of activity without situating them within larger narrative frameworks. Some of these films included men playing cards, workers leaving a factory, men watching a cockfight, a boat leaving a port, or most famously, a train arriving at the Ciotat Station. Early film exhibition practices amplified the aleatory nature of the films themselves. Actualities were featured, as Tom Gunning and Miriam Hansen have explained, as "one attraction on the vaudeville programme, surrounded by a mass of unrelated acts in a non-narrative and even nearly illogical succession of performances."[29] They were exhibited at such venues as "variety shows, dime museums," summer parks, "fairgrounds, and traveling shows," and they were arranged "in the most random manner possible."[30] Not only is Oxford's first Opera House precisely the sort of venue that would feature actualities alongside live performances but "the show" traveling through town on April 7, 1928, the novel's present day—the show Luster wishes to attend using his lost coin as price of entry—would also feature such films at the turn of the century.

The actuality is constitutively unplotted, predicated on a formal principle of indication rather than narration. Mary Ann Doane draws on Charles Sanders Peirce's semiology of the index to describe the particular problem the actuality poses to narrative meaning. For Peirce time consists of an indivisible continuum (what Henri Bergson would call *durée*) unable to be separated into successive instants. In denying the possibility of an instant in time, Peirce also denies the possibility of full immediacy; the pure present thus "can yield," in Doane's words, "no adequate sign of itself."[31] The index is a kind of sign, according to Peirce, that attains as immediate contact with the pure present as possible. Examples include a pointing finger, Doane explains, a footprint, a weathercock, the demonstrative pronoun "this" and the adverb "here," and the photographic image. The index "designates something without describing it"; it directs our attention to a thing without interpreting it, saying "this is here, look at it."[32] The demonstrative pronoun "this," for instance, merely "designates a specific and singular object or situation." It is understandable "only within a given discourse."[33] Indices point to the existence of something, but they do not interpret that thing (e.g., sound is an index that only "a given discourse" will help register as fury).

Siegfried Kracauer found the indexicality of the photographic image to be unsettling. Whereas human memory selects and preserves significant moments, the photograph archives indiscriminately. Walter Benjamin's notion of the "optical unconscious" is predicated precisely on the photograph's capacity to observe and archive what the human eye, constitutively selective, will often leave unnoticed. Still photographs are always haunted by their historicity; the moment they have captured is now gone—they mark a "this-has-been," in Barthes's formulation.[34] Film, however, maintains the illusion of presence by virtue of its capacity to represent movement, what Stein would call the "continuous present." The "movie spectator," as Christian Metz put it, "is absorbed, not by a 'has been there,' but by a sense of 'There it is.'" Because "the spectator," he says, "always sees movement as being present," they do not see film as "the trace of a past motion" but as an "impression" of present reality."[35]

Pier Paolo Pasolini's remarks on a much later actuality film than those of the Lumières—Abraham Zapruder's film of John F. Kennedy's assassination—effectively theorize how such an indexical impression of reality jeopardizes narrative sense.

> This extreme language of action with which Kennedy is expressed to the spectators remains indecisive and meaningless in the presence in which it is perceived by the senses and/or filmed. Like every language of action, *it requires something more*. It requires systematization with regard to both itself and the objective world; it must be related to other languages of action . . . to the actions of those at that moment surrounding him, for example, to those of his assassin, or assassins. . . . As long as such actions remain unrelated—they are fragmentary and incomplete languages, all but incomprehensible.[36]

Like Zapruder's and the Lumières' actualities, Benjy's section provides an "incomplete language of action," indicating occurrences without contextualizing them. It provides, rather, a surplus of proairetic data stripped of hermeneutic charge. As Faulkner told Jean Stein vanden Heuvel in an interview for the *Paris Review*, "I had begun to tell the story" through the eyes of Benjy, "since I felt that it would be more effective as told by someone capable only of knowing *what* happened but not *why*."[37] Stripped of its hermeneutic function, a proairetic unit such as "a man was killed" is semantically indeterminate beyond the meaning of the words themselves. Within the context of a plot, however, "a man was killed" can have devastating meaning. Benjy's statement "The room went away, but I didn't hush, and the room came back and Dilsey came and sat on the bed, looking at me" is no more narratively informative than the moment when he burns his hand in the fire: "I could still hear the clock between my voice. . . . My voice was going loud every time. . . . My voice went louder then and my hand tried to go back to my mouth, but Dilsey held it. My voice went loud."[38] Benjy gives us an incomplete language of action that needs to be put in relation to other languages in order to amass hermeneutic meaning.

The most prominent instance of such hermeneutic poverty in Benjy's section is when he observes his niece, Quentin II, robbing Jason—a robbery that, when narrated by Jason in his section, proves to be a climactic event. When Benjy observes her descending the tree outside her window and running across the yard to Jason's room, he delivers the scene in starkly proairetic terms:

> *I hushed, and then Luster stopped, his head toward the window. Then he went to the window and looked out. He came back and took my arm. Here she come, he said. Be quiet now. We went to the window and looked out. It came out of Quentin's window and climbed across into the tree. We watched the tree shaking. The shaking went down the tree, then it came out and we watched it go away across the grass. Then we couldn't see it.*[39]

The moment Benjy witnesses here is monumental in terms of its implications for the Compson family. Caddy's illegitimate daughter, Quentin II, named after her uncle Quentin, who committed suicide after his first year at Harvard, is taking back financial agency from her other uncle, Jason, who has been keeping for himself the money Caddy sends him regularly to support her. It is an event that will go on to undermine Jason's authority materially and thus definitively; as such, it is arguably the moment at which the legacy of the Compson family is fully superseded by a new socioeconomic regime. But Benjy's mode of narrating it mutes those implications; Quentin II becomes simply "it," her movements an indication merely of kinetic activity—"the shaking went down the tree." The narration needs, in Pasolini's terms, "something more" to imbue it with hermeneutic sense.

Thus, rather than narration, Benjy's section amounts to what André Gaudreault in the context of early film has called "monstration," an act of showing scenes rather than telling or emplotting them.[40] Of a piece with that will to show is Benjy's passive mode of reception. Quentin II unknowingly gives voice to Benjy's lack of perceptual mastery of his experience, deepening his association with the cinema of attractions. Frustrated and perhaps embarrassed at having been caught with a carnie affiliated with the traveling show passing through town (a character Faulkner simply calls "the man with the red tie"), Quentin II complains to Jason and Dilsey, "*You all send him to spy on me. I hate this house. I'm going to run away.*"[41] But Benjy in truth does not "spy," he simply sees. The remark highlights the difference between passively witnessing and actively searching with one's gaze, a distinction crucial to early cinematic spectatorship. The exhibitions' disjointed structure produced unpredictable temporal "eruptions" rather than narrative development, Gunning explains. Instead of the "linear progression of plotting and causality," early cinematic exhibitions featured "staccato jolts."[42] Built on formal principles less causative than constellational and associative, the temporal disjunctions of the early narrative cinema were markedly different from the commitment to continuity and motivation found in later narrative and classical cinema.

These formats prompted a specific form of spectatorship. The attraction "solicits surprise," Gunning argues, "astonishment, or pure curiosity instead of following the enigmas on which narrative depends." The spectator of early cinema surrenders her perception to the "unpredictability of the instant," a "succession of excitements and frustrations whose order cannot be predicted by narrative logic and whose pleasures are never sure of being prolonged."[43] Like early spectators, Benjy does not exercise narrative mastery over his impressions. He yields himself over to the lightest push or pull in any given spatial or temporal direction. Benjy allows for transitions without resistance, and unlike his brother Quentin, he does not search his mind for one memory in particular. This perceptual difference between Quentin and Benjy parallels that between classical and early cinematic viewers: "if the classical spectator enjoys apparent mastery of the narrative thread of a film . . . the viewer of the cinema of attractions plays a very different game . . . one strongly lacking predictability or a sense of mastery."[44] The nonlinear and labyrinthine structure of Benjy's section—itself organized by unpredictable jolts from one moment in time to another—reproduces the nonlinearity of these early exhibitions. His abandon to formlessness is thematized, for instance, in the episode of his intoxication with Quentin and T.P. during Caddy's wedding: "Quentin held my arm and we went toward the barn. Then the barn wasn't there and we had to wait until it came back"; "It was still going around, and then the shapes began."[45] His spectatorial surrender is also evident in the delight he takes in witnessing the flux of shadows, shapes, and lights when he goes to sleep.

But although Benjy does not present his observations according to a narrative hierarchy that would imbue certain elements with hermeneutic meaning over others, the section brims with feelings that Benjy cannot effectively manage. A slipper, the smell of trees, turning left instead of right at the monument in town, the sight of the swing, the pasture—these send him either into spells of desperate sadness and panic or states of rapt and dreamy calm. Hence, there *is* a system of hierarchization in his section, albeit not a narrative one. The order that dominates is affective, not hermeneutic.

In dislocating affective from narrative explanation, *The Sound and the Fury* appeals again to the early cinema. It is dangerous to speculate about the exact reactions of early film audiences (though the myth of the terrified novice has been definitively debunked), but film historians generally agree that they reacted with wonder at the workings of the cinematograph, and this had largely to do with the standard practice of early screenings. The exhibitor would begin by projecting the image in its still form and subsequently spurring the photograph into motion.[46] Audiences would often scream or "sit aghast" in both mesmerized curiosity at the workings of the cinematic apparatus and playfully anxious knowledge of the illusion of the image.[47] This affectively rich response was accompanied by, if not dependent on, a lack of involvement with the narrative content of the image. "Rather than being an involvement with narrative action," Gunning writes, the cinema of attractions elicits the viewer's "curiosity" concerning the image itself as an artificial object. The spectator "remains aware of the act of looking" and "does not get lost in a fictional world and its drama."[48] The sensory dexterity of the early film spectator exemplifies what Benjamin calls "reception in distraction," a modern sensory "vigilance" marked by an ability to be both "carried away and in control."[49]

In the passage when Benjy is sitting in the carriage with his mother, for instance, he receives in distraction—notes but does not narrativize—the kaleidoscopic rhythms, positionings, and brightnesses of the shapes and shadows, exemplifying what Benjamin considered this new form of spontaneous apperception encouraged by film:

> "You, T.P." Mother said, clutching me. I could hear Queenie's feet and the bright shapes went smooth and steady on both sides, the shadows of them flowing across Queenie's back. They went on like the bright tops of wheels. Then those on one side stopped at the tall white post where the soldier was. But on the other side they went on smooth and steady, but a little slower. . . . The shapes flowed on. The ones on the

other side began again, bright and fast and smooth, like when Caddy says we are going to sleep.[50]

But while Benjy is often tranquil, he is just as often radically uncomfortable and overwhelmed. Faulkner transposes the playful astonishment of the cinema of attractions into Benjy's profound unease. Fredric Jameson claims that Faulkner was instrumental in "lifting" the "taboo" of affect that held together the ideological "regime" of "Balzacian *récit*," that he helped emancipate the modern novel from the hermeneutic bondage of the classical text.[51] But the intensity of Benjy's bewilderment, panic, and grief suggests otherwise. In the final scene of the novel, for example, Benjy's wails take on monumental proportions: "Bellow on bellow, his voice mounted, with scarce interval for breath. There was more than astonishment in it, it was horror . . . agony eyeless, tongueless."[52] Affect does not herald such an unequivocal liberation; Benjy is an example of a modernist *character* who contends—as a form of psychic wound—with the consequences of losing novelistic plot.

Because losing the plot, in Benjy's case, is tantamount to losing his sister. When she was still at home, Caddy was Benjy's source of narrative meanings. She provided him with social frameworks that would allow him to make sense of his observations and experiences. When he runs out into the cold to meet her, she socially contextualizes his actions: "Did you think it would be Christmas when I came home from school. Is that what you thought. Christmas is the day after tomorrow. Santy Claus, Benjy. Santy Claus."[53] Or in the children's deliberation on their grandmother's death, Caddy draws the appropriate distinctions between human and animal styles of burial and decomposition that Benjy cannot make: "How can buzzards get in where Damuddy is. Father wouldn't let them. Would you let a buzzard undress you," she pointedly asks Jason.[54] Elsewhere, Caddy contextualizes Benjy's physical sensation of cold: "'Keep your hands in your pockets good, now.' . . . 'It's froze.' . . . Look.' She broke the top of the water and held a piece of it to my face. 'Ice. That means how cold it is.'"[55]

That Benjy's section ends abruptly, if not arbitrarily, has significant implications for the philosophy of time and meaning that the section proposes. "It is absolutely necessary to die," Pasolini writes in a similar vein as Peter Brooks and Frank Kermode, "*because while living we lack meaning.*" Death, according to Pasolini, "*performs a lightning quick montage on our lives*; . . . it chooses our truly significant moments (no longer changeable by other possible contrary or incoherent moments) and places them in sequence, converting our present, which is infinite, unstable and uncertain, and thus linguistically indescribable, into a clear, stable, certain, and thus linguistically describable past. . . . *It is thanks to death that our lives become expressive.*"[56] Benjy's section has presented moments of history as temporally interchangeable and thus constitutionally disorganized. He has lent formal expression to the contingency that Mr. Compson repeatedly tries to convince Quentin characterizes history and social reality. He persistently points to the constructedness of the social norms to which Quentin clings, the fact that they change according to the whims of a given moment in time and thus do not possess the permanent value Quentin seeks. Indeed, if Benjy's section has presented a crisis of meaning, it is because it has posed a challenge to the possibility of meaningful, formative change. Benjy's depiction of the world as an indexical archive—history as simply a series of occurrences having happened—denies change its formative potency. The temporal disorder of Benjy's section, like that of early films and exhibition practices, renders change ubiquitous but meaningless. His flashbacks do not fulfill what Gérard Genette calls the "explanatory" function of the analepses typical of classical texts.[57] Instead of producing narrative meaning, the temporal changes in Benjy's section flag change for its own sake. The structural logic of the changes is addition and accumulation, not clarification or explanation. Quentin's father tells him that "victory is an illusion" and that "no battle is ever won . . . they are not even fought."[58] If Benjy had language in the way that his father does, he might insist that battles *are* fought but that their outcomes do not affect the relentless passage of time. A battle fought would be merely one more observable and archivable element of history, a thing to be noted. Only death, an end, would engender change—a possibility to which his brother Quentin clings dearly.

"I WAS. I AM NOT."

Quentin tries to recuperate plotted order from what seems to him to be a world evacuated of narrative supports since his sister's loss of virginity out of wedlock. We might read Quentin's clamor for narrative meaning in the context of an increasing turn in early film history toward an interest in the formal and normative limits of the *event*. The nonnarrative format of film and its modes of exhibition began to decline sometime between 1902 and 1907, in large part because the novelty of the cinematograph had begun to wear off, and the then-burgeoning film industry relied more heavily on storytelling to increase and maintain specifically bourgeois patronage.[59] Early attempts to generate narrative meaning in cinema resulted in films that showcased "the grandiose tropes of life, death, waste, and eternity," such as Thomas Edison's *Electrocuting an Elephant* (1903) and *Execution of Czolgoz, with Panorama of Auborn Prison* (1901).[60] Though still within the actuality genre, these films were among the first critical steps toward narrative cinema, incorporating narrative progression primarily through the use of cuts. These cuts—constitutively selective in their move to omit what is insignificant to the main event—show the process by which film practitioners were attempting to wrangle the contingent flow of visual data into narrative shape, to make plots, however rudimentary, out of the surplus of visual details by organizing them around a significant occurrence. Whereas earlier actualities celebrated the ability merely to show audiences anything at all, these films relished in the ability to show audiences something important.[61]

The distinction between the Lumière Brothers' 1896 *Demolition of a Wall* and the Edison film company's 1903 *Electrocuting an Elephant* exemplifies this transition that started to take hold in film history and its development toward plot, one that illuminates the difference between Benjy's and Quentin's modes of perception. In *Demolition of a Wall*, a small group of men take down the side of a building with pickaxes and a stationary bulldozer and then hack away at the rubble. Halfway through this ninety-second film, the image starts to run in reverse: the men walk backward, their pickaxes spring back up in ludic reversal, and the wall pops up into place as if it had never been destroyed (fig. 30).

Electrocuting an Elephant, meanwhile, documents the real-life execution of a circus elephant named Topsy, who was sentenced to death allegedly for having aggressed patrons. In the first shot of the film, Topsy lumbers toward the camera in a medium long shot; she is led by one man and followed by three others. The second and final shot is a long shot of her standing alone as she is administered an electrical current. Surrounded by rising smoke, she first stiffens, then falls to the ground and lies dead. Tremors slightly jerk her limbs until she falls completely still. The film ends at approximately seventy-five seconds (fig. 31).

While both films still belong to the "cinema of attractions"—Topsy's death, after all, elicits precisely the sort of shock early films were known for—*Demolition of a Wall* deals solely in a ludic aesthetics of display and exhibition, while *Electrocuting an Elephant* begins to subordinate spectacle to the demands of storytelling. *Electrocuting an Elephant* is not yet a fully fleshed-out story. It is a formally bare, matter-of-fact demonstration of spectacular violence. But it is considered an important advance in the genealogy of narrative film in part because the cut omits the portion of time unnecessary to the portrayal of Topsy's execution. The cut eliminates what Doane calls "dead time."[62] We are given what we need to understand

FIGURE 30. *Demolition of a Wall* (Lumière Brothers, 1896). Men hacking at wall; men pushing down wall; men hacking at toppled wall; men working in reverse; wall pops back up; wall back in original position.

FIGURE 31. *Electrocuting an Elephant* (Thomas Edison, 1903). First cell is shot 1. Topsy is led to her execution. Next three cells are shot 2. Topsy is administered electricity, falls, and lies on the ground dead.

what is happening: Topsy walks toward something/Topsy is at her destination. More importantly for our purposes, however, is that the embryonic narrative apparent in *Electrocuting an Elephant* can be traced to its interest in the irreversibility of consequences, both in its thematic content and as a formal principle of causality. The Lumière film first establishes consequences—the wall falls because the men knock it down—but then refuses their permanence. The first-ever reverse-motion film, *Demolition of a Wall* restores the edifice to its former state, reversing time and erasing the effects it itself has caused. By contrast *Electrocuting an Elephant* punitively insists on the *ir*reversibility of effects. Topsy is shown to reap the consequences of her alleged transgression, which the film's form unforgivingly confirms as final. Not only does the film resist springing Topsy back to life, as it very well could have. It also emphasizes the irrevocability of her offense, not least by lingering for an uncomfortably long time on the image of her dead body. Not despite, but precisely because, the film would have been played multiple times back to back, it showcases what André Bazin calls cinema's "exorbitant privilege of repeating" the image of death, "the unique moment par excellence."[63]

In the significant case of *Electrocuting an Elephant*, the process of distinguishing formal limits—of establishing a distinction between what is worth filming and what isn't—also assumes, if not creates, normative dimensions. Here, the faint emergence of a story—Who is this elephant? Where is she going? Why is she being killed?—is afforded by the allocation of blame. The formal operation of causality—an elephant walks from point A to point B, is electrocuted, and dies—is twinned to an administration of consequences: Topsy hurt customers and therefore she must be killed. In this film—which Faulkner may very well have seen at the Old Opera House—the articulation of a normative world, one in which one's actions have not only formal but also moral consequences, is intrinsic to the institutional development of plot.

This twinning of formal constraint to incrimination takes on the proportions of an obsession in Quentin's section. When he observes a seemingly insignificant bird, for instance, like spectators of narrative cinema, he searches for plot development, believing himself to be watched:

> A sparrow slanted across the sunlight, onto the window ledge, and cocked his head at me. . . . First he'd watch me with one eye, then flick! And it would be the other one, his throat pumping faster than any pulse. The hour began to strike. The sparrow quit swapping eyes and watched me steadily with the same one until the chimes ceased, as if he were listening too. Then he flicked off the ledge and was gone.[64]

In Quentin's mind, the bird alights on this ledge as if to get a closer look at him. Its changing ocular perspectives and pumping throat indicate to Quentin some panicked cognitive process. Finally, the bird takes off precisely at the moment when the clock chimes cease, as if to arrive somewhere punctually to report an urgent message about Quentin. Moreover, Faulkner's choice to use the word *flick* to describe the bird's optic activity is suggestive; considering its proximity to *flicker* (a slang word, eventually abbreviated, used to describe early films), it is as if Quentin feels he is being *filmed*. Benjy also mentions a bird in his section: "It [the flag] was red, flapping on the pasture. Then there was a bird slanting and tilting on it. Luster threw. The flag flopped on the bright grass and the trees. I held to the fence."[65] Quentin lends intention to the bird's actions, all but anthropomorphizing its movements; he confers significance onto an otherwise contingent occurrence. Benjy, meanwhile, allows for the bird's existence to remain disconnected from his other observations, hanging there adjacently with the flag, the grass, and the trees. While for Benjy the bird is one among a number of visual details, Quentin narrativizes it, forcing it to symbolically participate in his search for judgment and desire for incrimination. Benjy might struggle to manage his surroundings (he does have to hold to the fence as he watches the bird) but he relinquishes perceptual control to the flux of details. Quentin, on the other hand, tries to gain formal mastery over those details by seeking experiential intensities. As in the genre of the death-and-execution film, Quentin reaches for "grandiose tropes" such as incest, divine judgment, and ultimately suicide so as to shock meaning, as it were, into that flux.

Unlike his brother Benjy, Quentin imbues seemingly insignificant events with hermeneutic meaning, integrating his observations and fleeting experiences into his fabricated incest plot. These include the moment with the sparrow but also his physical attack of Gerald Bland, thinking he was Caddy's lover Dalton Ames, or his insistence that the Black man sitting on a mule waiting for the train to move looks as if he "had been built there... like a sign up there saying You are home again."[66] Quentin responds in panic to hermeneutically impoverished excesses of presence, seeking to confer significance on his experience by effecting measurable change. The form of change Quentin actively seeks is not sociopolitical, economic, familial, or psychological: to the contrary, in a very important sense he wants nothing *to have changed.*[67] Quentin seeks *narrative* change: the meaningful transformation that constitutes the structure of a narrative event. As Stephen Heath has argued, "a narrative action is... a relation of transformation such that [its execution] determines a state S' different to an initial state S."[68] Quentin is drawn to sex and death because he is convinced that they permanently measure a form of narrative transformation, one that the excess of presence represented in Benjy's section makes unavailable.

The language Quentin uses in regard to sex and death suggests indeed that it is their shared transformative power that appeals to him. Quentin longs to lose his virginity (like Caddy), and his father tells him "It was men invented virginity not women... it's like death: only a state in which the others are left," a remark that, typical of Mr. Compson's insouciance, points to the status of virginity as a social fiction. He even denies death the significance with which Quentin imbues it, suggesting that it is "only a state," but, in Quentin's mind, at least one that measurably signifies permanent difference. Unwilling to accept his father's theory of the fictionality of virginity, Quentin replies: "Why couldn't it have been me and not her who is unvirgin and he said, That's why that's sad too; nothing is even worth the changing of it."[69] Otherwise put, even if Quentin were to become "unvirgin," it would not effect an authentic transformation. The prefix "un" suggests that to his mind, having sexual intercourse performs a measurable transformation from a previous state. As if inspired by his father's take on death, Quentin articulates his turn to suicide in terms that emphasize its ability to measure difference empirically. As his section draws to its close, he thinks, "A quarter hour yet. And then I'll not be. The peacefullest words. Peacefullest words . . . I was. I am not."[70] In both cases, the ability to say *I was a virgin and now and I am not* and *I was alive and now I am not*, draws Quentin to these two acts. In both, *S* would successfully turn into *S'*.

Change for its own sake, however, is not enough for Quentin. What he wants is that careful calibration of occurrence to significance that throughout this book I have been calling consequences. In the Edison film, the "what happens next" internal to the mechanics of plot is genetically linked to a sense of "what *should* happen next," not just in terms of Aristotelian verisimilitude—which early film's trick effects often flouted unapologetically, as in the case of *Demolition of a Wall*—but in terms of normative limits. The normative project represented in the execution of Topsy is linked to a formal economy of significance. What allows a plot to start to take hold is the film's assumption of the intractable formativity of causes. Not only does it "matter" that Topsy hurt customers but her execution also matters in a more strictly formal sense. Just as the film does not allow Topsy to retract her actions the way that *Demolition of a Wall* allows its construction workers to retract theirs, she is not brought back to life. The event of her execution matters formally in a way that the falling of the wall does not. She remains dead; the wall pops right back up.

Quentin, accordingly, locates permanent effects in major breaches of what is normatively acceptable: his desire for sex thus must be incestuous, a transgression of the incest taboo. In the scene at the squire's office when he has been accused of stealing the little Italian girl (an accidental occurrence Quentin absorbs into his narrative of sibling incest), he distorts the episode into an opportunity to suffer judgment and incrimination. He converts an otherwise contingent event into one of supreme meaning.

> He [the squire] opened a huge dusty book and drew it to him and dipped a foul pen into an inkwell with what looked like coal dust. . . .
> "The prisoner's name," the squire said. I told him. He wrote it slowly into the book, the pen scratching with excruciating deliberation. . . .
> "Age," the squire said. I told him. He wrote that, his mouth moving as he wrote. "Occupation." I told him. . . .
> "What was you doing, exactly?" I told him.[71]

His mad elation at having been incriminated ("I began to laugh," or "'Good afternoon,' I said, raising my hat. 'I'm under arrest'") and his readiness to offer his personal information to be written down in the "huge dusty book" suggest that he is looking above all to incur consequences[72]—that his actions would have durable effect, that he could affect S such that it would permanently become S'.

THE SHOW MUST GO ON

Emplotment reaches a maniacal extreme in *The Sound and the Fury* in the figure of Jason, whose section is at once the most comprehensible and the most violent of the three brothers'. Jason no longer allows for formal insignificance. To him, everything signifies, everything and everyone participates in his narrative of victimization. "Telling a story," Bordwell writes, is "the basic formal concern" of the classical cinema,[73] and integral to the execution of that aim is the principle of motivation. "Motivation is the process by which a narrative justifies its story material and the plot's presentation of that story material."[74] In a transitional film like *Electrocuting an Elephant*, the placement of the cut and the specific shot scales are motivated by the embryonic narrative of execution the film conveys (e.g., an earlier cut or more distant shots of Topsy may have compromised our narrative investment in her, just as closer shots would potentially have obscured her from view). But in later narrative and eventually classical films such as those shown at the Lyric, that motivational principle is even more prevalent, making for a much tighter narrative aesthetic. "Every element introduced" in the narrative cinema, Stephen Heath writes, "must be practicable in the development of the narrative, must be taken up again and be 'finished off' as an evident function in its progress, its resolution."[75] One example is in *Lilac Time* (George Fitzmaurice, 1928), a World War I drama that played at the Lyric in winter 1928 and that Faulkner would most probably have seen considering it traces the heroic escapades of a British aviator, played by Gary Cooper, a position Faulkner wished he had had and an actor he would go on to admire in *Sergeant York* (Hawks, 1941).[76] A scene at the beginning of the film, in which an aviator flies back to base in the French countryside so that he can die in the company of his crew's caretaker, Jeannie (Colleen Moore), is motivated by a reiteration of that scene at the end of the film. This time it is Cooper (the first dead soldier's replacement) who is hit by German forces and crashes down to the French base, thought dead and eventually revived to reunite with Jeannie, who had become his love interest. The inclusion of the first scene is motivated by its repetition, with a difference, that establishes Cooper's superiority as an aviator in similar circumstances, presents and then quells the possibility that Jeannie will sustain a second heartbreak, and above all lends narrative unity to a military conflict notorious for its destruction of and disregard for such formal integrity.

Jason takes this narrative logic of motivation—of *motive*—to its extreme. Consumed by what Matthews calls a "paranoid sense of persecution,"[77] Jason engages in constant and aggressive hermeneutic activity whereby every detail of his past and present seems the symptom and cause of his deprivation relative to those around him. Quentin longs for empirically measurable narrative order—an event that would matter so much as to permanently change the course of time. Jason, meanwhile, perceives all incidents as telling one totalizing story of injustice and dispossession; the world, it seems to him, is motivated against him. Overactively picking up on what he perceives as narrative cues, Jason engages in a pathological form of storytelling that in its rejection of the insignificant, Faulkner associates with the narrative cinema.

Jason believes himself to have fallen victim to several inequities: the financial and emotional dependence of the women in his family and their ostentatious behavior; what he considers the indolence of African Americans; the New York "Jews" and other "foreigners" who reap parasitic benefits from the US economy; and finally, his father's alcoholism, whose expense, Jason complains, precluded the possibility of his attending Harvard like Quentin. His sense of victimization informs even minute inconveniences: "I went on out the back to back the car out, then I had to go all the way round to the front before I found [Luster and Benjy]." He perceives such minutiae as microcosmic instances of vaster inequities. When he finally does find Luster and Benjy, for instance, he notices that Luster has not put the tire on the car despite his request, an oversight Jason sees as indicative of all African Americans' shiftlessness and unreliability. He uses the opportunity to bemoan the financial burden they pose him. "'I thought I told you to put that tire on the back of the car,' I says. 'I ain't had time,' Luster says. 'Ain't nobody to watch him till mammy git don in de kitchen.' 'Yes,' I says. I feed a whole damn kitchen full of n——s to follow him, but if I want an automobile tire changed, I have to do it myself."[78] When Luster provides a legitimate explanation (that he had no one with whom to leave Benjy), Jason instantly incorporates Benjy into his narrative of dispossession. "What the hell makes you want to keep him around here where people can see him? . . . It's bad enough on Sundays, with that damn field full of people that haven't got a side show and six n——s to feed, knocking a dam oversize mothball around."[79] This further propels Jason into an exaggerated, imaginary scenario in which Benjy will cause a series of unwanted expenses: "First thing I know they're going to begin charging me golf dues, then Mother and Dilsey'll have to get a couple of china door knobs and a walking stick and work it out, unless I play at night with a lantern. Then they'll send us all to Jackson, maybe."[80]

His disparaging invocations of amusement park entertainment (the "side show" and the "lantern") and his relentless integration of his experiences into his personal story of persecution are not conceptually divorced from one another. Jason's contempt for the traveling show that comes to town and the associations of nonnarrativity that that show historically evokes extend from his unrestricted hermeneutic pursuits.

Jason's scorn for popular entertainment is rooted in his fear of public exposure. His sense that the drama of his family's decline is being witnessed, watched, and that the once-great Compsons might now be on display as an object of an audience's gaze persistently incites his rage. One of his primary complaints about Luster is that he cares for Benjy in plain view, "where people can see him." Or when he argues with Quentin II over whether it is he or Caddy who is responsible for her expenses, "there was about a dozen people looking," making him "so mad for a minute it kind of blinded me." On his way to depositing her at school, he deliberately takes "the back street" so as to "dodge" the public space of "the square."[81] Publicity unsettles Jason, the prospect of the Compson family degenerating into an attraction, a fear that finds most potent expression in his choice to deem them pejoratively all a "side show." It makes sense, then, that Benjy and Quentin II are the characters who incite Jason's contempt the most. He associates his brother explicitly with amusement park entertainment, suggesting to his mother to "rent him out to a sideshow; there must be folks somewhere that would pay a dime to see him."[82] And his periodic remarks concerning Quentin II's revealing clothing and makeup ("that stuff on your face does hide more of you than anything else you've got on," or "her face [was] all painted up like a dam clown's") invoke stage makeup and picture her not only as a sex worker but also as a vaudeville or circus actress.[83] Finally, the presence in the novel's background of the man with the red tie invokes a host of associations with carnivals, circuses, traveling shows, all of which were part of early film culture.

Early, prenarrative film is discussed in terms of a "cinema of attractions" because it was formally predicated on an aesthetics of exhibitionism, or what Gunning calls a "display" of "visibility." As we have already discussed, the visual pleasure associated with early cinema had to do not with narrative immersion, but with the joy of visual spectacle. As a result, early films regularly and comfortably called attention to their own artificiality, best exemplified in the "recurring look at the camera."[84] Early erotic films vigorously exploited this technique. In *The Bride Retires* (1902), for instance, a woman looks and winks at the camera as she undresses for bed, ostensibly for her new husband but actually for the audience.[85] It is against the backdrop of this history that we should read Jason's simultaneous discomfort and fascination with Quentin II's powerful stare and exposed body, especially given her affiliation with the traveling show. In the midst of their violent quarrel over her tardiness for school, Jason remarks, "She looked at me, the cup in her hand. She brushed her hair back from her face, her kimono slipping off her shoulder. . . . She quit looking at me. She looked at Dilsey. . . . She dropped the cup. It broke on the floor and she jerked back, looking at me."[86] Jason and Quentin II reproduce a perverse version of the relationship between the spectator and actor of such early erotic films, bonded together in a nearly incestuous rapport through their mutual stares: "She didn't say anything. She was fastening her kimono up under her chin, pulling it tight around her, looking at me . . . she quit fighting and watched me, her eyes getting wide and dark."[87]

It is no coincidence that Jason's arguably most egregious act of violence in the novel is when he burns Luster's tickets to the show right in front of him, given how the show is a symbol of hermeneutic poverty and narrative disorder. By rendering Jason both the most comprehensible and the most destructive of the Compson brothers, Faulkner aligns narrative unity with violence. Jason's section thus validates Heath's observation that violence always inheres in the construction of narrative precisely because of its transformative structure: a narrative is "always a violence," he writes, "the interruption of the homogeneity of S . . . the homogeneity—S itself—being recognized in retrospect from that violence, that interruption."[88] In the case of *The Sound and the Fury*, Faulkner makes that prenarrative homogeneity and subsequent narrative violence intensely literal (as does *Lilac Time*, in fact, where Cooper's fully bandaged head in the final image of his embrace with Colleen Moore tacitly twins the violence of the Great War to the love plot's formal resolution—the narrative's wrapping up, as it were). Benjy's section is indeed homogeneous, treating the significant and insignificant with the same attention. It is not until we reach Jason's hateful and fully comprehensible section that the unadulterated quality of that descriptive homogeneity comes fully into view. Quentin's desperate search for narrative structure results in self-destruction; Jason's narrative of persecution punishes a full range of individuals and groups. It abolishes the possibility of the unparticipating detail. Jason's greed is the financial translation of a narrative issue: his interpretive habits enable an extremely economical storytelling—everything counts, and nothing is wasted.

TO SLOW DOWN

In *The Sound and the Fury*, formal traces of early film and film culture invoke a textual excess that threatens narrative meaning but in doing so also forecloses the psychic structures underpinning patriarchal, white supremacist narratives of dispossession and victimhood. Through the figures of Quentin and Jason, Faulkner appears to suggest that film loses touch with its ethically emancipatory potential when it gains plot, pitting as he does, in his first major work of modernist fiction, narrativization as a willful, paranoid act of sensemaking whose totalizing denial of contingency is the formal extension of the most violent ideologies of the Old South. But the temporality and formal problems posed by early film—an unmanageable excess of continuous presence—remain central to Faulkner's next modernist novel, *As I Lay Dying*, and in a way that complicates the neat denunciation of plot and plotting integral to *The Sound and the Fury*. More so than in that novel, Faulkner recognizes in *As I Lay Dying* the distinction between the formal horizons of the novel as a genre and the experience of living one's life—however fictional—without the solace of narrative or even merely aesthetic design. Through an extended engagement with present-tense narration, Faulkner acknowledges that it is one thing to write fragmented prose and another entirely to be caught in a flux of unplotted experience.

The materialist turn in Faulkner criticism awakened the field to the ways that Darl's linguistic indulgences could be regarded as indicative of a purely if not perilously aestheticist modernism, a drastic instantiation of the modernist doctrine of aesthetic autonomy in conflict with the novel's inscriptions of the uneven economic and social development of the New South.[89] Yet while Darl's abstractions certainly "de-substantializ[e]" the material world in a way that dislocates the lived from the aesthetic,[90] the ideological underpinnings of those linguistic adornments are cut with a fundamentally realist impulse. Quentin attempts to wrest narrative sense from temporal flux and in the process refuses to "receive in distraction." Darl, similarly, is engaging in the kind of aesthetic contemplation Benjamin argued was inherent to the discourse networks of the nineteenth century rather than those of the age of mechanical reproducibility, which thrive on precisely the sort of sensorial onslaught that Darl, like Quentin, attempts to avoid.[91] Darl may be wresting art from reality, but he is waging that battle along a temporal axis, attempting to recover narratable and aestheticizable experience by wresting the time needed for aesthetic contemplation. Darl's effete aestheticism is just as much a sign of a vestigial realism clamoring for the privilege of preterit retrospection as it is a relishing in a self-insulated modernist negation, if not more so.

Early on in *As I Lay Dying*, Darl invokes an image of his brother Cash so aestheticized that it strains its own grammar. "Standing in a litter of chips, he is fitting two of the boards together. Between the shadow spaces they are yellow as gold, like soft gold, bearing on their flanks in smooth undulations the marks of the adze blade: a good carpenter, Cash is."[92] Turning back midsentence to add texture to his simile—"yellow as gold, like soft gold"—Darl encumbers the immediacy of the present with a figurative and stylistic richness that it cannot comfortably accommodate, drawing attention to the strained, if not impossible temporal conditions of his narration. *Récit*, as Jameson has argued, is the retrospective posture of narrative's enunciative moment; it finds its grammatical home in the preterit tense, the tense of completed action that renders time and events immutable. The body in the present eludes the reifying effects of realist narration. Unruly, free, unconscious of itself, and not yet differentiated from all that surrounds it, the body in the present, Jameson argues, resists the confines of preterit narration that would ossify its impersonal corporeality into character, its inchoate sensations into namable emotions.[93] Literature's modernity is predicated, in Jameson's view, on claiming the presence of—and the present of—the body as a means of challenging, if not toppling, the regime of the *récit*, or its "tyranny," as Jacques Rancière has relatedly put it by way of Virginia Woolf.[94]

But the tenderness of Darl's amended simile reveals that the retrospective temporality of *récit* provides aesthetic labor what it needs most: time—time that Darl does not have, present as he is to the actions he narrates, but that he nevertheless wrests from some temporal reserve that the novel persistently requests of us imaginatively to allow. Though the preterit tense is the grammatical proxy for an ideology productive of precisely the bourgeois individualism that Faulkner has set out to critique, *As I Lay Dying* nevertheless suggests that it is that grammar that provides, or indicates the availability of, a period of delay in which the raw material of *histoire* can be shaped—like pieces of wood into planks for a coffin—into an arrangement that confirms their irrevocability. Remarking on the time required for aesthetic work would be unwarranted, were *As I Lay Dying* not so fundamentally concerned with the effort of labor, with sweat (or its absence; Anse so rarely works), with the time it takes to produce something beautiful for a thing that is passing away, be it a coffin for a mother's body or words for embodied time. Or of course, *As I Lay Dying* itself, which has accrued its own mythology in terms of the time it took Faulkner to compose it. While readers are used to thinking of Darl as reflective of his author, the way he labors over words is more indicative of the Faulkner who toiled over the Great Books for years, finally to have that come to fruition, according to his own account, in *The Sound and the Fury*, rather than the one who over the course of approximately eight lightning weeks and with minimal revisions produced *As I Lay Dying*.[95]

That effortlessness and automaticity of aesthetic labor—the way that, as André Bleikasten has put it, the novel "appears to have imposed itself of its own accord"[96]—does not carry over into Darl's more cumbersome artistic work, which right from the opening scene draws attention to itself as work, albeit uncommodified, comparable to but also incompatible with embodied effort. In the lore of the production of *As I Lay Dying*, Faulkner emerges as a medium through which the novel materialized itself. Inside its diegetic world, however, Darl's aesthetic contrivances bear the marks, as it were, of the adze blade. The opening scene draws attention to that work by cleaving a distance between language and action, exposing the spatial and temporal gap that prevails between narration and event, recognizing narration as a form of exertion. Weaving in and out of one another's way, Jewel and Darl walk the path from the field to their home, Jewel initially trailing behind his brother. But as they approach the old cottonhouse on the way to the barn and begin to hear Cash's adze hacking methodically at the planks of Addie's coffin, he outstrips Darl. Darl circumvents the dilapidated structure, taking the path that travels along its edge; Jewel walks straight through via the two windows directly opposite one another in alignment with the path outside. Jewel emerges from the cottonhouse ahead of his brother, walking in front of Darl until he stops to drink water from the spring with a gourd. That Darl does not stop to drink suggests that Jewel was exerting more physical effort, tacitly racing with his brother, who is not reciprocating the competition. Darl's choice to walk around the cottonhouse—to describe it with his walk the way a pen would describe a circle—is consistent with the fact that it is he who narrates the scene, speaking around it, as it were, instead of yielding himself to it. Jewel, on the other hand, does not narrate the scene because he is busy barreling through it, moving the action forward with each energetic stride.[97]

Jewel's steps are no doubt more in touch with the grammatical fabric of the scene than Darl's luxuriating narration. Delivered entirely in the present tense—"the cottonhouse is," "we reach," "I turn," "we go"—the scene asks for an elevated pace evocative of physical effort. And Darl's unhurried gait, as well as his equally unhurried imagery—"empty and shimmering dilapidation in the sunlight," "pale eyes set into his wooden face"[98]—tugs at that pace, resisting not just the alacrity of his brother but also the briskness of the grammatical tense itself. Nevertheless, his similes and metaphors parallel Jewel's effort in the work they are demanding the present tense to perform. Darl may be walking at a more leisurely clip than his brother, but with phrases such as "with the rigid gravity of a cigar store Indian dressed in patched overalls and endued with life from the hips down," he is nonetheless muscling the present tense into slowing down so that it can accommodate his imagery. It is as if Darl narrates in the present tense in spite of himself, overcompensating for its speed by saddling it with what Ezra Pound might call the "frills and festoons of language."[99] While Jewel silently retreats into action, stalking through the windows of the cottonhouse with a facial and corporeal deadpan evocative of Buster Keaton, Darl narrates with a volume of figurative language that burdens the scene's tense, resisting the verbs' celerity as well as the kinetic pull of the path beneath his feet.

The dilatory effect of Darl's language is especially pronounced when Faulkner provides more candid deictic evidence of Darl's presence to his scenes of aesthetic reverie. For instance, in the section where he contemplates the buzzards that have been attracted by the smell of Addie's corpse, Jewel reticently broods as Darl narrates: "High above the house, against the quick thick sky, they hang in narrowing circles. From here they are no more than specs, implacable, patient, portentous."[100] The voiceless consonance of "quick thick" in the first sentence already begins to obstruct the linguistic flow, but it is the paratactic accumulation of adjectives at the end of the second—"implacable, patient, portentous"—whose deceleration chafes most remarkably against the deictic word *here*. Making more literal what had remained suggestive in Benjy's section, the word *here* indexically anchors Darl's body to the site of his aesthetic contemplation, justifying the tense of the verbs *hang* and *are*, even as it generates a conflict between the fact of Darl's present body and the temporal stretch of his language, validating the contention among critics that Faulkner systematically obscures the source of utterance in this novel. That indeterminacy derives precisely from Darl's resistance to, if not denial of, his own presence to the fabula he is narrating, a fabula in and of which he is still, in spite of himself, a part. The enunciative aporias that Darl's manipulation of the present tense stitch into the text result from his effort to collapse fabula (the events themselves as they occur chronologically) into syuzhet (their narrative arrangement): to refuse his own substance by folding the time of the lived into the time of the telling.

Darl's difficulty with accepting the embodied terms of present-tense narration indexes a more general conflict with the aesthetic conditions of his possibility. Darl's is a temporality of refusal, delay, and contemplation that reaches for the perspectival advantage of retrospective signification whose narrative posture is rooted in formal realism. His apparent attempts to position himself differently with respect to his own experience than simply being in it must be understood within the context of realism's negotiation of narrative time and the aesthetic orthodoxy of retrospection toward which his linguistic protractions aspire. Classical realist narration predicated its epistemic authority on radically distancing the temporalities of fabula and syuzhet via the preterit tense, which it raised to the level of grammatical doctrine. The paradigmatic formal realism of Honoré de Balzac, for instance, adheres with little exception to the preterit. The opening line of his novel *Louis Lambert* (1832), for example, reads "Louis Lambert was born [*naquit*], in 1797, at Montoire, a small town in the Vendomois." The use of the French *passé simple* (or *passé historique* as it is sometimes called), rather than the more recent and unstable *passé composé* "est né," makes this distancing even more noticeable—since "naquit" locates "was born" in a distant and immutable past over which the narrator has absolute epistemic dominion. Realism's prohibition of what Jameson calls the "formal taboo" of the present derives from its intolerance of uncertainty, the adherence, as Philip Weinstein has argued, to a Cartesian epistemology founded on a belief in the knowability of reality, a totality it assumes human reason is able to apprehend. The kind of present tense that does emerge in Balzacian realism, far from an admission of uncertainty, most often serves the purpose of historical comparison. In *Lost Illusions* (1843), for instance, the narrator periodically breaks from the story of Lucien de Rubempré in order to articulate the difference between the era of the novel's fabula and that of "today." The present tense Balzac permits in such moments facilitates critique of postrevolutionary French society; it demonstrates the acuity and range of the narrator's ken rather than its limits.

More complexly than just pointing up the subjectivity and unreliability of the modernist narrator, the present tense in *As I Lay Dying* does away with the distance between the time of the fabula and that of the narrative enunciation, effectively pulling the former into the latter. The denial of the preterit thus has the effect of compressing the three-dimensional narrative architecture of the classical realist novel into a flat verticality: the fabula, now collapsed into the narrative enunciation, pushes into or along with the passage of time in the same direction and kinetic gesture, whereas in formal realism, the narrative emerges within the canopied space between the preterit narrative enunciation and the fabula to which it reaches back.

A spatial understanding of narrative is especially salient when one recalls that Benjamin saw the modern perceptual apparatus most potently manifest in architecture.[101] In his deliberation on the transformation of modes of aesthetic participation, Benjamin argues that architecture appeals to the body to experience it rather than to the eyes to contemplate it; excessive attention to a work of architecture compromises its inherent appeal to embodied experience, its demand to be inhabited rather than thought. He sets the "casual noticing" of the modern masses against the acts of "attentive observation" that characterized the premodernist aesthetic order. The "tasks," he continues, "which face the [modern] human apparatus of perception... cannot be performed solely by optical means—that is, by way of contemplation. They are mastered gradually—taking their cue from tactile reception—through habit."[102] Benjamin's meditation on architecture sheds light on Jewel's summary sacrifice of contemplation for action when he charges through the dilapidated structure of the cottonhouse. The automaticity of Jewel's movements suggests habituation—that he has walked through those windows on other occasions, as well, if not ritualized the act. Jewel's comfort with inhabiting the present through habitual action aligns him with Benjy, who also receives "in distraction." Meanwhile, Darl's avoidance of the building suggests a refusal of the dialectic of tactility and attention that constitutes modern perception and a choice, instead, to circumvent it. The perceptual demands of architecture that Benjamin sees as representative of the modern discourse network adopt especial significance when one recalls that other piece of architecture looming over *As I Lay Dying*, which Darl does not simply avoid, but violently destroys. Darl's burning of Gillespie's barn is a rejection of an embodied mode of aesthetic participation. It is the immolation of an architectural structure whose absence leaves room for Darl to erect the formal edifice of preterit narration in its stead—an act of narrative surrogacy that also sheds important light on Quentin's self-destructive search for plot.

Darl's inability or unwillingness to come into contact with the world without exacting the time to transform it—his refusal to accept the narrative terms of embodied presence—reaches a fever pitch in what is in effect a Pyrrhic transcendence of embodied experience through the arsonous destruction of an inhabitable space. There is a certain muted glee with which he narrates as the skeletal structure of the building gradually vanishes: "We watch through the dissolving proscenium of the doorway"; "Jewel has paused, looking up, and suddenly we watch the entire floor to the loft dissolve. It just turns to fire; a faint litter of sparks rains down."[103] The barn burning is taken to be a symptom of Darl's madness and the last straw that sends him to Jackson; it is also the point at which he replaces one structure for another. Having destroyed an architectural site of tactile, habituated labor—represented by the milking stool Jewel splinters to use as a prod but whose habitual purpose is to facilitate repetitious work whose grammatical proxy is the present—Darl erects a formal structure in its place. Shortly after having burned the barn, Darl begins to narrate himself in the past tense and in the third person, forging a spatial architecture of realist novelistic form to take the place of the symbol of rote, habituated labor whose automaticities are the province of the modern discourse network. If one of Darl's wishes has been to "just ravel out into time," then retrospective narrative affords him precisely that opportunity for self-extension: a raveling out into two consciousnesses—one living, one telling—that the present tense could not enable.[104] "They put him on the train, laughing, down the long car laughing, the heads turning like the heads of owls when he passed. 'What are you laughing at?' I said. . . . They pulled two seats together so Darl could sit by the window to laugh."[105] Darl's final section reads like a defunct realism, his descent into madness the consequence of his pursuit of access to preterit self-narration in the context of a discourse network no longer permissive of such formal purchase on experience. And readers are left to wonder whether his laughter is as manic as it ostensibly appears or if it is not a deranged and joyful assent to his imaginative denial of the existential present.

"TOO SOON TOO SOON TOO SOON"

There are some characters, in addition to Jewel, for whom the present tense does not generate discomfort. For instance, the way Cash's aphoristic list hangs suspended and contingent outside of time and space produces no crisis in him. To the contrary, Cash moves through the novel with remarkable evenness, barely reacting to the catastrophes that befall him, including his injured, rotting leg. The rote labor of his adze hacking, too, indicates dexterity with unintentional, habituated action.[106] Tull, as well, seems to navigate comfortably both present-tense and past-tense narration, slipping in and out of them with vertiginous regularity. Phrases such as "Anse meets us at the door" and "the boy is not there" are swiftly followed by conversions to "Peabody told about how he come into the kitchen, hollering, swarming and clawing at Cora," without the least indication of internal or formal emergency.[107] And yet Tull's rumination on crossing the bridge toward Jefferson offers insight into the broader stakes of Darl's difficulty managing the present. In the vulnerability of Tull's following passage, Faulkner acknowledges that in formally emancipating the novel from the constraints of the preterit, he is also leaving his characters with only the solace, fragile and intermittent, of one another, subjecting his creations to a kind of primordial abandonment.

> It was like when we was across, up out of the water again and the hard earth under us, that I was surprised. It was like we hadn't expected the bridge to end on the other bank, on something tame like the hard earth again that we had tromped on before this time and knowed well. Like it couldn't be me here, because I'd have had better sense than to done

what I just done. And when I looked back and saw the other bank and saw my mule standing there where I used to be and knew that I'd have to get back there someway, I knew it couldn't be, because I just couldn't think of anything that could make me cross the bridge ever even once. Yet here I was, and the fellow that could make himself cross it twice couldn't be me, not even if Cora told him to.

It was that boy. I said "here; you better take a holt of my hand" and he waited and held to me. I be durn if it wasn't like he come back and got me; like he was saying They wont nothing hurt you. Like he was saying about a fine place he knowed where Christmas come twice with Thanksgiving and lasts on through the winter and the spring and the summer, and if I just stayed with him I'd be all right too.[108]

An oft-noted feature of *As I Lay Dying* is Faulkner's felt absence from the text, the detachment of the novel's language from not just the characters but also Faulkner himself.[109] In keeping, however, with the paradoxes of modernist impersonality, the ostensible autonomy of *As I Lay Dying* from its maker is an effect of its exhaustive suffusion with his signature, the transfiguration of Faulkner into style.

But in preoccupying itself with stylistic performance, it is as if the novel leaves the characters to make their own way through narrative time. *As I Lay Dying* may be a veritable storehouse of Faulkner's modernist techniques, a stylistic tour de force; but as such, it all the more powerfully underscores the thrownness (to borrow Zachary Tavlin's Heideggerian language) of these characters into a series of traumas and calamities over which there presides no author, let alone omniscient narrator, to cradle their experiences within a narrative teleology. The quiet gratitude Tull feels toward Vardaman for providing him the comfort he did not even know he needed captures the defenselessness of that solitude as he and the Bundrens pass over and through the "thick dark current" of the river, whose relentless undertow comes to represent novelistic time itself.[110] In leaving the characters to fend for themselves, Faulkner acknowledges that formal departure from the realist preterit involves a certain cruelty on the part of the modernist creator toward her characters, whose status as discursive formations may be all the more apparent in modernism but whose embodied reality is all the more pronounced and thus urgently vulnerable.

But despite Faulkner's relinquishment of his characters' narrative trajectories for the sake of style, *As I Lay Dying* remains one of his most teleological novels. The novel's style certainly obfuscates the time and place of events, and typical to Faulkner, often the alienating effects of the style can distract from the events themselves. Nevertheless, the novel has a clear beginning, middle, and end organized along the axis of a coherent chronology of occurrences. In short, compared with *The Sound and the Fury* and the later *Absalom, Absalom!*, *As I Lay Dying* is a plotted novel. But if Faulkner's sacrifice of preterit omniscient narration for a transfiguration into style leaves the characters in a present that they must desperately try to manage, then what is often considered the bizarre, nigh-comical perseverance of the Bundrens is a resolution not just to reach Jefferson but also to try to make do with their formal circumstances and to arrive at the end of the novel itself. In insisting on burying Addie in Jefferson, the Bundrens are also seeing to it that they reach the end of their own plot. And the clumsiness of their trajectory—their nearly fatal encounter with the flooding river, Cash's injury, the loss of their animals, and so forth—is a casualty, *en abyme*, of what such characters in search of an author would have to endure to get there. And in keeping with the dark humor of the novel, once they do finally reach the end, they essentially botch it: Anse procures another wife, and they are, in effect, right back where they started—as if the novel never even happened.

Faulkner is just as interested in acknowledging the existential consequences of the departure from preterit narration for his characters as he is in exploring its emancipatory promise for the novel as a genre—recognizing that what may very well be a source of tragedy and panic for one might engender new formal horizons for the other. Though Faulkner may be using present-tense narration in *As I Lay Dying* as a way to announce the novel's antirealism, he is also aware that that formal choice may come at the expense of his characters' ability to gain traction on novelistic time without, as it were, drowning in it.[111]

Dewey Dell articulates the alarm of that detachment from an authorial maker most lucidly as she narrates from the wagon on the way to ford the river. Organizing her thoughts around the distinction between living and unliving things, she thinks to herself, "The signboard comes in sight. It is looking out at the road now, because it can wait. New Hope. 3 mi. it will say. New Hope. 3 mi. New Hope 3 mi. And then the road will begin, curving away into the trees, empty with waiting, saying New Hope three miles."[112] There is a peculiar displacement of agency in this passage, rendering sentient the inanimate sign and road: the sign "comes into sight"; it "is looking out" because "it can wait"; the sign "will say," the road "will begin . . . empty with waiting." Reminiscent of Darl's nocturnal ruminations on "emptying himself for sleep" and Vardaman's observation that "the air is empty for rain,"[113] the lexicon of emptiness, which assumes its opposite, fullness, creates a formal framework of before and after. Dewey Dell's language thus maps onto the inanimate world the metaphysics of being and not being—anteriority and posteriority—that distinguish Addie's mortality at the center of the novel. But in imagining what the sign will say (3 mi.) and, implicitly, what the road will be "filled" with (the Bundren wagon), Dewey Dell is also tracking the passage of time. Her anticipation of the evidence of their journey's progress is banal, but it gives way to a devastated existential rumination on mortality as she discovers, as if for the first time, that to be a living body in the present is also to confront one's finitude.

For when in reference to the road she says "because it can wait," she tacitly acknowledges that there are things in the world that cannot. The inanimate sign can wait to be read, just as the road can wait to be filled with the Bundren wagon. And from within this rumination on the privilege of inanimateness—that to be inanimate means to be able to prepare for being experienced, for experiencing—emerges Dewey Dell's most anguished passage in the novel, where she gives language to her mourning for her mother in a way that no other Bundren has been able to.

> I heard that my mother is dead. I wish I had time to let her die. I wish I had time to wish I had. It is because in the wild and outraged earth too soon too soon too soon. It's not that I wouldn't and will not it's that it is too soon too soon too soon.
> Now it begins to say it. New Hope three miles. New Hope three miles. *That's what they mean by the womb of time: the agony and the despair of spreading bones, the hard girdle in which lie the outraged entrails of events.*[114]

When she says that she "heard" that her mother was dead, Dewey Dell is of course not referring to being absent from her mother's deathbed, since we know she was there. Rather, Dewey Dell refers to the velocity of Addie's death, her inability to apprehend it—to wait and thus prepare for it—as would the sign to say "3 mi." to passersby or the road to be filled with animate travelers. She would not prolong Addie's life; rather, when she thinks, "I wish I had time to let her die. I wish I had time to wish I had," Dewey Dell is discovering that the womb of time, constantly birthing the next instant, is by its very nature in a perpetual state of pushing her into the present, robbing her of the time for comprehension, let alone retrospection. As if by logical deduction, she then contemplates the simple, though crushing metaphysical fact that inanimate objects, unlike living beings, do not experience time—are not subject to the intolerable cruelty of its unceasing births, like the "engendering gusts" of sparks from the burning barn[115]—because signs and roads in fact do not "wait" or "say" or "look" but simply exist in dumb insentience. Dewey Dell thus awakens, with ever more agony, to her own sentience and, by extension, her own mortality. She then turns to God—"I believe in God, God. God, I believe in God."[116]

Like Doctor Matthew O'Connor's appeals to God in Barnes's *Nightwood*, Dewey Dell's Steinian repetitions exude panicked doubt in the existence of divinity, as the novel collapses her recognition of the absence of God into a recognition, too, that the preterit narration that would have afforded her the "time to let [Addie] die" and the "time to wish" that she had the time is merely a fantasy of an afterlife—a position only fictively beyond or after the present. In her apostrophic appeals to a higher power that would provide retrospective assurance for godless beings in time—as if appealing to Faulkner himself—Dewey Dell identifies the present not as freedom but as panic, not as formal deliverance but as existential grief.

THE BRIDGE

In the absence of the preterit, the characters of *As I Lay Dying* are left to move themselves from one point of novelistic time to another, where the flooding of the bridge symbolizes the evacuation of a narrative infrastructure engineered by an author. In addition to establishing the immutability of events, the preterit was in essence a bridging device, an apparatus for connecting events to one another in a causal chain. From the modernist point of view, as Rancière has argued, the structural integrity of the nineteenth-century realist novel depended on a "strong connection of causes and effects" manufactured by what Woolf called "some powerful and unscrupulous tyrant . . . to provide a plot."[117] By virtue of its determination to break with the realist tradition, "modern fiction has no proper mode of linkage"[118] and thus has to find alternative ways of bridging textual moments to each other without resorting to the familiar kinetics of plot. It would be hard to dispute that a modernist novel whose central action involves the inundation of a bridge is preoccupied with the problematization of realist "linkage" and thus causation. But what we find in *As I Lay Dying* is an account of the pain and difficulty of that process; again and again in this novel, characters not only manage to push themselves through plotted time but they also forge bonds of causation where such bonds feel absent or inaccessible. For these characters, the logic of adjacency, correlation, or constellation produces panic and fear, culminating in a tropology of blame.

In *Nightwood*, as we discussed in chapter 2, the Doctor inculpates himself so as to give Nora Flood a reason for her heartbreak; he tells her it was he who introduced Robin Vote to Jenny Petherbridge and in so doing allows Nora momentarily to direct her feelings of betrayal toward him, a locatable source, rather than toward Robin, whose actions persistently elude narrative explanation. Blame is central, too, to *As I Lay Dying*, but to different effect. In *Nightwood*, the Doctor's expression of guilt is an act of self-sacrifice; he risks incurring Nora's anger so as to give her a reason where causal structures have been replaced by tautologies. Robin left Nora because she left her, just as Robin left Felix because she left him. In *As I Lay Dying*, blame becomes a surrogate for the causal structures the present tense cannot accommodate; it is the expression of the characters' attempts to create palliative etiologies *for themselves* where Faulkner refuses to give them. Indeed, if the question lingers as to whether the present tense can bear the full weight of modernist antirealism—whether genre, or mode, is reducible to tense—that burden becomes clear in the instances of the misallocation of blame throughout the novel. It is the epistemic consequence of Faulkner's relinquishment of preterit narration, for bound up within the preterit's retrospective posture was also realism's primary vehicle for the assignment of causality. The instances of blame assignment that pepper the novel suggest that rather than surrendering themselves to a textual chaos—such as we find in Benjy's section or what Woolf calls the "incessant shower of innumerable atoms" that "fall upon the mind"—the characters are reaching for realist forms of causal linkage.[119]

The implications of what Weinstein calls the "strategies" of "psychic displacement" through which the characters of *As I Lay Dying* try to manage their grief—the full extent of the forms they take and their stakes for the vaster scheme of Faulkner's modernism—have yet to be fully understood.[120] The characters of *As I Lay Dying* try provisionally, albeit unsuccessfully, to resolve the tensions generated by the present by relying on diachronic formulations of culpability. Deprived of the realist retrospection whose raison d'être is to forge a narrative system of explanation, the characters writhe in a present they cannot understand and thus depend on blame to manufacture etiological narratives that will mitigate their suffering.

The novel's most conspicuous and memorable instance of misallocation of blame is when Vardaman holds Peabody responsible for Addie's death. "You kilt my maw!" he screams, as he hits the obese doctor with the stick he has snatched from the barn, "You kilt her!"[121] The affective resonance of Vardaman's "kilt," whose emphatic pastness is underscored by its phonetic misspelling, derives from the fact that Faulkner renders the madness of Vardaman's grief not by naming it but by using the present tense to show the child's inability to name it himself. "Then I begin to run," he narrates, upon Addie's death "I run toward the back and come to the edge of the porch and stop. Then I begin to cry. . . . I can hear the bed and her face and them and I can feel the floor"; and later, "I am not crying now. I am not anything. . . . I am not anything. I am quiet."[122] But out of the deluge of Vardaman's staccato present-tense declaratives eventually rushes forth a line of reasoning for Addie's death, as if he detects something soothing about designating its cause. "That came and did it," he narrates suddenly in past tense, "when she was all right but he came and did it. 'That fat son of a bitch.'"[123] What Vardaman knows is that Addie was alive before Peabody arrived, and she was dead once he was there. He conjures a relation of causality from an otherwise paratactic correlation of events, taming the incomprehensibility of Addie's death by assigning it a readily locatable source. The conversion to past-tense narration, far from an incidental grammatical gesture, suggests Vardaman's ache for a narrative armature that would help explain the sudden loss of his mother. Where Darl wrests art from the swiftness of experience, Vardaman allocates blame—the closest thing he has to the formal order afforded by *récit*—to render comprehensible the sheer contingency of death whose metaphysics he spends the whole novel trying to understand.

But Vardaman's misrecognition is not idiosyncratic; it is representative of how blame works in *As I Lay Dying*. Anse's complaint that the road built near his home led to his incurring expenses under new laws in the modernizing South, for instance, is no less misplaced a form of blame than Vardaman's. Nor, for that matter, is Cora's shrill insistence that she bore no sons because the Lord did not see fit for it to be so, or Dewey Dell's thought that Peabody could give her an abortion "if he just would," as if by some mental acrobatics she sees him as responsible for her pregnancy.[124] Or even the way Addie localizes the disenfranchisement she experiences as a poor woman in the Southern patriarchy into a fierce hatred for her husband and the regret of one decision—"And so I took Anse."[125] All of these gestures are fundamentally analeptic, attempts to establish an anteriority capable of explaining the suffering or disenfranchisement of the present moment. In this way the present tense of *As I Lay Dying* indeed may come to bear the weight of history, a history in and among which the characters find themselves and whose vertiginous transitions they are trying to navigate. When Anse says "Durn that road. . . . A-laying there, right up to my door, where every bad luck that comes and goes is bound to find it,"[126] he is creating a palliative narrative that will mitigate his anxiety at the thought that his family, in Matthews's words, is becoming a "sociological corpse" by virtue of the economic transformations of the New South.[127] In their rush to determine the sources of their hardship, the characters in essence try to embed themselves within a chain of realist causality, situating their experiences within a narrative continuity that the novel's constant recursions to the present tense otherwise sever from them. The pervasive image throughout the novel of Anse rubbing his knees while looking out onto the land is an obverse reflection of Darl's parallel struggle to reckon with the materiality of the present, Darl's recourse to art no less self-deceptive than Anse's blaming of the road for what is at bottom his terror of uncertainty for his future.

Throughout his career, Faulkner takes interest in the ways that cultural, social, and historical narratives are created—how reputations develop, how gossip travels, how fears take hold through the capitulation and recapitulation of personal, regional, and national stories. In reference to *Light in August*, Peter Lurie argues that to convey the cultural mechanisms of social and racial surveillance, Faulkner positions us "as looking *at* and, most often, looking *for* [Joe] Christmas in an implicitly violent way."[128] This hermeneutic tendency of Faulknerian apprehension—the narrativizing proclivity of his characters' judgment—is a recurring feature in Faulkner's oeuvre and is indeed often bent toward violence, most powerfully, as we saw, in the case of Jason Compson. Through those hermeneutic gestures, Faulkner also insists, however, that modernism confront that despite the mandate to break with realist story, human communities—at least those that preoccupy Faulkner—thirst for and are constituted by narrative. Or more accurately, realist story came about as a formal answer to a cultural and social need whose potential violence Faulkner acknowledges but whose inescapability he also confesses. This may be one of the reasons why, apart from *Absalom, Absalom!*, Faulkner returns to a largely realist style throughout the rest of his career, refusing to "sacrifice story to technical virtuosity."[129] Or why Addie, the character most attuned to the flimsiness of language compared with the efficacy of action—who from the grave complains "how words go up in a thin line, quick and harmless, and how terribly doing goes along the earth"—still exerts the novel's most powerful force of narrative causality with her request to be buried in Jefferson.[130]

By having the characters of *The Sound and the Fury* and *As I Lay Dying* attempt to regain either aesthetic or epistemic purchase on the otherwise inchoate or overwhelming onrush of the present—to make a "scratch," as Judith Sutpen of *Absalom, Absalom!* would go on say, "that undying mark on the blank face of the oblivion to which we are all doomed"[131]—Faulkner contemplates the fundamental proximity of, on the one hand, modernism's commitment to lending coherence and meaning to modernity and, on the other, realism's mandate to impose order where it, too, saw chaos. And perhaps what makes Faulkner's modernism—as well as that of Larsen and Barnes—so distinctive is his willingness, even at his most experimental moments, to confess that constitutive embarrassment: that even though modernism as a literary moment and movement may be under pressure to withdraw realist forms of linkage, those joints will somehow still get crafted, however precariously, if for no other reason than that we so often want and need them to.

INDULGENCE BY PROXY

Attempts to locate the precise traces of Faulkner's Hollywood writing have been haunted by the particularities of the screenplay as a genre, that porous, ever-"unfinished" object constantly under construction and always destined for transformation, if not disappearance, into another text.[132] Different Hollywood studios' aesthetic specificities (e.g., the centrality of stars at MGM, the signature grit of Warner Brothers) also put enormous constraint on individual creativity, leaving authors' personal style as "no more than an inflection," as Thomas Schatz puts it, "on an established studio style" that was so corporately controlled that the commercial screenplay has even been referred to as a "corporate art."[133] The screenplay is a constitutively collaborative structure, a fact that Faulkner regularly bemoaned but could not avoid.[134] From an institutional standpoint, the names that appear (or don't) on the final screenplay—itself a contradiction in terms—are (as was the case with Zoë Akins, on *Camille*) often the source of personal resentment, institutional strife, even legal action. Faulkner was a "motion picture doctor"[135] for approximately fifty films at their different stages of development, and for a number of different directors and studios.[136] He ended up being credited for only six of them: *Today We Live* (Howard Hawks, 1933), *The Road to Glory* (Hawks, 1936), *Slave Ship* (Tay Garnett, 1938), *To Have and Have Not* (Hawks, 1944), *The Big Sleep* (Hawks, 1946), and *Land of the Pharaohs* (Hawks, 1955). In short, because of the collaborative, corporate, and self-effacing nature of the classical Hollywood screenplay, it is "nearly impossible to identify Faulkner's precise contributions" to the films he wrote for, a methodological problem enhanced by Faulkner's own deflections of responsibility.[137] Determining what was or was not Faulkner's Hollywood touch has always been to a great extent speculative. We can't know with certainty the full extent of what he did or didn't do there, and we can't take his word for it either.

The story typically goes that Faulkner hated working for the Hollywood studios, that he compared it, hyperbolically and inappropriately, to slave labor, and that what he did do for the big studios (MGM, Twentieth-Century Fox, and Warner Brothers, in particular) should be understood in terms of the struggles of an art novelist to smuggle his high-modernist sensibility into the commercial screenplays when he could. It was alienated labor he performed because he needed to make money to support his family and house back in Oxford that he could never quite afford, and so he made screenwriting bearable when possible by stitching into the screenplays fleeting outcroppings of a critical sensibility—adding to *Today We Live* a self-reflective meditation on MGM's imposition of a female love interest (Joan Crawford) when there was none in his original short story, "The Turnabout," from which it was adapted, or basking in the narrative contortions of *The Big Sleep*, laying bare the continuities between the narrative obscurantism of high literary modernism and the detective genre Raymond Chandler's source text was so central in modernizing (to name just two examples).[138] Whatever genuine interest Faulkner may have had in the silver screen, we're often told, did not involve the fantasies of narrative unity offered by the Hollywood dream factory.

But we have seen that Faulkner's first two high-modernist efforts systematically stage characters' desire for the forms of causation and narrative unity associated with bourgeois plot—the desire for time to sweep experience clean, as Virginia Woolf might put it, into manageable wholes over which these characters might exercise epistemic power, through which they may experience existential comfort. We also know that by the time Faulkner was writing *The Sound and the Fury* and *As I Lay Dying* (and Nella Larsen *Quicksand* and Djuna Barnes *Nightwood*) that bourgeois plot and its principles of unity, motivation, and consequence had become the primary dominion of the classical Hollywood cinema. If we can indeed never be sure what is Faulkner and what isn't in Hollywood, may we not leave open the possibility that he also wrote—and enjoyed with complex comfort—the moments when the narrative comes together rather than when it falls apart? Could he not have written—and experienced with private pangs of relief—the scene of Lauren Bacall and Humphry Bogart coming together at the end of *To Have and Have Not*, slinking off into their uncertain but coupled future? Could he not have written, too, the scene at the end of *The Big Sleep*, where Bogart and Bacall again unite, their final image the wildly implausible and no less satisfying conclusion that pours forth from a morass of textual density; that of Barbara Stanwyck and Joel McCrea in a storm-soaked embrace at the end of *Banjo on My Knee* (John Cromwell, 1936); of Richard Green and Nancy Kelly as naval officers Perry Green and Susan Leeds in *Submarine Patrol* (John Ford, 1938) (yet another film Faulkner doctored), yelling to each other from different ships that they love each other and that they'll wait for each other? And so on.

If he did not write these and other unifying scenes—and there is no reason to believe with any measure of certainty that he didn't—then could he not have enjoyed watching them with the same need for comfort that characters from Quentin, Jason, and Darl to Tull, Vardaman, and Dewey Dell express in the fleeting moments where they manage to seize narrative sense for themselves—however violently, misdirectedly, even unsuccessfully—where their author has withdrawn it? In the opening of *The Big Sleep*, General Sternwood (Charles Waldron)—who looks like a parodic image of Faulkner himself—sits in a wheel chair in the conservatory of his mansion and though he himself abstains because of health concerns, he offers the private detective Marlowe (Bogart) a brandy and tells him he may smoke if he wishes. "A nice state of affairs," the General remarks sardonically, "when a man has to indulge his vices by proxy." Could Faulkner not also have been indulging in such pleasures by proxy—the pleasure of watching a narrative come to an assuring close through watching, even writing, its achievement in others, getting from the screen what he so regularly withheld from his own modernist characters? If so, then it would mean that the Faulkner who wrote for the movies was not very different from the one who went to them growing up in Oxford, those movies whose alluring fantasies of narrative unity made their way into some of the least "trash and junk" writing he ever produced.

■ ■

At approximately the mathematical center of Roberto Rossellini's watershed neorealist World War II drama, *Roma, città aperta* (*Rome, Open City*, 1945), what the film had prepared us to consider a love story between two Resistance fighters, Francesco (Francesco Grandjacquet) and his pregnant fiancée Pina (Anna Magnani), is abruptly cut short. Francesco has been captured by German SS troops for his suspected protection of communist and antifascist leader Giorgio Manfredi (Marcello Pagliero) and is being driven away along with other insurgents. In an act of blind terror and love, Pina frees herself from the grasp of an officer by slapping him in the face, sprints into the street as the van speeds away, and is instantly shot dead. Caught in a frontal long shot by Ubaldo Arata's camera, Pina's final moment is of her grasping helplessly at the air, at Francesco, at a life they could have had but that the war aborts just as it does their unborn child (fig. 32).

Her gesture captures, too, the dread of Dewey Dell: "too soon too soon too soon." "It is because in the wild and outraged earth too soon too soon too soon. . . . *That's what they mean by the womb of time: the agony and the despair of spreading bones, the hard girdle in which lie the outraged entrails of events.*"[139] Just as Faulkner leaves his characters to weather a present tense they manage only with enormous difficulty, abandoned to a stream

FIGURE 32. Pina grasping at Francesco in *Rome, Open City* (Roberto Rossellini, 1945).

of experience unmoored from authorial protection, Pina's raised hand asks for formal solace.

The object of her panicked stare is Francesco, but it is also Rossellini, Arata, the production team, us. Pina reaches forward in search of a more merciful authorship, a supplication that the film, like Faulkner in *As I Lay Dying*, answers only through internal and thus inadequate means. As Pina's living son Marcello charges to her side screaming "Mama! Mama! Mama!"—themselves echoes of Dewey Dell's "too soon too soon" or Vardaman's "You kilt her!"—the priest Don Pietro Pallegrini (Aldo Fabrizi) holds her limp body in an inverted pose of the Pietà.

An avid reader of Faulkner, Rossellini was one of the grandfathers of Italian neorealism, a transformative cinematic movement beginning in the 1940s that capitalized on film's capacity for the automatic capture of reality and that laid the groundwork for film's own properly modernist moment in the midcentury.[140] Drawing on the poetic realism of filmmakers such as Jean Renoir and Marcel Carné, neorealism was praised most famously by *Cahier du cinéma*'s André Bazin for calling systematically on film's documentary proclivities, disrupting narrative unity, relying regularly on nonprofessional actors, and privileging on-location shooting rather than the artificial worlds of the studio. *Rome, Open City*, for instance, was itself shot too soon—not only in the streets of Rome but also as the war was still happening. The brutal preclusion of Pina's and Francesco's love story thus extends from the film's critical interrogation of artifice, the power of the love story in particular to obscure the horrors of war, poverty, and economic desperation. In the classical Hollywood melodramas of Garbo, the love story is the sole motivating force of the films' narratives and potent in its capacity to render inconsequential the prohibitions of material reality (so, too, in *Lilac Time*, where Gary Cooper's character is effectively brought back from the dead to reunite with his wartime lover, Jeannie). *Rome, Open City*, meanwhile, kills off Pina halfway through the film so as to liberate our affective investments from the immersive grip of the love plot and instead force us to confront the indifference of war to expectations of narrative wholeness and romantic attachment.

This book concludes by discussing a midcentury filmmaker intimately familiar with the poetic and neorealist traditions but best known for indulging in the affordances of artifice and the emotional heights of romantic love. In his complex engagement with the dialectic of realism and aesthetic illusion, Max Ophuls's cinema suggests that even knowledge of the violence underpinning that most ideologically powerful of all plots—the cinematic love story—is not enough to dispel our desire for its fulfillment. For Rossellini indeed does not succeed in liberating our affective investments. Pina's pose is a mirror image of our own, reaching out toward the screen, horrified that her and Francesco's story ends here, right now, too soon.

CODA

Max Ophuls
On Love and Finitude

> *When the commonplace "We all must die" transforms itself suddenly into the acute consciousness "I must die—and soon," then death grapples us, and his fingers are cruel; afterwards he may come to fold us in his arms as our mother did, and our last moment of dim earthly discerning may be like the first.*
>
> GEORGE ELIOT, *Middlemarch*

We end this story by seeing how plot became an object of ambivalence in cinema's own properly modernist moment of the midcentury and how it became entangled with a concern with love and the end, our ends. Here we will go inside longing, allowing the acute immersive faculties of film to temporarily suspend our ability—or desire—to theorize. We will do so by way of the films of German-born filmmaker Max Ophuls, particularly his second French period and more specifically still his most cherished masterpiece, *The Earrings of Madame de . . .* (1953).

Theorizations of the time line of cinema's modernism abound, and they are by no means synonymous with those of literature's now emphatically plural modernisms.[1] Moves similar in spirit to the new modernist studies' temporal, geographical, and disciplinary expansion of literary modernism have been made in film studies, a disciplinary practice exacerbated, no doubt, by the fact that according to some (such as Sergei Eisenstein), film augurs an intrinsic aesthetic modernity, and according to others (such as Michael Fried), is inherently antimodernist because of its immersive faculties.[2] Scholars have made compelling arguments for the aesthetic modernism of films as disparate in style, theme, and release date as Robert Bresson's *Au hasard Balthazar* (1966) and Robert Wiene's *The Cabinet of Dr. Caligari* (1920), Fernand Léger's *Ballet mécanique* (1925) and Akira Kurosawa's *Rashomon* (1950), Luis Buñuel's *Un chien andalou* (1929) and Stan Brakhage's *Mothlight* (1963).[3]

I focus on Ophuls not because he represents cinematic modernism in any paradigmatic sense, though his most influential work did emerge in the 1950s, the period of the so-called great auteurs, which Fredric Jameson has argued is cinema's outwardly recognizable modernist moment.[4] To the contrary, although Ophuls is now recognized as a master filmmaker whose signature tracking shots and self-conscious embrace of artifice have exercised tremendous influence on the history of global art cinema, his work was long accused of frivolity, empty formalism, and effeminate unseriousness. Like George Cukor and to a lesser extent Josef von Sternberg, Ophuls was considered a so-called women's director—one thought to tell stories about women for women—and this damned him to the critical margins.

But we will see that Ophuls's work is essential to an examination of modernism, ambivalence, and cinematic storytelling precisely because his films are marked by a modernist sensibility while *not* encouraging in its viewers anything approaching exhaustive ironic detachment. Indeed, the political provocation of Ophuls's late cinema lies in how it elicits in its viewers a combination of criticality and what are often considered its various antitheses: immersion, identification, and profound investment. Ophuls's love stories—particularly the love story between Louise de . . . and the Baron Donati—get us to feel the desire for formal wholeness while also letting us know the material realities of political violence and colonial brutality that that wholeness supports. Through a mode of knowing identification, self-reflective immersion, *Madame de . . .* (as it is called in the original French) shows us what it feels like to *be* one who—like the characters of Larsen, Barnes, and Faulkner—seeks the solace of consequence despite all that it costs. And Ophuls accomplishes this, we will see, through a radical amplification of cinema's immersive powers. He elicits in us a mode of identification so intensified that it puts us in touch with our own mortality and in so doing makes the stakes of the lovers' union, the success of the love plot, feel a disarmingly urgent necessity.

Ophuls is often venerated for the irony with which he approaches his subject matter. His signature long tracking shots, along with his penchant for ornate interiors, elaborate sets, and brilliant costumes that bring to life the fin de siècle European scenarios to which he repeatedly returned, have given his cinema the reputation of having a distinctively synthetic quality, profoundly in touch with its own status as artifice. Often contrasted with the grandfather of French poetic realism, Jean Renoir, Ophuls had long been criticized for exhibiting a decadent "emptiness of technique,"[5] indulging in a cinematic formalism that Lindsay Anderson, in an especially damning review in *Sight and Sound* in 1954, called a "distracting" and "gratuitous" "visual *frou-frou*."[6] But once championed by the *Cahiers du cinéma* editorial group, that same textual excess that his detractors condemned became the basis for his celebration as a modernist. Implicitly referring to *Lola Montes* (1955)—Ophuls's final film and the one that put him on the avant-garde's radar—early advocate Claude Beylie, for instance, writes that "even as he exalts spectacle (if only in the delirium of his camera), Ophuls denounces its profound vanity." It is as if Ophuls "denies the cinema," Beylie concludes, "after having affirmed it to its highest degree."[7] And the ironic distance that his films seem to take from the romantic and spectacular excesses they depict, a penchant for critical estrangement that so many have been wont to find in Ophuls, is supported by the aesthetic archive that shaped him, not least his early embeddedness within the German avant-garde and his fondness for literary figures such as Guy de Maupassant, Stendhal, Gustave Flaubert, and Austrian satirist Arthur Schnitzler, all of whose works deeply shaped his cinema in the form of overt reference or source material for adaptation.[8]

Central to the discussion of Ophulsian formalism has been what many consider to be the "antipsychological bias" of his films' treatment of character.[9] Deleuze refers to Ophuls's films as "crystalline perfections" that "let no outside subsist: there is no outside of . . . the [Ophulsian] film set," he claims, "but only an obverse where the characters who disappear or die go, abandoned by life which thrusts itself back into the film set."[10] The orb-like enclosure of Ophulsian artifice indeed powerfully brings into view the synthetic nature of his characters. Whether perceived as suggestive functions of masterful composition or bloodless forces of mere form, Ophuls's characters are markedly evident as textual formations—so much like characters that any sense of their personhood remains tenuous.

Accordingly, Ophuls's cinema tends to have a tenuous relationship, too, to plot. To be sure, his films do not lack plot. The ones he made for Hollywood in the 1940s, for instance, are heavily plotted not least because of the creative mandates of the studios. And even in the films where he was able to exercise more creative freedom, plot is never jettisoned entirely (though certain films have especially episodic structures, such as *La ronde*, *Lola Montes*, and *Le plaisir*).[11] Rather, Ophuls's films typically accentuate the *fact* that plots organize narrative movement to such a degree that he rarely allows us to lose sight of their structural seams. And often plot emerges in Ophuls's cinema as a source of social and formal restriction, an artificial and sometimes even fatal form of aesthetic bondage.

His *La signora di tutti* (1934), a damning representation of the vampiric demands of the mainstream film industry, is exemplary in this regard. Based on the melodramatic novel of the same name by Salvatore Gotta, the film forecloses narrative immersion in its plot by thematizing the formal operations at work in plotting. The film centers on a screen actress named Gaby Doriot (Isa Miranda) who gets systematically absorbed into sexual scandals despite her attempts to live an uneventful life. Bringing calamity wherever she goes—the juiciest plots one could ask for, replete with infidelity, filial betrayal, and suicide—Gaby comes to represent a casualty of the process of narrativization Ophuls sees as obsessing the mainstream film industry at the expense of its female stars. Because Ophuls showed interest throughout his career in the lives of women and the condition of womanhood, feminist film theory has had a long and intimate history with his work and has made the most productive and perceptive use of the overtly synthetic quality of his characters and plots, doing much to rescue Ophuls from his prior marginalization on the grounds not just of his formalism but also his investment in melodrama. Part of the theoretical and political effort of feminist approaches to Ophuls has involved showing how the synthetic quality of his characters allows them to operate not as singular individuals with psychic depth but as synecdochic representatives of forces—social, economic, political, and formal—much vaster than themselves.

But in the process of unpacking those synecdochic functions, feminist film theory, like the midcentury avant-garde before it, has tended to disavow the pathetic intensity of Ophuls's cinema, largely theorizing away the affective heights of his cinema by insisting on his ironic treatment of that melodramatic pathos, recuperating it as politically emancipatory, or explaining it in terms of the formal affordances of camera movement, thus relegating it to the safely modernist register of film form and style.[12] The "interest of Ophuls' films lies," Susan White writes, "in their analytical approach to the process of marginalization." "Ophuls was a modernist," Mulvey claims even more straightforwardly; "Although he loved the kind of cinema, these melodramas of romantic failure, through which he earned his living and found creative expression, evidence exists across his films that he always looked ironically both on the illusion of love and the cinema illusion."[13] Despite its flair for the affective heights of romance and melodrama, Ophuls's cinema has remained, in our collective critical imagination, immanently analytical.

And *The Earrings of Madame de . . .*—his "compendium," as Mulvey puts it, in which themes that preoccupied him for his entire career come to full aesthetic fruition[14]—is thought to be arguably his most sophisticated analysis. "If the military man," Mulvey writes, referring to the protagonist's husband, General André de . . . , represents "the stop of death that will bring its story to its end," then "the 'womanizer,'" figured in the character of the Baron Donati, "brings motion to the story through his ability to create emotion." In *Madame de* . . . , "Ophuls frames abstract and structural problems: the relation of desire to narrative drive or of death to narrative's termination, and these problems cannot be detached from the movement of the cinema itself, the destiny of the motion picture machine, in which the narrative function of emotion is to enable the film to blossom into sequences of pure cinematic movement."[15] Mulvey's argument (like many other feminist readings of Ophuls) is so convincing as to feel incontrovertible. But in lifting all story material to the level of discourse—explaining content in terms inevitably of form and the materiality of cinematicity—these arguments corral the ecstatic heights of the film's stories. In explaining those heights as thematic extensions of film form, they explain away the affective excesses of the failed love story on which Ophuls has indeed given us ironic perspective but to whose outcomes we nevertheless grow deeply attached.

Ophuls's cinema (and certainly *Madame de* . . .) *is* deeply analytical—arguably so much so as to anticipate, with Nabokovian shrewdness, its own hermeneutics. But over and above the analytical quality of Ophuls's films there remains an irreducible affective residue linked to plot that we must confront if we are to grasp the full terms and force of the Ophulsian provocation. Disavowing, or theorizing away, what *Madame de* . . . makes us *feel* compromises our understanding of it. Ophuls was just as invested in Balzacian melodrama as he was in Schnitzlerian critique, just as indebted to the Romantic excesses of Goethe as he was to the acerbic cynicism of Maupassant and the analytical reserve of Stendhal. His aesthetic archive, which we've long acknowledged was deeply informed by European (proto) modernism skeptical of the nineteenth-century pleasures of plot, was also textured with aesthetic traditions for which plot, emotion, identification, and aesthetic immersion were not treated with irony. Ophuls was just as invested in the immersive dramas of the *texte de plaisir* as he was in the stylistic negativity of the *texte de jouissance*,[16] and this ambivalence emerges in comments he made about the cinematic medium, for which he left his career in the theater: "Technology has reached a stage in our profession," he remarked of film, "where it is a threat to our heart"; "drama," he also said, "cannot be mass produced."[17] In downplaying the significance of these elements of Ophuls's aesthetic sensibility—his investment in "the heart," in "drama"—or in recuperating the Ophulsian dramatic as merely ironic—or bent, as Heather Love might put it, toward "political utility"—we lose sight of the provocatively difficult, ambivalent position Ophuls puts us in, which is to make us long for the very thing we know to do harm.

Madame de . . . is especially exemplary of this powerful double feeling. Just as the film lays bare the imperial violence and gendered oppression on which the formation of the liberal individual and the romance plot is predicated, it elicits in us the desire for the lovers nevertheless to have gotten together. The film expresses ambivalence toward the structures of imperial and patriarchal violence it shows to underpin cinematic spectacle and the love plot; and, more powerfully still, it elicits that ambivalence in *us*. No matter how analytical his cinema may be, how negatively it pushes against the forms of bourgeois normativity that were embedded, too, within classical cinematic style, it nevertheless draws from us a disarming desire not just for plot, but, as in the case of *Madame de . . .* , for the lovers' union, arguably the most conservative of plot structures. *Madame de . . .* simultaneously exposes the psychic, social, and political apparatuses of oppression and property relations that form the basis of the romance plot and forces us to confront our desire for the terms of that plot nevertheless to be fulfilled. In lingering on rather than denying the obduracy of that longing—despite the film's careful exposure of what the lovers' union would symbolically support, its exposure of *whom* we are identifying with—we gain access not just to a critical perspective on the various forms of unfreedom embodied in the love plot but also, and far more powerfully, to what it feels like to want it anyway.

Ophuls accomplishes this through the deployment of a haptic aurality that indexes the sentient presence of the body of his protagonist, Louise. In love and in pain, Louise's body, which has otherwise appeared immaculately constructed, becomes suddenly and strangely audible to us in a way that elicits a terrifying, rather than soothing, identification—one based less in the mimetic nature of character and more arrestingly and uncomfortably in a recognition of what Toril Moi, borrowing from Stanley Cavell, would call the "finitude" of personhood.[18] Emphatically not escapist (where escapism suggests a temporary and pleasurable attenuation of the self), the identification Ophuls encourages with the character of Louise provokes a radical recognition of the material and temporal boundaries of the self, the hic et nunc of the mortal body, not just hers, but ours, as we watch and hear hers. This form of identification elicits the "stupid" or "simple metaphysics" Roland Barthes considered photography to call forth but that film does as well.[19] And that metaphysics finds articulation in phrases devastating in their plainness, such as "I have a body, too. I, too, am living. I, like her, will die one day." The effect of this vertiginous grappling with one's mortal limits, to borrow George Eliot's term from my opening epigraph—or what Jean-Paul Sartre would refer to as nausea—is that Ophuls encourages us not just to examine intellectually the love plot as a proxy for apparatuses of political violence and social constraint but to grow affectively intimate with the urgency of the desire for the lover's union: to feel what it would feel like to have that union be a vital need. To *be* the one loving, the one losing.

Plotting out deep amorous spaces through an aesthetics of depth and natural space, Ophuls articulates a kind of love plot—more specifically, a kind of causality generated by love—capable of effecting novelty in a world shown to be otherwise run by a regime of narrative and historical sameness and, by extension, a meaningless cyclicality of desire. As such, this love, predicated on nonattainment—the loss of the beloved—is shown to have the potential of undoing the very structures of patriarchal capitalism and imperial conquest governing the world of the characters. In giving us access to the affective urgency of that allure—in imbuing us with the affective urgency of the lover—Ophuls asks us to grow familiar with so as to understand better what the feeling is like, what the existential stakes are felt to be, of being drawn to the very experiences that soothe but that further entrench a politics of unfreedom.

THE PLOT

A well-known cinematic tour de force among film scholars but perhaps new to scholars of literary modernism, *Madame de . . .* is Ophuls's penultimate film and what many consider to be his masterwork, "the final and definitive version" of the triangular love story he was experimenting with since his first film, *Liebelei* (1932), adapted from Schnitzler's play of the same name.[20] Liberally adapted from a 1951 novella by Louise de Vilmorin, *Madame de . . .* follows the life of French aristocrat the Countess Louise de . . . (Danielle Darrieux) and her husband, General André de . . . (Charles Boyer). The couple exhibits the distant cordiality of the typical Ophulsian upper-class couple. They barely touch, they sleep in separate rooms, and their exchanges of witty and superficial banter suggest a convenient social and political partnership rather than a passionate romance. One day, unbeknownst to André, Louise sells the earrings he gave her as a wedding gift so that she can pay off her debts. She successfully sustains the lie, convincing André that she has lost the jewels, until an article in the newspaper speculates that they have been stolen. The jeweler returns the earrings to André despite having promised Louise his discretion; André, out of respect for the jeweler and to protect his own image as a knowing husband, repurchases them and silently plants them among Louise's belongings. Upon finding them, Louise—famous for her perfidies—masks her bewilderment with feigned surprise, and the case seems to be closed. André then decides to give the earrings to his mistress (Lia Di Leo), of whom he's grown tired, and she takes them with her on a trip to Constantinople. While there, she gambles away her money and to compensate for her losses sells the earrings. They are then bought by the Italian Baron, Fabrizio Donati (played by Italian neorealist director and film star Vittorio De Sica and thought by many to be based on Stendhal's Fabrizio del Dongo of *The Charterhouse of Parma*). The Baron travels to France by way of Switzerland, where he meets Louise. They fall in love, he gifts her the earrings, and she pretends never to have seen them before. André sees her wearing the earrings, and knowing that she must have acquired them from the Baron, tells the Baron of their origin. When given the chance to tell the Baron the truth, Louise lies and says that they were a gift from her mother. The Baron ends the affair, feeling that the authenticity of their love has been irreparably betrayed by her deception, from which he had thought himself protected. Made jealous by Louise's grief, André forces Louise to gift the earrings to his niece. Louise obeys. The niece sells the earrings back to the jeweler out of financial need. Unable to recover from her heartache, Louise sells her belongings in order to repurchase the earrings. André challenges the Baron to a duel in which the Baron is killed by André's first shot. Louise rushes through the forest to try to stop the duel, but dies, presumably of an overwhelmed heart, moments after hearing the shot from off-screen that kills Donati.

Evidently concerned with the narrative contortions generated by chance, coincidence, and repetition, *Madame de . . .* , as critics have long noted, makes explicit from its very opening title card the processes of narrativization that it deploys.[21] The title card reads, "Madame de . . . était une femme très élégante, très brillante, très fêtée. Elle semblait promise à une jolie vie sans histoire." While some English subtitles translate "sans histoire" into the more figurative "uncomplicated," the term translates into English, literally, as "without story."[22] The phrase "Madame de . . . was seemingly destined to a delightful life without story" gets at the heart of the film's meditation on the friction between rote domestic plots and a form of cinematic expression based in the autonomous movement of the camera. Through set design and camera movement, *Madame de . . .* depicts the relationship between cinema and narrativity as fundamentally conflicted. Dealing in a suggestive visual essentialism, *Madame de . . .* casts film and plot as antagonistic forces working against one another, where the "cinematic" emerges as a mode based in the freedom of movement while plot gets conflated with what we might call casual domestic stories, happenings that, though they take narrative shape, are nevertheless so habitual as to lack permanent effects. If, to borrow Tzvetan Todorov's formulation, narrative is the process by which an initial equilibrium is transformed and reestablished into a second, slightly modified equilibrium, then we might say that the world of *Madame de...* is structured such that it reestablishes equilibrium quickly and easily. And this is because the initial equilibrium is so structurally powerful—built as it is on a foundation of aristocratic patriarchal imperialism—that the disturbances are themselves endemic to, anticipated by, that equilibrium and thus do not cause structurally disruptive effects. In other words, like in *Quicksand*, *Nightwood*, and Benjy's section of *The Sound and the Fury*, although effects abound and changes are felt, those changes are easily and systematically reintegrated into a regime of affective and narrative sameness. Plot in *Madame de...* flourishes, but—until the arrival of the Baron—is proleptically anticipated and thus lacking in any real consequences.

This anticipatory narrativity is conveyed from the film's opening scene. The title card initiating the action of the film reads, "Probably nothing would have happened, had it not been for these jewels." In immediate response to the deictic reference to "these jewels," the opening shot fades in on a close-up of Louise's gloved hand opening the bottom drawer of a jewelry box and hanging suspended over a pair of earrings (fig. 33). Sparkling in their delicate bulk, the earrings momentarily exude haptic fascination, resisting narrative value. Still in close-up, the hand reaches for the earrings and instantly draws back, as if refusing to enlist the shiny tokens

FIGURE 33. Louise's hand goes to take the earrings from the jewelry box but hesitates, in *Madame de...* (Max Ophuls, 1953).

in an object drama. Louise then says from off-screen, "What's annoying is that they're the ones he gave me the day after our wedding." The earrings are thus commandeered by what we now know will be an ensuing plot, yanked from their proairetic facticity into a hermeneutic economy of narrative stakes.

Right from the opening shot, then, the film preempts the arrival of what Gérard Genette would call the "singulative" event that propels the plot forward, the extraordinary occurrence that breaks the quotidian, "iterative" actions of everyday life and that catalyzes plot.[23] Once the opening shot fades in, we already know that it is "these jewels" that will launch the action forward. Plot in this film clearly does not operate according to the principle of deferred significance, where knowledge is acquired over the course of the unfolding of the story. Rather, *Madame de . . .* suggests that events are already determined from the outset, and our actions merely block out, like actors on a stage, scripts that have already been written proleptically. ("The theater is an awesome thing," Robert Kuhlenkampf [Jean-Louis Barreault] tells his mistress, the actress Charlotte [Isa Miranda] in *La ronde*, "we know in advance everything that we will say.")

Plot in *Madame de . . .* may thus be a certain disturbance of the everyday, but it is a contained disturbance. While it may not be every day that Louise contemplates selling her earrings, the singularity of her decision to sell them on this day is subdued by Ophuls's choice to give the viewer the epistemic privilege of knowing what we are going to see before we see it, of knowing what Louise will do even before she does. Her breezy insouciance suggests that though there might be a degree of uncertainty and risk in selling her earrings, she does not envision this choice as disrupting her quotidian rhythms. The intrusion of the earrings' plot into the iterative scripts of Louise's life has led critics such as White to argue that the jewels "cleave in twain the otherwise undifferentiated life of a young married woman, making possible the beginning of a tale."[24] But it is not so much that Louise's life is undifferentiated as that the differentiations that do punctuate her life are, like others this book has explored, recessive, inconsequential. Their consequences, rather, are muffled by the broader system of meaning and morality that contains them. When Louise tosses the earrings into her purse, sweeps down the stairs, shuffles into the living room to have breakfast, her movements have all the ease and automaticity of familiar routines. The opening scene teaches us that the sequences of events motivating Louise's moral world and generating its stories are impermanent in their ramifications—kinetic and self-reproducing but impoverished in their ability to *effect*.

In other words, the domestic narratives of minor perfidy and betrayal that motivate Louise's and André's world do generate causality (e.g., Louise sells her earrings because she has accrued debt; the jeweler brings them back to André because he worries for his reputation). But it is a causality ultimately bereft of lasting ramifications. Little *matters* in the narrative economy of the film, and this has in large part to do with the permissiveness of its moral world. Louise's betrayal—not to mention the jeweler's, since he'd promised Louise his discretion—falls within what Daniel Morgan rightly calls the film's "acceptable forms of lying and deceit," barely offending André, who tolerates his wife's periodic disloyalties, which he has learned to expect with icy elegance.[25] Far from resulting in a narrative upheaval, the event produces in the couple an easy reconciliation. Louise apologizes to André for having lost the jewels, and as she extinguishes the candles to prepare for sleep, says, "We'll not talk about this story anymore, all right?" "Never!" André responds, "What's done is done," and with that the issue is put to bed. The "story" of the lost earrings is contained, having caused no disruption of the social, political, and aesthetic order. The earrings' initial trajectory—from André to Louise (before the film begins), from Louise to the jeweler, from the jeweler back to André—leaves uninterrupted the relentless continuity and self-perpetuation of aristocratic mores and conventions. To the contrary, the earrings are at first instrumental in showcasing—in their cyclical choreography mimetic of the signature Ophulsian waltz—how those mores operate and what their spatial and ethical limits are.

The productive, but stifled narrative causality determining the initial cycle of the earrings is rendered, too, at the level of cinematography and its relation to the film set. The famous opening long take of the film is shot remarkably closely, such that we are not given an establishing shot of Louise's boudoir, or even of Louise herself, until considerably late in the opening sequence. The scene opens and the camera tracks, pans, and tilts almost entirely in close-up—sometimes dollying out to as far as a medium shot but not out to a long shot of Louise until two minutes and thirty-five seconds into the scene. The effect of this choice is that though we recognize that the objects are exquisite, our extreme and sustained proximity to them is startling, if not suffocating. Christian Matras's cinematography is thus delicately strangling, like the diamond choker we witness Louise dangling against her throat (fig. 34). The closeness of the shot is accentuated by the recurring motif of the mirrors that adorn Louise's boudoir—and, too, in the specific mirror whose tight but gorgeous borders frame Louise's face in figure 34. Whereas naked walls would risk going unnoticed, the mirrors enclose the diegetic world by conspicuously reflecting it back onto itself, sealing it off, as Deleuze might say, from any

FIGURE 34. Louise dangling a diamond choker against her neck in *Madame de . . . .*

force that would disturb the unfolding of the narrative within. The mirrors provide limits to the kinetic and visual range of the camera by imposing a noticeable barrier to the degree of depth it can reach, reminding us of the confines of the space.

The movement of the camera, as David Bordwell argued so long ago, is among the many strategies of encouraging viewers to forget the flatness of the screen and to buy into the illusion of spatial depth. If manipulated in such a way as to mimic human movement (such as pans and tilts), the camera serves as "a persuasive surrogate for our subjective movement through an objective world." "The cues" generated by the moving camera, he continues, "supply a compelling experience of moving through space."[26] He submits that it is the tracking shot—Ophuls' signature technique—that is most effective in generating the illusion of depth. "We always noted," Bordwell quotes from filmmaker Allan Dwan, "that if we dollied past a tree, it became solid and round instead of flat."[27] In a classical film, these techniques are used to generate a successful illusion of a deep scenographic space within which we ourselves might move. Pushing those techniques to their limits, Ophuls, too, puts us in the space but makes us feel just how crowded and shallow it is. Typical of much of Ophuls's cinema, it is as if when the camera moves around the mirrored rooms of Louise's boudoir it is shooting inside the restricted but beautiful interior of an enormous box. Morgan has argued that the virtuosity of Ophuls's camera movements lay in its ability to offer an alternative, floating perspective on the moral world of the characters, expressing a position from which we can examine their ethical limits;[28] but here, precisely in its nigh-constant movement, Ophuls's camera lends a claustrophobic feeling to the interiors within which it circulates (recall, too, how the delirious camera movement inside the nightclub of *Le plaisir*'s "Le masque" episode is a stylistic extension of the old man's spinning to the point of such exhaustion that his mask of youth nearly suffocates him to death). Like Louise's curtailed strides within the narrowed boundaries of her day dress—to whose audible swishes we will return later in this chapter—the camera can move and see only so much.

SHALLOW DEPTHS

Central to this book's inquiry, especially in our considerations of Larsen and Barnes, was the problem of the dimensionality of character as it pertains both to the protagonists of the nineteenth-century bildungsroman and to the effects of visual verisimilitude in the dominant narrative cinema. The problem of dimensionality—what I called Helga Crane's inconceivable dimensionality, or the status of Barnes's characters as ubersynthetic, words flat on the page—is critical, too, to *Madame de . . . .* In this film, spatial depths—or their inhibition—become a key factor in the aesthetic language through which Ophuls articulates the limitations placed on the causal efficacy of narrative action and by extension Louise's affective repertoire. Spatial depth at the level of decor and mise-en-scène becomes a visual metaphor for character.

There is indeed a refusal of depth in Louise's boudoir, and counterintuitively so, considering the extent to which Jean d'Eaubonne's set design accentuates the motif of the compartment. The compartments that proliferate throughout the first long take—jewelry boxes, containers, closets—reduce to surfaces, since what occupies them suppresses the volumes they promise. The jewelry box in the opening shot, for example, is filled with multiple chambers (fig. 33). But they are all conspicuously shallow, and many of them contain jewelry that, by ricocheting the light from the lamps off themselves, appear as tiny reflective surfaces. Other of the box's compartments are closed by little doors with miniature scenes painted on them that encourage the look to rest on top rather than enter into the small apertures into which two of them allow a teasing glimpse. Similarly, when Louise opens her first closet, it is onto a wall of closed

FIGURE 35. Drawers inside Louise's closet in *Madame de...* .

drawers; and her last two closets are so stuffed with clothing that they, too, suppress their depth, an effect accentuated by the extreme tightness of the framing (fig. 35). As a result, even though Louise's hand glides over and touches intermittently the materials she inspects, there is a slippery dumbness to the objects, a strange deathly quality to them (her dresses so many empty skins, her furs so many dead ones), since the structures and textures that ostensibly provide depth instead seem to collapse into two dimensions. We are dealing, in Louise's boudoir, in a form of depthless depth, self-negating volumes.

An aesthetics of shallow depth was in fact what Ophuls had in mind when conceiving of the character of Louise. According to his costume designer, George Annenkov, Ophuls explained to Darrieux that her goal must be to capture the "emptiness" of Louise's life as a countess. "You must ... incarnate *emptiness*, inexistence," he told her. "Not fill the emptiness," he insisted, but "*be* it." You must be "inexistence ... extravagantly dressed," he told her.[29] Like the depthless compartments that populate her boudoir, the architecture of Louise's character is based on a fundamental spatial contradiction. Not unlike Helga, Louise is at once vacated and pure surface, both a volume and a plane—a self-contradiction represented in the flat shadow cast by her body against the drawers in her closet in figure 35, whose closed doors confirm the unavailability of the recesses they presage.

It is represented, too, in the feathers sticking out of those drawers, which seems to say: yes, we are full, but we are full of fluff. An emptiness extravagantly dressed. If depth of character is generated over time and through experience, but plot in this film operates cyclically and without world-disrupting consequences, then Louise's emptiness (expertly performed by Darrieux) is only logical, and the limits placed on the camera's movement and visual reach reflect those etiological limits.

Indeed, Louise's voluminous flatness—her "inexistent" emptiness—follows from how we have seen plot function in this film. The quickness and ease with which the first cycle of the earrings was initiated, allowed to operate, and then ended suggests a vision of plot as a limited semantic container. Just as the camera does not have much room to move or depths to see, plot in this film tethers experience to systems of explanation such as familial or religious authority, harnessing Louise's desires and motivations to mechanisms of narrative containment. As she contemplates her decision to pawn the earrings, she hums to herself that were her mother there, she would offer maternal advice, or when her Bible falls on the ground as she combs through her closet, she says that she needs it now more than ever. And when she goes to the church to ask Saint Genevieve to make the jeweler buy her earrings, she calls on divine intervention to keep her actions and their outcomes yoked to cosmically organizing apparatuses. (The Church's loss of collective authority is signified by the emptiness of the church but for one praying soldier who sneaks a peek at Louise's rear end as she shuffles down the aisle).

Plot and plotting in *Madame de . . .* , then, find their corollary in an aesthetics of choked depths in which productive but ultimately stifled systems of causality circulate. Ophuls thus transports to the cinema a Flaubertian critique of the *texte de plaisir*, where the depthless depths of the decor, the fluff-filled void of Louise's character (whose proximity to Emma Bovary has long been noted), and the smothered causality of the narrative actions illuminate the spatial confines of the "readerly" text. (What are the dumb objects in Louise's boudoir if not also invocations of the young Charles Bovary's equally inscrutable hat?)[30] Ophuls's cinema indeed throws into relief the confines of the readerly text—held together by what Barthes calls a "logical paste" and always "preparing its defense against the enemy that may force it to acknowledge the scandal of some illogicality"[31]—as themselves *spatial* confines, since the film set becomes a figure in its own right, persistently drawing attention to itself and the ways it immures its subjects within narrative forms.

The little we have discussed gives reason to look somewhat askance at the standard take on Ophuls as the consummate filmmaker of artifice, since his interiors—so often metonyms for the set—emerge in his films again and again as aesthetically productive but ultimately restrictive, if not fatal, spaces. Ophuls's interpreters often discuss his work in terms of a distinct "will to compose" linked to his background in the theater. The "tight weave of Ophuls' compositions," the sense they give of artificial enclosure and insulation from living nature,[32] has led scholars to believe that Ophuls's cinema belongs to the realm of "baroque architecture" rather than neorealism or the detached observational register of the cinéma vérité. The Ophulsian baroque is a "form," Beylie writes, "that contrasts with life"; his reliance on the motifs of staircases, cages, and mirrors demonstrates his will to exaggerate and contort reality, rather than to deliver it, believing as he does that "reality is less beautiful than its reflection."[33] But as we have already seen in the case of *Madame de . . .*, his attitude toward the ornate interiors that populate his films was far more complicated than these accounts might lead us to believe, since the set emerges as a gorgeous but strangling enclosure, leaving the outside to hold the promise of liberation.

Examples of suffocating interiors abound in Ophuls's oeuvre.[34] But *La signora di tutti* is the most salient precursor to *Madame de . . .* in the way that it presents the natural world—the outside—as a potential space of refuge from plot. Whereas plot in *Madame de . . .* grows affiliated with rote narratives of aristocratic domesticity, in *La signora di tutti* plot becomes synonymous with scandal, lethal narratives of gendered shame, the fallen woman, and the femme fatale. The utopian alternative—a state of contingency unburdened by narrative responsibility—grows stylistically associated with organic matter and the haptic, a visuality that resists narrative sense, eliciting longing for optical touch rather than knowledge of plot. Ophuls maps Gaby's longing for a life safe from narrative intrigue onto a stylistic drama of a filmic contingency persistently violated and destroyed by the contrivances of film production. Understanding this will, in turn, allow us to understand more fully the significance of the figure of nature in *Madame de . . .* and what kinds of plots and passions it promises.

A BRIEF EXCURSION INTO THE GARDEN

The primal scandal or consequential event that disturbs the initial equilibrium of Gaby Doriot's life in *La signora di tutti* happens before the film begins: when she is a young schoolgirl, her music teacher, Professor Sommi, falls in love with her despite being married with children. Sommi abandons his family and moves abroad, leaving her to experience the social consequences of the unrealized affair. The event makes Gaby the center of malicious gossip—popular interest that anticipates her eventual status as a movie star. In its critique of the narrative sensationalism of the mainstream cinema, *La signora di tutti* casts Gaby's desire to attain a state of contingency irrecuperable by the operations of plot and plotting in terms of a longing for another cinematic style. Ophuls comes to associate Gaby with a force within the filmic medium itself toward a kind of aimless recording anathema to the plot-cranking apparatus of the mainstream film industry. In a pivotal scene early in the film in which Gaby's family discusses strategies for smothering the rumors that have begun to depict Gaby as a sexual deviant, Ophuls establishes a relationship between Gaby and a realist aesthetics, an editing and cinematography that taps into the lyricism of objects resistant to narrative frames of reference. The night the family learns of Gaby's alleged affair with Sommi, Gaby's father gets up from the dinner table, calling Gaby's stepmother and sister Anna into an adjacent room while Gaby is left to clean up. Anna comes back momentarily to remind Gaby to eat, then retreats again and closes the door behind her. Ophuls then divides the scene into two separate planes, one visual, one aural.

The camera stays on Gaby tidying up the dining room while we hear her family in the kitchen heatedly discussing—narrating—the scandal. However, instead of showing us what is indisputably the center of narrative action (the family argument), the camera stays on Gaby performing a series of mundane tasks, as if shooting the wrong material. The camera resists capturing the plot, in other words, preferring instead to linger on the narratively unintriguing movements of housework: we watch as Gaby methodically picks up the plates, places them in a tray, and walks out of the dining room and into the kitchen on the other end of the house. Crucially, the camera remains in the dining room so as to capture her in a deep-focus extreme long shot, accentuating the depth of field (fig. 36). Markedly realist in its aesthetics, the shot, never cutting once, stays on her as she first places the plates on the kitchen counter in the deep background and then walks back toward the dining room with the empty tray hanging at her side, stopping on her way to pet the family dog leashed to a coat stand situated halfway. When Gaby finally returns to the dining room, we hear the family argument escalating to the point where it sounds like her father has struck Anna. But we cannot be sure, since Ophuls still displaces this narrative intrigue from our visual attention. The long take stays on Gaby and her domestic work, even catching the slight flinch of her body as she hears Anna being struck.

It is the trope of the garden, however, the world of organic matter, that comes to promise Gaby seclusion from narratability. It emerges as a utopic

FIGURE 36. Gaby in the kitchen at the far end of the hallway in *La signora di tutti* (Max Ophuls, 1934).

plot of land to be roamed and cultivated rather than imbued with narrative significance. But it is indeed merely a promise, since even as the garden offers a haven from the narratives of the fallen woman that threaten to subsume her—affiliated as it becomes with an extranarrative visual and haptic utopia—it is vulnerable to violation by the optics, if not mechanics, of filming.

One day, Gaby is working in the garden behind her family home when a group of young men on the opposite side of the gate gossip about her audibly. One of the young men is named Roberto Nanni, who wants to invite her to a dance. His friend protests, reminding him of her alleged affair with Sommi. A fistfight ensues, but one of the men manages to throw a wooden ruler over the gate, and it falls among the flowers and soil that Gaby is tilling. The men run off, and the camera dollies in to a close-up of the flowerbed where Gaby looks for the ruler. The camera momentarily hesitates over a daisy plant in extreme close-up, so close that the image momentarily blurs. It hovers there for a full two seconds as the tiny flowers bob to and fro before panning slightly to the left to show Gaby's soil-covered hands in close-up holding the ruler. As Gaby stands up, the camera stays in close-up on her hands—stays, in fact, for an unnecessarily long time, since the ruler has only the letters *R* and *N* written on it and are legible at an instant (fig. 37). The length of the close-up grants the viewer the time to look—as we had just moments ago looked at the cluster of bouncing daisies or, in the prior scene, at Gaby as she performed housework—at the soil encrusted on Gaby's hands. It allows us the time to notice the contrast between the unformed earth caked on her flesh and the ruler's artificially worked wood. The ruler, moreover, is flat, both in its shape and its visual appeal. One reads it immediately and without difficulty, the eye sliding swiftly across the letters. By contrast, the textured, or what Giuliana Bruno might call the "topographical," nuance of the soil is visually compelling in its layering, distinctively haptic in its draw for us to feel it with our eyes.[35]

First theorized by Austrian art historian Aloïs Reigl (and most influentially discussed in recent film theory by Laura U. Marks in her *The Skin of the Film*), the haptic refers to a kind of visuality that synaesthetically conjures the act of touching.[36] It is a mode of perception that evokes a sense of contact rather than distant observation, a visual "caress," to borrow Marks's phrase, of the object of vision. Writing specifically about early

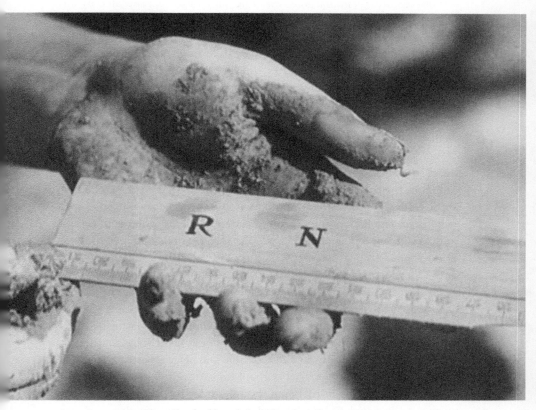

FIGURE 37. Gaby's soil-caked hands holding the ruler the men have tossed into the garden in *La signora di tutti*.

cinema, Antonia Lant and Noël Burch view film's access to haptic visuality as the result of its unique spatiality. Film is an "utterly flat medium of presentation," Lant writes, "insubstantial, without texture or material." But the cinematic image nevertheless evokes "a fuller illusion of the physicality and exactness" of things "than any prior art."[37] We see the juxtaposition of these two visual and spatial modes—film's "false depth" as Michel Chion puts it[38]—in the image of Gaby's hands holding the ruler, one haptic and evocative of three-dimensionality, the other flat and observationally distant. A moist clump of soil sticks between the thumb and forefinger of her right hand; a short string of root hangs off her left thumb. Threatening meaning with an excess of mimesis, these details produce a Barthesian "third meaning" that works in excess of narrative signification and invites our haptic engagement by offering the illusion of depth, fullness, and textural variety. Whereas we *feel* the encrustations of soil with our eyes, the gaze slips past or off the ruler. The ruler is slick, uniform, and without texture. Its implacable two-dimensionality is accentuated by the shadow it casts on Gaby's left fingers that curl around its bottom edge; the shadows highlight the contrast between the ruler's stubborn frontality and the articulated depth of her hand in space, referring back, in miniature, to the spatial distinction between the flatness of the door Anna closes behind her and the depth of the hallway whose length Gaby travels back and forth.

Rather than a symbol of her soiled reputation, then, the haptic earth encrusted on Gaby's hands is a stylistic extension of her yearning to transcend the narratable and to exist outside of plots. When the ruler lands in the garden, Gaby's father asks, "Has something been ruined?" And though she assures him no, she is tragically wrong, since the penetration of the garden by the ruler heralds the reintroduction of lethal plots—embodied in the worked, broken wood—into her utopically unstoried life out of the public eye. The flatness of the ruler nestled inside the volume of Gaby's soil-caked hand foreshadows the way her image will be flattened into the iconography of movie posters (see fig. 38). Indeed, elaborating this scene's foreshadowing of Gaby's fate as a film star, Ophuls even works into it the mechanics and spatiality of cinematic looking, staging the scene according to a strategic division of planes: Gaby is behind a gate—a screen—while the men in front of it gossip and fight over her without addressing her. This small audience, in other words, talks about her as if she were not there at all, as if she were inhabiting a different time and place altogether and thus making of her the present absence that forms the ontological basis of the cinematic image. The intrusion of the ruler into the garden thus augurs the process by which Gaby will herself be robbed of volume, flattened into a technologically reproducible image.

FIGURE 38. Gaby's face on a poster once she has become a movie star in *La signora di tutti*.

The figure of the garden as a potentially utopic space outside scandal emerges again in the scene when Gaby and Roberto (the "R N" of the wooden ruler) begin what promises at first to be a romance free of disturbance. As they roam flaneuristically in Roberto's gardens, Ophuls constructs a haptic cinema of experience—reciprocal and phenomenological—that flouts the stylistic mandates of the classical cinema. Together, the couple paces along a garden path surrounded by plants. They slowly advance in a medium tracking shot, the camera placed behind the plants on their left. The plants intermittently obstruct our view of the couple, emphasizing the multiple planes and deep staging of the scene. The placement of the camera behind the plants elicits our desire to reach out and push them to the side so that we can see Gaby and Roberto without visual impediment. It thus reminds us of our bodies as spectators, flouting the unspoken rule in classical continuity editing to afford a perspective on the narrative action that allows the viewer to disavow their empirical body in the theater.

In forcing us to become aware of our own visual limitations, Ophuls poses an epistemic challenge to the kind of cinematic viewing dominant in the classical continuity system. Christian Metz canonically claims that the narrative fluidity generated by continuity editing erases the empirical boundaries of the viewing body. The editorial techniques of classical style, he submits, are designed to create such a degree of stylistic and narrative transparency that the spectator is allowed to disavow the technical workings of the film's mechanical procedures and instead identify with the camera itself as an "all-perceiving subject" who sees and knows all. Classical style places its viewer in the "ideal" position to view the narrative action, Bordwell argued in his pioneering work *Narration in the Fiction Film* (1985). It is an optimal orientation toward the profilmic events that allows the viewer to see and know what is happening when it is happening and with the utmost visual and aural clarity.[39] Driven by what Doane calls narrative "epistemophilia"—the drive or obsession to know—classical style endows the viewer with maximum epistemic privilege, enabling us optimally to apprehend the meaning of the events within the causal chain of the story rather than drawing distracting attention to our physical position vis-à-vis the projected image.[40] In short, seeing, in the classical continuity system, is understanding, and understanding is following the plot.

By allowing the plants in the garden regularly to obfuscate our view of Gaby and Roberto—plants that are haptically intriguing in their own right—Ophuls makes us aware of the epistemic limits enforced on us by the limits of our empirical viewing bodies. We, like his camera, can see and know only so much. As a result, he goes some way toward putting us inside the diegetic world itself. Whereas the ruler scene was organized around the boys' nosy, probing interest in Gaby as an object of gossip, here Ophuls generates an epistemology of curiosity and reciprocity. We want to know more about Gaby and Roberto, but not in order to weaponize our knowledge—rather, to understand them better and exist temporarily alongside them. Ophuls thus effects in the viewer a sense of simultaneity with the couple that exceeds the typical identification with the camera as a transcendent viewing subject and instead places our viewing body in their same space and time. The garden scene thus validates Bruno's claim that the haptic invokes a sense of inhabitation, the sense that we can live inside the image, thinning the distinction between our world and the world of the film.[41] The lack of extradiegetic music, too, plays a key role in giving us a sense of being inside the scene: we hear nothing but their voices and the gravel crunching under their feet. By placing us within the scene—in and among Roberto and Gaby rather than observing them from the voyeuristically "ideal" position of a transcendent subject—Ophuls fosters an alternative relationship to the audiovisual experience of film than epistemophilia. He develops an aesthetic that Miriam Hansen, following Walter Benjamin, would probably call a "cinema of experience," based less in the acquisition of knowledge and more in the reciprocity of symbolically mutual gazes and physiognomically heterogeneous audiovisuality.[42]

He encourages us to indulge in the haptic temptations of the plant life, to enjoy the metronomic sounds of the couple's footsteps on the stones. Rather than demanding of us to understand the scene in narrative terms, the camerawork, slow pace, and mise-en-scène encourage us to experience the scene as a lulling environment of contingent multiplicities.

But precisely in its exaggerated sequestration from the social dangers elsewhere at work in the world of the film—the perfection of its promise to offer Gaby refuge from the despair brought on by social infamy—the scene of Roberto and Gaby's walk also suggests a deceiving dream. Even the haptic utopia of the garden—whose visual and aural contingencies provide an organic haven from the fabricated plots of sexual scandal burdening Gaby outside its walls—is ultimately overridden by the more powerful and unforgiving allegory of the biblical garden and the fall into knowledge, where doom-laden historical time has already infiltrated the dilatory time of a temporary and false paradise. *La signora di tutti* thus registers the fragility of that paradisal cinema of experience, the impossibility of a sustained existence in that haptic arena of curiosity and touch, in terms unique to the medial materiality of film. Gaby's "fall from grace" is conveyed as a fall into technological reproducibility, as Doane rightly suggests, no longer textured with the contingent hapticities of human flesh—the caked soil on Gaby's hand effectively serving as an exaggeration of her own skin—but distanced by the technical processes of mechanical reproduction.[43]

Crucially for our purposes, it is the Nonni house that comes to represent interior spaces as architectural extensions of the always narratively potentialized space of the film set. Ophuls would repeatedly visit the theme of a woman's desire for freedom from an imprisoning house. In *Caught*, for instance, the character of Leonora Eames (Barbara Bel Geddes) is held hostage by the narcissistic millionaire Smith Ohlrig (Robert Ryan) in his mansion and eventually rescued by her love interest, pediatrician Doctor Larry Quinada (James Mason).[44] Or the edifice of the Maison Tellier brothel in *Le plaisir*, for instance, which is always shot from the outside, that makes the sex workers inside appear as so many birds in a cage. And the model Joséphine's attempted suicide by defenestration in the "Le modèle" episode of *Le plaisir*, too, barely mediates its critique of the interior as a space productive of art—the window she leaps from belongs to her artist's studio—but hostile to subjective flourishing.

But nowhere else in Ophuls's body of work is the interior of a home made to appear so discernibly representative of the enclosure of the film set as in the pivotal scene at the end of *La signora di tutti*. Roberto has left for a trip to Rome, and in his absence, his father, Leonardo, falls in love with Gaby despite his marriage to Alma, a disabled, middle-aged woman who has become a close friend of Gaby. Though Gaby initially tries to fend Leonardo off, she eventually gives in to his advances after a tragic episode in which Alma falls down a flight of stairs to her death when recognizing Leonardo's betrayal. Gaby and Leonardo go on a long voyage in order to allow the dust to settle after Alma's death, and in a key scene of their return, the Nonni house transforms in Gaby's mind from a home into a setting, from a place of residence into a mise-en-scène.

She and Leonardo walk into the living room to discover that the butler has placed cloths over the furniture and that the warm lighting of the table and desk lamps have been turned off in favor of harsh overhead lights. When Leonardo asks why the lighting has been left this way, the butler turns on the lamps and extinguishes the overheads. Leonardo then asks after his mail, and the butler informs him that it is in "lo studio," the Italian word both for "study" and for "studio." As the butler says the words "lo studio," he reaches over and works a pulley that raises the curtain on the outside of an enormous windowed wall spanning one side of the room looking out onto the balcony. This shot, coupled with the following low-angle long shot of Gaby looking up at Alma's portrait overhanging the fireplace, accentuates the placement of Gaby's body in the space, making the room look like an enormous film set whose covered furniture and harsh house lights suggest that it is between scenes and waiting for occupation by its next actors (fig. 39). Quickly afterward, Gaby reads a telegraph from Roberto, who tells her and Leonardo to terminate their contact with him—the final disruption to whatever uneventful equilibrium Gaby may have found on her peripatetic journey and the disruption that catapults her descent into madness. Ophuls conveys Gaby's insanity in terms of the world itself—not just the world of the film but also the world outside it—becoming overtaken by diegetic demands.

Gaby grows overcome with feverish anger at this reimposition of a melodramatic narrative of sexual deviance. She turns that anger toward the house. "I can't live in this house," she pleads, "I want to leave. It's impossible, take me away, I want to leave." As her rage climaxes, we hear what sounds like a suspenseful underscore of violins, at first barely audible but gradually increasing in volume. But Gaby hears the music, first thinking that it is emanating from the fireplace or somewhere else in the house. It turns out that it is extradiegetic music that only she can hear. Extradiegetic music typically works to enclose the diegetic world in a sequestered fictional space. "Background music," as Chion puts it, is "triaged to another place, an imaginary one."[45] It is a framing device that, like the filmic frame of classical style, creates formal boundaries between us and the

FIGURE 39. Gaby looking up at Alma's portrait in the Nonni house in *La signora di tutti*.

image on screen and contributes to the illusion of a neatly and transparently sutured fictional world. Thus, when Gaby hears the music that no other character can—except for the viewers of *La signora di tutti*—she has in essence gained access to the film's *editing*, grown eerily in touch with the very mechanisms of film production that persistently draw her within plots of sexual scandal, adultery, and familial betrayal. As opposed to the scene of Gaby and Roberto's walk in the garden, where the erosion of the boundary between diegetic and extradiegetic space generated a sensuous visual and aural site in which to explore multiple topographies of objects and sounds, the scene of Gaby's psychotic break, conveyed by the disruption of the acoustic "triage" Chion argues is essential to the maintenance of a transparent narrative world, suggests a complete collapse of nonnarratable experience into the narratable. *All* the world has now become a nightmarishly diegetic enclosure. In Gaby's futile attempt to exist for any extended duration of time outside the terms of scandalous narratives, she tries to flee the house, rattling the ornate bars of the property and screaming "I want to leave! I want to leave!" Left with no social or spatial refuge from plot—which has grown entirely synonymous with the narrative of the fallen woman and the deceptive femme fatale—Gaby removes herself to the studios of the French and Italian mainstream cinema, which, Ophuls seems to suggest, in its exploitation of female sexuality for narrative intrigue may be the only place Gaby can conceivably exist.

We will return to the use of sound, because aurality will play a key role, too, in *Madame de . . .* 's critique of the formal confines of plot and the social coercion involved in plotting. It will play a key role, as well, in imagining how identification and immersion can be ethically productive rather than just "stupefying" forms of engagement with plot, as Bertold Brecht would put it. First, however, it is important to note that *La signora di tutti* does not find a way out of or a solution to the problem it has detected as central to the process of narrativization. In this film plot becomes synonymous with narratives of gendered shame: to be emplotted is to be the center of malicious, exploitative attention. And this is not a problem the film considers specific to Gaby. Her status as "everybody's woman" suggests the ability to "abstract," as Doane puts it, Gaby's experience to a broader critique of the violence of narrative itself—especially as narrative is adhered to in classical cinematic style, as Stephen Heath argues and as we discussed in chapter 3.[46] The film is unwavering in its suspicion of plot and plotting as institutionally ordained narrative operations that enlist and ensnare the very women the industry exploits for commercial gain. In this sense, *La signora di tutti* offers a Mulveyan critique avant la lettre, proposing that the apparatus of mainstream cinematic narrative pleasure is predicated on the psychic destruction of women. Ophuls tells this story—of the social and psychic perils of story—from the perspective of a femme fatale who would prefer not to be the femme fatale. Doane remarks on the "process" by which the film "abstract[s] the woman and transform[s] her into a signifier of generalized desire" and how that desire "is supplemented by the production of a discourse about mechanical reproduction and its techniques of abstraction."[47] It is toward the operations of plot that the film levels that critique. Gaby would prefer to exist outside plot and the coercive mechanics of plotting—to be not "everybody's woman," but no one's woman—to be, in the critical idiom I have been using throughout this book, inconsequential.

As we have seen, the film virtuosically maps that search for a transcendent state outside narrative onto a stylistic language of natural space and depth of field, a lyricism and hapticity of objects and sounds in constant defense against what the film depicts as the industry's forced "order of forms" ever invested in exploiting its objects for its own narrative pleasure and commercial gain.[48] *La signora di tutti* thus impresses us as "certain," to borrow Clare Hemmings's term, in its indictment of plot as a formal force of patriarchal oppression, and this extends, too, to what potential—or lack of potential—it sees in romantic or affective attachment. It is attachment, as Doane suggests, that in *La signora di tutti* is the very culprit in the sense that male desire is the centripetal force that relentlessly draws Gaby to the center of scandal. Thus, in one sense, it is true that this film paradigmatically represents Ophuls's lamentation of the consequences of mechanical reproduction—recall his comment that "drama cannot be mass produced." "One of the dangers of technology," Doane writes of this film, "is the annihilation of difference, of uniqueness."[49] But it is also the case that despite being "everybody's woman," Gaby is woefully special, consequential in the extreme: she is the woman for whom men will leave their wives, abandon their sons, even die. To keep plot at bay and remain safely unimportant, the film suggests, would involve keeping desire at bay as well. The absoluteness with which the film sees no alternative to the psychic violence of plot and the fatality of desire is evidenced in Gaby's suicide—the only way to exist outside narrative, the film grimly suggests, is not to exist at all. The kind of spectatorship *La signora di tutti* encourages, by extension, is one of profound critical estrangement. In proposing that the processes by which narrative intrigue is generated in mainstream cinema are oppressive, if not fatal, *La signora di tutti* pushes us away from itself. It shows us the forms of psychic damage and subjective erasure on which the very apparatus of immersion is so often founded.[50]

Madame de . . . , meanwhile, discovers other possibilities for immersion and identification. And these are irrevocably bound up in its discovery, too, of other possibilities for affective attachment and by extension for plot. Though the very titles of the two films evince Ophuls's broader interest in anonymity and inconsequentiality (think, too, of *Letter from an Unknown Woman*), *La signora di tutti* and *Madame de . . .* are not often read together.[51] However, *Madame de . . .* revisits and revises *La signora di tutti*'s lack of faith in the ethics of plot, proposing a possible solution. That solution, however, is one that we are invited to appreciate analytically but—this is key—not ultimately to *want*. *Madame de . . .* , like *La signora di tutti*, investigates a dialectical relationship between natural space and constructed interiors. It stages a tension between a realist style based in deep staging, deep focus, and hapticity and one that prioritizes the set and the narrativization of visual data and experience into enclosed aesthetic wholes. Like *La signora di tutti*, *Madame de . . .* ponders the promise of an alternative, transcendent mode of being unencumbered by the formal and social confines of plot through a visual interrogation of spatial depth and the natural world. *Madame de . . .* finds possibility not in desire but in love. But rather than name an impasse, as *La signora di tutti* does, *Madame de . . .* proposes an alternative kind of causality, of consequentiality, than the one it acknowledges is entangled with the history of Western imperialism and patriarchal capitalism. It does so through an aesthetics of not just love and death but of love and depth. A word about love is thus in order.

LOVE

Love and desire, though conflatable in many circumstances, hold discrete values in Ophuls's cinema and critically so in *Madame de* . . . . Love is often considered difficult to describe, or so private, sentimental, even mawkish an experience as to be unworthy of critical description. The first view, which Barthes put forward most famously in *Fragments: A Lover's Discourse* (1977), is predicated on the assumption that love is theoretically interesting—so much so that it is difficult to theorize. The loose and baggy theorization of amorous affection in Barthes's text reflects the elusiveness of love as a category of experience. The elliptical loquacity of *A Lover's Discourse* shows love to be productive of theory, requiring philosophical exegesis precisely because its mysterious hold on us can at once be so fugitive and so tenacious. But an equally prevalent view, on the wane since at least the rise of so-called weak theory, is quite the opposite: that love is so simple, if not stupid, a thing to talk about that it stops up theoretical inquiry. There's nothing to theorize about love, some contend, because it is a cliché the discussion of which is best saved for the book club rather than the conference venue or the lecture hall.[52] Love talk—like character talk—smacks of unprofessionalism, the kind of affective investments one feels in the privacy of one's home rather than on the critical page.[53]

Enfolded into this second reason—that love is too banal a matter to discuss with any sort of critical rigor—is a third reason, not often stated explicitly but that implicitly has to do with what Moi argues is love's seeming resistance to formalist analysis in the style often considered central to professional literary criticism. Despite the long tradition of philosophical inquiry into the nature of love, Moi suggests, literary critics have largely relegated love to the status of mere content and therefore not ripe for analysis in the same way as are, say, structure and style.[54] What Moi does not say outright but that Berlant does is that by virtue of being associated with content, love tends to be understood as thriving unapologetically in the realm of plot, that other jejune and feminized feature of fiction that we've been taught to ignore, especially in modernism. Love, in other words, has a history of being thought theoretically uninteresting because of its affiliation, as we discussed in the context of Djuna Barnes, with love plots. ("What does it mean about love," Berlant asks, "that its expressions tend to be so *conventional*, so bound up . . . in plots?")[55] It is the masterful structure and style of Jane Austen's novels, for instance, that critics should pay attention to, not the affective content of the love plots between Darcy and Elizabeth, Elinor and Edward, and Catherine and Henry. The proper film critic, similarly, would resist immersion in the love plot of, say, *It's a Wonderful Life* and search instead for what Kristin Thompson calls the "excess" of filmic representation that the love plot cannot manage to contain, the formal and material contingencies that spill over the image's illusory homogeneity and that perhaps only the trained eye can catch.[56]

That tendency to recoil at the mention of love is not unrelated to the modernist ironization of affective investment. As Moi shows, professional literary criticism itself emerged at the same time as high literary modernism. Professional literary criticism adopted high modernism's same tenets of ironic dispassion and impersonality both as a reflection of modernism's emphasis on form and as an attempt to promote this new experimental—and thus serious/masculine/rigorous—body of fiction. In studying love, as in studying plots, one performs the worst kind of critical *bovarysme*.

It is rather desire that, especially in the hands of psychoanalytic, feminist, and queer theorists, has been given the negative power deserving of a modernist aesthetics and sensibility. Associated with the drives and the libido, desire is oriented toward objects but is ultimately a compensatory affect resulting from the traumatic loss of the primal nourishing object (e.g., the mother's breast). As such, desire is metonymic and iterative, expressing an irrevocable distance between the subject and its original object of attachment. Desire contributes to the formation of the self, but importantly, its constitutive nonfulfillment leaves the subject open and unfinished. "The formalism of desire," Berlant writes, "thus both produces perversion and manifests itself in narratives that aim toward normalcy but, paradoxically, never reach completion: even 'normal' desire [as opposed to nonnormative, queer desire, for instance] operates incrementally, restlessly testing out its objects."[57]

The deferred formalism of desire is largely what has led it to be viewed in critical theory as harboring politically radical potential. On its own, desire's formal centrifugality gives it the power to negate the psychic, corporeal, and ideological constraints of the symbolic order. The symbolic mediates and mitigates desire's negativity, channeling it into the more socially acceptable formalisms of teleology and closure. It is because desire is an open text—leading, in Deleuze and Felix Guattari's words, to ever-changing "rhizomatic" configurations[58]—that it has been so productive for theorists of modernism, not to mention of Ophuls. The openness of desire formally aligns with the dominant understanding of modernist *écriture*; the negative politics thought to underpin the anarchic pleasures of desire align, too, with those typically thought to motivate modernist aesthetics. It is hard, for instance, to imagine a more accurate description of Robin Vote's movements throughout *Nightwood* than as a "formalism of desire."

The dominant understanding of love, by contrast, is formally reparative,[59] binding, and socially stabilizing, mediated through and represented in mass culture as what allows romance plots to take shape. Romantic love, Berlant writes, "tend[s] to disavow erotic ambivalence and install, in its place, a love plot—a temporal sequence in which erotic antagonism or anxiety is overcome by events that lead to fulfillment."[60] Love thus domesticates the anarchism of desire by working it through the institutional funnel of the heteronormative bourgeois marriage. Whereas love is a cohesive agent—middle class, middlebrow, feminine, and thus affirmative, positivistic, and sociopolitically complicit—desire is wild and marginal and thus negative, antinormative, and transgressive. Love is subordinate to form; desire breaks it. Love tames, desire negates.[61]

But love is more complicated than that, or at least it is for Max Ophuls.[62] The very first page of *Fragments: A Lover's Discourse* shows us that precisely because of its privacy and ineffability, love frustrates form. The theoretical hyperproductivity of that text—its status as a torrent of entries rather than a streamlined theoretical argument—is a formal reflection of the antisystemic nature of love itself, an attempt on Barthes's part to "simulat[e]" rather than "describe" the erratic, self-sabotaging, desperate discourse of the lover. "What is proposed" in *A Lover's Discourse*, he writes, is a "portrait—but not a psychological portrait"—rather, a "structural" one that "offers the reader a discursive site: the site of someone speaking within himself . . . confronting the other (the loved object), who does not speak."[63] What is needed when attempting to theorize love, then, is a spatial rather than a psychological inquiry: "une place de parole," as it appears in the French.[64] The interiority generated by this space—this place—is not the interiority of the bourgeois subject. The "I" iterated by the lover, for Barthes, is not the self-possessing autonomous individual but a mad I who speaks to themselves and has lost their autonomy, their very existence hanging on the other, who is not there. Barthes creates a discursive place—a plot of theoretical space—whose depths are not psychological but topographical, whose reaches can accommodate the lover's various "gymnastic" movements, their "running[s] here and there, comings and goings." But love does not escape plot for Barthes. To the contrary, it causes plots to proliferate to the point of chaos, and this "choreographic" frenzy necessitates a vast and yawning space that Barthes produces in discursive form.[65]

And while Barthes's remarks remind us of how complex love can be,

Mari Ruti's in *The Ethics of Opting Out* (2017) remind us, conversely, of how banal sex and desire can be. Taking Edelmanian queer theory to task for fetishizing *jouissance* as inherently traumatizing and negative—the jouissance of orgasm dealing one "unbearable" blows that "shock" and decenter the very basis of the subject—Ruti writes of what she sees as the flashy theoretical rhetoric surrounding discussions of desire. It is worth quoting at length:

> Unbearable? Seriously? . . . My skepticism of this argument may be due to my Scandinavian matter-of-factness about sex, for I have never found my "enjoyment" (jouissance) particularly unbearable. What exactly is it about sex that is supposedly so deeply traumatizing? I am not here referring to the injurious stigmas attached to queer sexuality by the heteronormative social order but to the idea—promoted not just by Edelman but also by critics such as Bersani and Halperin—that there is something about the sheer experience of sex that is *intrinsically* traumatizing. It seems to me that (consensual) sex does not necessarily do much damage to our sense of self. It may decenter us momentarily but it does not inevitably leave any lasting imprint of trauma: often we simply just tidy up our hair, give our clothes a good shake, and get going with the rest of our (more or less coherent) lives.[66]

One need only recall the opening scene of *Lola Montes*, in which Lola lies in a posture of unimpressed postcoital fatigue, or the ludic sexual romps animating *La ronde* and *Le plaisir*, to observe that there is nothing especially Scandinavian about Ruti's more ordinary approach to sex, sexuality, and desire than the dramatically negative ones historically championed in much queer theory and modernist studies. To the contrary, in especially Ophuls's second French period, it is rather desire that has grown so habitual as to be considered banal, old hat. *Le plaisir*, for instance, whose episode "La Maison Tellier" centers the activities of a town brothel, shows carnal desire to be the itch one scratches before returning home to eat dinner with the wife and kids; *La ronde*, meanwhile, depicts desire as the thing that everyone has and sex the thing that everyone does, but neither disrupts the social and economic order holding the world of the characters together. Soldiers sleep with maids, bourgeois wives cuckold their husbands with students, actresses sleep with army generals, and the world goes on and on in the same way it otherwise would. "*La Ronde*," Ophuls told Jacques Rivette and François Truffaut, "is opposed to love," and "its cynicism is not the fruit of lived experience." "Pleasure [*la jouissance*] is a fact," the Count tells his lover, the actress Charlotte, "it's like intoxication; it is there and then it is not." Desire in *La ronde* is so prevalent as to be mundane; everyone is fucking everyone, and no one fucking cares.[67]

And carnal desire is everywhere in *Madame de . . .* , albeit quietly so. We are made to understand that André and Louise engage regularly in extramarital affairs and flirtations. As they exit the opera house toward the beginning of the film, for instance, André gently insists that they go home instead of to the café because "all of her suitors are annoying" him. But the palpable ease with which he makes the comment suggests his general comfort with her extramarital attentions. Their carnal desires, most prominently represented in the figure of André's mistress whom he shuttles off to Turkey, are precisely not disruptive to the social order. To the contrary, as Morgan has pointed out, they form an important part of its foundation. Desire is the norm in *Madame de . . .* , as it is in much of Ophuls's work. Love is not. It is the fact that Louise and the Baron fall madly in love with one another that gives their affective attachment the force it needs to generate world-disrupting consequences. Building on visual themes we witnessed in *La signora di tutti*, Ophuls conveys this through an aesthetics of depth and natural space.

A DEPTH THAT TELLS A DIFFERENT STORY

As we have seen in our discussion of *Madame de . . .* so far, Ophuls makes the artificial enclosure of the film set all too conspicuous, affiliating its boundaries and the rote narratives of domestic betrayal and reconciliation that circulate inside it with the spatial confines of the readerly text. However, the initial cycle of the earrings occupies only the first twenty-six minutes of the film. The rest is spent offering an aesthetic solution to the formal impasse this first section produces. It finds its solution in the exploration of a different kind of depth—not shallow and readerly but deictic, spatial, contingent. Through an aesthetics of spatial depth and contingency, the film discovers another form of narrative structure, one that has world-disrupting ramifications. This form of consequentiality ultimately provides an alternative model of political subjectivity to that assumed in the nineteenth-century novel and the classical Hollywood cinema. The first sign that some contingent force may threaten the rote functioning of Louise and André's life is the introduction of the Baron, played by Vittorio De Sica.

De Sica is a significant choice for Ophuls to have made for *Madame de . . .* . He was both a glamour icon in prewar Italian cinema (which Ophuls would surely have known, not least because he made *La signora di tutti* in Italy at the height of De Sica's fame), and he was one of the most prominent filmmakers of the Italian neorealist movement. Very much influenced by the poetic realism of Renoir in particular, neorealism was lauded by the critics of *Cahiers du cinéma* for its commitment to shooting on location, hiring untrained actors (Anna Magnani's debut performance as Pina in Roberto Rossellini's *Rome, Open City* [1945] is just one example of the extreme success of that strategy), and relinquishing narrative formulas for episodic and often very loosely formed narratives. It was a cinematic movement born out of a dedication to a degree of social realism its proponents thought missing from contemporary film, one that would attest specifically to the lived hardships of those undergoing the brutalities of the Second World War and the forms of poverty and desperation that emerged in its wake. De Sica's *Bicycle Thieves* (1948), for example, follows a sequence of events in the lives of a poor father and son in post–World War II Rome as they try to locate a bicycle that was stolen from them on the father's first day of work at a new job. Shot on location in the streets of Rome, the film resists integrating its events into a tight narrative whole. Rather, the episodes hang loosely together and remain despairingly unresolved at the end. The father and son are unable to track down the bicycle, and thus even more dire poverty lies imminently ahead as they walk off into an urban crowd. In André Bazin's words, *Ladri di biciclette* "unfolds on the level of pure accident," and "no one seems to have arranged [the incidents in the film] on any dramatic spectrum."[68] With not a single scene shot in a studio (as in most Italian neorealist films), *Ladri di biciclette* exemplifies what Bazin considered neorealism's ability to release cinema from the burdens of artificial design and restore it instead to what he considered— with his typical essentialism long since discredited—its original affiliation with the chance and contingency we saw at play, too, in Faulkner's invocation of early film in chapter 3. Indeed, though theoretical accounts such as Bazin's about the so-called originary purpose of cinema no longer hold, what does remain relevant in the case of *Madame de . . .* and Ophuls's choice to cast De Sica as Louise's love object is neorealism's impulse to limit, as much as possible, the interventions of artifice into the automatic capture of physical and aural existence.[69] And *Madame de . . .* , too, deals in a kind of provocative essentialism in the service of rendering in stylistic terms Louise's struggle to release herself from André through contact with a liberated intensity.

The aesthetic disruption that the Baron represents is signaled in the scene we are first introduced to him. In a Swiss train station on his way to Paris, the Baron catches sight of Louise and quite literally tries to stage a chance encounter. Directing the customs agent to "Speak louder! Louder! I want this woman to hear! Count, count the articles!" he tries to manufacture a chance meeting between him and Louise, which does not end up coming to fruition. Louise is allowed to pass through customs without delay, while Donati is held back and instructed to show his passport. Donati's struggle to cross the national boundary into the world of the film suggests the broader extent to which the aesthetics of chance and contingency itself struggles to penetrate the aesthetic interior of this film obsessed with narrative control through the anticipation and containment of potentially disruptive events. While Donati frantically searches his belongings for his passport, Louise waits for her train on the other side of the glass partition. In a crowded long shot, Louise stands on the left side of the frame, framed within a window—as if stuck in one of the film's photograms—while on the right, the customs agent refuses the Baron entry (fig. 40). In struggling to integrate the Baron—De Sica, really—into its aesthetic framework, the film conveys not just the social but also the aesthetic threat he poses to a world whose plots are so tightly woven and predetermined. In the very next scene, their carriages crash into one another by accident on the city street.

The film's struggle to integrate De Sica and the antisystemic contingencies he augurs gets coded as a stylistic encounter between the theatricized enclosure of the film set and the moving camera. That formal encounter is made most explicit in the scene where Louise announces to André that she

FIGURE 40. The Baron Donati tries to orchestrate a chance encounter with Louise in *Madame de . . . .*

will depart for a voyage to calm her upset nerves. Breaking the unspoken rule of reticence, André confronts Louise about her affair with the Baron, encouraging her to calibrate better her behavior around him, since their affection has become apparent as more than an innocent tryst. In the scene where she announces her intention to take her solitary voyage, the agon between her and André gets mapped onto a tension between the camera and the set. When Louise tells André her decision to take a small vacation, his first response is to close the door behind him, conspicuously enclosing himself and Louise within the scenographic space of their private apartments. As he steadily interrogates her, he advances in medium close-up as the camera dollies farther and farther back into the rooms. In fact the camera never gives us the reverse-angle shot of Louise as the two talk, which would be the standard move in continuity editing. Instead, the camera stays on André; it tracks backward as he continues to advance and occasionally cuts on action as he passes from one room to the next. The camera stays on him for a full two minutes and twenty-seven seconds.

Louise remains persistently off-screen, but we hear her disembodied voice responding to André. The effect is of André conversing with the camera itself and of Louise's voice lending the camera's subdued movements the audible expression of wanting to flee. "I want to leave," says Louise, echoing Gaby Doriot, "I need to take care of myself. I want to leave." Ophuls never does cut to a reverse-angle shot of Louise. Instead, she suddenly appears in the right side of the frame when the camera tracks André approaching her bed. Louise suddenly appears lying in bed in a two shot, with her cornered at the far end of the room and André looming ominously at the foot of the bed. Thin curtains hang down on either side of her body, framing her as if she were on a stage (fig. 41). André—here seen not just as spectator, but also director—would indeed prefer to keep Louise within these suppressed spatial depths, fully in control of her movements. Literalizing that figurative control, André forbids Louise's departure and bounds throughout their quarters, shutting all of the windows and enclosing her within. The final shot of the scene is a medium shot of the window—from the outside looking in—as André effectively excommunicates the camera along with the contingencies of the exterior world. Ophuls thus depicts André's effort to confine Louise to their domestic emplotment as a reduction of scenographic space.

Appropriately, Louise's love for the Baron grows affiliated with a visual style of yawning spatial depths. The event that first evinces the extent of her affection for him, for instance, relies on an extreme long shot of him surrounded by natural space. Louise accompanies the men on their hunt (itself an invocation of quintessential Renoir). As the party prepares to

FIGURE 41. André stands at the foot of Louise's bed; she suddenly appears in the frame in *Madame de . . . .*

return to their estate, Donati cannot be found. One of the attendants finally spots him, and Louise uses one of the spyglasses on hand to see him in the far distance (a direct reference to Renoir's *Rules of the Game* [1939], where Christine is handed a spyglass during the hunt to observe a squirrel without disturbing it but then also catches a glimpse in the distance of her husband and his lover in an embrace). We cut from a medium shot of Louise searching from atop her horse to a point of view shot of Donati falling from his horse in the middle of an open field (figs. 42, 43). As he falls, Louise is overcome with concern and faints, almost falling from her own horse. The vast and natural setting—the visual antithesis of the sepulchral interiors she shares with André—becomes the stylistic backdrop of the love between her and the Baron, suggesting both a spatial and affective liberation from the shallow depths of her life with her husband. When Louise finally does manage to take a trip to collect herself, she chooses to go to the Italian lakes. And here, Ophuls allows us to catch a fuller glimpse of what Deleuze refers to as the forbidden "obverse" of the film set. The realist aesthetic toward which the film conspicuously turns in this moment on the lakeshore invokes not just the Baron but the cinematic realism of De Sica himself, suggesting a departure from a style bound by artifice. There, amid the strewn detritus and bedraggled fishing nets—boundaryless and

FIGURE 42. Louise tries to spot the Baron in the far distance in *Madame de* . . . .

FIGURE 43. Reverse-angle extreme long shot of the Baron (left) falling from his horse in *Madame de* . . . .

FIGURE 44. Louise pacing the shore of the Italian lakes in *Madame de* . . . .

dilatory—Louise fully confronts what she herself, in an unsent love letter to Donati, calls "la profondeur," "the depth," of her "friendship, which has become my love" (fig. 44).

What ultimately drives Louise and the Baron apart is her recidivistic recourse to deception and thus an aesthetics of artifice. At the last ball of the film, he asks where she first received the earrings, despite having just been informed by André of their origins. She lies to him, telling him that they were a gift from her mother. The Baron's reason for leaving Louise at this point in the film has been much debated. Some consider it to be the result of the bruised ego of a "womanizer" recognizing that his "possession" of Louise is merely shared—a reading supported by De Sica's star text: he is a glamorous figure pursuing intrigues. Others consider the failure of their union to be the result of social "complications" brought on by the unorthodoxy of their affections.[70] But while Stefan Brand of *Letter from an Unknown Woman* may very well strike us as a womanizer, we would be missing something important about *Madame de* . . . were we to attribute the same label to the Baron. It is not that the Baron realizes that he does not have full possession of Louise that drives him away. His status as a diplomat is crucial here; he is a pacifist, uninvested in territorial ownership and conquest—"If diplomats were doing their job, we wouldn't need so much military," he tells André in a tense exchange. Further, the Baron is associated not just with Italy but with Switzerland as well, where we first meet him, where he first meets Louise, and which established its political neutrality as a result of Napoleon Bonaparte's defeat at Waterloo that so haunts André as well as the subsequent 1815 Treaty of Paris. And though his resistance to imperial ownership certainly, as Mulvey suggests, puts him in touch with a dilatory temporality resistant to narrative integration, De Sica's performance imbues the Baron with none of the callous narcissism of Stefan Brand. Louise and the Baron have already consummated their affections—a cut from inside to the outside of the carriage in which they meet after her return from the lakes suggests as much. Possessive desire is not what motivates the Baron. It is that he loves her. He is hurt that she is lying to him. He feels betrayed by her recourse to the artifice and deception from which he had thought their love protected him. "I lose my way a bit," he tells Louise, bewildered, in despair, "amid all your fabrications." What drives the Baron away is watching his beloved unable to tell him the truth. In short, what has happened here, what *love* has started to accomplish here is a developmental narrative in which Donati's psychic status has changed: he is no longer concerned to engage in the social world of polite lies but places value on—and needs to know—the truth.

Indeed, from within their separation, Ophuls lays the groundwork for a kind of causality disarticulated from the totalizing and rote structures of readerly narrative the film has shown to physically delimit and affectively deaden its subjects. *Madame de . . .* shows readerly narrativity to be infinitely cyclical, self-perpetuating, and self-contained—so many Ophulsian waltzes. This has led critics such as Vincent Amiel to claim that "on the dance floor, in the circus ring, on the social scene, events follow and repeat one another to infinity, unmodified by their own history." Such "stories," he concludes, "leave no traces." Ophuls reserves another kind of event, Amiel argues, for the domain of nature, a "defining event" that *"puts its stamp* on individuals."[71] In his use of the term *traces*, Amiel may very well be thinking of Annenkov's book on his experience working with Ophuls. There is a passage in the novella *Madame de . . .* , Annenkov reports, that apparently organized Ophuls's entire approach to the film. "By the sea"—the novella's equivalent of the film's scene at the lake—Louise is described by de Vilmorin as having the following thoughts: "Suddenly she had the impression of no longer having any importance; she asked herself what she was doing on earth and why she existed; she felt lost in an infinite universe."[72] "Nothing but this" was to guide their approach to the film, Annenkov reports Ophuls's words to him before filming:

the complete meaninglessness of this woman's life, accentuated by her elegance and her valets. What purpose does she serve? And not just her, but all people of her kind, this entire society, women who gossip, flirt, men who go to the club, on the hunt, play billiards. What do they do that's meaningful? Nothing. They're born, they live, they die, surrounded by valets but without leaving traces. It is not life, it is an existence. Even less: an inexistence.[73]

Organizing the aesthetic vision of this film, then, was Ophuls's interest in depicting a world bereft of meaning where the tautological inanity of carnal desire and the empty pleasures of conspicuous consumption accentuate the absence of any meaningful system of narrative design. Ironically, as we have seen, Ophuls renders that absence of narrative sense through the *over*production of narrative sense: the initial cycle of the earrings shows the ease and automaticity with which plots of domestic betrayal and reconciliation emerge, generate disturbance, and then retreat into inconsequentiality. But unlike *La signora di tutti*, which remains committed to its critique of plotting as an aesthetic proxy for gendered forms of psychic and social unfreedom, *Madame de . . .* ultimately sheds its stance of ironic detachment and proposes passionate love as a radically singular but formative experience capable of lending causal sense to an abandoned empirical world and of reconfiguring its political terms.

It has long been noted that Ophuls had a lifelong fascination with Stendhal's treatise *De l'amour* (1822). The spiritual antecedent of the "Swann in Love" section of Marcel Proust's *Swann's Way* and Barthes's *A Lover's Discourse*, *De l'amour* is Stendhal's attempt to name and thus somehow conceptualize his amorous and unrequited obsession with a young Milanese woman named Mathilde Dembowski. (She had been married to a Polish officer.) The erratic, "composite" nature of the treatise's form led it to become one of Stendhal's least successful works; but that form reflects the author's clamor to get the sort of analytical grip we see on display in his novels on an affect that continues to resist his conceptualizations. "The reader requires more than intelligence," he writes, "to follow a philosophical examination of this sentiment with interest."[74] Led by three "attempts" at a preface, *De l'amour* consists of two volumes of sixty chapters of varying lengths, some of which contain lists, definitions, and citations, others that present personal experiences, and still others that present analytical prose, before the final pages devolve into a series of loosely related fragments. Signaled instantly by its very struggle to begin, the discursive frenzy of *De l'amour*—creating what Barthes would call a "place de parole"—is the result of the fact that the kind of love Stendhal was most interested to capture linguistically is what he calls in the treatise "passionate love." As opposed to "vanity-love," felt by "the majority of men, especially in France," who "both desire and possess a fashionable woman, much in the way one might own a fine horse," passionate love elicits a kind of madness and has little to do with what Stendhal generally dismisses as the baser and far less interesting category of "physical love." Further, unlike "mannered love," in which "there is no place at all for anything unpleasant—for that would be a breach of etiquette, of good taste, of delicacy," passionate love is indecorous, "carr[ying] us away against our own real interests." For Stendhal, mannered and vanity love—clearly what we might ascribe to André—are largely interdependent ("take away vanity and there is little left of mannered love," he writes), while it is passionate love that he deems "real."[75] Indeed, for Stendhal, as for Ophuls, love does not carry the same valence as it does in contemporary critical theory, which, as we've seen, largely treats it as the conservative shadow of the politically emancipatory intensities of desire. For Stendhal—as for Goethe, with whom Ophuls also had a lifelong aesthetic intimacy—love is what undoes us, "carries us away against our interests"—a phrase whose quietly wild jamming of adverb and preposition suggests the decentralizing effect of love on language and the self.

The passionate love between Louise and the Baron is perhaps best represented in the nonsensical phrase that becomes their intimate incantation: "Je ne vous aime pas." *I don't love you.* She repeats it to him throughout the film, indulging in an at times playful, at times pained self-contradiction to express her love, denying what is so obviously the case through an attenuation of meaning reminiscent of the sense-straining grammatical cluster—"away against"—of Stendhal's description of passionate love. The Baron begs her to speak the phrase to him while they lie together in the carriage upon her return from the lakes, Louise's splayed body rocking and draping across his, accentuating the power of passionate love to compromise corporeal decorum.

It would thus be wrong to see merely a false consciousness at the center of the love story between Louise and the Baron, to exhibit an overly academic resistance to feeling *with* them what they are feeling. Feeling with them, rather than against them, allows us to see how Louise and the Baron augur a radically singular and threatening structure of feeling and behavior that departs, as Morgan argues, from the system of meaning that otherwise organizes the characters' world and that starts to shake its foundations. In the ramifying tremors of that contingency, a new form of narrative structure—a consequential, formative causality with both historically and aesthetically emancipatory potential—takes root. Whereas *Signora* could not imagine a social or formal alternative to the lethal plots that ensnared Gaby—plot in that film always being subsumed by the interests of commercial exploitation and social censure—*Madame de . . .* forges a structure of narrative causality imminently singular in its refusal of readerly subordination, its attendant forms of social oppression, and, as we will see, imperial violence.

The formative causality augured by Louise and Donati's passionate love is first suggested when, out of anger and jealousy, André performs his first and only inessential action extraneous to any narrative purpose. He buys back the earrings from the jeweler (to whom the Baron had resold them as a gesture of ending his affair with Louise) and shows them to her. He watches her as the keepsake both devastates and elates her. Out of spite, André gratuitously punishes his wife; he forces her to give the earrings as a gift to their impoverished niece, who ultimately sells them back to the jeweler to use the money for more necessary articles. As André leads Louise to the niece's door, they have an interaction that echoes, some twenty-five years later, the exchange in *The Sound and the Fury* in which Mr. Compson insists to Quentin that the relentless passage of time would erase everything that is important to us and that we leave no traces behind us. "You think you are experiencing a great pain," André tells Louise, "and you think that I'm adding to it. But in a few days," he assures her icily, "you'll be the first to laugh at your feelings today. And these earrings," he continues, "to which you've attached so much importance, will appear to your eyes as nothing more than a few pieces of broken glass." Louise, however, whispers in breathy anger, "Je ne te pardonnerai jamais. Jamais"—"I will never forgive you. Never." She insists, in other words, that André's punishment will have permanently formative effects, that they *will* leave a trace. André tries to maintain the cyclical and infinitely inconsequential temporal logic of "mannered" plot, sensing that its social and narrative premises are being definitively threatened. But Louise's rage augurs the emergence of a structure of transcendent causality that can penetrate the incessant flow of decorous custom—that can *mean* something, cleave the passage of time such that it is "never" the same. It is that desire for consequence—to have mattered, to have had her love with Donati make a mark on the otherwise flattened surface of that ever-unending waltz of ongoing time and history, a scratch on the tablet of existence—that places Louise alongside those other modernist characters who hold fast to whatever vestigial remnants of plot they can recover and toward whom this book has turned its attention.

It is indeed within the context of the Flaubertian, Stendhalian, and Marxian disappointments in the failures of the modern liberal nation-state to deliver on its revolutionary hopes that we must understand *Madame de* . . . . Despite the fact that de Vilmorin's novella was set some indistinct time in the 1930s or 1940s, the film *Madame de* . . . sets the action during the French Third Republic of the late nineteenth century. This period witnessed the totalitarian suppression of the socialist revolutionary Paris Commune as well as considerable French colonial expansion in Asia and Africa. Though André is a general of the French army under the Third Republic, he represents a conservative nostalgia for the even earlier regime of Napoleon Bonaparte, suggesting to Louise at one point that the emperor was wrong only twice in his life: once when he said that "in love, the only victory is flight," and again "at Waterloo," Bonaparte's famously lost battle, which André elegizes in a painting in his study. André thus represents the strain of authoritarian French politics that epitomized—to figures such as Stendhal, Flaubert, Baudelaire, and Marx—the inability of revolution to generate novelty and the extent to which the culture of bourgeois commercialism, temporally and narratively, mimics the regime of sameness and repetition represented in that failure. In his *Eighteenth Brumaire* (1852), Marx described the period after the French Revolution of 1848 as a moment of recognition that the Napoleonic state was a terrain of dooming similitude, a society of "passions without truth, truth without passions; heroes without deeds of heroism, history without events; a course of development only driven forward by the calendar, and made wearisome by the constant repetition of the same tension and relaxation."[76] What better way to symbolize this historical changelessness that "has been painted grey on grey"—what Ophuls in his remarks to Annenkov would refer to as "inexistence"—than the seemingly frivolous Ophulsian waltz and the inconsequential narratives around whose circumferences they repetitively circulate? It is in this context of the late nineteenth-century lost hope in the possibility of genuine historical change that the inconsequential narratives determining Louise's life—and the consequential, trace-making love between her and the Baron—take on their full importance.

Flaubert, as we discussed in the introduction to this book, capitulated to that failure, compensating for his sense of political disempowerment and disappointment by mastering it through irony. He stopped short of imagining a possible political beyond (much to Georg Lukács's chagrin), setting the tradition of modernist ironic impersonality in motion by refusing to indulge in what for him seemed like the naive fantasy of teleological plot. Instead, events proliferate without any meaningful ends, contained within a vast narrative compartment of bourgeois clichés. Accordingly, the only forms of political selfhood Flaubert allowed himself to imagine, alternative to the possessive liberal individual whose politics he watched reproduce the authoritarianisms of monarchism, were the political apathetic (Frédéric Moreau); the romantic not yet sufficiently disillusioned by the onset of bourgeois modernity and its various assaults on romantic ideals (Emma Bovary); or the clerks too stupid to perceive their own platitudes (Bouvard and Pécuchet). And though the frivolity of Emma Bovary is certainly present in Louise, Louise's despair ultimately lays the groundwork for a different, more politically potentialized subjectivity. An acerbic and brilliant Flaubertian critical intransigence characterizes *La signora di tutti*—and a similar, Schnitzlerian one permeates *La ronde*, where sex and unfettered desire form the basis of a negative form of life but not new modes of selfhood or social order. And that Flaubertian loss of faith is rearticulated in the beginning two acts of *Madame de* . . . . But Ophuls begins to construct a different kind of subjectivity than that presupposed by the nineteenth-century European literary tradition. In the relationship between Louise and Donati—and the formative causality that their love engenders—Ophuls speculates about the possibility of an alternative model of selfhood to the possessive liberal individual. For as Louise falls more and more in love with Donati—and especially once she is forced to relinquish him ("Je ne suis déjà plus là," he tells her, "I'm not here anymore," "et je ne suis plus avec vous, Louise," "and I'm no longer with you")—she starts to cast off her mannered self-possession and become more materially human.

We have been cautioned against something resembling this view. What is often discussed as Ophuls's obsession with the materiality of the cinematic medium has led us to be suspicious of anything that looks like the "realistic fallacy," whereby we forget, or choose to forget, that characters are not persons and instead treat them as having life and breath outside of their activity as textual beings.[77] Therefore, to speak of Louise's humanness—or even worse, to get affectively invested in her outcomes—is itself perceived as the result of a false consciousness, a failure on the part of the critic to resist the mystifications of fiction. But to dismiss the category of the human, the person, in *Madame de* . . . as merely naive is to lose sight of the way that through the very materiality of the cinematic medium, Ophuls gives us access to Louise's living body (and to a very different effect than Josef von Sternberg with Dietrich). Louise does achieve something through suffering, but that thing is not "personality depth," which White rightly treats with suspicion.[78] A formation born out of the eighteenth- and nineteenth-century novel, "personality depth," as we have mentioned throughout this book, is predicated on the formativity of events: one develops personality over time and through experience. Further, as we discussed in chapter 1, the notion of personality as it was engendered by the late eighteenth- and nineteenth-century novel corresponds, too, to a form of political subjectivity subordinate to the state and its social and economic interests. To have a personality is to have the right to own. And this is a primary reason, as we have seen, that love—an attachment formation typically viewed as premised on at least the fantasy if not the reality of being loved back and having those feelings institutionally acknowledged—is often considered to be the more politically conservative cousin of desire. Whereas the kind of ownership associated with desire is fleeting, orgasmic, institutionally unsanctioned, and therefore constitutively impermanent, the marriage contract institutionally consecrates and makes permanent the ownership associated with love, grafting affective ownership onto the logic of proprietary investment. Louise precisely does *not* achieve personality depth. The entire film has been spent exposing—by way of an aesthetic economy of choked voids that refuse depth even as they promise it—the notion of personality depth as a discursive formation predicated on the gendered restriction of social mobility and affective repertoire. *Madame de . . .* has thus ironized the entire formal apparatus generative of so-called personalities in the literary realist tradition. As such, it has indeed laid bare the distinction between characters and persons. "I'm not especially fond of the character you've made of me," André tells Louise in a rare moment of vulnerability, "but I pretended to be him, so as not to displease you. But it's not what I would have chosen." Rather than personality depth, what Louise starts to achieve toward the end of the film is something on the order of existential personhood.

This is nowhere more evident than in Louise's reaction upon receiving the earrings again from André before he forces her to give them to her niece. She lies in her nightgown, her hair undone, without makeup or jewelry, reclining on a chaise longue. When André shows her the earrings, she clutches them to her face, taking in several deep, audible breaths. The earrings rattle around in her hands as she breathes them in, as if inhaling the memory of Donati into her lungs. When André takes them back from her—arguably his cruelest gesture in the film, reminiscent of Jason Compson throwing the tickets to the show into the stove fire—she seizes her face with one hand while audibly breathing back mucus collected in her throat and nostrils, as tears stream down her disheveled face (fig. 45). Here, Louise, whose movements have otherwise been supremely calculated and contrived, comes undone. The development of her anguished facial expressions indicates a complete loss of self-possession, exemplifying what Béla Balàzs famously calls the expressive "polyphony" of the human face on screen, the "chord of emotions" that the cinema is able to capture in the visage.[79] In her remarkable subtlety, Darrieux conveys the

FIGURE 45. Louise grabs her face, audibly breathing back mucus gathered in her throat and nostrils, in *Madame de . . . .*

mixture of misery and ecstasy that the earrings—now an extension of Donati himself—evoke in Louise, how his absence that they now index strips her of all mannered corporeality. Louise's unmannered, indecorous body emerges precisely out of the experience of having lost possession of her love object. Perhaps, the film suggests, in a world such as this, in which love has been appropriated into the political framework of liberal imperialism, the most negative way to love would be to love from afar—to love, merely and desperately, the things that the beloved has touched.

Similar to the way that Marguerite Gautier's rotting, consumptive body in Alexandre Dumas's novel we discussed in chapter 1 threw into relief the invisible formal borders that contain literary character in the nineteenth-century novel, the excesses of Louise's body cleave a distance between the phenomenology of persons and the discursivity of character—of "personality"—as it has been reified throughout the film. *Madame de . . .* achieves this visually: the tears that appear glistening on Louise's cheeks do not so much fall as secrete from her face, now alive with visible wrinkles of contorted skin. But it is more the aurality of the scene that asserts her departure from the confines of character. In their haptic subtleties, the sounds Louise makes reveal her to be a spatial vessel no longer of character but of bodily functions. Here emerges a sense of interiority not secured by the physical boundaries of the film set or liberal notions of personality—as did the final image of Garbo in *Camille*—but by the porous and vulnerable membranes of the living body. Her audible inhales and exhales provide the haptic index of her working lungs, the drawing back of her mucus testifies to the cavities of her sinuses (fig. 45). The soft rattling of the earrings professes to the living shelter of her cupped hands. (Later, when she rushes to Donati's home to beg him not to fight in the duel and is stopped by his butler, we hear the shortness of her breath and the pharyngeal strain of her nigh shriek: "I know he's here; he gave you orders not to let me in, didn't he? Didn't he??"). Sound accomplishes something vertiginous here: what Vivian Sobchack would call the actor Darrieux's "pre-personal" body, her material body before it is understood as a conceptual entity, is exposing something like *Louise*'s pre-personal body.

For Jean-Luc Nancy, it is listening rather than hearing that in the context of philosophy generates an ethical epistemology not of sensemaking but of the senses.[80] Hearing is, for him, what philosophers do while waiting to philosophize, an ego-oriented acoustic suspension. Meanwhile, the philosopher who listens leaves herself open to the shared space of meaning, "straining toward" the source of sound or silence.[81] But in these final scenes, it is the suddenness with which we hear and continue to hear Louise—hearing her body there in those rooms, as if for the first time—that forces us to encounter her differently than we have thus far. We have listened to Louise as she periodically hums her signature musical refrain (a recurring echo of the film score); we have listened to the whisking of her day dress as she trots off to sell her earrings; listened as she lies to André, to the Baron. But here, we are suddenly made to *hear* the sounds her body makes—then the latch of the door, as André leaves the room, the latch of the door again as he closes it behind him—as these sounds echo throughout the room, whose resonant emptiness, now made visible through a cut to a medium shot of Louise in pain alone, mimics the empty womb of its childless inhabitant. Hearing here is not passive or uncaring. Rather, hearing Louise now makes us arrestingly conscious of her, awake to her. We hear the limits of her physical body and confront, by extension, what Moi would call the temporal and spatial dimensions of her finitude: the fact that she will die one day, as will the ones—but more importantly the one—she loves, and that her body is and will always be distinct from his, that she is "bodily, existential[ly] separate" from her beloved.[82] We are forced into the traumatic acknowledgment that all are forced into, but perhaps more so those who passionately love: that she cannot, as Moi might argue, "merge" with him, that their bodies cannot inhabit one another. ("My life was lived ... *through* you," writes the anonymous woman to the protagonist

FIGURE 46. Louise clutches the door and repeats to the Baron, "Je ne vous aime pas," in *Madame de* . . . .

of Stefan Zweig's *Letter from an Unknown Woman*.[83]) That brutal membrane between loving body and loving body is accentuated by the dumb and impermeable door Louise presses herself against as she whispers to him her incantation "je ne vous aime pas je ne vous aime pas" and also in the glass door in the Baron's home, whose delicacy mocks their discreteness from one another rather than make it less painful (fig. 46). Hearing Louise's suffering body confronting its physical and temporal limits, we apprehend her no longer as human in the liberal humanist sense of the term but as a finite, mortal, loving body.

The kind of identification these sounds of Louise's suffering body elicits in us is not immersive in the typical sense of the term. Rather, it is based in a recognition of existential separateness. We do not imagine ourselves as Louise, symbolically identifying with her as we would with a heroine in a classical narrative film, immersed in a drama whose invisible edges encourage us to place ourselves imaginatively in her skin. *Madame de* . . . is, as we have seen, a film that reckons with the borders between people, the frontiers that keep us separate. Therefore, neither is the film's affective pull on us based in a fantasy of merger. Rather, the sort of identification it elicits in us is a radical and vertiginous—nauseating, if you will—grappling with our own spatial and temporal limits. For Barthes, the testimonial nature of celluloid photography gives photographs the power to provoke in us what he calls a "'stupid' or simple metaphysics," by which he means contemplations so basic to human existence that they appear substanceless. "*They were there*," Barthes confesses to often thinking, when looking at subjects in a photograph, be they a person, a place, or a thing; and "why is it," he finds himself pondering subsequently, "that I am alive *here and now*?" These contemplations, he claims, are born out of photography's special capacity to conjure a "mystery of concomitance," of relationality—that was there then, I am here now.[84] Hearing Louise's body working to sustain its heartbreak draws from us such stupid Barthesian metaphysics of the sort this book has encouraged us not to ignore and that finds articulation in phrases devastating in their plainness, such as *I have a body, too. I, too, am living. I, like her, will die one day. Her lungs, like my lungs, will stop one day forever; one day those inundated glands, like mine, will dry out.* It is in this way that our investment in the plot's outcomes is generated: from a sense not of what we want for Louise but from a sense—with all the existential urgency of traumatic recognition—of what we would want for ourselves. To have been with the beloved, no matter what the cost.

And the film, importantly, does not allow us to forget the cost. It alerts us to the forms of brutality on which the lover's union would be predicated. Just as the figure of nature emerges in Ophuls's cinema precisely as a figure—to produce the effect of a "location-shock" as he told Rivette and Truffaut[85]—Louise's body is *made* audible to us. Ophuls makes sure, through the amplification of sound, that we will hear her body straining, breathing, dying, and as such suggests that though the body may appear as immediate, it is always informed by structures of history. While film, Sobchack writes, seems to give access to the experiencing body as "direct" material, "our experiences" are themselves "mediated and qualified by our engagements not only through the various transformative technologies of perception and expression but also by historical and cultural systems that constrain both the inner limits of our perception and the outer limits of our world."[86] And through its own visual excesses, the film makes clear what historical and cultural systems—or more accurately, what structures of political violence—Louise's suffering would promise symbolically to contest. By extension, it also makes clear precisely on what structures of political violence Louise's and therefore our relief from suffering—her union with the beloved—would rely.

As Louise loses what is most dear to her, her material, carnal humanness grows more evident. The less attached to signifiers of liberal possessiveness she becomes—she sells all of her belongings to buy back the Baron's keepsake, her closets shown now to be gapingly deep—the more she loses her autonomy. Whereas Marguerite's weakness at the end of Cukor's *Camille* remained conspicuously stylized (Garbo literally preparing for her close-up), Louise's is urgent; she can barely stand up, leaning on anything and everything around her. So different from Gaby's suicide, which was the only way out of a social and commercial world from which she could never wrest personal autonomy, Louise's deterioration symbolizes a renunciation of the very terms of autonomous selfhood. Like *The Lady of the Camellias, Madame de . . .* lays bare the forms of social repression and political violence internal to the modern concept of personal autonomy and the individual's right to property.

The film even indicates what political promise such a dis-integration of the possessive self and the relinquishment of property relations—material or affective—would entail. To be "human" in the liberal humanist sense, Sylvia Wynter reminds us, is to be a beneficiary of the social distinctions that determine liberal imperialism.[87] This is the implicit political force behind Franco Moretti's claim that one of the primary projects of the bildungsroman was to lend narrative shape to the "intrinsically boundless dynamism" and "protean elusiveness" of Europe after the first French Revolution so that modernity could be "made human."[88] To be human in the nineteenth-century European imagination was to be a subject of the state set against and above forms of life considered subhuman—such as the colonial subjects of the Caribbean, Africa, and Asia—traces of whose conquest adorn the rooms of André's home. However empty the lives of these aristocrats may be, they are indeed anything but traceless; we simply are not allowed to see the traces they have left. The radical trace of Louise and the Baron's passionate love gestures toward the radical trace left, too, by French imperial conquest on the vast swathes of the globe the film refers to quietly but nonnegligibly—those vast geopolitical spaces that do indeed exist outside the orb-like interiors of the film set and that those interiors merely mask with desperate and eloquent trickery. André's enormous weapons framing his even more enormous painting of Napoleon's army (fig. 47)—and more importantly still, the leopard-skin upholstery of Louise's chaise longue (fig. 45)—point to the ravaged, worked, and owned lands and bodies on whose backs the wealth inside these gorgeous interiors is made and against whom the very notion of the liberal self is defined. Thus, the undermining of Louise's autonomous subjectivity as it grows metaphorically indistinct from the Baron's—as if the same bullet that kills him in his duel with André ends her too—offers a reappraisal and potential reconfiguration of the terms of the liberal self and the forms of corporeal ownership, racialized violence, and imperial conquest that underpin both it and the fascist regimes of *Madame de . . .* 's contemporary

FIGURE 47. André's weapons hang next to his painting of Napoleon's army in *Madame de . . . .*

postwar moment. Predicated on nonattainment and the attenuation of the self, the failure of Louise and the Baron's love holds within it the potential for a form of life alternative to these terms.

But the point, as I have been stressing and that I insist we confront if we are to take in the monumentally challenging position in which Ophuls puts his viewers, is that none of this is enough to change what the film leaves us wanting. Over and above our recognition of the kinds of imperial violence that afford people like Louise and André such dazzling interiors and belongings with which to fill them—that afford them, too, the negative terms with which to identify their own humanity—is our implacable desire for the lovers nevertheless to have gotten together, for that subjective merger symbolized in their joint deaths to have been literalized in their material union. Most provocatively, the emerging expressions of Louise's carnal presence, as they work away at the polish of her character, peel back, as it were, the image of Louise to more conspicuously reveal the person Darrieux, who was a collaborator with the Vichy regime and (unlike Dietrich, who refused) appeared in Berlin to support the war effort, footage of which would go on to appear in *The Sorrow and the Pity* (1969) directed by Ophuls's son Marcel, which traces the history of Vichy-Nazi collusion. Unlike Ophuls the Jewish exile and Boyer the active and outspoken antifascist, Darrieux was a Nazi sympathizer, a representative of the continuation of the logics of instrumental reason and conquest in the contemporary lives of *Madame de . . .* 's viewers. Ophuls knew this, everyone did; Darrieux did not hide it. But the point is that we nevertheless still ask why, when Louise goes to beg the Baron not to duel André, could the Baron not reach his hand across to her as he had so many times before and promise her he won't fight and that they'll leave this place forever? He tells her she is "more beautiful than she has ever been"; surely, he still loves her. As it is in all of his films, the hand of Ophuls is everywhere present in *Madame de . . .* , even in its ostensible explorations of chance, the natural, and the antisystemic. What are the chances, for example, that the carriages of Louise and the Baron would crash into one another on just *that* corner? That they would both be at *that* train station in Basel, during *that* precise hour of *that* day? Ophuls makes his signature intractably evident, making us all the more aware of what the film is not giving us and for what it leaves us longing.[89] And a lack of attention, as Carl Plantinga would argue, to this affective dimension of the film would lead us only partially to understand its provocation or to misunderstand it altogether.[90] Like the "away against" of Stendhalian passionate love, Ophuls jams two things together and makes us confront their terrible parataxis: this thing rests on a world of wrongdoing; we want this thing.

In the final pages of *The Political Unconscious*, Fredric Jameson brings to climactic conclusion his remarks on the extraordinarily powerful means by which ideology inscribes itself into culture. Thinking through Benjamin's own terribly paratactical meditation from *Theses on the Philosophy of History* that there "has never been a document of culture which was not at one and the same time a document of barbarism," Jameson writes, "It is increasingly clear in today's world (if it had ever been in doubt) that a Left which cannot grasp the immense Utopian appeal of nationalism (any more than it can grasp that of religion or of fascism) can scarcely hope to 'reappropriate' such collective energies and must effectively doom itself to political impotence."[91] In other words, if the goal of those political bodies dedicated to forging forms of life based in social, political, and economic equality is not to denounce emptily or celebrate the periodic disempowerment of those structures dedicated to the lust for power, then they must affectively inhabit those structures. One must understand them, those bodies, from the inside and to imagine what it feels like to be promised something very valuable by them—be it community, a sense of historical purpose, or a vision of a world that holds the interests of you and your loved ones safe and dear. It is not enough simply to see one's life as having a narrative arc. It is to how the story might end that we cleave, to where those narrative energies might deposit us, in what circumstances they will finally place us. The depth of our investment in those outcomes is often directly proportional to our investment in the structures that promise to ensure them.

Max Ophuls knew perhaps more than many what it feels like to wonder about the outcomes of one's life and whether they will correspond to what one might want them to be. Rejected early on by a mercantile family disapproving of his aesthetic pursuits, forced into political exile and a nomadic existence in Europe and the United States during the Nazi occupation, periodically unable to secure work, and long marginalized for his aesthetic achievements, Ophuls's life was itself filled with the sorts of narrative disruptions and fragmentations one might expect to characterize the life of a European Jewish émigré in the early midcentury. The very proliferation of names he espoused throughout his career—changed from the original Oppenheimer to, variously, Ophuls, Ophüls, and Opuls—suggests, as White has duly noted, the unrest characterizing the trajectory of his life, the unsettlement of his lived experience over time, as well as the very real material unsafeties he was persistently dodging.[92] As a European Jew, Ophuls also knew all too well how horrifically powerful the narratives of racial, ethnic, and social belonging and historical purpose offered by a politics of totalitarianism were, and to what terrible lengths those narratives would go to make themselves appear as so many beautiful sheltering enclosures. In making us long for the lovers' union—in making us feel its formidable appeal to our basic, indeed, simple and stupid desires: *I, too, will die one day; I, too, will have wanted to be with my beloved while we are both still living, breathing*—Ophuls shows us what it is like to feel one's life at stake in the pursuit of an outcome. He moves us to consider that although there may be alternative plots to pursue, shapes that the narratives of our lives might take that do fewer people harm, including ourselves, we must at the very least begin from the premise—if what we really want is to create something different—that often we long for the thing that makes us feel better sooner, no matter the cost.

Thus, by way of Ophuls's mixture of modernist detachment and melodramatic investment, we will arrive at the broadest implications of the argument of this book. A German Jew who produced most of his work in exile from the Nazi occupation—its afterlives have been reemerging across the Western world during the years I have spent writing this book—Ophuls would have been especially attuned to what in the "Work of Art" essay Benjamin called the "aestheticization of politics." Ophuls's cinema suggests that actual political change—the production of novelty, rather than the perpetuation of the same tensions and relaxations that Marx describes in the *Eighteenth Brumaire* and that find their embodiment in the endlessly circulating figure of the Ophulsian waltz—might need be predicated on self-incrimination, an admission to one's own ugly feelings. The passage from one equilibrium to a second constitutively different equilibrium that does not reproduce the violences of the first might, *Madame de...* suggests in a Benjaminian and Arendtian gesture, need to start with the basic and difficult, because self-incriminating recognition that regimes predicated on the exclusion, subjugation, exploitation, even extermination of others build their success on their *aesthetic* appeal. That they obfuscate their violence through forms of aesthetic fascination that often have very much to do with the narratives they tell about the outcomes they could ensure, the formal assurances they give to those they wish to draw in that if just certain things were to happen, and in the right order, then all will be all right, one's sense of belonging, purpose, and security restored. Cinema, by virtue of its ability to take us—even the most critical among us—somewhere else, to allow us temporarily to be someone else, to let us feel momentarily like our wildest dreams might come true and if they don't, then all will be lost, is especially well suited to confronting us with this recognition.

Acknowledgments

No plot orders these acknowledgments. But the names that appear here comprise a group of brilliant and generous individuals, to each and every one of whom I am enormously grateful and without whom, in some way or another, I could not have written this book.

My friendship with Virginie Maillard, a peer at the International Theater School Jacques Lecoq so many years ago, feels written in the stars. The imprint of that friendship is evident to me, and hopefully to her, everywhere in this book. Our discussions about Kafka, Melville, *le masque neutre*, the relation of the body on stage to the space around it, were among the first that taught me what thought could look and feel like outside the confines of the university. That has never left me, and I hope it never will.

My professors and peers in the English department at Boston University and the broader Boston academic community helped shaped me and my thinking. The companionship of Greg Chase, Shannon Draucker, Emily Gowen, Sarah Hosein, Annael Jonas-Paneth, Jon Najarian, Melissa Schoenberger, and Patty and Patrick Whitmarsh was life-giving. Being the student of Robert Chodat, Jonathan Foltz, Susan Mizruchi, Anita Patterson, Carrie Preston, Joseph Rezek, and John Paul Riquelme within my alma mater, as well as Boston's wider intellectual community, which also included Yoon Sun Lee, Deidre Lynch, Richard Moran, John Plotz, and others, was an honor and a privilege.

In many ways this book reflects two formative intellectual experiences, one at the School of Criticism and Theory, the other at the Futures of American Studies Institute. Being in conversation with Elizabeth Maddock Dillon, Heather Love, Sébastien Fanzun, Hamza Radid, and Kyle Kaplan cracked open my thinking in ways I couldn't have anticipated. And Peter Gordon is a hallmark for me of the power of clear and precise articulation of thought. I'm honored to call him a teacher, a mentor, and an interlocutor.

Yoon Sun Lee and Deidre Lynch's Zoom version of the Novel Theory Seminar at the Mahindra Center at Harvard gave me something to look forward to during the peak quarantine years of the pandemic, during which time I was completing this manuscript. The conversations we all had together—including with Stuart Burrows, Tara Menon, Hilary Schor, Timothy Bewes, Chloë Kitzinger, and others—are among the few things I miss from that dark time of quarantine.

Portions of this book were completed with support from the Boston University Humanities Center as well as the Huntington Library. I would also like to express my gratitude to the librarians at the Beinecke Rare Book and Manuscript Library, the Hornbake Library at the University of Maryland, the Harry Ransom Center at the University of Texas, Austin, the Huntington Library, the Library of Congress, the Margaret Herrick Library, the Marlene Dietrich Collection at the Deutsche Kinemathek, the Schomburg Center for Research in Black Culture, and the libraries at the University of Delaware and the University of Mississippi for giving me access to archival materials while I was conducting my research. I am grateful, as well, to *Modernism/modernity*, *Textual Practice*, and *Arizona Quarterly* for graciously permitting separate publication of material previously published in these journals.

My colleagues at the University of Nevada, Reno, Katherine Fusco, Michael Branch, Lynda Olsen, James Mardock, Jen Hill, Stephen Pasqualina, and Daniel Morse modeled what it is to be a colleague in this difficult and shrinking profession. And more closely, Nasia Anam, Cathy and Maddie Chaput, Lydia Huerta, Ruthie Meadows, Ignacio Montoya, Anushka Peres, Jim Webber, Catrina, and Star: thank you for your friendship, your time, patience, and love.

I'm grateful for the kindness, support, and generosity of friends, colleagues, and mentors in the profession at large, people who have taught me more than they realize. These include Nancy Armstrong, Amy Elkins, Agata Frymus, Joshua Landy, Grace Lavery, Cara Lewis, Peter Lurie, Kartik Nair, Julie Beth Napolin, Erin Spampinato, and Jay Watson. Daniel Morgan and Allyson Nadia Field, your work inspires me and your generosity has been stunning. And my colleagues at Bryn Mawr College and in the broader Philadelphia community have already made me feel welcomed: Alex Alberro, Nora Alter, Piyali Bhattacharya, Jenny Bradbury, Chris Cagle, Jed Esty, Chloe Flower, John Ghazvinian, Colby Gordon, Jennifer Hartford Vargas, Kathleen Karlyn, Homay King, C. C. McKee, Gerry Prince, Paul Saint-Amour, Rubina K. Salikuddin, Aytug Sasmaz, Bethany Schneider, Jay Shelat, Jess Shollenberger, Julien Sueadeau, Jamie K. Taylor, Tariq Thachil,

Kate Thomas, Alicia Walker, Rafael Walker, Sarah Wasserman, and Patricia White. I am very lucky and grateful to be in conversation with all of you.

Michael Bérubé's support of my work over the years has been a gift for which I am honored and grateful. He models what being a good citizen in this endangered profession looks like, and I hope I can emulate his generosity even partially. Bud Bynack's eye for logic and rhetoric, as well as his willingness to keep me accountable to writing deadlines, allowed me to complete this manuscript in a timely manner. I'm grateful for his time, attention, and expertise. The pandemic took so much away, but it gave me a friendship with Alix Beeston deep in its intellectual intimacy and personal trust. Thank you, Alix, for all the ways you've tirelessly supported me through these long few years. The generosity of Sarah Gleeson-White knows no bounds; I am grateful for her friendship, coeditorship, and mentorship. I could not have gotten to this point without her institutional and personal support. My fellow travelers Beilah, Faye, Karen, Malkah, and Robin have kept me afloat. Howard Eiland and Julia Brown's ability to read literature for the real lives animated by the words on the page is an example for me of why the death of humanistic thought would amount to the end of us. Thank you for your intellectual mentorship and your friendship. And without John T. Matthews, I would not have had the courage to listen to my own writing voice. Jack's support and intellectual mentorship took myriad and remarkable forms, but the most powerful was in simply assuming the best of me. Thank you, Jack, from the bottom of my heart.

I'm enormously grateful to Alan Thomas at the University of Chicago Press for believing in this project and shepherding it through its various stages of development; to Randy Petilos and the rest of the team—Sara Bakerman, Beth Ina, freelance copyeditor Steve LaRue, and Meredith Nini—for managing its passage into production and fruition; and, finally, to the anonymous readers who gave me feedback that allowed the book to become what it was meant to.

Without the support, guidance, and love of my family—Mom, Dad, Kaveh, Patrick, Caitlin, Felor, Azi, Pino, Chelgis, and Golchin—I would be lost. This book is dedicated to Babajoon; but it is also dedicated to you.

And last, I would like to thank Justin Gifford, who is my home. He provides my life the frame without which it would all be a pile of words, held together by nothing but the book binding.

Notes

INTRODUCTION

1. Emily Holmes Coleman to Djuna Barnes, May 2, 1935, box 3, folder 7, Djuna Barnes Papers, Special Collections, University of Maryland, Hornbake Library, College Park, MD.
2. Emily Holmes Coleman to Djuna Barnes, August 1, 1935, box 3, folder 7, Djuna Barnes Papers, Special Collections, University of Maryland, Hornbake Library, College Park, MD.
3. Emily Holmes Coleman to Djuna Barnes, October 27, 1935, box 3, folder 8, Djuna Barnes Papers, Special Collections, University of Maryland, Hornbake Library, College Park, MD.
4. Emily Holmes Coleman to Djuna Barnes, August 1, 1935.
5. Adorno's critique of narrative unity spans across his entire oeuvre, and it is intimately related to his critique of metaphysics and the concept as it emerges as a vehicle of human knowledge in Kantian epistemology. However, for an especially concentrated articulation of this critique as it pertains to narrative coherence and plot, see the "Coherence and Meaning" section of his *Aesthetic Theory*, ed. Gretel Adorno and Rolf Tiedemann, ed. and trans. Robert Hullot-Kentor (Minneapolis: University of Minnesota Press, 1997), 136–63, and Theodor Adorno and Max Horkheimer, "The Culture Industry: Enlightenment as Mass Deception," in *The Dialectic of Enlightenment: Philosophical Fragments*, ed. Gunzelin Schmid Noerr, trans. Edmund Jephcott (Stanford, CA: Stanford University Press, 2002), 94–136.
6. See Bertolt Brecht, "The Modern Theatre Is the Epic Theatre," in *Brecht on Theatre: The Development of an Aesthetic*, ed. and trans. John Willett (New York: Hill & Wang, 1992), 33–42.
7. Joseph Frank, "Spatial Form in Modern Literature: An Essay in Two Parts," *Sewanee Review* 53, no. 2 (Spring 1945): 221–40; Edmund Wilson, *Axel's Castle: A Study in the Imaginative Literature of 1870–1930* (New York: Charles Scribner's Sons, 1931), 1.
8. Georg Lukács, "The Ideology of Modernism," in *The Meaning of Contemporary Realism*, trans. John Mander and Necke Mander (London: Merlin Press, 1962), 17–46. For his elaboration of the so-called descriptive method, see Georg Lukács,

"Narrate or Describe?," in *Writer and Critic: and Other Essays*, ed. and trans. Arthur Kahn (London: Merlin Press, 1970), 110–148.

9. Virginia Woolf, "Modern Fiction," in *Virginia Woolf: Selected Essays*, ed. David Bradshaw (Oxford: Oxford University Press, 2008), 8, 9.

10. Henry James, "Preface to Roderick Hudson," *The Art of the Novel: Prefaces by Henry James*, ed. R. P. Blackmur (Chicago: University of Chicago Press, 2011), 5.

11. Filippo Tommaso Marinetti, "First Futurist Political Manifesto," in *F. T. Marinetti: Critical Writings*, ed. Günter Berghaus, trans. Dough Thompson (New York: Farrar, Straus, and Giroux, 2006), 49.

12. Djuna Barnes to Emily Holmes Coleman, August 19, 1935, MSS 105, series 1.2, folder 11, Emily Coleman Papers, Special Collections, University of Delaware Library, Museums and Press, Newark, DE.

13. The idea that life is bereft of plot is not, of course, original to Woolf or James. Theories suggesting the same abound. See, for instance, Roger Fry's theory of art as an elaboration of our "imaginative" rather than "actual" life. Roger Fry, "An Essay in Aesthetics," *New Quarterly* 2 (April 1909), 171–90. And more famously, reading novels, for Walter Benjamin, is an act of "consuming" the deaths of characters in the vicarious hope of gaining access to knowledge of our own death, which remains unavailable to us as we are living. Walter Benjamin, "The Storyteller: Observations on the Work of Nikolai Leskov," in *Walter Benjamin: Selected Writings*, vol. 3, *1935–1938*, ed. and trans. Howard Eiland and Michael Jennings (Cambridge, MA: Harvard University Press, 2006). Pier Paolo Pasolini elaborates this idea, too, in his "Observations on the Long Take," which I discuss at length in chapter three.

14. Coleridge, Samuel Taylor. *Coleridge's Shakespeare Criticism*, vol. 1, ed. Thomas Middleton Rayson (London: Constable, 1960), 116. E. M. Forster, *Aspects of the Novel*, ed. Oliver Stallybrass (1927; New York: Penguin, 2005), 40. For more on Coleridge's comments on volition and the novel, particularly as it pertains to the emergence of fictionality, see Cathy Gallagher, "The Rise of Fictionality," in *The Novel*, vol. 1, ed. Franco Moretti (Princeton, NJ: Princeton University Press, 2006), 347–49.

15. Benjamin, "The Storyteller."

16. D. A. Miller, *The Novel and the Police* (Berkeley: University of California Press, 1988), 26.

17. Scholars have shown nineteenth-century novelistic plot in a far more complex, even sympathetic light than what we might call the "complicity model," offering rich complications, if not powerful refutations, of the Barthesian and Millerian view that nineteenth-century plot was coextensive with coercive social and normative control. See, for instance, Stephanie Insley Hernishow, *Born Yesterday: Inexperience and the Early Realist Novel* (Baltimore: Johns Hopkins University Press, 2020); Anna Kornbluh, *The Order of Forms: Realism, Formalism, and Social Space* (Chicago: University of Chicago Press, 2019); Caroline Levine, *The Serious Pleasures of Suspense: Victorian Realism and Narrative Doubt* (Charlottesville: University of Virginia Press, 2003); Jesse Rosenthal, *Good Form: The Ethical Experience of the Victorian Novel* (Princeton, NJ: Princeton University Press, 2017).

18. Kornbluh, *The Order of Forms*, 2.

19. Brian Richardson might describe these structural substitutes as forms of "non-plot-based narrative progression." Brian Richardson, *A Poetics of Plot for the Twenty-First Century: Theorizing Unruly Narratives* (Columbus: Ohio State University Press, 2019), 83–97.

20. See Jacques Rancière, *The Edges of Fiction*, trans. Steve Corcoran (Cambridge: Polity Press, 2020).

21. The term *media ecology* was first coined in 1968 by media theorist Neil Postman, inspired by Marshall McLuhan's work in *Understanding Media* (1964). Julian Murphet (himself influenced by Raymond Williams, Fredric Jameson, and Friedrich Kittler) uses it in the discussion of modernist literature in particular as part of a broad network of new technological media. See Julian Murphet, *Multimedia Modernism: Literature and the Anglo-American Avant-Garde* (Cambridge: Cambridge University Press, 2009), 8; Mark Wollaeger, *Modernism, Media, and Propaganda: British Narrative From 1900 to 1945* (Princeton, NJ: Princeton University Press, 2006), xvi; Friedrich Kittler, *Gramophone, Film, Typewriter*, trans. Geoffrey Winthrop-Young and Michael Wutz (Stanford, CA: Stanford University Press, 1999).

22. Cara L. Lewis, *Dynamic Form: How Intermediality Made Modernism* (Ithaca, NY: Cornell University Press, 2020).

23. For details of this formal and institutional development, see Tom Gunning, *D. W. Griffith and the Origins of American Narrative Film: The Early Years at Biograph* (Chicago: University of Illinois Press, 1991); Mary Ann Doane, *The Emergence of Cinematic Time: Modernity, Contingency, and the Archive* (Cambridge, MA: Harvard University Press, 2002).

24. See Thomas Elsaessear, *Film History as Media Archaeology: Tracking Digital Cinema* (Amsterdam: Amsterdam University Press, 2016).

25. Judith Mayne, *Private Novels, Public Films* (Athens: University of Georgia Press, 1988), 3. See John Fell's and Robert C. Allen's older but still illuminating studies of the relationship between the burgeoning narrative cinema and the theater. Robert C. Allen, *Vaudeville and Film, 1895–1915: A Study in Media Interaction* (New York: Arno Press, 1980); John Fell, *Film and the Narrative Tradition* (Norman: University of Oklahoma Press, 1974).

26. Vachel Lindsay, *The Art of the Moving Picture* (1915; New York: Liveright, 1970), 197–98.

27. See Mayne, *Private Novels, Public Films*; David Bordwell, Janet Staiger, and Kristin Thompson, *The Classical Hollywood Cinema: Film Style and Mode of Production to 1960* (New York: Columbia University Press, 1985).

28. See, for instance, Tom Gunning, *D.W. Griffith and the Origins of Narrative Film* (Urbana: University of Illinois Press, 1991); Miriam Hansen, *Babel and Babylon: Spectatorship in American Silent Film* (Cambridge, MA: Harvard University Press, 1994); Lee Grieveson, *Policing Cinema: Movies and Censorship in Early Twentieth-Century America* (Berkeley: University of California Press, 2004).

29. Sergei Eisenstein, "Dickens, Griffith, and the Film Today," in *Film Form*, ed. and trans. Jay Leyda (New York: Harcourt, 1977), 206.

30. Walter Benjamin, "The Work of Art in the Age of Its Technological Reproducibility," in *Walter Benjamin: Selected Writings*, vol. 4, *1938–1940*, ed. Howard

Eiland and Michael Jennings, trans., Edmund Jephcott (Cambridge, MA: Harvard University Press, 2003), 263–64.

31. Christian Metz, *The Imaginary Signifier: Psychoanalysis and the Signifier*, trans., Celia Britton, Annwyl Williams, Ben Brewster, and Alfred Guzzetti (Bloomington: Indiana University Press, 1977), 93.

32. David Trotter, *Cinema and Modernism* (Malden, MA: Blackwell, 2007), 10.

33. Paul Ricoeur, *Time and Narrative*, vol. 1, trans. Kathleen McLaughlin and David Pellauer (Chicago: University of Chicago Press, 1984), 3, emphasis added.

34. James MacDowell, *Happy Endings in Hollywood Cinema: Cliché, Convention, and the Final Couple* (Edinburgh: Edinburgh University Press, 2013).

35. Mayne, *Private Novels, Public Films*.

36. Gregory Castle, *Reading the Modernist Bildungsroman* (Gainesville: University Press of Florida, 2006), 3.

37. Peter Brooks, *Reading for the Plot: Design and Intention in Narrative* (Cambridge, MA: Harvard University Press, 1984), 5.

38. James Phelan, *Reading Plots, Reading People: Character, Progression, and the Interpretation of Narrative* (Chicago: University of Chicago Press, 1989).

39. Ian Watt, *Conrad in the Nineteenth Century* (Berkeley: University of California Press, 1979), 169.

40. Tzvetan Todorov, *The Poetics of Prose*, trans. Richard Howard (Ithaca, NY: Cornell University Press, 1977), 111.

41. Gérard Genette, *Narrative Discourse: An Essay in Method*, trans. Jane E. Lewin (Ithaca, NY: Cornell University Press, 1983).

42. Aristotle, *Poetics*, trans. Malcom Heath (New York: Penguin, 1996), 18–19.

43. Karl Marx, *The Eighteenth Brumaire of Louis Bonaparte*, trans. Ben Fowkes, in *Surveys from Exile*, ed. David Fernbach (New York: Penguin, 1973), 170. For Peter Nicholls's discussion of this quotation in relation to modernist aesthetics, see Peter Nicholls, *Modernisms: A Literary Guide* (London: Palgrave Macmillan, 2009), 6–7.

44. Gertrude Stein, "Composition as Explanation," in *Selected Writings of Gertrude Stein*, ed. Carl Van Vechten (New York: Vintage, 1990), 518. Stein was important to American avant-garde filmmaker Stan Brakhage, whose cinema Annette Michelson refers to as generating "the sense of a continuous present, of a filmic time which devours memory and expectation in the presentation of presentness." Annette Michelson, "Camera Lucida/Camera Obscura," in *On the Wings of Hypothesis: Collected Writings on Soviet Cinema*, ed. Rachel Churner (Cambridge, MA: MIT Press, 2020), 39. For more on Michelson's critique of Brakhage's aesthetics of the present, see Daniel Morgan, "Modernism Is Not for Children: Reckoning with Annette Michelson" (lecture, University of Chicago, Chicago, IL, November 3, 2021).

45. Deidre Lynch, *The Economy of Character: Novels, Market Culture, and the Business of Inner Meaning* (Chicago: University of Chicago Press, 1998), 14.

46. Michael Sayeau, *Against the Event: The Everyday and the Evolution of Modernist Narrative* (Oxford: Oxford University Press, 2013), 13.

47. It was "accepted consensus" in the Aristotelian frame that most people do not act but rather participate in ordinary, repetitive activity prescribed by their lower station; their lives were thought, in other words, to reside solely in the

iterative; the singulative is relegated to the special (read, politically powerful). Rancière, *The Edges of Fiction*, 8, 9

48. Rancière, *The Edges of Fiction*, 10.

49. Rancière, 9.

50. See Rancière, *Edges of Fiction*, but also *The Future of the Image* (London: Verso, 2019) and especially *The Lost Thread: The Democracy of Modern Fiction*, trans. Steven Corcoran (London: Bloomsbury, 2016).

51. For a reading of the trope of stillness in *To the Lighthouse* as it relates to the history and aesthetics of still life painting, see Cara Lewis, *Dynamic Form: How Intermediality Made Modernism* (Ithaca, NY: Cornell University Press, 2020), 72–77.

52. See Toril Moi, "Rethinking Character," in *Character: Three Inquiries in Literary Studies* (Chicago: University of Chicago Press, 2020), 27–75. While the insistence on the textuality of character has been especially vehement in the study of modernism, a literary moment whose rise coincided, as Moi reminds us, with the professionalization of literary criticism, the fictionality of literary characters has been at the forefront of critics' and consumers' minds since at least the mid-eighteenth century. The naive reader who believes in the reality of the characters they read is a convenient fiction generated by early critical champions of modernism; the self-conscious pleasures of investment in characters as fictional entities was central to the very rise of the novel, as Catherine Gallagher, Deidre Lynch, and others have shown.

53. Mieke Bal, *Guidelines for Writing a PhD Thesis within ASCA* (Amsterdam: Amsterdam School for Cultural Analysis, 2006), 30, quoted by Moi in "Rethinking Character," 28.

54. Phelan, *Reading Plots, Reading People*; John Frow, *Character and Person* (Oxford: Oxford University Press, 2014).

55. For that reason, it would be less nonsensical to ask "*Would* Anna like kiwis?" if and only if, for example, it were written in *Anna Karenina* that she likes other kinds of similarly tangy fruit. These examples are a play on those that L. C. Knights performs in his famous 1933 attack on the study of character in Shakespeare criticism, *How Many Children Had Lady Macbeth? An Essay on the Theory and Practice of Shakespeare Criticism* (Cambridge: Minority Press, 1933), quoted in Toril Moi and Alex Woloch, *The One vs. the Many: Minor Characters and the Space of the Protagonist in the Novel* (Princeton, NJ: Princeton University Press, 2003), 16.

56. Vivian Sobchack, "The Actor's Four Bodies," in *Acting and Performance in Moving Image Culture: Bodies, Screens, Renderings*, ed. Jörg Sternagel, Deborah Levitt, and Dieter Mersch (New Brunswick, NJ: Transaction, 2012), 439–40.

57. Woloch, *One vs. the Many*, 13.

58. Jonathan Foltz, *The Novel after Film: Modernism and the Decline of Autonomy* (Oxford: Oxford University Press, 2018); Trotter, *Cinema and Modernism*; Laura Marcus, *The Tenth Muse: Writing about Cinema in the Modernist Period* (Oxford: Oxford University Press, 2010). An important exception to the earlier trend of centering avant-garde visual culture when thinking through the relationship between modernist literature and film, and one that influenced Trotter's important study, is Garrett Stewart, *Between Film and Screen: Modernism's Photo Synthesis* (Chicago: University of Chicago Press, 2008).

59. Narrative film, writes Foltz, "was poised to strike novelists not primarily as an alternative form of narrative art" but as an example of "narrative lapse" whose formal "unconventionality" offered modernists alternative examples of narrative disassemblage. Foltz, *The Novel after Film*, 6, 5. And in its capacity to record not stories, but "existence as such," Trotter argues, popular film offered a media-historical parallel to literary modernism's "fragmentary and encyclopedic" aesthetics; Trotter, *Cinema and Modernism*, 1, 4.

60. Andreas Huyssen, *After the Great Divide: Modernism, Mass Culture, Postmodernism* (Bloomington: Indiana University Press, 1986).

61. Natalia Cecire, *Experimental: American Literature and the Aesthetics of Knowledge* (Baltimore: Johns Hopkins University Press, 2019); Moi, "Rethinking Character," 32.

62. See, for instance, Sara Marcus, *Cinematic Modernisms* (Cambridge: Cambridge University Press, 2000); Michael North, *Machine-Age Comedy* (Oxford: Oxford University Press, 2008). For a recent and excellent account of Clair's avant-garde comedy, see Malcolm Turvey, *Play Time: Jacques Tati and Comedic Modernism* (New York: Columbia University Press, 2020), 45–52.

63. Miriam Hansen, "The Mass Production of the Senses: Classical Cinema as Vernacular Modernism," *Modernism/modernity* 6, no. 2 (1999): 59-77.

64. "In Hollywood cinema, there are no subversive films, only subversive moments. For social and economic reasons, no Hollywood film can provide a distinct and coherent alternative to the classical model. . . . So powerful is the classical paradigm that it regulates what may violate it." David Bordwell, Janet Staiger, and Kristin Thompson, *The Classical Hollywood Cinema: Film Style and Mode of Production to 1960* (New York: Columbia University Press, 1985), 81.

65. David Bordwell's own forthcoming book, *Perplexing Plots* (New York: Columbia University Press), accounts more exhaustively for the narrative complexities of several genres in the classical period, including, most obviously, film noir.

66. Hansen, "Mass Production of the Senses," 60.

67. Raymond Williams, "When Was Modernism?," *Politics of Modernism: Against the New Conformists* (London: Verso, 2007), 31–37.

68. Sergei Eisenstein, "Dickens, Griffith, and the Film Today," in *Film Form*, ed. and trans. Jay Leyda (New York: Harcourt, 1977), 195–255.

69. Judith Mayne, *Private Novels, Public Films* (Athens: University of Georgia Press, 1988), 9.

70. Toni Morrison, *The Bluest Eye* (1970; New York: Vintage International, 2007), 122.

71. See Lauren Berlant, *Cruel Optimism* (Durham, NC: Duke University Press, 2011), but especially Lauren Berlant, *The Female Complaint: The Unfinished Business of Sentimentality in American Culture* (Durham, NC: Duke University Press, 2008).

72. James Baldwin, *The Devil Finds Work* (1976; New York: Vintage International, 2011), 30.

73. Mao and Walkowitz coined the phrase to refer to the oppositional stance of the then newly pluralized "modernisms" vis-à-vis the network of economic, social, and aesthetic forces against which aesthetic modernity was thought to position itself (i.e., capitalism, the bourgeoisie, mass culture)—what they call the

"bad artistic behavior" constituting the "modernist affront." The phrase was also meant to flag how modernism's badness itself eventually went bad. At some point relatively early in its development, modernism started to be considered quite good, and the intensity of its affront "withered," Mao and Walkowitz write, "under the sun of esteem." Douglas Mao and Rebecca Walkowitz, eds., *Bad Modernisms* (Durham, NC: Duke University Press, 2006), 2–4.

74. Clare Hemmings, *Considering Emma Goldman: Feminist Political Ambivalence and the Imaginative Archive* (Durham, NC: Duke University Press, 2018), 5–6.

75. Sianne Ngai, *Ugly Feelings* (Cambridge, MA: Harvard University Press, 2005).

76. Morrison, *The Bluest Eye*, 122–23.

77. Morrison, 123.

78. Jaqueline Najuma Stewart, *Migrating to the Movies: Cinema and Black Urban Modernity* (Berkeley: University of California Press, 2005), 17. Anna Everett, *Returning the Gaze: A Genealogy of Black Film Criticism, 1909–1949* (Durham, NC: Duke University Press, 2001); Charlene Regester, "From the Buzzard's Roost: Black Movie-Going in Durham and Other North Carolina Cities during the Early Period of American Cinema," *Film History* 17, no. 1 (2005): 113–24.

79. bell hooks, *Black Looks: Race and Representation* (Boston: South End, 1992); Manthia Diawara, "Black Spectatorship: Problems of Identification and Resistance," *Black American Cinema*, ed. Manthia Diawara (New York: Routledge, 1993).

80. Baldwin, *The Devil Finds Work*, 7. For the most recent reading of the significance of Bette Davis to the history of African American cinematic spectatorship, see Julia Stern, *Bette Davis Black and White* (Chicago: University of Chicago Press, 2021).

81. José Esteban Muñoz, *Disidentifications: Queers of Color and the Performance of Politics* (Minneapolis: University of Minnesota Press, 1999), 15–18.

82. Baldwin, *The Devil Finds Work*, 8.

83. Berlant, *Cruel Optimism*, 39.

84. Stewart, *Migrating to the Movies*, 98.

85. Jean Epstein, "Magnification," *October* 3 (Spring 1977): 14.

86. Morrison, *The Bluest Eye*, 123.

87. Morrison, 126.

88. Sarah Keller, *Anxious Cinephilia: Pleasure and Peril at the Movies* (New York: Columbia University Press, 2020), 27.

89. Keller, 10. See Nico Baumbach, "All That Heaven Allows: What Is, or What Was Cinephilia?," *Film Comment* 48, no. 2 (March/April 2012): 46–53.

90. Anna Kornbluh, *The Order of Forms: Realism, Formalism, and Social Space* (Chicago: University of Chicago Press, 2019).

91. Deidre Lynch, *The Economy of Character: Novels, Market Culture, and the Business of Inner Meaning* (Chicago: University of Chicago Press, 1998), 5.

92. This sobering reality is at the heart of Morrison's own as well as Sharon Patricia Holland's more recent discussion of the perils of the discursive turn in theories of the body and identity. It is present, too, in Sylvia Wynter's critique of antihumanism and posthumanism and in bell hooks's of the overvaluation of states of difference and decenteredness in postmodern theory. And it is at the heart, finally, of Mari Ruti's claims in *The Ethics of Opting Out: Queer Theory's*

Defiant Subjects (New York: Columbia University Press, 2017) concerning what she calls the "fetishization of negativity" in the Edelmanian tradition in queer theory, which in its assaults on the centered subject and the valuation of states of nonrelationality and subjective failure loses touch with how desirable, if not necessary, states of relationality, centered selfhood, and success are to those who have had nonrelationality, social and psychic fragmentation, and material failure enforced on them and how some measure of formal solidity does, in an importantly ordinary sense, organize our everyday experiences as human beings. Toni Morrison, "Unspeakable Things Unspoken: The Afro-American Presence in American Literature," *Michigan Quarterly Review* 28, no. 1 (1989): 1–34; Sharon Patricia Holland, *The Erotic Life of Racism* (Durham, NC: Duke University Press, 2012); bell hooks, "Postmodern Blackness," *Postmodern Culture* 1, no. 1 (1990); Sylvia Wynter, "Unsettling the Coloniality of Being/Power/Truth/Freedom: Towards the Human, after Man, Its Overrepresentation—An Argument," *CR: The New Centennial Review* 3, no. 3 (2003): 257–337; Ruti, *Ethics of Opting Out*, 174.

93. James Baldwin, *Go Tell It on the Mountain* (1953; New York: Vintage International, 2013), 28.

94. Morrison, *The Bluest Eye*, 115, 117, 123.

95. Frank Kermode, *The Sense of an Ending: Studies in the Theory of Fiction* (Oxford: Oxford University Press, 2000), 44.

96. See, for instance, Dennis Broe, *Birth of the Binge: Serial TV and the End of Leisure* (Detroit: Wayne State University Press, 2019); *Binge-Watching and Contemporary Television Studies*, ed. Mareike Jenner (Edinburgh: Edinburgh University Press, 2021); Tanya Horecks, *Justice on Demand: True Crime in the Digital Streaming Era* (Detroit: Wayne State University Press, 2019); Siegfried Kracauer, "Cult of Distraction," in *The Mass Ornament: Weimar Essays*, ed. and trans. Thomas Y. Levin (Cambridge, MA: Harvard University Press, 1995), 323–28.

97. Milena Jesenská, "The Cinema" (1920), in *The Promise of Cinema: German Film Theory, 1907–1933*, ed. Anton Kaes, Nicholas Baer, and Michael Cowan (Berkeley: University of California Press, 2016), 166.

98. In *Cruel Optimism*, Berlant locates that complicated persistence in the contemporary postwelfare state, but in *Female Complaint*, they find an earlier phase in classical Hollywood sentimentalism.

99. Kobena Mercer, "Skin Head Sex Thing: Racial Difference and the Homoerotic Imaginary," in *Only Skin Deep: Changing Visions of the American Self*, ed. Coco Fusco and Brian Wallis (New York: Harry N. Abrams, 2003), 143; Kyle Kaplan, "The Ambivalent Erotics of *Hotpants*: Peter de Rome and the Soundtrack of Liberation," *Women and Music: A Journal of Gender and Culture* 22 (2018): 93.

100. Annette Kuhn, *An Everyday Magic: Cinema and Cultural Memory* (London: I. B. Tauris, 2002). For more on this methodological problem, see Janet Staiger, *Interpreting Films: Studies in the Historical Reception of American Cinema* (Princeton, NJ: Princeton University Press, 1992); "The Handmaiden of Villainy: Methods and Problems in Studying the Historical Reception of Film," *Wide Angle* 8, no. 1 (1986): 19–28; "The Perversity of Spectators: Expanding the History of Classical Hollywood Cinema," in *Moving Images: Culture and the Mind*, ed. Ib Bondebjerg (Luton: University of Luton Press, 2000), 19–30; and Robert C. Allen, "From Exhibition

to Reception: Reflections on the Audience in Film History," in *Screen Histories: A Screen Reader*, ed. Annette Kuhn and Jackie Stacey (Oxford: Oxford University Press, 1998), 13–21.

101. Keller, *Anxious Cinephilia*.

102. Christian Keathley, *Cinephilia and History: Or, the Wind in the Trees* (Bloomington: Indiana University Press, 2005); Eugenie Brinkema, *The Forms of the Affects* (Durham, NC: Duke University Press, 2014).

103. See Foltz, *The Novel after Film*; Trotter, *Cinema and Modernism*; Marcus, *The Tenth Muse*. Similarly, Kafka's comments on the cinema in his letters and early diaries are a reliable fund for Hanns Zichler as he interprets what the movies did or did not mean to the Czech author. Hanns Zichler, *Kafka Goes to the Movies*, trans. Susan H. Gillespie (Chicago: University of Chicago Press, 2003).

104. Thadious Davis and George Hutchinson mention Larsen's viewings of *Camille* in their biographies. Thadious Davis, *Nella Larsen: Novelist of the Harlem Renaissance* (Baton Rouge: Louisiana State University Press, 1994), 423; George Hutchinson, *In Search of Nella Larsen: A Biography of the Color Line* (Cambridge, MA: Belknap Press, 2006), 445.

105. Laura Helton's work on the archival practices of historian, activist, and collector Arturo Alfonso Schomburg, for instance, has shown that archival absences are often the result of selective curation, the reflection of a set of choices, rather than a narrative of ignored history. See Laura Helton, "Schomburg's Library and the Price of Black History," *African American Review* 54, no. 1/2 (Spring/Summer 2021): 109–28.

106. As in the work of Saidiya Hartman, Allyson Nadia Field, and Jacqueline Stewart.

107. Saidiya Hartman, *Wayward Lives, Beautiful Experiments: Intimate Histories of Riotous Black Girls, Troublesome Women, and Queer Radicals* (New York: W. W. Norton, 2019), xiv; Allyson Nadia Field, *Uplift Cinema: The Emergence of African American Film and the Possibility of Black Modernity* (Durham, NC: Duke University Press, 2015); Stewart, *Migrating to the Movies*.

108. I develop this claim about the speculative nature of aesthetic criticism in Pardis Dabashi, "Introduction to 'Cultures of Argument': The Loose Garments of Argument," *PMLA* 135, no. 5 (2020): 946–55.

109. S. Pearl Brilmyer, Filippo Trentin, and Zairong Xiang, "Introduction: The Ontology of the Couple," in "The Ontology of the Couple," ed. S. Pearl Brilmyer, Filippo Trentin, and Zairong Xiang, special issue, *GLQ: A Journal of Lesbian and Gay Studies* 25, no. 2 (April 2019): 217. For an extensive theoretical investigation of long-term queer relationship, including but not limited to monogamy, see *Long Term: Essays on Queer Commitment*, eds. Scott Herring and Lee Wallace (Durham, NC: Duke University Press, 2021).

110. Dabashi, "Introduction to 'Cultures of Argument.'"

CHAPTER ONE

1. Thadious Davis, *Nella Larsen: Novelist of the Harlem Renaissance* (Baton Rouge: Louisiana State University Press, 1994), 423. George Hutchinson, *In Search*

of Nella Larsen: A Biography of the Color Line (Cambridge, MA: Belknap Press of Harvard University Press, 2006), 445.

2. Gregory Castle, *Reading the Modernist Bildungsroman* (Gainesville: University of Florida Press, 2006), 1. Fredric Jameson, *Antinomies of Realism* (London: Verso, 2013), 35. See also Jacques Rancière, "The Thread of the Novel," *Novel: A Forum on Fiction* 47, no. 2 (2014): 196–209; Michael Sayeau, *Against the Event: The Everyday and the Evolution of Modernist Narrative* (Oxford: Oxford University Press, 2013). For work on the modernist bildungsroman that privileges negativity, see also Thomas L. Jeffers, *Apprenticeship: The Bildungsroman from Goethe to Santayana* (London: Palgrave Macmillan, 2005), and "Modernist Life Narratives: Bildungsroman, Biography, Autobiography," ed. John Paul Riquelme, special issue of *MFS: Modern Fiction Studies* 59, no. 3 (Fall 2013).

3. Castle, *Reading the Modernist Bildungsroman*, 3.

4. In this, I take Jed Esty's political impulse one step further. More attuned to the political implications of modernism's invalidation of the so-called regime of realist narration, Esty examines the entanglements of modernism's "resist[ance to] the tyranny of plot" with modern colonialism; he studies "the disruption of developmental time" in modernism as "reciprocal allegories of self-making and nation-building." Jed Esty, *Unseasonable Youth: Modernism, Colonialism, and the Fiction of Development* (Oxford: Oxford University Press, 2013), 2.

5. James Phelan, *Reading People, Reading Plots: Character, Progression, and the Interpretation of Narrative* (Chicago: University of Chicago Press, 1989).

6. Mieke Bal, *Guidelines for Writing a PhD Thesis within ASCA* (Amsterdam: Amsterdam School for Cultural Analysis, 2006), 30.

7. Toril Moi, "Rethinking Character," in *Character: Three Inquiries in Literary Studies* (Chicago: University of Chicago Press, 2020), 27–75.

8. Sharon Patricia Holland, *The Erotic Life of Racism* (Durham, NC: Duke University Press, 2012); bell hooks, "Postmodern Blackness," *Postmodern Culture* 1, no. 1 (1990); Lynne Huffer, *Are the Lips a Grave? A Queer Feminist on the Ethics of Sex* (New York: Columbia University Press, 2013); Heather Love, *Feeling Backward: Loss and the Politics of Queer History* (Cambridge, MA: Harvard University Press, 2007); Toni Morrison, "Unspeakable Things Unspoken: The Afro-American Presence in American Literature," *Michigan Quarterly Review* 28, no. 1 (1989): 1–34; José Muñoz, *Cruising Utopia: The Then and There of Queer Futurity* (New York: New York University Press, 2009); Mari Ruti, *The Ethics of Opting Out: Queer Theory's Defiant Subjects* (New York: Columbia University Press, 2017); Robyn Wiegman and Elizabeth A. Wilson, "Introduction: Antinormativity's Queer Conventions," *differences* 26, no. 1 (2015): 1–25; Sylvia Wynter, "Unsettling the Coloniality of Being/Power/Truth/Freedom: Towards the Human, After Man, Its Overrepresentation—An Argument," *CR: The New Centennial Review* 3, no. 3 (2003): 257–337.

9. Houston Baker, quoted in Adam McKible and Suzanne W. Churchill, "Introduction: In Conversation: The Harlem Renaissance and the New Modernist Studies," *Modernism/modernity* 20, no. 3 (September 2013): 427–31 (429).

10. Michael Bibby, "The Disinterested and Fine: New Negro Renaissance Poetry and the Racial Formation of Modernist Studies," *Modernism/modernity* 20, no. 3 (September 2013): 490–93.

11. For more on this critical history, see K. Merinda Simmons and James A. Clark, eds., *Race and New Modernisms*, (London: Bloomsbury), 2019).

12. I elaborate this point in my introduction.

13. Two examples of this important new work are Octavio R. Gonzelez, *Misfit Modernism: Queer Forms of Double Exile in the Twentieth-Century Novel* (University Park: Pennsylvania State University, 2020); and Natalia Cecire, *Experimental: American Literature and the Aesthetics of Knowledge* (Baltimore: Johns Hopkins University Press, 2019).

14. José Esteban Muñoz, *Disidentifications: Queers of Color and the Performance of Politics* (Minneapolis: University of Minnesota Press, 1999).

15. Judith Mayne, *Private Novels, Public Films* (Athens: University of Georgia Press, 1988), 9.

16. Alix Beeston, *In and Out of Sight: Modernist Writing and the Photographic Unseen* (Oxford: Oxford University Press, 2018); Wai Chee Dimock, "A Theory of Resonance," *PMLA* 112, no. 5 (October 1997): 1060–71; David Eng, *The Feeling of Kinship: Queer Liberalism and the Racialization of Intimacy* (Durham, NC: Duke University Press, 2010); Allyson Nadia Field, *Uplift Cinema: The Emergence of African American Film and the Possibility of Black Modernity* (Durham, NC: Duke University Press, 2015); Saidiya Hartman, *Wayward Lives, Beautiful Experiments: Intimate Histories of Riotous Black Girls, Troublesome Women, and Queer Radicals* (New York: W. W. Norton, 2019); Julie Beth Napolin, *The Fact of Resonance: Modernist Acoustics and Narrative Form* (New York: Fordham University Press, 2020); Jacqueline Najuma Stewart, *Migrating to the Movies: Cinema and Black Urban Modernity* (Berkeley: University of California Press, 2005).

17. Joseph North, *Literary Criticism: A Concise Political History* (Cambridge, MA: Harvard University Press, 2017); see introductions to David Trotter, *Cinema and Modernism* (Malden, MA: Blackwell, 2007), and Laura Marcus, *The Tenth Muse: Writing about Cinema and the Modernist Period* (Oxford: Oxford University Press, 2007). The most recent articulation of that historicist imperative emerges in Jonathan Foltz, *The Novel after Film: Modernism and the Decline of Autonomy* (Oxford: Oxford University Press, 2018).

18. Dimock, "A Theory of Resonance," 1061; Beeston, *In and Out of Sight*, 26. For more on the critical value of decontextualizing modernist texts, see Michaela Bronstein, *Out of Context: The Uses of Modernist Fiction* (Oxford: Oxford University Press, 2018).

19. Hartman, *Wayward Lives, Beautiful Experiments*, xiii.

20. Hartman, xiv.

21. Dimock, "A Theory of Resonance," 1068; Eng, *The Feeling of Kinship*, 183–84.

22. Hutchinson, *In Search of Nella Larsen*, 445.

23. Field, *Uplift Cinema*, 25; Stewart, *Migrating to the Movies*, xviii.

24. See Patrick McGilligan, *George Cukor: A Double Life, A Biography of the Gentleman Director* (New York: St. Martin's Press, 1992); Alan Kreizenbeck, *Zoë Akins: Broadway Playwright* (Westport, CT: Praeger, 2004). Akins is officially credited as one of three screenwriters for *Camille* (the other two are Frances Marion and James Hilton). However, it is clear from Akins's archive that she was the only significant writer on the project and that the accreditation of Marion and Hilton

was the source of a major dispute between her and MGM after the release of the film. In a letter to Alice Kauser on December 30, 1937, she writes that agent George Volck's office "failed me miserably by permitting the studio to put anybody's name on 'Camille' except my own, as they had the absolute word of George Cukor that not one line was shot except what I wrote." Zoë Akins to Alice Hauser, ZA 1856, box 78, The Huntington Library, San Marino, California.

25. Early draft of opening title cards for *Camille* by Zoë Akins, 1936, box 182, folder 4, Zoë Akins Papers, The Huntington Library, San Marino, California.

26. Dimock, "A Theory of Resonance," 1064–65.

27. Nancy Armstrong, *How Novels Think: The Limits of Individualism from 1719–1900* (New York: Columbia University Press, 2006), 3.

28. Armstrong, 33.

29. For an account of a similar set of formal and characterological problems in the context of the early realist novel, see Stephanie Insley Hernishow, *Born Yesterday: Inexperience and the Early Realist Novel* (Baltimore: Johns Hopkins University Press, 2020).

30. Jennifer L. Fleissner, *Maladies of the Will: The American Novel and the Modernity Problem* (Chicago: University of Chicago Press, 2022).

31. Larsen, *Quicksand* (New York: W. W. Norton, 2019), 43, 59, 100.

32. Walter Benjamin, "The Storyteller: Reflections on the Works of Nikolai Leskov," trans. Harry Zohn, *Walter Benjamin: Selected Writings*, vol. 3: *1935–1938*, ed. Howard Eiland and Michael Jennings (Cambridge, MA: Belknap Press of Harvard University Press, 2006), 156.

33. Virginia Woolf, *To the Lighthouse* (San Diego, CA: Harcourt Brace, 1989), 112.

34. Rafael Walker has commented, relatedly, that often the objects that surround Helga are "more potent agents than their nominal owner." Rafael Walker, "Nella Larsen Reconsidered: The Trouble with Desire in *Quicksand* and *Passing*," *MELUS* 41, no. 1 (Spring 2016): 169.

35. Larsen, *Quicksand*, 19, 38.

36. Cherene Sherrard-Johnson, *Portraits of the New Negro Woman: Visual and Literary Culture in the Harlem Renaissance* (New Brunswick, NJ: Rutgers University Press, 2007), 22.

37. Larsen, *Quicksand*, 7–9.

38. Ann E. Hostetler, "The Aesthetics of Race and Gender in Nella Larsen's *Quicksand*," *PMLA* 105, no. 1 (January 1990): 35.

39. Larsen, *Quicksand*, 10.

40. Marjorie Rosen, *Popcorn Venus: Women, Movies, and the American Dream* (New York: Avon, 1973), 169.

41. *New York Times*, July 6, 1927, 23, quoted by Rosen, *Popcorn Venus*, 92.

42. Michelle Henning, "The Floating Face: Garbo, Photography and Death Masks," *Photographies* 10, no. 2 (2017): 157–78.

43. Antonia Lant, "Haptical Cinema," *October* 74 (Autumn 1995): 45. For more on cinematic hapticity and dimensionality, particularly in early, preclassical film, see Noël Burch, "Building a Haptic Space," in *Life to Those Shadows*, ed. and trans. Ben Brewster (Berkeley: University of California Press, 1990), 62–85. For other, more recent discussions of hapticity in film, see Jennifer M. Barker, *The Tactile*

Eye: Touch and the Cinematic Experience (Berkeley: University of California Press, 2009); Laura U. Marks, *The Skin of the Film: Intercultural Cinema, Embodiment, and the Senses* (Durham, NC: Duke University Press, 2000); and *Touch: Sensuous Theory and Multisensory Media* (Minneapolis: University of Minnesota Press, 2002); Vivian Sobchak, *Carnal Thoughts: Embodiment and Moving Image Culture* (Berkeley: University of California Press, 2004).

44. Christian Metz, *The Imaginary Signifier: Psychoanalysis and the Cinema*, trans. Celia Britton, Annwyl Williams, Ben Brewster, and Alfred Guzzetti (Bloomington: Indiana University Press, 1982), 45.

45. Michel Chion, *The Voice in Cinema*, trans. Claudia Gorbman (New York: Columbia University Press), 3.

46. Larsen, *Quicksand*, 7.

47. Laura E. Tanner, "Intimate Geography: The Body, Race, and Space in Larsen's *Quicksand*," *Texas Studies in Literature and Language* 51, no. 1 (Summer 2009): 187.

48. Larsen, *Quicksand*, 88, 106.

49. Angsar Nünning and Kai Marcel Sicks, *Turning Points: Concepts and Narratives of Change in Literature and Other Media* (Berlin: De Gruyter, 2017), introduction.

50. Franco Moretti, *The Way of the World: The Bildungsroman in European Culture* (London: Verso, 2000), 44, 48.

51. Larsen, *Quicksand*, 96.

52. Larsen, *Quicksand*, 95.

53. Jacquelyn Y. McLendon drew this comparison first in *The Politics of Color in the Fiction of Jessie Fauset and Nella Larsen* (Charlottesville,: University of Virginia Press, 1995), 89.

54. Larsen, *Quicksand*, 105–106.

55. Fredric Jameson, *Antinomies of Realism* (London: Verso, 2013).

56. Hence the importance of Walker's argument concerning the place of desire in Larsen's fiction. Helga Crane engages in "desperate efforts to become a self-defined agent," he writes, to "assume the position of self-conscious subject." One of the primary tragedies of *Quicksand*, for Walker—and I agree with him—is that the "synthesis" of the two parts of her identity into one coherent self proves impossible. Walker, "Nella Larsen Reconsidered," 168, 169.

57. Larsen, *Quicksand*, 111.

58. Gabrielle McIntire, "Toward a Narratology of Passing: Epistemology, Race, and Misrecognition in Nella Larsen's *Passing*," *Callaloo* 35, no. 3 (Summer 2012): 778.

59. Frances Ellen Watkins Harper, *Iola Leroy; Or, Shadows Uplifted* (New York, Penguin Books, 2010), 44.

60. William Wells Brown, *Clotel; Or, The President's Daughter* (New York, Penguin Books, 2004), 49.

61. Jessie Fauset, *Plum Bun: A Novel without A Moral* (Boston: Beacon Press, 1990).

62. Deborah E. McDowell, introduction to *Quicksand* and *Passing*, by Nella Larsen, ed. Deborah E. McDowell (New Brunswick, NJ: Rutgers University Press, 1986), ix–xxxv.

63. Nella Larsen, *Passing* (New York: Penguin Books, 1997), 17–18.

64. Ralina L. Joseph, *Transcending Blackness: From the New Millennium Mulatta to the Exceptional Multiracial* (Durham, NC: Duke University Press, 2013), ix.

65. Adrian Piper, "Passing for White, Passing for Black," *Transition* 58 (1992): 6.

66. Gayle Wald, *Crossing the Line: Racial Passing in 20th-Century U.S. Literature and Culture* (Durham, NC: Duke University Press, 2000), 6. The hermeneutic challenge central to passing is what has led many critics, most canonically Claudia Tate, to claim that Larsen's *Passing* is a novel fundamentally about interpretation. See Claudia Tate, "Nella Larsen's *Passing*: A Problem of Interpretation," *Black American Literature Forum* 14, no. 4 (Winter 1980): 142–46. For a more recent and also excellent account of interpretive difficulty in *Passing*, see McIntire, "Toward a Narratology of Passing."

67. Joseph, *Transcending Blackness*, ix.

68. Toni Morrison, *The Bluest Eye* (1970; New York: Vintage International, 2007), 16. For whiteness and classical Hollywood, see *Classical Hollywood, Classic Whiteness*, ed. Daniel Bernardi (Minneapolis: University of Minnesota Press, 2001); Richard Dyer, *White: Essays on Race and Culture* (London: Routledge, 1997); *The Birth of Whiteness: Race and the Emergence of U.S. Cinema*, ed. Daniel Bernardi (New Brunswick, NJ: Rutgers University Press, 1996).

69. Bernardi, *Classic Hollywood, Classic Whiteness*, xvii.

70. Arne Olave Lunde, *Nordic Exposures: Scandinavian Identities in Classical Hollywood Cinema* (Seattle: University of Washington Press, 2010), 3.

71. Michael Krützen, *The Most Beautiful Woman on the Screen: The Fabrication of the Star Greta Garbo* (Frankfurt: Peter Lang, 1992), 69; Lunde, *Nordic Exposures*, 93–94; for more on Garbo's extremely restrictive diet, see Karen Swenson, *Greta Garbo: A Life Apart* (New York: Scribner, 1997).

72. Swenson, *Greta Garbo*, 62. Though there is no certainty as to the meaning of the name, it is thought to descend from the term *garbon*, "a mysterious sprite that sometimes comes out at night to dance to the moonbeams. This elfin creature was a descendant of the dreaded *gabilun* of Swedish and German folklore." Robert Payne, *The Great Garbo* (New York: Cooper Square Press, 2002), 59. There is also debate as to the origin of the choice of the name. While for Swenson it was the creation of Pollack and Garbo, for Payne it was Stiller who came up with it (Payne, 59). Regardless, there's little in Garbo's biographical accounts to suggest that she was unwilling to make the change or uncomfortable with the name itself.

73. Dyer, *White: Essays on Race and Culture*.

74. Lunde, *Nordic Exposures*, 103.

75. Lunde, 94. Roland Barthes, "The Face of Garbo," *Mythologies*, trans. Annette Lavers (New York: Hill & Wang), 56–57.

76. Swenson, *Greta Garbo*, 217.

77. Lunde, *Nordic Exposures*, 94.

78. Larsen, *Passing*, 17–18.

79. Larsen, *Passing*, 30.

80. For a reading of Garbo as an important icon of lesbian cinephilia in the classical Hollywood period, especially alongside Marlene Dietrich and Katherine Hepburn, see Patricia White, *UnInvited: Classical Hollywood Cinema and Lesbian Representability* (Bloomington: Indiana University Press, 1999).

81. Betsy Erkkila, "Greta Garbo: Sailing beyond the Frame," *Critical Inquiry* 11, no. 4 (June 1985), 598, 602.

82. Jinny Huh, *The Arresting Eye: Race and the Anxiety of Detection* (Charlottesville: University of Virginia Press, 2015).

83. Roland Barthes, *S/Z: An Essay*, trans. Richard Miller (New York: Hill & Wang, 1975), 17.

84. Larsen, *Passing*, 111.

85. Virginia Lee Warren, "A New England School Boy Who Liked to Draw Became the Hollywood Fashion King," *Washington Post*, January 4, 1934, 11.

86. See Helen Louise Walker, "Stars or Stooges," *Silver Screen*, November 1936, 22–23.

87. George Hutchinson, *In Search of Nella Larsen: A Biography of the Color Line* (Cambridge, MA: Belknap Press of Harvard University Press, 2006), 46–47.

88. Werner Sollors, *Neither Black Nor White Yet Both: Thematic Explorations of Interracial Literature* (Oxford: Oxford University Press, 1997).

89. Michael Gillespie, *Film Blackness: American Cinema and the Idea of Black Film* (Durham, NC: Duke University Press, 2016), 2–6.

90. Gillespie, 15.

91. Larsen, *Quicksand*, 51. Not insignificantly, Marlene Dietrich, whom we will discuss at length in chapter 2, wears a pair of sequined gloves as undercover Agent X-27 in *Dishonored* (Josef von Sternberg, 1931), a film with a very similar plot to *Mata Hari*. Those sequins, whose rows of tiny oscillating disks produce the same chromatic duality as Mata's velvet and mesh, may be viewed as a precursor to the more explicit racial masquerade on display in the famous musical number in *Blonde Venus* (Josef von Sternberg, 1932), where Dietrich strips off a gorilla suit to slowly reveal her searing white skin beneath. For pioneering work on clothing, skin, and race on screen, see Anne Anlin Cheng, *Ornamentalism* (New York: Oxford University Press, 2019); *Second Skin: Josephine Baker & the Modern Surface* (New York: Oxford University Press, 2011).

92. The classic argument for Garbo as Art Deco icon appears in Lucy Fischer, "Greta Garbo and Silent Cinema: The Actress as Art Deco Icon," *Camera Obscura* 16, no. 3 (2001): 82–111.

93. Sylvia Ullback, "Garbo's Glamor . . . Mystery or Misery?," *Photoplay* 1, no. 6 (December 1936): 56.

94. For a reading of Clare as a vampiric figure, see Cherene Sherrard-Johnson, *Portraits of the New Negro Woman: Visual and Literary Culture in the Harlem Renaissance* (New Brunswick, NJ: Rutgers University Press, 2007), 859–62.

95. In Sun Yu's similarly plotted film *Daybreak* (1933), starring the iconic actress Li Lili, Yu solves the problem of the final couple somewhat differently, by having the two die together by firing squad.

96. Larsen, *Passing*, 111.

97. It is no surprise that Garbo and prominent German expressionistic filmmaker F. W. Murnau (a friend of Mauritz Stiller) were admirers of one another and that upon Murnau's tragic, early death, Garbo commissioned a death mask of his face and kept it on her desk her entire career in Hollywood.

98. On the importance of causality to the Hollywood ending, see especially

David Bordwell's "Happily Ever After, Part Two," *Velvet Light Trap* 19 (1982): 2–7. Bordwell's essay comes in response to Fritz Lang's canonical essay on happy endings that he wants to insist are motivated rather than tacked on. Fritz Lang, "Happily Ever After" (1948), in *Film Makers on Filmmaking*, ed. Harry Geduld (London: Pelican Books, 1969). For more recent accounts of the Hollywood happy ending, see James MacDowell, *Happy Endings in Hollywood Cinema: Cliché, Convention, and the Final Couple* (Edinburgh: University of Edinburgh Press, 2013); Richard Neupert, *The End: Narration and Closure in the Cinema* (Detroit, MI: Wayne State University Press, 1995).

99. Bordwell, "Happily Ever After, Part Two," 2.

100. Alexandre Dumas, *The Lady of the Camellias*, trans. Liesl Schillinger (New York: Penguin, 2013), 205.

101. Linda Alexander, *Reluctant Witness: Robert Taylor, Hollywood, and Communism* (Albany, GA: Bearmanor, 2016); Jane Ellen Wayne, *Robert Taylor: The Man with the Perfect Face* (New York: St. Martin's, 1989).

102. *Hollywood* 26, no. 2 (February 1937): 4.

103. Dumas, 39.

104. Dumas, 194, 200–201.

105. For a reading of the ambivalence permeating the scene at the Circus, see Terri Francis, "Embodied Fictions, Melancholy Migrations: Josephine Baker's Cinematic Celebrity," *MFS: Modern Fiction Studies* 51, no. 4 (Winter 2005): 826.

106. See Hutchinson, *In Search of Nella Larsen*, chaps. 20–22.

107. Lauren Berlant, *The Female Complaint: The Unfinished Business of Sentimentality in American Culture* (Durham, NC: Duke University Press, 2008); and *Cruel Optimism* (Durham, NC: Duke University Press, 2011).

108. Hutchinson, 458–79.

PREMIÈRE ENTR'ACTE

1. In the novel, Irene reads the letter herself, a scene that opens the novel. In Hall's adaptation, Irene's husband Brian reads the letter to Irene while they are in bed. For an interpretation of the implications of this change to Larsen's original, see Rafael Walker, "Passing into Film: Rebecca Hall's Adaptation of Nella Larsen," *Modernism/modernity Print Plus* 6, no. 2 (November 10, 2021), https://modernismmodernity.org/forums/posts/walker-passing-film-hall-adaptation-larsen#_ednref8.

2. Nella Larsen, *Passing* (New York: Penguin, 1997), 112.

3. Laura Mulvey, "Afterthoughts on 'Visual Pleasure and the Narrative Cinema' Inspired by *Duel in the Sun*," *Framework: The Journal of Cinema and Media* 15–17 (Summer 1981): 12–15.

CHAPTER TWO

1. Adrienne Rich, "Compulsory Heterosexuality and Lesbian Existence," *Signs* 5, no. 4 (Summer 1980): 631–60.

2. See Kevin Ohi, *Henry James and the Queerness of Style* (Minneapolis: Univer-

sity of Minnesota Press, 2011). See also Eve Kosofsky Sedgwick, *The Epistemology of the Closet* (Berkeley: University of California Press, 1990).

3. D. A. Miller, *The Novel and the Police* (Berkeley: University of California Press, 1988), 26.

4. For an illuminating reading of the place of *Nightwood* in Joseph Frank's "spatial form" essay and its various developments, see Brian Glavey, *The Wallflower Avant-Garde: Modernism, Sexuality, and Queer Ekphrasis* (New York: Oxford University Press, 2015), 51–54; Joseph Frank, "Spatial Form in Modern Literature: An Essay in Three Parts," *Sewanee Review* 53, no. 2 (1945): 221–40; no. 3 (1945): 443–56; no. 4 (1948): 643–53; Scott Herring, *Queering the Underworld: Slumming, Literature, and the Undoing of Lesbian and Gay History* (Chicago: University of Chicago Press, 2007), 111; Julie Taylor, *Djuna Barnes and Affective Modernism* (Edinburgh: Edinburgh University Press, 2012), 12. The tradition of seeing Barnes's fiction as offering an alternative to, if not fully repudiating, the heteronormative constraints embodied in nineteenth-century literary form is long standing, and so to name all instances of its critical articulation would be excessive. And it is important to keep in mind, as well, the divide in Barnes criticism between gay and lesbian criticism and queer theoretical approaches, one that is perhaps most evident in Scott Herring's *Queering the Underworld*, which departs emphatically from the gay/lesbian analytic frame that dominated Barnes studies since arguably the feminist recovery of her work in the 1980s and 90s by scholars such as Mary Lynn Broe and Jane Marcus. But key instances of scholarship that argues for Barnesian form as emphatically antiheteronormative, even across the gay/lesbian and queer divide, include Julie Abraham, *Are Girls Necessary? Lesbian Writing and Modern Histories* (New York: Routledge, 1996); Shari Benstock, *Women of the Left Bank: Paris, 1900–1945* (Austin: University of Texas Press, 1986); Joseph Allen Boone, *Libidinal Currents: Sexuality and the Shaping of Modernism* (Chicago: University of Chicago Press, 1998); the essays in *Silence and Power: A Reevaluation of Djuna Barnes*, ed. Mary Lynn Broe (Carbondale: Southern Illinois University Press, 1991); Mary E. Galvin, *Queer Poetics: Five Modernist Women Writers* (Westport, CT: Praeger, 1998); and Bonnie Kime Scott, *The Gender of Modernism: An Anthology* (Bloomington: Indiana University Press, 1990).

5. Katherine A. Fama, "Melancholic Remedies: Djuna Barnes's *Nightwood* as Narrative Theory," *Journal of Modern Literature* 37, no. 2 (Winter 2014): 41; Glavey, *The Wallflower Avant-Garde* (51); Daniela Caselli, "'If Some Strong Woman': Djuna Barnes's Great Capacity for All Things Uncertain," in *Shattered Objects: Djuna Barnes's Modernism*, ed. Elizabeth Pender and Cathryn Setz (University Park: Pennsylvania State University Press, 2019), 147–61. Caselli borrows the term *aesthetics of uncertainty* from Janet Wolff, *The Aesthetic of Uncertainty* (New York: Columbia University Press, 2008). Caselli develops her theory of Barnes as fitting uneasily within standard conceptions of modernism in her book *Improper Modernism: The Bewildering Corpus of Djuna Barnes* (London: Routledge, 2009). Tyrus Miller would go so far as to say that Barnes occupies a form of "late modernism" that borders on postmodernism. See Tyrus Miller, *Politics, Fiction, and the Arts between the World Wars* (Berkeley: University of California Press, 1999), 121–68.

6. Djuna Barnes to Emily Holmes Coleman, November 8, 1935, folder 12,

box 2, series 1.2, Emily Holmes Coleman Papers, Special Collections, University of Delaware Library, quoted in Elizabeth Pender and Cathryn Setz, introduction to *Shattered Objects: Djuna Barnes's Modernism*, ed. Elizabeth Pender and Cathryn Setz (University Park: Pennsylvania State University Press, 2019), 1, and in Kate Armond, "Allegory and Dismemberment: Reading Djuna Barnes's *Nightwood* through the Forms of the Baroque Trauerspiel," *Textual Practice* 26, no. 3 (2012): 867, and in Mary Lynn Broe and Angela J. C. Ingram, *Women's Writing in Exile* (Chapel Hill: University of North Carolina Press, 1989), 51.

7. S. Pearl Brilmyer, Filippo Trentin, and Zairong Xiang, "Introduction: The Ontology of the Couple," in "The Ontology of the Couple," ed. S. Pearl Brilmyer, Filippo Trentin, and Zairong Xiang, special issue, *GLQ: A Journal of Lesbian and Gay Studies*, 25, no. 2 (April 2019): 217.

8. Phillip Herring, *Djuna: The Life and Work of Djuna Barnes* (New York: Penguin, 1996), 160.

9. Dorothy Manners, *Motion Picture* 11, no. 6 (January 1931): 50.

10. *Photoplay*, 39, no. 2 (January 1931): 15. Katherine Albert, "She Threatens Garbo's Throne," *Photoplay* 39, no. 1 (December 1930): 60. The comparison between Dietrich and Garbo was a veritable institution, fueled by publicity venues such as *Photoplay*, *Modern Screen*, and *Motion Picture*. One especially striking example is a Garbo fan letter titled "Fie! For Shame!" published in *Photoplay* that reads, "Miss Dietrich has come too late. We worship only one idol and she is Garbo. We resent the intrusion of this Marlene Dietrich. There is no place for her in our hearts. We do not want her"; *Photoplay* 39, no. 3 (February 1931): 10. For more on the public dynamic and institutional competition between the images of Dietrich and Garbo, see Joseph Garncarz, "Playing Garbo: How Marlene Dietrich Conquered Hollywood," in *Dietrich Icon*, ed. Gerd Gemünden and Mary R. Desjardins (Durham, NC: Duke University Press, 2007), 103–18; see also Alexander Doty, "Marlene Dietrich and Greta Garbo: The Sexy Hausfrau versus the Swedish Sphinx," in *Glamour in the Golden Age: Movie Stars of the 1930s*, ed. Adrienne McLean (New Brunswick, NJ: Rutgers University Press, 2010), 108–28.

11. Steven Bach, *Marlene Dietrich: Life and Legend* (Minneapolis: University of Minnesota Press, 2011), 172–73, 203–7.

12. Jane Marcus, "Laughing at Leviticus: *Nightwood* as Woman's Circus Epic," in *Silence and Power: A Reevaluation of Djuna Barnes*, ed. Mary Lynn Broe (Carbondale: Southern Illinois University Press, 1991), 236–37; for other mention of Dietrich during the feminist recovery era of Barnes scholarship, see also Nancy Levine, "I've Always Suffered from Sirens: The Cinema Vamp and Djuna Barnes's *Nightwood*," *Women's Studies: An Interdisciplinary Journal* 16, no. 3/4 (March 1989), 273. For more recent examples see Laura Winkiel, "Circuses and Spectacles: Public Culture in *Nightwood*," *Journal of Modern Literature* 21, no. 1 (Fall 1997): 22; Alex Goody, *Modernist Articulations: A Cultural Study of Djuna Barnes, Mina Loy, and Gertrude Stein* (New York: Palgrave Macmillan, 2007), 172. For other scholarship on film, film culture, and film technology in relation to Barnes, see Alex Goody, "Spectacle, Technology, and Performing Bodies: Djuna Barnes at Coney Island," *Modernist Cultures* 7, no. 2 (October 2012): 205–30; Melissa Hardie, "Djuna Barnes: The Flower of Her Secret," in *Shattered Objects: Djuna Barnes's Modernism*, ed.

Elizabeth Pender and Cathryn Setz (University Park: Pennsylvania State University Press, 2019), 178–92; Deborah Tyler-Bennett, "'Thick within Our Hair': Djuna Barnes's Gothic Lovers," in *Gothic Modernisms*, ed. Andrew Smith and Jeff Wallace (London: Palgrave Macmillan, 2001), 95–110.

13. Djuna Barnes, "Playgoer's Almanac," *Theatre Guild Magazine* 8, no. 4 (January 1931): 34–35. Series 3, folder 56, Djuna Barnes Papers, Hornbake Library, University of Maryland. She remarked very briefly on Dietrich's legs in *The Blue Angel* in the March 1931 iteration of "Playgoer's Almanac."

14. *Photoplay* 39, no.1 (December 1930): 54.

15. Heather Love, "Playing for Keeps," *GLQ: A Journal of Lesbian and Gay Studies* 25, no. 2 (2019): 258.

16. Djuna Barnes, *Nightwood* (1936; New York: New Directions, 2006), 160.

17. Barnes, 137.

18. Herring, *Queering the Underworld*, 174.

19. Anne-Lise François, *Open Secrets: The Literature of Uncounted Experience* (Stanford, CA: Stanford University Press, 2008).

20. Barnes, *Nightwood*, 41.

21. Barnes, 13.

22. Barnes, 90.

23. Barnes, 47.

24. Barnes, 85–86.

25. Barnes, 45.

26. Dora Zhang, *Strange Likeness: Description and the Modernist Novel* (Chicago: University of Chicago Press, 2020), 12; Glavey, *The Wallflower Avant-Garde*, 60.

27. James Phelan, *Reading People, Reading Plots: Character, Progression, and the Interpretation of Narrative* (Chicago: University of Chicago Press, 1989), 2–14.

28. Sarah Henstra, "Looking the Part: Performative Narration in Djuna Barnes's *Nightwood* and Katherine Mansfield's *Je ne parle pas français*," *Twentieth Century Literature* 46, no. 2 (2000): 128; Barnes, *Nightwood*, 16–17.

29. Barnes, *Nightwood*, 37–8.

30. Winkiel, "Circuses and Spectacles," 22.

31. Barnes, *Nightwood*, 38, emphasis added.

32. Barnes, 38.

33. Barnes, 155; James Phillip, *Sternberg and Dietrich: The Phenomenology of Spectacle* (Oxford: Oxford University Press, 2019), 3.

34. Barnes, *Nightwood*, 46.

35. Bach, *Marlene Dietrich*, 57, 77.

36. *Photoplay* 38, no. 5 (October 1930): 21.

37. Maurice Chevalier, quoted by Bach, *Marlene Dietrich*, 153; Pare Loretz quoted by Bach, 161.

38. Barnes, *Nightwood*, 48, 51.

39. The term Marcus uses to describe especially the scene introducing Robin in "La somnambule."

40. John Baxter, *Von Sternberg* (Lexington: University Press of Kentucky, 2010), 13.

41. For Dietrich's performances under the constraints of the Hays Code, see Gaylyn Studlar, "Marlene Dietrich and the Erotics of Code-Bound Hollywood,"

Dietrich Icon, ed. Gerd Gemünden and Mary R. Desjardins (Durham, NC: Duke University Press, 2007), 211–38.

42. Christian Metz, *The Imaginary Signifier: Psychoanalysis and the Cinema*, trans. Celia Britton, Ben Brewster, Alfred Guzzetti, and Annwyl Williams (Bloomington: Indiana University Press, 1975).

43. Marlene Dietrich, *Marlene* (New York: Grove Press, 1987), 81.

44. Josef von Sternberg, *Fun in a Chinese Laundry* (San Francisco: Mercury House, 1988), 265.

45. Carole Zucker, *The Idea of the Image: Josef von Sternberg's Dietrich Films* (London: Associated University Presses, 1988), 28.

46. Zucker, *Idea of the Image*, 28.

47. Herman G. Weinberg, *Josef von Sternberg: A Critical Study* (New York: E. P. Dutton, 1967), 62.

48. Barnes, *Nightwood*, 45, 65.

49. Barnes, 51, 173.

50. Mieke Bal, *Guidelines for Writing a PhD Thesis within ASCA* (Amsterdam: Amsterdam School of Cultural Analysis, 2006), 30, quoted in Toril Moi, "Rethinking Character," in *Character: Three Inquiries in Literary Studies* (Chicago: University of Chicago Press, 2019), 28.

51. Charles Grivel, *Production de l'intérêt romanesque* (1973), quoted in Toril Moi, "Rethinking Character," 28, and in Catherine Gallagher, "The Rise of Fictionality," in *The Novel*, ed. Franco Moretti (Princeton, NJ: Princeton University Press, 2006), 350.

52. Toril Moi, "Rethinking Character," 27–75.

53. Erwin Panofsky, "Style and Medium in the Motion Pictures," in *Three Essays on Style*, ed. Irving Lavin (1934; Cambridge, MA: MIT Press, 1997), 118.

54. Richard Dyer, *Stars* (1998; London: Palgrave Macmillan, 2011), 20. See also Stanley Cavell, *The World Viewed: Reflections on the Ontology of Film* (Cambridge, MA: Harvard University Press, 1979), chap. 4.

55. Cavell, *The World Viewed*, 27.

56. Djuna Barnes, "Playgoer's Almanac," *Theatre Guild Magazine*, September 1930, 32. Series 3, folder 56, Djuna Barnes Papers, Hornbake Library, University of Maryland.

57. This habit of Dietrich's was common knowledge in Hollywood, but for one especially acute account, see *The New Movie Magazine* 1, no. 2 (August 1932): 10.

58. This was widely publicized, but for one instance of journalistic coverage, see "Sues Marlene Dietrich," *New York Times*, August 8, 1931, 16. See also "Marlene Calls Charges in Lawsuit 'Absurd,'" *Washington Post*, August 9, 1931, 8.

59. Sarah Hamilton, "Dietrich: Woman of Contrasts," *Movie Mirror* 1, no. 1 (November 1931): 29.

60. Djuna Barnes, "Playgoer's Almanac," *Theatre Guild Magazine* 8, no. 4 (January 1931): 34–35. Series 3, folder 56, Djuna Barnes Papers, Hornbake Library, University of Maryland.

61. For an account of the sexual dimensions of that effect of restraint, see Gaylyn Studlar's exquisite, canonical *In the Realm of Pleasure: Von Sternberg, Dietrich, and the Masochistic Aesthetic* (New York: Columbia University Press, 1992).

62. Doty, "Marlene Dietrich and Greta Garbo," 109. For more on the cultural and textual significance of Dietrich's voice, see Amy Lawrence, "Marlene Dietrich: The Voice as Mask," in *Dietrich Icon*, ed. Gerd Gemünden and Mary R. Desjardins (Durham, NC: Duke University Press, 2007), 79–99.

63. For Barnes's comments on Garbo's voice, see the introduction.

64. Bach, *Marlene Dietrich*, 90.

65. "Frau Dietrich Comes, Sex Press Matter, and Sweet Marie," *Pittsburgh Post-Gazette*, December 6, 1930, 10.

66. In Dietrich's own words, "*The Blue Angel* was something completely different, the role of an ordinary, brazen, sexy and impetuous floozie, the very opposite of the 'mysterious woman' that von Sternberg wanted me to play in *Morocco*." Marlene Dietrich, *Marlene*, trans., Salvator Attanasio (New York: Grove Press, 1989), 77. And Paramount was financially invested in that mysterious reticence. Though *The Blue Angel* was made before *Morocco*, Hollywood released *Morocco* first for fear that Paramount Studios' new star would be perceived as too "brazen and vulgar" and therefore not an effective rival to their main competition, MGM's always demure and urbane Garbo. For more on the history of these different release dates, the comparisons between Dietrich and Garbo, and the press's role in that public dynamic, see Doty, "Marlene Dietrich and Greta Garbo"; see also Joseph Garncarz, "Playing Garbo," and Patrice Petro, "*The Blue Angel* in Multiple Language Versions: The Inner Thighs of Miss Dietrich," in *Dietrich Icon*, ed. Gerd Gemünden and Mary R. Desjardins (Durham, NC: Duke University Press, 2007), 103–18, and 141–61, respectively.

67. Lutz Koepnick, "Dietrich's Face," in *Dietrich Icon*, 50. For an extended analysis of the transformation of Dietrich's performance style from *Morocco* onward, see Zucker, *Idea of the Image*, 89–96.

68. Bach, *Marlene Dietrich*, 88.

69. *Variety*, November 19, 1930.

70. "A lot of people say that you can't photograph thought, but you certainly can if you have a Gary Cooper," said King Vidor. Interviews by Nancy Dowd and David Shepard in *King Vidor*, Director's Guild of America Oral History Series (Metuchen, NJ: Scarecrow Press, 1988), 152–53.

71. Corey K. Creekmur, "Gary Cooper: Rugged Elegance," *Glamour in a Golden Age: Movie Stars of the 1930s*, ed. Adrienne L. McLean (New Brunswick, NJ: Rutgers University Press, 2012), 76.

72. Creekmur, "Gary Cooper," 66–83; Jeffrey A. Brown, "'Putting on the Ritz': Masculinity and the Young Gary Cooper," *Screen* 36, no. 3 (Summer 1995): 194.

73. Creekmur, "Gary Cooper," 76.

74. See Brown, "'Putting on the Ritz.'"

75. Patricia White, *UnInvited: Classical Hollywood Cinema and Lesbian Representability* (Bloomington: Indiana University Press, 1999), 55. We might say that the editing of this sequence anticipates *Meeting of Two Queens* (Cecilia Barriga, 1991). A compilation tape made by Spanish video artist Cecilia Barriga, the film splices a series of images and scenes from the films of Dietrich and Garbo, making it seem as if the two stars—icons of queer, particularly lesbian, cinephilia, as Patricia White has argued, are in an embrace across an editorial distance. For an

illuminating reading of this film in the context of a discussion of lesbian spectatorship, see White, 53–58.

76. James MacDowell, *Happy Endings in Hollywood Cinema: Cliché, Convention, and the Final Couple* (Edinburgh: Edinburgh University Press, 2013).

77. Alice A. Kuzniar, "'It's Not Often That I Want a Man': Reading for a Queer Marlene," in *Dietrich Icon*, ed. Gerd Gemünden and Mary R. Desjardins (Durham, NC: Duke University Press, 2007), 248, 254.

78. Kuzniar, "'It's Not Often That I Want a Man,'" 243.

79. A similar dynamic, especially between Dietrich and Marshall, appears in *Angel* (Ernst Lubitsch, 1937), in which they also costarred (the analogy to Grant's character is there played by Melvyn Douglas). Dietrich's and Marshall's screen chemistry notoriously left much to be desired.

80. Barnes, *Nightwood*, 42, 44–45, 52.

81. Katherine A. Fama, "Melancholic Remedies: Djuna Barnes's *Nightwood* as Narrative Theory," *Journal of Modern Literature* 37, no. 2 (Winter 2014): 47; Barnes, *Nightwood*, 147.

82. Barnes, *Nightwood*, 48, 52, 77.

83. See Lee Edelman, *No Future: Queer Theory and the Death Drive* (Durham, NC: Duke University Press, 2004).

84. Bonnie Roos, *Djuna Barnes's* Nightwood*: The World and Politics of Peace* (London: Bloomsbury, 2014), 5.

85. Scott Herring, *Queering the Underworld: Slumming, Literature, and the Undoing of Lesbian and Gay History* (Chicago: University of Chicago Press, 2007), 21.

86. Barnes, *Nightwood*, 12.

87. Barnes, 28.

88. For more on the relation of plot to social climbing, see Wendy Veronica Xin, "Reading for the Plotter," *New Literary History* 49, no. 1 (Winter 2018): 93–118.

89. Barnes, *Nightwood*, 99, 144.

90. Barnes, 144.

91. Letter to Emily Coleman, November 22, 1935, quoted by Phillip Herring, *Djuna: The Life and Work of Djuna Barnes* (New York: Penguin, 1996), 160.

92. Diaries of Emily Holmes Coleman (unpublished manuscript, University of Delaware Library), 209–10, quoted in Herring, *Djuna*, 160.

93. Herring, *Queering the Underworld*, 190–92.

94. Barnes, *Nightwood*, 107, 110.

95. A valuable line of inquiry, which I unfortunately do not have the space to pursue here, would be to locate the points of convergence between Doctor's desire for normative plotting I am describing here and Emma Heaney's reading of the Doctor's "frustrated impossible desire" for experiences of normative domesticity typically associated with straight cis women. Emma Heaney, *The New Woman: Literary Modernism, Queer Theory, and the Transfeminine Allegory* (Evanston, IL: Northwestern University Press, 2017), 136.

96. Barnes, *Nightwood*, 43.

97. Barnes, 25.

98. Barnes to Christine Koschel, quoted in Daniela Caselli, *Improper Modernism: The Bewildering Corpus of Djuna Barnes* (London: Routledge, 2009), 3.

DEUXIÈME ENTR'ACTE

1. William Faulkner, *Absalom, Absalom!* (1936; New York: Vintage International, 1990), 102.

CHAPTER THREE

1. William Faulkner, quoted by Joseph Blotner, *Faulkner: A Biography* (New York: Random House, 1974), 1216.
2. See Tom Gunning, *D. W. Griffith and the Origins of American Narrative Film: The Early Years at Biograph* (Chicago: University of Illinois Press, 1991).
3. See Sergei Eisenstein, "Montage of Attractions, An Essay," in *The Film Sense*, ed. and trans. Jay Leyda (New York: Harcourt Brace, 1970), 230–33.
4. See Gunning, *D. W. Griffith*.
5. Sarah Gleeson-White, ed., *William Faulkner at Twentieth-Century Fox: The Annotated Screenplays* (Oxford: Oxford University Press, 2017); Stefan Solomon, *William Faulkner in Hollywood: Screenwriting for the Studios* (Athens: University of Georgia Press, 2017); Jordan Brower, "Hollywood Signs: A Literary History of the Studio System," book manuscript in progress.
6. A prominent example of criticism that has privileged *The Birth of a Nation* is Peter Lurie's tremendous work of film-theoretical scholarship on Faulkner, *Vision's Immanence: Faulkner, Film, and the Popular Imagination* (Baltimore: Johns Hopkins University Press, 2004).
7. Jane Gaines, *Fire and Desire: Mixed-Race Movies in the Silent Era* (Chicago: University of Chicago Press, 2001), 93.
8. Gaines, 93.
9. The extant copies of the *Mississippian* and the *Oxford Eagle* through 1929, the year *The Sound and the Fury* was published, advertise fifty-three titles. Many thanks to the librarians at the J. D. Williams Library at the University of Mississippi for their help locating the microfilms for the *Mississippian* and the *Oxford Eagle*, especially Jennifer Ford. Between the years 1915 and 1930, there was only one (albeit very enthusiastic) advertisement in the *Oxford Eagle* for a showing of *The Birth of a Nation* at the Lyric, and that was in 1926—no more or less than any other film showing between those dates. The January 22, 1926, issue of the *Oxford Eagle* advertised *The Birth of a Nation* as "The Greatest and Most Enduring Motion Picture Ever Produced" and informed its readers that it would be playing at the Lyric on "Tuesday Night." *Oxford Eagle*, January 22, 1926, 5.
10. Many thanks to William Lewis, owner of Neilson Department Store in Oxford, MS, whose conversations with me in August 2020 allowed me to discover this history. For the presence and location of the Opera House in the town square of Oxford, see Oxford Lafayette County Heritage Foundation, Lafayette County Historic Maps Project, https://olhf.maps.arcgis.com/apps/webappviewer/index.html?id=f8a3a37e4df94764bbf665bd392a997c.
11. See Gleeson-White, *William Faulkner at Twentieth-Century Fox*; Solomon, *William Faulkner in Hollywood*.
12. William Faulkner, *The Sound and the Fury* (1929; New York: Vintage International, 1984), 177.

13. For motivation and the classical Hollywood cinema, see David Bordwell, "Story Causality and Motivation," in David Bordwell, Janet Staiger, and Kristin Thompson, *The Classical Hollywood Cinema: Film Style and Mode of Production to 1960* (New York: Columbia University Press, 1985), 19.

14. Gertrude Stein, "Composition as Explanation," in *Selected Writings of Gertrude Stein*, ed. Carl Van Vechten (New York: Vintage, 1990), 518.

15. Philip Weinstein, *Becoming Faulkner: The Art and Life of William Faulkner* (Oxford: Oxford University Press, 2010), 8–10.

16. Weinstein, 8.

17. Lee Edelman, *No Future: Queer Theory and the Death Drive* (Durham, NC: Duke University Press, 2004), 29. For more on Barnes's fiction in relation to Edelmanian critique of reproductive futurity, see Brian Glavey, *The Wallflower Avant-Garde: Modernism, Sexuality, and Queer Ekphrasis* (New York: Oxford University Press, 2015).

18. Jed Esty uses this phrase in the context of British and global Anglophone literature. See Jed Esty, *Unseasonable Youth: Modernism, Colonialism, and the Fiction of Development* (Oxford: Oxford University Press, 2013).

19. Rafael Walker, "Nella Larsen Reconsidered: The Trouble with Desire in *Quicksand* and *Passing*," *MELUS* 41, no. 1 (Spring 2016): 173.

20. Gregory Castle, *Reading the Modernist Bildungsroman* (Gainesville: University Press of Florida, 2006), 71.

21. Djuna Barnes, *Nightwood* (1936; New York: New Directions, 2006), 115.

22. Heather Love, *Feeling Backward: Loss and the Politics of Queer History* (Cambridge, MA: Harvard University Press, 2007), 3–4.

23. Barnes, *Nightwood*, 114.

24. Barnes, 167.

25. Tellingly, the six characters in search of an author in Luigi Pirandello's play are a dysfunctional family.

26. Weinstein, *Becoming Faulkner*, 62.

27. James M. Mellard has also usefully examined the various aesthetic modes present in *As I Lay Dying*, teasing out its various engagements with the representational strategies and ideological assumptions of not just modernism but also realism and naturalism. James M. Mellard, "Realism, Naturalism, Modernism: Residual, Dominant, and Emergent Ideologies in *As I Lay Dying*," in *Faulkner and Ideology*, ed. Donald Kartiganer and Anne J. Abadie (Jackson: University Press of Mississippi, 1995), 217–37.

28. Faulkner, *The Sound and the Fury*, 14.

29. Tom Gunning, "Cinema of Attractions: Early Film, Its Spectator and the Avant-Garde," in *Early Cinema: Space, Frame, Narrative*, ed. Thomas Elsaesser and Adam Barker (London: BFI, 1990), 56–62 (60).

30. Miriam Hansen, *Babel and Babylon: Spectatorship in American Silent Film* (Cambridge, MA: Harvard University Press, 1991), 29.

31. Mary Ann Doane, *The Emergence of Cinematic Time: Modernity, Contingency, the Archive* (Cambridge, MA: Harvard University Press, 2002), 91.

32. Doane, 92.

33. Doane, 93.

34. Roland Barthes, *Camera Lucida*, trans. Richard Howard (New York: Hill & Wang, 1981), 79.

35. Christian Metz, *Film Language: A Semiotics of the Cinema*, trans. Michael Taylor (Chicago: University of Chicago Press, 1974), 6, 8.

36. Pier Paolo Pasolini, "Observations on the Long Take," trans. Norman MacAfee and Craig Owens, *October* 13 (1980), 3–6 (4), emphasis in original.

37. William Faulkner, "Interview with Jean Stein vanden Heuvel (1956)," in *The Lion in the Garden: Interviews with William Faulkner, 1926–1962*, ed. James B. Meriwether and Michael Millgate (New York: Random House, 1968), 245, emphasis added.

38. Faulkner, *The Sound and the Fury*, 44, 59.

39. Faulkner, 74.

40. André Gaudreault, *From Plato to Lumière: Narration and Monstration in Literature and Cinema*, trans. Timothy Barnard (1988; Toronto: University of Toronto Press, 2009), 72–80.

41. Faulkner, *The Sound and the Fury*, 71.

42. Tom Gunning, "'Now You See It, Now You Don't': The Temporality of the Cinema of Attractions," *Velvet Light Trap* 32, no. 3 (1993): 3–12 (7).

43. Gunning, 10–11.

44. Gunning, 11.

45. Faulkner, *The Sound and the Fury*, 21–22.

46. See Gunning, "An Aesthetic of Astonishment: Early Film and the (In)Credulous Spectator," in *Film Theory and Criticism: Critical Concepts in Media and Cultural Studies*, ed. Philip Simpson, Andrew Utterson, and K. J. Shepherdson (London: Routledge, 2004), 78–95.

47. Gunning, 84.

48. Gunning, 84.

49. Howard Eiland, "Reception in Distraction," *boundary 2* 30, no. 1 (2003): 56n10.

50. Faulkner, *The Sound and the Fury*, 11–12.

51. Fredric Jameson, *Antinomies of Realism* (London, Verso, 2013), 177.

52. Faulkner, *The Sound and the Fury*, 320.

53. Faulkner, 7.

54. Faulkner, 36.

55. Faulkner, 13.

56. Pasolini, "Observations on the Long Take," 6, emphasis in original.

57. Gerard Genette, *Narrative Discourse: An Essay on Method*, trans. Jane E. Lewin (Ithaca, NY: Cornell University Press, 1993), 71–98 (79).

58. Faulkner, *The Sound and the Fury*, 76.

59. See Doane, *Emergence of Cinematic Time*, chap. 5; Gunning, *D. W. Griffith*, 89–129.

60. Doane, *Emergence of Cinematic Time*, 141.

61. For a full account of the significance of death, editing, and the event in the execution genre, see Doane, chap. 5.

62. For an extended reading of the narrative function of cutting in this film, see Doane, chap. 5.

63. André Bazin, "Death Every Afternoon," in *Rites of Realism: Essays on Corporeal Cinema*, ed. Ivone Margulies, trans. Mark A. Cohen (Durham, NC: Duke University Press, 2003), 30.

64. Faulkner, *The Sound and the Fury*, 79.

65. Faulkner, 4.

66. Faulkner, 86.

67. John T. Matthews is right, for instance, that Quentin yearns to recover the physical and psychological intimacies of childhood and that his "obsession with virginity marks his inability to move from childhood into adulthood." John T. Matthews, *Faulkner and the Lost Cause* (Boston: Twayne, 1991), 47.

68. Stephen Heath, *Questions of Cinema* (Bloomington: Indiana University Press, 1981), 136.

69. Faulkner, *The Sound and the Fury*, 78.

70. Faulkner, 174.

71. Faulkner, 142.

72. Faulkner, 140, 141.

73. David Bordwell, "An Excessively Obvious Cinema," in David Bordwell, Janet Staiger, and Kristin Thompson, *The Classical Hollywood Cinema: Film Style and Mode of Production to 1960* (New York: Columbia University Press, 1985), 3.

74. David Bordwell, "Story Causality and Motivation," in David Bordwell, Janet Staiger, and Kristin Thompson, *The Classical Hollywood Cinema: Film Style and Mode of Production to 1960* (New York: Columbia University Press, 1985), 19.

75. Heath, *Questions of Cinema*, 134.

76. The *Oxford Eagle*, November 1, 1928, 5; Many thanks to the librarians at the Moving Picture Collection in the Library of Congress for giving me access to this film; for more on Faulkner's interest in *Sergeant York*, see Stefan Solomon, *William Faulkner in Hollywood: Screenwriting for the Studios* (Athens: University of Georgia Press, 2017), 117–20.

77. Matthews, *Faulkner and the Lost Cause*, 64.

78. Faulkner, *The Sound and the Fury*, 186.

79. Faulkner, 187.

80. Faulkner, 187.

81. Faulkner, 188.

82. Faulkner, 187.

83. Faulkner, 187, 232.

84. Tom Gunning, "Cinema of Attractions: Early Film, Its Spectator and the Avant-Garde," in *Early Cinema: Space, Frame, Narrative*, ed. Thomas Elsaesser and Adam Barker (London: BFI, 1990), 57.

85. However, as Gunning notes, these erotic films were also among the first to develop film technique in service of what would later become classical cinema's reliance on character identification. That is because even though the wife looks at the camera as she undresses, our gaze is mediated through the character of the husband, who is inside the shot as well but whose point of view we are presumed to adopt. As a result, a film like *The Bride Retires*, like others in the "peeping tom" genre Gunning identifies, "moves toward the construction of a diegetic world that mediates the spectator's relation to the film through a character's relation to a

dramatic situation." Tom Gunning, "What I Saw From the Rear Window of the Hôtel des Folie-Dramatiques, or the Story Point of View Films Told," in *Ce que je vois de mon ciné... : La Représentation du regard dans le cinéma des premiers temps*, ed. André Gaudreault (Paris: Méridiens Klincksieck, 1988), 37.

86. Faulkner, *The Sound and the Fury*, 183.

87. Faulkner, 184.

88. Heath, *Questions of Cinema*, 136.

89. The most elegant and influential articulation of this view comes from Matthews, who argues that Darl's "regular efforts to expunge a certain kind of reality through aesthetic treatment" represents a "falsifying modernism" that is "overly aesthetic" in its retreat from the historical circumstances with which the Bundrens are coming to terms. John T. Matthews, "*As I Lay Dying* in the Machine Age," *boundary 2* 19, no. 1 (1992): 88–90. More recently, Ted Atkinson has repeated the sentiment in his suggestion that Darl's aesthetic work testifies to how "entranced" he is "by the [modernist] ideology of autonomy." Ted Atkinson, "The Ideology of Autonomy: Form and Function in *As I Lay Dying*," *Faulkner Journal* 2, no. 1/2 (2005–6): 22.

90. Matthews, "*As I Lay Dying* in the Machine Age," 88.

91. I borrow the concept of a "discourse network" from Friedrich Kittler. See the introduction.

92. William Faulkner, *As I Lay Dying* (1930; New York: Vintage, 1991), 4.

93. Jameson, *Antinomies of Realism*, 35.

94. Jacques Rancière, "The Thread of the Novel," *Novel: A Forum on Fiction* 47, no. 2 (2014): 197.

95. In his introduction to *The Sound and the Fury*, Faulkner wrote that upon writing the novel, "I discovered then that I had gone through all that I had ever read, from Henry James through Henty to newspaper murders, without making any distinction or digesting any of it, as a moth or a goat might. After *The Sound and the Fury* and without heeding to open another book and in a series of delayed repercussions like summer thunder, I discovered the Flauberts and Dostoievskys and Conrads whose books I had read ten years ago."

96. André Bleikasten, *The Ink of Melancholy: Faulkner's Novels from* The Sound and the Fury *to* Light in August (Bloomington: Indiana University Press, 1990), 151.

97. For a Heideggerian reading of embodiment and time in this scene and others in *As I Lay Dying*, see Zachary Tavlin, "'Ravel Out into Time': Phenomenology and Temporality in *As I Lay Dying*," *Mississippi Quarterly* 68, no. 1/2 (2015): 83–100.

98. Faulkner, *As I Lay Dying*, 4.

99. Ezra Pound, "Elizabethan Classicists," *Egoist* 4 (1917): 136.

100. Faulkner, *As I Lay Dying*, 94.

101. By invoking spatiality, I am not suggesting that we apply Joseph Frank's canonical term "spatial form"—which he reserved for modernism—to realism. Frank argues that the linear sequentiality of realism gives way to the spatial topography of works such as *The Waste Land*, *Ulysses*, or *Nightwood*. I am making a point orthogonal to Frank's, that realist plot is generated within the space between retrospective omniscient narration and the events themselves—in essence, plot is an effect of the narrative enunciation craning back toward the fabula.

102. Walter Benjamin, "The Work of Art in the Age of Its Technological Reproducibility," in *Walter Benjamin: Selected Writings*, vol. 4, *1938–1940*, ed. Howard Eiland and Michael W. Jennings, trans., Edmund Jephcott (Cambridge, MA: Harvard University Press, 2003), 266–68.

103. Faulkner, *As I Lay Dying*, 220–21.

104. Faulkner, 208.

105. Faulkner, 253.

106. See Tavlin, "'Ravel Out into Time.'"

107. Faulkner, *As I Lay Dying*, 86.

108. Faulkner, 139.

109. That detachment, in Eric Sundquist's words, "astutely challenges" the notion of "a narrative consciousness formed by a supposed union between the author and his language, a union formalized and made conventional by the standard device of omniscient, or at least partly omniscient, narration, which the novel explicitly discards and disavows." Eric Sundquist, *Faulkner: The House Divided* (Baltimore: Johns Hopkins University Press, 1983), 29.

110. Faulkner, *As I Lay Dying*, 141.

111. For an extended and illuminating reading of how the present tense can represent the challenge of gaining epistemic mastery over one's lived experience, see James Phelan, "Present Tense Narration, Mimesis, the Narrative Norm, and the Positioning of the Reader in *Waiting for the Barbarians*," in *Understanding Narrative*, ed. James Phelan and Peter J. Rabinowitz (Columbus: Ohio State University Press, 1994), 222–45. See also Susan Fleischman, *Tense and Narrativity: From Medieval Performance to Modern Fiction* (Austin: University of Texas Press, 1990).

112. Faulkner, *As I Lay Dying*, 120.

113. Faulkner, 55.

114. Faulkner, 120–21.

115. Faulkner, 222.

116. Faulkner, 122. Candace Waid sees in these repetitive utterances Dewey Dell's emancipation from Faulkner's productive but exploitative aesthetic paradigm that, in Waid's view, tethers Dewey Dell's creative energies to her "dead mother" and "artist brother." Heretofore penetrated by the voice and preoccupations of Addie and Darl, Dewey Dell now cuts herself free of her aesthetic bond to mother and brother, summoning a "religious trinity" (in the three successive "Gods" following the first) to take the place of the "aesthetic triumvirate" now rendered null. But, as I argue here, this is not an authentic moment of divine contact. Candace Waid, *The Signifying Eye: Seeing Faulkner's Art* (Athens: University of Georgia Press, 2013), 110.

117. Woolf quoted in Rancière, "Thread of the Novel," 197.

118. Rancière, 206.

119. Rancière, 160–61; Woolf quoted 196.

120. Philip Weinstein, *Becoming Faulkner: The Art and Life of William Faulkner* (Oxford: Oxford University Press, 2010), 63.

121. Faulkner, *As I Lay Dying*, 44–45.

122. Faulkner, 53, 56.

123. Faulkner, 54.

124. Faulkner, 63.
125. Faulkner, 170.
126. Faulkner, 35.
127. Matthews, "*As I Lay Dying* in the Machine Age," 93.
128. Peter Lurie, *Vision's Immanence: Faulkner, Film, and the Popular Imagination* (Baltimore: Johns Hopkins University Press, 2004), 69.
129. Matthews, "Faulkner to Film in the Fifties," in *William Faulkner in the Media Ecology*, ed. Julian Murphet and Stefan Solomon (Baton Rouge: Louisiana State University Press, 2015), 30.
130. Faulkner, *As I Lay Dying*, 173. For a reading of the efficacy of language in *As I Lay Dying*, particularly its relation to Wittgensteinian ordinary language philosophy, see Greg Chase, "Acknowledging Addie's Pain: Language, Wittgenstein, and *As I Lay Dying*," *Twentieth-Century Literature* 63, no. 2 (2017): 167–90.
131. Faulkner, *Absalom, Absalom!* (1936; New York: Vintage, 1990), 102.
132. Stefan Solomon, *William Faulkner in Hollywood: Screenwriting for the Studios* (Athens: University of Georgia Press, 2017), 8; Pier Paolo Pasolini, "The Screenplay as a 'Structure That Wants to Be Another Structure," in *Heretical Empiricism*, ed. and trans. Ben Lawton and Louise K. Barnett (Bloomington: Indiana University Press, 1988), 193.
133. Thomas Schatz, *The Genius of the System: Hollywood Filmmaking in the Studio Era* (New York: Pantheon Books, 1988), 6. Jerome Christensen, *America's Corporate Art: The Studio Authorship of Hollywood Motion Pictures* (Stanford, CA: Stanford University Press, 2021), 2. See also Solomon, *William Faulkner in Hollywood*, 11.
134. Solomon, *William Faulkner in Hollywood*, 10.
135. William Faulkner, *The Lion in the Garden: Interviews with William Faulkner, 1926–1962*, ed. James B. Meriwether and Michael Millgate (New York: Random House, 1968), 57.
136. Solomon, *William Faulkner in Hollywood*, 3.
137. Solomon, 11.
138. See, for instance, John T. Matthews, "Faulkner and the Culture Industry," *The Cambridge Companion to William Faulkner*, ed. Philip Weinstein (Cambridge: Cambridge University Press, 2006), 51–74.
139. William Faulkner, *As I Lay Dying* (1930; New York: Vintage International, 1990), 120–21.
140. Faulkner, along with John Dos Passos and Ernest Hemingway, were central literary figures in André Bazin's theorizations of neorealist aesthetics. See André Bazin, *What Is Cinema*, 2 vols., trans. Hugh Gray (1967–71; Berkeley: University of California Press, 2005).

CODA

1. For more on the asynchronous genealogies of literature's and cinema's modernisms, see Fredric Jameson, *Signatures of the Visible* (London: Routledge, 1992), 213–314.
2. "Modernity," Murray Pomerance writes, for instance, "can hardly be spoken of outside of cinema." Murray Pomerance, ed. *Cinema and Modernity* (New Bruns-

wick: Rutgers University Press, 2006), 4. For more on Fried's views concerning cinema's innate antimodernism, see Daniel Morgan, "Missed Connections," *Nonsite*, no. 22 (November 1, 2017), https://nonsite.org/missed-connections/.

3. See for instance, Ted Perry, ed. *Masterpieces of Modernist Cinema* (Bloomington: Indiana University Press, 2006). These broad disciplinary debates are still very much alive, unsettled, and ongoing, as evidenced by Malcolm Turvey's recent interrogations of what constitutes cinematic modernism by way of earlier theorizations by David Bordwell, P. Adams Sitney, and András Bálint Kovács, as well as by Daniel Morgan's recent expansion of the film-theoretical genealogy of modernism to include thinkers such as Stanley Cavell, Michael Fried, and Annette Michelson, who are often understudied or considered altogether antimodernist in their approaches to cinema. Malcolm Turvey, *Play Time: Jacques Tati and Comedic Modernism* (New York: Columbia University Press, 2020), 10–20; Morgan, "Missed Connections"; "Modernist Investigations: A Reading of *The World Viewed*," *Discourse* 42, no. 1/2 (Winter/Spring 2020): 209–40.

4. Jameson, *Signatures of the Visible*.

5. Mary Ann Doane, *Femmes Fatales: Feminism, Film Theory, Pscyhoanalysis* (New York: Routledge, 1991), 120.

6. Lindsay Anderson, "*Madame de . . . ,*" *Sight and Sound*, April–June 1954, 196. Citing Anderson's review, Richard Porton argues that what might seem like the "ecstatic" tenor of the enthusiasm expressed by contemporary admirers of Ophuls has largely to do with the vehemence with which he had previously been denounced. See Richard Porton, "More Than 'Visual Froufrou': The Politics of Passion in the Films of Max Ophuls," *Cinéaste*, Fall 2020, 8.

7. Claude Beylie, *Max Ophuls* (Paris: Éditions Seghers, 1963), 11. All French translations throughout this chapter are my own unless otherwise specified.

8. For critical work that examines this ironic distance in Ophuls, see, for instance, Beylie, Gilles Deleuze, Andrew Sarris, Kaja Silverman, Mary Ann Doane, Gertrud Koch, and Laura Mulvey.

9. Susan M. White, *The Cinema of Max Ophuls: Magisterial Vision and the Figure of Woman* (New York: Columbia University Press, 1995), 56.

10. Gilles Deleuze, *Cinema 2: The Time Image* (Minneapolis: University of Minnesota Press, 1986), 83.

11. As critics have long noted, it is also true that the films he made for Hollywood systematically disrupt the narrative and aesthetic expectations of classical style. For an extended study of Ophuls's work in Hollywood, see Lutz Bacher, *Max Ophuls in the Hollywood Studios* (New Brunswick, NJ: Rutgers University Press, 1996). White's *Cinema of Max Ophuls* and Mulvey's recent essays on Ophuls also examine the narratively disruptive features of his Hollywood films. More recently, Karl Schoonover has performed a brilliant reading of how Ophuls challenges the terms of classical style in his Hollywood films, especially his women's noir, *The Reckless Moment*. See Karl Schoonover, "Cinema of Disposal: Max Ophuls and Accumulation in America," *differences: a journal of feminist cultural studies* 29, no. 1 (2018): 33–65.

12. They "reveal," White continues, "how women at every class level figure in the operation of fictionality, representation itself, and the process of exchange

upon which patriarchal capitalism is based." White, *Cinema of Max Ophuls*, 6. Kaja Silverman argues that Ophuls's oeuvre offers a meditation on the gendered terms of cinematic suture, a "disquisition about the status of the female image in classical cinema." Kaja Silverman, *The Subject of Semiotics* (New York: Oxford University Press, 1983), 226.

13. Laura Mulvey, "The Earrings of Madame de . . . ," *Film Quarterly* 62, no. 4 (Summer 2009): 19.

14. Mulvey, 16.

15. Mulvey, 16.

16. Roland Barthes, *Le plaisir du texte* (Paris: Éditions du Seuil, 1973).

17. Max Ophuls, "Thoughts on Film," in *Ophuls*, ed. Paul Willemen (London: British Film Institute, 1978), 43, 45.

18. Toril Moi, "From Femininity to Finitude: Freud, Lacan, and Feminism, Again," *Signs: Journal of Women in Culture and Society* 29, no. 3 (2004): 871.

19. Roland Barthes, *Camera Lucida: Reflections on Photography*, trans. Richard Howard (New York: Hill & Wang, 2010), 85.

20. Mulvey, "*Earrings of Madame de* . . . ," 16; Laura Mulvey, "Love, History, and Max Ophuls: Repetition and Difference in Three Films of Doomed Romance," *Film & History: An Interdisciplinary Journal* 43, no. 1 (Spring 2013): 11.

21. The most comprehensive account of the work of coincidence, chance, and repetition in *Madame de* . . . is still to be found in Mary Ann Doane, "The Dialogical Text: Film Irony and the Spectator" (PhD diss. University of Iowa, 1979).

22. White, *Cinema of Max Ophuls*, 55.

23. Gerard Genette, *Narrative Discourse: An Essay on Method*, trans. Jane E. Lewin (Ithaca, NY: Cornell University Press, 1993), 114.

24. White, *Cinema of Max Ophuls*, 55.

25. Daniel Morgan, "Max Ophuls and the Limits of Virtuosity: On the Aesthetics and Ethics of Camera Movement," *Critical Inquiry* 38 (Autumn 2011): 144.

26. Daniel Morgan has recently put compelling pressure on this canonical view of the moving camera as enacting a surrogate perspective on profilmic events. See Daniel Morgan *The Lure of the Image: Epistemic Fantasies of the Moving Camera* (Oakland: University of California Press, 2021).

27. David Bordwell, "Camera Movement and Cinematic Space," *Ciné-Tracts*, no. 2 (Summer 1977): 23.

28. Morgan, *Lure of the Image*, chap. 5.

29. George Annenkov, *Max Ophuls* (Paris: Le Terrain Vague, 1962), 67; my translations throughout this chapter.

30. But it has also been noted that the reference to *Madame Bovary* is stronger in *La ronde*, where the only married couple (both members adulterous) are named Emma and Charles.

31. Roland Barthes, *S/Z: An Essay*, trans. Richard Miller (New York: Hill & Wang), 156.

32. Vincent Amiel, "Nature and Artifice in Max Ophuls' Cinema," *Arizona Quarterly* 60, no. 5 (2004): 149.

33. Claude Beylie, *Max Ophuls* (Paris: Éditions Seghers, 1963), 9–10, 98–101. Koch finds in Ophuls an impulse toward "a completely aesthetic form of life,

broken by no reality principle." Gertrude Koch, "Positivierung der Gefühle: Zu den Schnitzler-Verfimungen von Max Ophüls," in *Arthur Schnitzler in neuer Sicht*, ed. Harmut Scheible (Munich: Wilhelm Fink, 1981), 314. Susan M. White's translation found in White, *Cinema of Max Ophuls*. Allan Larson Williams similarly argues that in Ophuls's work, "any literal rendering of reality" is "mocked." Allan Larson Williams, *Max Ophuls and the Cinema of Desire: Style and Spectacle in Four Films, 1948–1955* (New York: Arno Press, 1980), 148.

34. The labyrinthine sets of *Lola Montes*, for instance, provide a world of only false refuges, reflecting the imprisoning quality of Lola's love affairs with possessive men as well as the circular and humiliating space of the Mammoth Circus, at which the ringmaster (Peter Ustinov) tells the scandalous story of Lola's life as she performs physical feats. And as Karl Schoonover has recently shown, the obstructive mise-en-scène and overflowing interiors of particularly *A Reckless Moment* indicate Ophuls's sense that subjects are overrun with refuse that never truly disappears, histories that never completely die. Later on in this chapter, I will also turn more directly to the work of Vincent Amiel, who, too, has lent important nuance to the dominant view of Ophuls as merely mocking the natural.

35. Giuliana Bruno, *Atlas of Emotion: Journeys in Art, Architecture, and Film* (London: Verso, 2002), 6.

36. See Aloïs Riegl, *Problems of Style: Foundations for a History of Ornament*, trans. Evelyn Kain (Princeton: Princeton University Press, 1993; first published 1893 in German by G. Siemans [Berlin]); *Late Roman Art Industry*, trans. Rolf Winkes (Giorgio Bretschneider Editore, 1985; first published 1901 in German by Kaiserlich-Königlichen hof- und Staatsdruckerei [Vienna]); Laura U. Marks, *The Skin of the Film: Intercultural Cinema, Embodiment, and the Senses* (Durham, NC: Duke University Press, 2000). Other, more recent discussions of hapticity in film can be found in such as books as Jennifer M. Barker, *The Tactile Eye: Touch and the Cinematic Experience* (Berkeley: University of California Press, 2009); Laura U. Marks, *Touch: Sensuous Theory and Multisensory Media* (Minneapolis: University of Minnesota Press, 2002); and Vivian Sobchak, *Carnal Thoughts: Embodiment and Moving Image Culture* (Berkeley: University of California Press, 2004).

37. Antonia Lant, "Haptical Cinema," *October* 74 (1995): 45. See also Noël Burch, "Building a Haptic Space," in *Life to Those Shadows*, ed. and trans. Ben Brewster (Berkeley: University of California Press, 1990), 62–85.

38. Michel Chion, *The Voice in Cinema*, trans. Claudia Gorbman (New York: Columbia University Press, 1999), 3.

39. David Bordwell, *Narration in the Fiction Film* (Madison: University of Wisconsin Press, 1985), 7.

40. While I am drawing on Doane's term *epistemophilia* to discuss the more general obsession with knowledge that drives classical style, it's important to note that Doane uses the term in the context of her discussion of the femme fatale and the gendered obsession with knowing the woman that often organizes cinematic looking in film noir. See Mary Ann Doane, *Femmes Fatales: Feminism, Film Theory, Pscyhoanalysis* (New York: Routledge, 1991), 1.

41. Bruno, *Atlas of Emotion*, 250. For a discussion of the way that films generate

narrative "worlds," see Daniel Yacavone, *Film Worlds: A Philosophical Aesthetics of Cinema* (New York: Columbia University Press, 2014).

42. Miriam Hansen, "Benjamin, Cinema, and Experience: The 'Blue Flower' in the Land of Technology," *New German Critique* 40 (1987): 195.

43. Doane, *Femmes Fatales*, 122.

44. For more on the use of space in *Caught*, see Marshall Deutelbaum, "Leonora's Place: The Spatial Logic of *Caught*," *Arizona Quarterly* 60, no. 5 (2005): 87–96.

45. Chion, *Voice of the Cinema*, 3. Building on earlier critiques of the distinction between diegetic and nondiegetic (what many now call "extradiegetic") space that Étienne Souriau canonized in his 1953 *L'univers filmique*, recent scholars of film music and sound studies have put pressure on the notion of extradiegetic music, arguing that the distinction does not convincingly hold, since in many instances it's not in fact clear whether the characters can hear the music or not. For an especially astute representation of this argument, see Ben Winters, "The Non-Diegetic Fallacy: Film, Music, and Narrative Space," *Music and Letters* 91, no. 2 (2010): 224–44. I would argue, however, that in a film such as *La signora di tutti*, the diegetic-extradiegetic distinction remains useful, since it is a film whose drama is founded on the protagonist's inability to escape diegetic demands.

46. Doane, *Femmes Fatales*, 119–41. Stephen Heath refers to narrative as inherently entailing violence. A "narrative action," he writes, "is a series of elements held in a relation of transformation such that their consecution—the movement of the transformation from the ones to the others—determines a state S' different from an initial state S. . . . A beginning, therefore, is always a violence, the interruption of the homogeneity of S (once again, the homogeneity—S itself—being recognized in retrospect from that violence, that interruption)." Stephen Heath, *Questions of Cinema* (Bloomington: Indiana University Press, 1981), 136. I discuss the association of narrative with violence more at length in my discussion of Faulkner in chapter 3.

47. Doane, *Femmes Fatales*, 121–22.

48. Anna Kornbluh, *The Order of Forms: Realism, Formalism, and Social Space* (Chicago: University of Chicago Press, 2019).

49. Doane, *Femme Fatales*, 119.

50. This is no doubt why, as Doane argues, *La signora di tutti* was venerated as an art film but accused particularly often of being gratuitously formalist.

51. In her chapter on this film in her 1991 *Femme Fatales*, Doane refers to *La signora di tutti* as "seldom discussed" (119). With a few important exceptions, this has not changed, in large part because of how hard it was to access the film for many decades.

52. Deidre Lynch demonstrates that, paradoxically, literary scholars are "called on" to love their objects of study even as critical dispassion became a cornerstone of the discipline. Deidre Lynch, *Loving Literature: A Cultural History* (Chicago: University of Chicago Press, 2015).

53. The more pointed articulations of this view have emerged recently in the so-called method wars. For an exemplary expression of this view, see Bruce Robbins, "Not So Well Attached," *PMLA* 132, no. 2 (2017): 375. But again, this view is changing, and what is perhaps its last holdout is indeed in the more virulent

attacks on so-called post-critique. For just a few recent examples of studies interested in the theoretical and historical complexities of love—and thus the theoretical import of the study of love in and of itself—see Lisa Mendelman, *Modern Sentimentalism: Affect Irony, and Female Authorship in Interwar America* (Oxford: Oxford University Press, 2019); Emily Ogden, *On Not Knowing: How to Love and Other Essays* (Chicago: University of Chicago Press, 2022); John Frow, *Character & Person* (Oxford: Oxford University Press, 2014), chap. 1; Eugenie Brinkema, *Life-Destroying Diagrams* (Durham, NC: Duke University Press, 2022); Janine Utell, *James Joyce and the Revolt of Love: Marriage, Adultery, Desire* (New York: Palgrave, 2010).

54. Amanda Anderson, Rita Felski, and Toril Moi, *Character: Three Inquiries in Literary Studies* (Chicago: University of Chicago Press, 2019), 64.

55. Lauren Berlant, *Desire/Love* (New York: Punctum Books, 2012), 7.

56. Kristin Thompson, "The Concept of Cinematic Excess," *Ciné-Tracts*, no. 2 (Summer 1977): 54–63.

57. Berlant, *Desire/Love*, 43.

58. Gilles Deleuze and Felix Guattari, *Anti-Oedipus: Capitalism and Schizophrenia*, trans. Robert Hurley, Mark Seem, and Helen R. Lane (New York: Viking Press, 1977).

59. In the context of contemporary postcritical debates, for instance, love is a mode of attachment to texts that the culture and argumentative modalities of critical theory have forced us to relinquish. "But what about love?" Felski representatively asks in *The Limits of Critique* (2015). Cannot love, too, be a force that brings and binds us—indeed, "hooks" us—to our objects of critical inquiry rather than just the circumspection typical of the hermeneutics of suspicion? Rita Felski, *The Limits of Critique* (Chicago: University of Chicago Press, 2015), 17; *Hooked: Art and Attachment* (Chicago: University of Chicago Press, 2020).

60. Berlant, *Desire/Love*, 24.

61. For an examination of the categories of love and desire as they pertain to the institution of marriage in modernist aesthetics, see Utell.

62. Martha Nussbaum is right, for instance, to call love "that strange unmanageable phenomenon or form of life, source at once of illumination and confusion." Martha Nussbaum, *Love's Knowledge: Essays on Philosophy and Literature* (Oxford: Oxford University Press, 1992), 4. And Diedre Lynch is right, too, when she says that critics often forget that love "can be a matter of misrecognition, overvaluation, self-congratulation, aggressivity, transference, fetishism, and/or jealousy" and that "it too brings with it (sometimes unreasonable) intimacy expectations." Lynch, *Loving Literature*, 4. For a quite different, very recent account of love and its relation to form and, more specifically, formalism, see Brinkema, *Life-Destroying Diagrams*, 289–368.

63. Roland Barthes, *Fragments: A Lover's Discourse*, trans. Richard Howard (New York: Hill & Wang, 2010), 3.

64. Roland Barthes, *Fragments d'un discours amoureux* (Paris: Éditions du Seuil, 1977), 1.

65. Barthes, Fragments: A Lover's Discourse, 3.

66. Mari Ruti, *The Ethics of Opting Out: Queer Theory's Defiant Subjects* (New York: Columbia University Press, 2017), 138.

67. Max Ophuls, "Interview with Max Ophuls," in *Ophuls* (London: British Film Institute, 1978), 23.

68. André Bazin, *What Is Cinema*, vol. 2, trans. Hugh Gray (1971; Berkeley: University of California Press, 2005), 59.

69. For an especially useful account of the history of loss of faith in the realist theory of film, see Robert B. Ray, *How a Film Theory Got Lost and Other Mysteries in Cultural Studies* (Bloomington: Indiana University Press, 2001).

70. Laura Mulvey, "Love, History, and Max Ophuls: Repetition and Difference in Three Films of Doomed Romance," *Film & History: An Interdisciplinary Journal* 43, no. 1 (Spring 2013), 26; Daniel Morgan, "Max Ophuls and the Limits of Virtuosity: On the Aesthetics and Ethics of Camera Movement," *Critical Inquiry* 38 (Autumn 2011), 48.

71. Vincent Amiel, "Nature and Artifice in Max Ophuls' Cinema," *Arizona Quarterly* 60, no. 5 (2004), 155.

72. Louise de Vilmorin, *Madame de . . .* (Paris: Gallimard, 1951), 42, my translation.

73. George Annenkov, *Max Ophuls* (Paris: Le Terrain Vague, 1962), 66–67.

74. I borrow the term *composite* from Alix Beeston, *In and Out of Sight: Modernist Writing and the Photographic Unseen* (Oxford: Oxford University Press, 2018); Stendhal, *On Love*, trans., Gilbert and Suzanne Sale (New York: Penguin Classics, 2004), 28.

75. Stendhal, *On Love*, 43.

76. Karl Marx, *The Eighteenth Brumaire of Louis Bonaparte*, trans. Ben Fowkes, in *Surveys from Exile*, ed. David Fernbach (New York: Penguin, 1973), 170.

77. Mieke Bal, *Guidelines for Writing a PhD Thesis within ASCA* (Amsterdam: Amsterdam School for Cultural Analysis, 2006), 30.

78. To see "the point" of *Madame de . . .* as "the *achievement* of personality depth through suffering (overcoming the shallowness of vanity, the tendency to *perform* rather than to feel)" is, in her view, "to ignore the film's complex play with the instability of both 'character' and 'narrative.'" Susan M. White, *The Cinema of Max Ophuls: Magisterial Vision and the Figure of Woman* (New York: Columbia University Press, 1995), 56.

79. Béla Balàzs, *Béla Balàzs: Early Film Theory; Visible Man and The Spirit of Film* (New York: Berghahn Books, 2010), 34.

80. Jean-Luc Nancy, *Listening* (New York: Fordham University Press, 2007).

81. Nancy, *Listening*, 9.

82. Toril Moi, "From Femininity to Finitude: Freud, Lacan, and Feminism, Again," *Signs: Journal of Women in Culture and Society* 29, no. 3 (2004): 872.

83. Stefan Zweig, *Letter from an Unknown Woman*, trans. Anthea Bell (London: Pushkin Press, 2013), 31, emphasis added.

84. Roland Barthes, *Camera Lucida: Reflections on Photography*, trans. Richard Howard (New York: Hill & Wang, 2010), 82, 84–85.

85. Ophuls, "Interview with Max Ophuls," 27.

86. Vivian Sobchack, *Carnal Thoughts: Embodiment and Moving Image Culture* (Berkeley: University of California Press, 2004), 4.

87. Sylvia Wynter, "Unsettling the Coloniality of Being/Power/Truth/Freedom:

Towards the Human, After Man, Its Overrepresentation—An Argument," *CR: The New Centennial Review* 3, no. 3 (2003): 262.

88. Franco Moretti, *The Way of the World: The Bildungsroman in European Culture* (London: Verso, 2000), 5–6.

89. As Ophuls was wont to do with source material, he, Marcel Archant, and Annette Wademant changed the story considerably in their adaptation of *Madame de . . .* to the screen, quite to the displeasure of Louise de Vilmorin. He turned André from a businessman into a military general. He made André's mistress go to Constantinople, rather than South America. He compressed the elaborate subplot involving André's poor niece to a matter of mere minutes. And whereas in the book Louise dies in bed, the Baron on the one side of her and André on the other, Ophuls adds a duel—the narrative hallmark of his cinema—that in essence kills off both Louise and the Baron. Mulvey rightly refers to Ophuls' "repeated distortion of original texts." Mulvey, "Love, History, and Max Ophuls," 12.

90. Carl Plantinga, *Moving Viewers: American Film and the Spectator Experience* (Berkeley: University of California Press, 2009), 3–4.

91. Fredric Jameson, *The Political Unconscious: Narrative as a Socially Symbolic Act* (Ithaca, NY: Cornell University Press, 1981), 298.

92. White, *Cinema of Max Ophuls*, 8–11.

Index

Page numbers in italics refer to illustrations.

abandonment, 41, 120, 135–36, 163–64, 173–74, 179, 216
Absalom, Absalom! (Faulkner), 6–7, 129, 165, 170
abstractions, 14, 102, 157, 202
Acosta, Mercedes de, 65, 92
actuality genre, 141, 147
adjacency, 96, 116, 120, 167
Adorno, Theodor, 2, 4–5, 18, 20, 28, 235n5
Adrian (costume designer), 66–69
aesthetic criticism, 38, 243n108. *See also* literary criticism
aesthetics: and achievements, 45–47, 229; and amorous spaces, 183; and appeal, 230; of artifice, 214; of chance and contingency, 210; and choices, 1, 22, 104; of choked depths, 191; and classical style, 264n11; and closure, 76; and constraints, 5–6, 90–91, 102, 171; of contingency, 18; and contrivances, 159; and crisis, 47; and critical triumph, 45; and design, 157; "destituent," 5; of display and exhibition, 147; and disruption, 209; and economy of choked voids, 221; and emancipatory potential, 217–18; and hierarchies, 20; interstitial, 19; and intervention, 5; and labor, 138, 158–59;
and language, 189; ludic, 147; and modernism, 2–3, 9, 15, 17, 19–22, 28, 44, 46, 51, 94, 123, 157, 170, 177, 205–6, 238n43, 240–41n73, 240n59, 258n27, 261n89, 268n61; and participation, 161–62; and plot, 47, 191, 210, 216; political import of, 20; of possibility, 160; premodernist, 21, 161–62; proxy, 4, 216; representational, 20–22; and restriction, 47; and retrospection, 61, 157, 160; and reverie, 160; and sensibility, 12, 181, 205; and spatial depths, 189–91, 208; and strained grammar, 157; and stretches, 138; and traditions, 181; and triumph, 45; of triumvirate, 262n116; of unmanageable, 135
Affairs of Anatol, The (Demille film), 132
affirmation, 31
African Americans: and cinematic spectatorship, 31, 49, 241n80; and inequities, 154. *See also* Black
Agamben, Giorgio, 5
Ahmed, Sarah, 35–36
Akins, Zoë, 25, 50–51, 73, 171, 245–46nn24–25
alcoholism, 39, 154. *See also* substance abuse
Aldrich, Robert, 128–29

alienation effect *(Verfremdungseffect)*, 2
All about Eve (Mankiewicz film), 128–29
Allen, Robert C., 237n25
Altamonte, Onatorio, Count (fictional character), 98, 121
Always Audacious (Cruz film), 132
ambiguity, 73
ambivalence, 5–6, 8–9, 12, 22, 30, 33–42, 46–47, 67, 82, 85, 90, 177–78, 181–82, 206, 250n105
Amiel, Vincent, 215, 266n34
anagnorisis, 65
analogies, 8, 13, 24, 101–2, 256n79
Anderson, Lindsay, 178, 264n6
Anderson, Robert (fictional character), 59–60
Anderson, Tom (fictional character), 62
Angel (Lubitsch film), 256n79
Anna Christie (Brown film), 24, 64, 109
Anna Karenina (film), 64
Anna Karenina (Tolstoy), 16, 23, 239n55
Annenkov, George, 190, 215–16, 219
anonymity, 109, 223–24; and inconsequentiality, 203
antihumanism, and posthumanism, 241n92
apperception, spontaneous, 144–45
Arata, Ubaldo, 173–74
Archant, Marcel, 270n89
Arendt, Hannah, 230
aristocracy, 6, 22, 41–44, 75, 89, 94, 96, 121, 127–28, 139, 183–97, 192, 226; Black, 43
Aristotle, 2, 9, 15, 17, 19–20, 95, 152, 238n47
Armstrong, Nancy, 51
art: impulse to shatter in, 46–47; interior as space productive of, 199; precious ordering endemic to, 135; and thought, 34
art cinema, 178
Art Deco, 70, 249n92
artifice, 41, 98, 103, 175, 178–79, 191–92, 209, 212, 214–15

artificiality, 20, 103, 155
Art of the Moving Picture, The (Lindsay), 10
arts, of inconsequence, 1
As I Lay Dying (Faulkner), 15, 41, 133–38, 157–74, 258n27, 261n97, 263n130
Atkinson, Ted, 261n89
attentive observation, and casual noticing, 161–62
attenuation, of self, 36, 182, 226–27
Atwill, Lionel, 101
Au hasard Balthazar (Bresson film), 177
aurality, 41, 64, 182, 198, 202, 222
Austen, Jane, 57, 204–5
authoritarianism, 17, 219–20
authors: and characters, 22–26, 45, 61, 135–38, 173, 178–79, 258n25; and language, 262n109; modernist, 3, 5, 28
automaticities, 2, 159, 162–63, 186, 216
autonomy, 14, 45, 51, 57, 79, 136, 164, 184, 206, 225–26; aesthetic, 157; modernist ideology of, 261n89
avant garde: Barnes as, 125; cinema, 12–13; comedy, 240n62; directors, 102, 179; filmmaking, 26–28, 238n44, 239n58; midcentury, 180; montage, 28; Ophuls as, 179; visual culture, 26, 239n58
Axel's Castle (Wilson), 2

Bacall, Lauren, 172
Bach, Steven, 111
Bacher, Lutz, 264n11
Baker, Houston, 46
Bal, Mieke, 23, 45
Balàzs, Béla, 221
Baldwin, James, 29–35, 44
Ballet mécanique (Léger film), 102, 177
Balzac, Honoré de, 4, 24, 28, 53, 94, 121, 145, 161, 181
Banjo on My Knee (Cromwell film), 172
Barker, Jennifer M., 246–47n43
Barker, Reginald, 132
Barnes, Djuna, 1–3, 167, 250n4; aesthetics of, 5, 22, 101–2; and ambivalence, 8, 34, 39; ambivalent feelings

about queer antinormativity, 41; archives, 38, 40; aristocratic worlds of, 6; as avant garde, 125; bisexuality of, 114; characters of, 135–36, 178; and cinematic style, 102; and consequence, solace of, 178; and Dietrich, films of, 13, 34–36, 39–41, 87, 89–125, 127–28, 135, 137, 170–71, 189, 252n12; feminist recovery of, 92, 251n4, 252n12; fiction and movies, 39–41; and film, 252n12; formal tensions in work of, 90; on Garbo's voice, 255n63; and hermeneutic poverty of present, 35–36; and interpellation and hegemony, 36; as journalist, film and theater, 92, 110, 253n13; and linguistic excess, 92; and literary modernism, 21; and love plots, 204; and mimetic illusions, 106–7; and minoritarian subjectivity, 39; as modernist, 3–4, 8, 14, 21–22, 89, 91, 125, 170–71, 251n5; and moviegoing, 12–14, 34–36, 39–41, 91–93, 113, 123; and narrative unity, 14; novel-in-progress, 1–5, 19; novels of, 39; and overdescription, 119; and plot, 3–8, 26, 39, 89, 135; and plots of tortuous security, 87; and popular film, 12–13; and postmodernism, 251n5; radical experiments with narrative form, 5; and reproductive futurity, 258n17; romance plot, 26; semantic inundations, 122; stylistic excess and the irreverence of, 119; stylistic occlusion of, 101–2; and torment, security of, 87, 89–125; and ubersynthetic characters, 189; viscosity of, 102. *See also Nightwood* (Barnes novel)
Barreault, Jean-Louis, 186
Barriga, Cecilia, 255n75
Barthes, Roland, 4, 15–16, 45, 63, 65, 72, 120, 141, 182, 191, 196, 204, 206–7, 216–17, 224–25, 236n17
Bates, Norman (fictional character), 103
Baudelaire, Charles, 219

Baudry, Jean-Louis, 11
Baumbach, Nico, 34
Bazin, André, 13, 149, 174, 209, 263n140
Beaupré, Madeleine de (fictional character), 101
Beeston, Alix, 48, 233, 269n74
Bel Geddes, Barbara, 199
Belle of Alaska (Bennett film), 132
Bellew, John (fictional character), 65, 85
belonging, 47, 52, 82, 137, 229–30
Benjamin, Walter, 4, 11–13, 52–53, 141, 144–45, 157, 161–62, 198, 228–30, 236n13
Bennet, Elizabeth (fictional character), 23, 53
Bennett, Chester, 132
Bergson, Henri, 140
Berlant, Lauren, 8, 29–30, 33–34, 36, 82, 204–6, 242n98
Bernardi, Daniel, 62–63
betrayal, 67, 94, 96, 123–24, 137, 167–68, 180, 184, 186–87, 200–201, 208, 215–16
Beylie, Claude, 179, 192, 264n8
Bibby, Michael, 46
Bicycle Thieves/Ladri di biciclette (De Sica film), 209
Big Sleep (Chandler novel), 172
Big Sleep, The (Hawks film), 132, 171, 172–73
bildungsroman, 5, 8, 17, 26, 32, 40, 44–53, 57–61, 79, 82, 109, 135–36, 189, 226; classical, 49, 51, 73; modernist, 45, 49, 244n2; and plot, 44–45
binge-watching, and cult of distraction, 36
Biograph Studios, 131
biracial women, 40, 60, 62, 82, 135–36
Birth of a Nation, The (Griffith film), 132–33, 257n6, 257n9
bisexuality, 65, 92, 114
Black: ancestry, 62; aristocracy, 43; blood, in passing, 65; cultural production, 46; culture, 58; film culture in Chicago, 31; film historiography, 31, 38, 243n105; film production, 132; modernists, 46; respectability

Black (*continued*)
  politics, 52; spectatorship, 31, 49, 241n80; studies, 45–46. *See also* African Americans
Blackface, 70
blackness, film, 69–72
blame, 94, 150, 166–69
Blazing Saddles (Brooks film), 101
Bleikasten, André, 159
Blonde Venus (von Sternberg film), 70, 91–92, 98–99, *99*, 101, 116–18, *117*, 249n91
Bloom, Leopold (fictional character), 4, 19
Blue Angel, The (von Sternberg film), 91–92, 102, 111, 253n13, 255n66
Bluest Eye, The (Morrison), 1, 29–37, 62–63
Bogart, Humphrey, 172–73
Boleslawski, Richard, 24, 64
Bonaparte, Napoleon, 215, 219, 226–27
bondage: aesthetic, 179, 262n116; hermeneutic, 125, 145
Bordwell, David, 10, 27, 73, 153, 188, 198, 240n65, 249–50n98, 258n13, 264n3
Borzage, Frank, 101
bourgeois, 2, 5, 8–9, 12, 14, 18, 28, 40, 44, 49–52, 65, 73–80, 118, 122, 125, 146, 158, 172, 182, 206–7, 219–20, 240–41n73. *See also* middle class
Bovary, Charles (fictional character), 191
Bovary, Emma, Madame (fictional character), 191, 205, 220, 265n30
Bowie, David, 127–29
Bradley, Tom (fictional character), 101
Brakhage, Stan, 177, 238n44
Brand, Stefan (fictional character), 79, 214–15
Brecht, Bertolt, 2, 202
Breedlove, Pauline (fictional character), 30–37
Breedlove, Pecola (fictional character), 31
Bresson, Robert, 177
Bride Retires, The (film), 155, 260–61n85

Brilmyer, S. Pearl, 40, 91
Brinkema, Eugenie, 37–38, 268n62
Broe, Mary Lynn, 92, 251n4
Bronstein, Michaela, 245n18
Brooks, Mel, 101
Brooks, Peter, 13, 15–16, 51, 120, 145
Brown, Clarence, 24
Brown, Jeffrey A., 114
Brown, Tom (fictional character), 111–16, *115*
Brownface, 70
Bruno, Giuliana, 195, 198
Bull, Clarence Sinclair, 72, 74
Bundren, Addie (fictional character), 137, 159–60, 165–70, 262n116
Bundren, Anse (fictional character), 137, 158, 165, 169–70
Bundren, Darl (fictional character), 157–65, 169–70, 172–73, 261n89, 262n116
Bundren family (fictional characters), 137, 164–66, 261n89, 262n116
Buñuel, Luis, 102, 177
Burch, Noël, 195–96, 246n43

Cabinet of Dr. Caligari, The (Wiene film), 177
Cahiers du cinéma, 174, 178–79, 209
camera, as machine, 103
Camille (Cukor film), 24–25, 38, 40, 43–44, 47–56, *55*, *56*, 70, 73–82, *76*, *77*, *80*, 109, 112, 115, 125, 171, 222–26, 243n104, 245–45nn24–25
Cane (Toomer), stories and poems, 6
capitalism, 18–19, 26, 240–41n73; and imperialism, 183, 203–4; industrial, 138–39; inhumanities of, 22; and modernism, 18; and modernity, 2; patriarchal, 183, 203–4, 264–65n12
Carné, Marcel, 174
Caselli, Daniella, 90, 251n5
Castle, Gregory, 15, 45, 60
casual noticing, and attentive observation, 161–62
Catherine the Great (as fictional character in film), 104–9, *107*, *108*

INDEX | 275

Caught (Ophuls film), 199
causality/causation, 16–22, 57–58, 120–25, 128, 186–87; bonds of, 87, 124; and boundaries, 20; and characters, 20; and consequence, 16–17, 19, 72, 121, 203–4, 217–18; and constellation, 125, 143; and feeling, structure of, 123; formal economy of, 72; formal logic of, 47; formal operation of, 150; formal principle of, 149; formative, 19, 26, 217–18, 220; hermeneutic structures of, 122; and Hollywood endings, 72–73, 249–50n98; laws of, 73; and love, 125, 183; and modernism, 21; narrative, 18, 26, 40, 47, 65, 116, 120, 122, 170, 180, 187, 191, 215, 218; and narrative unity, 172; paratactic, 169; principles of, 20; and psychology, 6; and realism, 167–70; and relations of correlation, constellation, or parataxis, 7–8; significant, 16–17, 19; and staccato jolts, 143; structures of, 2–3, 6–8, 20, 26, 120, 122–23; systems of, 21, 191; teleological, 8, 61; transcendent, 218
Cavell, Stanley, 109–10, 182, 264n3
Cecire, Natalia, 27–29
certainty, 70; Cartesian, 48; epistemological, 123; racial, 72; rhetorics of, 41–42. *See also* uncertainty
Chandler, Raymond, 172
characters: and actors, 78, 109–10; and arts of inconsequence, 22–26; and authors, 22–26, 45, 61, 135–38, 173, 178–79, 258n25; and boundaries, 20; and causality, 20; and consequence, 15; deaths of, 236n13; desires of, 25, 96, 172; distributional matrix of, 25–26; extratextual presence, 24–25; as fictional entities, 239n52; as fictional entities/fictionality of, 239n52; as figurations of text, 109; heteronormative concepts of, 5; and identification, 260n85; illusion of, 24; instability of, 269n78; literary, 137; as literary stars (recurring), 24; mimetic immersion in, 98; modernist, 21, 145, 173, 218; and mourning, 21–22; and narrative, 269n78; narrative trajectories of, 164; and narrativizing proclivity of judgment, 170; ontology of, 23, 25; overtly synthetic quality of, 180; and palliative etiologies, 168; and personality, 57–58, 220–22; and personhood, 23–25, 179, 182, 221; and personified body, 23–25; and plot, 12, 45, 180; point of view of, 260–61n85; and readers, 53; and realistic fallacy, 45; in realist novels, 246n29; reality of, 25, 239n52; as real people, 23, 45; recurring, 24; in Shakespeare criticism, 239n55; social fraudulence of, 121; synthetic aspects of, 98; and text, distinct from one another, 109; textuality of, 239n52; textual ontology of, 23, 25; ubersynthetic, 189
Charterhouse of Parma, The (Stendhal), 184
Chevalier, Maurice, 101
chiaroscuro, 54, 67, 69, 80
Chion, Michel, 56, 196, 200–201
Christie, Anna (fictional character), 24, 64, 109
Churchill, Suzanne W., 46
cinema, 230; art, 178; of attractions, 9–10, 41, 131, 134, 142–45, 147, 155; classical, 27–28, 30–31, 134, 143, 153, 182, 197, 202, 260n85, 265n12; commercial, 12; of experience, 197–99; false depth of, 56; as flat medium of presentation, 56; global art, 178; immersive effects and powers, 11–12, 178, 181, 202; and modernism, 26–28, 30, 39, 48, 177–78, 263–64nn1–3; and novels, 12; perceptual wealth of, 56; prenarrative, 134, 155–56; as psychic retreat, 36; transitional period of, 9–10, 41. *See also* classical Hollywood cinema; film; motion pictures; moving pictures; narrative cinema and film; sound film (talkies)

"Cinema, The" (Woolf essay), 38
Cinema and Modernism (Trotter), 48
cinematic reception: and arts of inconsequence, 37–39; historiography of, 37–38
cinematography, 9–11, 29, 40–41, 67, 81–82, 105, 131, 144, 146, 187, 193
cinephilia, 33–34, 37, 248n80, 255n75
Civil War, 22, 138
Clair, René, 27, 240n62
classical Hollywood cinema, 8–13, 171–72, 264n11; brutal power of, 29; and class, 78, 81–82; as coercive, 35; endings, 72–73, 76, 78–82, 115, 249–50n98; extraordinary force of, 29; film exhibition, 131, 134, 140; as inconsequential, 29; and motivation, 134, 258n13; and narrative, 11–13, 15, 103, 131–34, 140; and novels, 208; and orientalist fetishism, 70; and Oxford, MS, film exhibition, 41, 132; and plot, 42, 44–45, 47, 49–50, 80–81, 103, 172; as powerful, 29; subversive moments in, 240n64; touch in, 112; transitional period, 9–10, 41; universalist concept of, 27. *See also* melodramas
Classical Hollywood Cinema, The (Bordwell, Staiger, Thompson), 27–28
Clotel; or, the President's Daughter (Brown), 62
Coleman, Emily Holmes, 1–5, 19, 39, 91, 122
Coleridge, Samuel Taylor, 4, 236n14
colonialism, 18, 21, 41, 50, 178, 219, 226, 244n4. *See also* imperialism; postcolonial studies
Comédie humaine (Balzac), 24, 121, 127
complicity: bourgeois, 5, 28; existential temptations of, 6; in novels, 236n17; of plot, 5–6, 236n17; and vernacular modernism, 28
Compson, Benjy (fictional character), 134, 137, 139–47, 150–51, 154–56, 160, 162, 168, 185

Compson, Caddy (fictional character), 134, 139–45, 151, 155
Compson, Jason (fictional character), 134, 137, 139, 142–45, 153–57, 170–73, 221
Compson, Quentin (fictional character), 7, 15, 134, 137, 139, 142–43, 146–47, 150–57, 162, 172–73, 218, 260n67
Compson family (fictional characters), 138–46, 155, 218
concealment, 4, 98
Conrad, Joseph, 6, 16, 96–97, 261n95
consciousness: double, 46; and human experience, 8; narrative, 262n109. *See also* self-: consciousness
consequence, 16–19, 152–53, 185; and aesthetics, 19; and biracial experience, 40; and causality, 16–17, 19, 72, 121, 203–4, 217–18; and characters, 15; and classical Hollywood cinema, 12, 72, 172, 208; erosion of, 19; and events, 16–17; existential, 165; in modernism, 17; moral, 150; and narrative, 41, 58, 73; in plot, 15–18, 80; and significance, 16–17, 128; solace of, 178; structures of, 15. *See also* inconsequence
consequential/inconsequential, 186; and literary modernism, 21; and modernist characters, 21; numerical relations between, 21
constellation, 7–8, 95, 125, 143, 167
contemplation, 52, 138, 157, 160–62, 166, 170, 186, 191, 225
contextualizing, 55, 141, 145, 245n18
Conway, Jack, 132
Cooper, Gary, 101, 111–16, *114*, *115*, 153, 156, 175, 255n70; as pretty cowboy, 114
corporeality, 52, 57, 79, 158, 160, 205, 217, 222, 226
correlation, 7–8, 167, 169
costumes and costuming, 40, 66–70, 75–76, 99, 178, 190
Cowley, Malcolm, 131

Crane, Helga (fictional character), 15, 47–61, 66, 70, 76, 79–82, 135–37, 189–90, 246n34, 247n56
Crawford, Joan, 172
critical theory, 205, 217, 268n59
criticism. *See* aesthetic criticism; historiographical criticism; literary criticism
Cromwell, John, 172
Cruz, James, 132
Cukor, George, 24–25, 40, 43–44, 49–50, 82, 128–29, 178, 226, 246n24
cult of distraction, and binge-watching, 36
culture, mass. *See* mass culture

Dabashi, Pardis, 243n108
Dalloway, Clarissa (fictional character), 4, 6
Dance of Life, The (film), 59
Daniels, William, 66
Dark Secrets (Fleming film), 132
Davis, Bette, 31–35; and African American cinematic spectatorship, 31–32, 241n80; beauty of, 31–32; disidentification with, 31–32
Davis, Thadious, 38, 243n104
Dayan, Daniel, 11
Daybreak (Yu film), 249n95
d'Eaubonne, Jean, 189
decenteredness, 45; and difference, 241n92; of empirical, 48; and plot, 9; of subject, 207
decontextualizing, modernist texts, 245n18
de Grasse, Joseph, 132
De l'amour (Stendhal), 216–17
Deleuze, Gilles, 179, 187–88, 205, 212, 264n8
Dell, Dewey (fictional character), 165–67, 169, 172–74, 262n116
Dembowski, Mathilde, 216
DeMille, Cecile B., 132
Demolition of a Wall (Lumière brothers film), 147–49, *148*, 152
demystification, 21

depression, 12, 39, 43, 48, 81
descriptive method, 2–3, 235–36n8
De Sica, Vittorio, 184, 208–15
desire, 247n56; and acquisition, 51; and aesthetics, 205–6, 268n61; anarchic pleasures of, 205–6; carnal, 207–8, 216; and classical Hollywood cinema, 35; and conspicuous consumption, 216; existential, 4; fatality of, 203; and feeling, 35; flashy theoretical rhetoric surrounding, 207; formalism of, 15, 205–6; hermeneutic, 90, 123; and inconsequential/inconsequentiality, 41; and incrimination, 150–51; and judgment, 150–51; literary forms of, 91; and love, 204–8, 268n61; narrative, 12, 15, 28, 96, 216; and narrative unity, 14, 138; negativity of, 205; and normativity, 256n95; and ownership, 221; and passionate love, 217; projections of, 78; psychoanalytic formalism of, 15; queer, 62, 65, 90, 119, 205; and sex, 206–8; tautological formalisms of, 41; wild, 85
Desire (Borzage film), 101
desires: of characters, 25, 96, 172
despair, 39, 43–44, 54, 136
detachment, 34, 59, 113, 164–65, 178, 181, 192, 216, 229, 262n109
detection, and passing, 65
detective: fiction, 65; genre, 172
determination, 51, 167
Devil Finds Work, The (Baldwin), 29–33
Devil Is a Woman, The (von Sternberg film), 91–92, 104
dialectics, 136, 203; of modernists, 18; of realism, 175; of tactility and attention, 162
Diawara, Manthia, 31
Dickens, Charles, 4, 10–11, 28–29, 32, 53
diegetic sound, 159, 187, 260–61n85; extra-, 198, 200–201, 267n45
Dietrich, Marlene, 39–40, 87, 227, 254n57; aesthetics of, 101–2; allure of, 110–11; in *Angel*, 256n79; bisexual-

278 | INDEX

Dietrich, Marlene (*continued*)
ity of, 92, 114; in *Blonde Venus*, 70, 91–92, 98–99, 101, 116–18, 249n91; in *Blue Angel, The*, 91–92, 102, 111, 253n13, 255n66; and cabaret, 110–11; as calm, 110; as carnal, 91; characters played, 26; as cool, distant, ironic, 18; in *Desire*, 101; in *Devil Is a Woman, The*, 91–92, 104; in *Dishonored*, 91–92, 249n91; as disinterested/noncommittal, 119; and disinterestedness/fatigue, 101; and distance, 93, 110, 124; and distraction, 110; documentary, as last film, 129–30; as elusive, 91; emotional minimalism of, 92, 111; as erotic object in film, 114; evasiveness of, 111; and fame, 110; family, 110; as femme fatale, 91–92; as first international movie star created by sound, 111; and Garbo, comparisons with, 91, 101, 252n10, 255–56n75, 255n66; as gorgeous girl with slumberous eyes, 101; and Hays Code, 102–3, 253n41; as icon, 255–56n75; indifference of, 87, 93, 101, 116, 118–19, 124–25, 128; inner expressions of face, 111; and irony, 128; in *Just a Gigolo*, 127–30, *129*; as knowing, distant, invested, 118; last fiction film, 127; legs, 253n13; and lesbian cinephilia, as icon of, 248–49n80, 255–56n75; as main love interest, at eighty years old, 130; masculine sexuality of, 101; minimalism of, 92–93, 111; and modernism, 92–93, 109–20, 125; in *Morocco*, 40, 91–93, 110–16, *112*, *113*, *115*, 118, 255nn66–67; as movie star, 111; mysterious reticence of, 255n66; name origins, 87; and nonchalance, 93; as public figure, 110; as queer icon, 40, 92, 255–56n75; quietude of, 93; quintessence of style on screen, 130; as ravishing sleepwalker, 101; restraint of, 110–11, 118–19; reticence of, 111, 255n66; in *Scarlet Empress, The*, 91–92, 102–9, *105*, *107*, *108*, 117; and security of torment, 89–125; sexually powerful restraint of, 110; in *Shanghai Express*, 40, 91–92, *100*; silences on screen, 87, 92, 94, 111, 118–19, 122; sly evasiveness of, 111; sly glances of, 125; and somnambulance, 101; in *Song of Songs*, 101; in *Stage Fright*, 101; as star, 102; stardom, 129; strange calm of, 110; and stylistic lyricism, 93; transformation of performance style, 255n67; voice, cultural, textual significance of, 255n62

difference: and decenteredness, 45, 241n92; and similarity, 93
dimensionality, 49, 56–58, 102, 189, 228, 246n43
Dimock, Wai Chee, 48–49, 51
disassemblage: and aesthetics, 5; and art forms, 29; and assemblage, 5, 29; narrative, 240n59; and plot, 5
disclosure, 16, 38, 65, 72, 75
discontinuities, 2, 9–10, 28–29, 96, 120
discourse: literary, 45; narrative, 16; networks, 157, 162–63, 261n91
disenfranchisement, 169
Dishonored (von Sternberg film), 91–92, 249n91
disidentification, 31–32, 36
Disidentifications (Muñoz), 36
disillusionment, 17–18, 31, 219–20
disinterest, 93–94, 101, 116, 119
dislocation, 51, 144, 157
displacements, 33, 52, 58–59, 90, 138–39, 165, 168
dispossession, 154, 156–57
dissatisfaction, 51, 118
dissociation, traumatic, 45
distraction: cult of, and binge-watching, 36; reception in, 144; and self-soothing, 12
disturbance, 85, 185–86, 197, 216
Doane, Mary Ann, 140, 147, 198–99, 202–3, 259nn61–62, 264n8, 265n21, 266n40, 267nn50–51

domestic fiction/domesticity, 5, 17, 21, 40–41, 52, 65, 89, 118, 122, 184–88, 192, 208, 216, 256n95, 260–61n85
Dongo, Fabrizio del (fictional character), 184
Doriot, Gaby (fictional character), 180, 192–203, *194*, *195*, *197*, *201*, 211, 218, 226
Dos Passos, John, 263n140
Dostoevsky, Fyodor, 261n95
double consciousness, 46
Douglas, Melvyn, 64, 256n79
dramas. *See* melodramas; romance dramas
Dreyer, Carl, 80
Dr. Jekyll and Mr. Hyde (Robertson film), 132
duality, 40, 49–50, 56, 62, 64–69, 249n91
Du Bois, W. E. B., 43, 46
duels, as narrative hallmark of Ophuls cinema, 184, 223, 226, 228, 270n89
Dumas, Alexandre, 25, 44, 49–50, 73–82, 222, 226
Duprat, Julie, 79
Duval, Armand (fictional character), 44, 73–80, *77*, 112
Dwan, Allan, 188
Dyer, Richard, 62–63, 109–10

Eames, Leonora (fictional character), 199
Earrings of Madame de . . . , The (Ophuls film), 41, 177–227, 185, 188, 190, 210, 212, 213, 214, 222, 224, 227, 265n21, 269n78, 270n89
écriture, modernist, 20, 22, 26, 90, 119, 205–6
Edelman, Lee, 120, 136, 207, 241–42n92, 258n17
Edison, Thomas, 146–47, 149, 152
effete aestheticism, 157
Eighteenth Brumaire (Marx), 17, 219, 229–30
Eisenstein, Sergei, 10–11, 28, 102, 131, 177
Electrocuting an Elephant (Edison film), 146–53, *149*; as transitional film, 153
Eliot, George, 177, 182
Eliot, T. S., 1–2, 13, 46
Elsaessear, Thomas, 10
embodiment, 23, 52, 110, 118, 229–30, 261n97
empirical, 12, 39, 48, 151–52, 154, 197–98, 216
emplotment, 134, 142, 153, 202, 211
emptiness, 165, 190–91, 223
Eng, David, 40, 48–49
Enlightenment: modernity, 18; subject, 19
epistemic, 32, 59–60, 121, 160–61, 168, 170, 172, 186, 197–98, 262n111
epistemology, 29, 37, 62, 123, 198, 223; Cartesian, 161; Kantian, 235n5
epistemophilia, 198, 266n40
equilibrium, 16, 72, 184–85, 192, 200, 230
Erkkila, Betsy, 65
erotic films, 155–56, 260n85
escapism: and fantasy, 138; and identification, 36; and mortality, 41; ritual of, 36; and self, 182
Escher, M. C., 105
essentialism: provocative, 209; visual, 184
Esty, Jed, 244n4, 258n18
Ethics of Opting Out, The (Ruti), 206–7
etiologies: and limits, 191; and narrative, 168; palliative, 26, 41, 168
Everett, Anna, 31
exclusion, 18–19, 38, 48, 134, 230
execution films, 14, 70, 146–47, 151, 153, 259n61
Execution of Czolgoz, with Panorama of Auborn Prison (Edison film), 146–47
exhibitionism: aesthetics of, 155; and display of visibility, 155
existential: allure, of plot, 5–6; bodily, 223; comfort, 172; and complicity, temptations of, 6; consequences, 165; desire, 4; despair, 136; grief, 167; index of, 4; longing for, 5; and

existential (*continued*)
mortality, rumination on, 166; personhood, 221; and present, 137, 163; promises, 8, 138; refuge, 47; separateness, 223–24; stakes, 183; and traumatic recognition, 225; urgency, 133, 225
experience, cinema of, 197–99
experimentalism, 27–28; aesthetic, 9; linguistic, 123; radical stylistic, 90–91
exploitation, 21, 155, 201–2, 218, 230, 262n116
exposure, 63–67, 70, 72, 75, 98, 155, 182

Fabrizi, Aldo, 174
fabula, 15–16, 96, 160–61, 261n101
Fama, Katherine A., 90, 119
Fanon, Frantz, 46
fantasies, 8–9, 11, 29–30, 33, 36, 40, 44, 78, 82, 85, 87, 114, 125, 138, 167, 172–73, 219, 221, 224
Faraday, Helen (fictional character), 92, 98–99, 99, 116–18
fascism, 2, 173, 226–28
Faulkner, John [brother], 132–33
Faulkner, William, 129; and aesthetics, 22, 263n140; and ambivalence, 8, 34; characters of, 135–38, 173, 178; and classical Hollywood cinema, 132, 171; and consequence, solace of, 178; and early film, 39, 41, 131–75; and family in novels, 137; film-theoretical scholarship on, 257n6; and hermeneutic poverty of present, 35–36; and indulgence by proxy, 171–73; and interpellation and hegemony, 36; and ironic distance, 133; on *is* vs. *was*, 131; and literary modernism, 21; and minoritarian subjectivity, 39; as modernist, 8, 14, 21–22, 41, 131–32, 134, 138, 157, 167, 170–72; as motion picture doctor, 171; and moviegoing, 12–13, 14, 34–36, 39, 132; and narrative cinema, 39; and narrative poverty, 41; and narratives, 170; and narrative unity, 14; New South of, 6, 157; novels of, 39; and Oxford, MS, 12, 41, 132–33, 140, 172–73, 257nn9–10; and palliative etiologies, 26, 41, 168; and plot, 4–8, 26, 134; and popular film, 12–13; and presentness, limits of, 26, 41, 131–75; and pulp fiction, 132; reading by, 261n95; screenplays, credits for, 171; screenwriting, 39, 132–33, 138, 171–73, 260n76; and violence, narrative with, 267n46; on *was* vs. *is*, 131; Yoknapatawpha County characters, 24
Fauset, Jessie, 62
feeling(s): and behavior, 217; and causality, 123; and desire, 35; and human experience, 30; and thoughts, 37–38; ugly, 30–31, 230. *See also specific feeling(s)*
Fell, John, 237n25
Felski, Rita, 268n59
Female Complaint, The (Berlant), 242n98
feminism, 92, 180–81, 205, 251n4, 252n12
femme fatales, 91–92, 192, 201–2, 266n40
Femme Fatales (Doane), 267n51
Feyder, Jacques, 24
fiction: detective, 65; modernist, decontextualizing of, 245n18; modern/modernist, 2–3, 5, 19–21, 34, 131–32, 134, 157, 167, 204; premodernist, 19; pulp, 132. *See also* novels
fictionality, 151, 236n14, 239n52, 264–65n12
Field, Allyson Nadia, 38, 48–49, 243n106
film: blackness, 69–72; and cultures of exhibition, 41; to entertain, 82; history, 10, 13, 26–27, 36, 38, 47–48, 131, 134, 137, 147; and literature, 13, 48–49, 92, 239n58, 263n1; and novels, 9, 39, 44, 49, 92, 208; and plot, 134; prenarrative, 134, 155–56;

and profilmic events, 198, 265n26; realist theory of, 269n69; studies, 27, 40, 177; subversive, 240n64; theory, 13, 269n69; and visual spectacle, 131. *See also* cinema; classical Hollywood cinema; motion pictures; moving pictures; narrative cinema/film; sound film (talkies)
film noir, 240n65, 264n11, 266n40
film reception. *See* cinematic reception
film theory, 195, 257n6, 264n3, 269n69
finitude, 166; and love, 41, 177–230; of personhood, 182. *See also* mortality
Finnegans Wake (Joyce), 6
Fischer, Lucy, 249n92
Fitzgerald, F. Scott, 6
Fitzmaurice, George, 68, 153
Flaubert, Gustave, 2–3, 14, 17, 179, 191, 218–20, 261n95
Fleissner, Jennifer L., 52
Fleming, Victor, 132
Flesh and the Devil (film), 64
Flood, Nora (fictional character), 15, 40, 89–90, 93–98, 106, 116, 120–24, 167–68
Foltz, Jonathan, 240n59, 245n17
Ford, Jennifer, 257n9
Ford, John, 132, 172
formalism, 267n50; cinematic, 134, 178; of desire, 15, 205–6; empty, 178; and love, 268n62; modernist, 45; Ophulsian, 178–80; psychoanalytic, 15; reparative, 90; Russian, 15–16; tautological, 41; of teleology and closure, 205
formlessness, 47, 143
Forster, E. M., 4, 6
Foucault, Michel, 10
fragmentation, 9, 13, 18, 22, 34–35, 45–46, 73, 95, 138–39, 229, 242n92
Fragments: A Lover's Discourse (Barthes), 204, 206
François, Anne-Lise, 96
Frank, Joseph, 2, 90, 251n4, 261n101

Freud, Sigmund, 16
Fried, Michael, 177, 264nn2–3
Friedman, Susan Stanford, 48
Frow, John, 23
Fry, Roger, 236n13
Futurist Manifesto, The (Marinetti), 3

Gaines, Jane, 132
Gallagher, Catherine (Cathy), 236n14, 239n52
Gance, Abel, 59
Garbo, Greta, 34–40, 43–83, 135, 137, 170–71, 189; as alluring, 110; androgynous and erotic potency of, 65; in *Anna Christie* (her first talkie), 24, 64, 109; in *Anna Karenina*, 64; and Art Deco, 70, 249n92; bisexuality of, 65; as blonde with brunette voice, 63; in *Camille*, 24–25, 38, 40, 44, 49, 51, 54–56, *55*, *56*, 70, 76–78, *77*, 80, 80–82, 109, 222–23; characters played, 26, 62; as cinematic image, 54; and classical Hollywood, 70; and death mask, 55; as demure and urbane, 255n66; and diet, restrictive, 248n71; and Dietrich, comparisons with, 91, 101, 252n10, 255–56n75, 255n66; emotional removal of, 65; as enigmatic, 91, 110; erotic and androgynous potency of, 65; as ethereal, 87; exoticism of, 70; extratextual presence, 24–25; eyelashes, long, 80; as fascinating and seductive, 64; first talkie, 64; in *Flesh and the Devil*, 64; as glamorous, 44, 78, 129; in *Grand Hotel*, 54; Gustafsson name change, 63; hyperwhiteness, 63; as icon, 55, 70, 78, 248–49n80, 255–56n75; impenetrability of, 65; and impression of voluminous warmth and promise, 83; in *Kiss, The*, 24, 64–69, *66*, *67*; languidness of, 54; and lesbian cinephilia, as icon of, 248–49n80, 255–56n75; in *Love*, 64; magnetism on screen, 65; marketability of, 63; in *Mata*

282 | INDEX

Garbo, Greta (*continued*)
  Hari, 64, 67–76, *68*, *69*, *71*, *74*, 80–81; melodramas of, 175; as memorable star persona, 63; as MGM's most profitable star, 63; and modernism, 80–81; and Murnau death mask, 249n97; in *Mysterious Lady, The* (silent film), 63, 64; name origins and change, 63, 248n72; in *Ninotchka*, 64–65; and orientalist fetishism, 70; and originless, ethereal pallor, 63; as otherworldly, 91; otherworldly largesse of, 65; in *Painted Veil, The*, 24, 64; pale exoticism of, 70; in *Passing*, 65; photographic iconography of, 55; in *Queen Christina*, 54, 64–65; queer energies and intensity of, 65; as queer icon, 255–56n75; screen presence, 65; as seductive and fascinating, 64; sexuality of, 65; in silent films, 63; as singularly ethereal, otherworldly, divinely untouchable, 54; star status, 66; as Swedish working class, 51; in *Temptress, The* (silent film), 63, 64; in *Torrent, The* (her first American feature), 63–64; in *Two-Faced Woman*, 64; vamp films, 64; voice, 63–64, 111, 255n63; warmth and promise, impression of, 83; and white beauty, 62–63, 82; in *Wild Orchids*, 64
Garnett, Tay, 171
Gaudreault, André, 142
Gautier, Marguerite (fictional character), 24–25, 49–51, 54–56, *55*, *56*, 73–82, *77*, *80*, 105–6, 109, 112, 125, 222, 226; as consumptive courtesan, 44
gender: performance, 139; politics, 133
gendered: cinematic looking in film noir, 266n40; of cinematic suture, 265n12; domestic life, 21; financial independence, 122; motherhood, 58; oppression, 181–82; shame, 192, 202; of social mobility and affective repertoire, 221; unfreedom, 216
Genette, Gérard, 15–16, 146, 186

Gilbert, Ethel Bedient, 43
Gilbert, John, 64–65, 92, 111
Gillespie, Michael, 69–70, 162
glamour, 214; aesthetic principle of, 129; and irrelevance, 129
Glavey, Brian, 90, 98, 251n4, 258n17
Godard, Jean-Luc, 46
Goethe, Johann Wolfgang von, 181, 217
Gone with the Wind (film), 43, 82
Goody, Alex, 92
Go Tell It on the Mountain (Baldwin), 32, 35
Gotta, Salvatore, 179
Grand Hotel (film), 54
grandiose tropes, 146–47, 151
Grandjacquet, Francesco, 173, 175
Grant, Cary, 98, 117, 256n79
Great Divide, The (Barker film), 132
Green, Rev. Pleasant, (fictional character), 52, 58
Green, Richard, 172
Greenburg, Adrian Adolph. *See* Adrian (costume designer)
grief, 87, 131, 145, 167–68, 184
Griffith, D. W., 28–29, 131–32
Grivel, Charles, 109
Guattari, Felix, 205
Guido II (fictional character), 95, 120, 135–37
Gunning, Tom, 9, 41, 131, 140, 143–44, 155, 237n23, 260–61n85

Hale, Louise Closser, 103
Hall, Rebecca, 85, 250n1
Hamilton, Sarah, 110
Hansen, Miriam, 27–28, 140, 198
hapticity: and aurality/sounds, 41, 182, 202, 222–23; in cinema/film, 197, 246–47n43, 266n36; and dimensionality, 246n43; and gardens/plants, 198–99; and inhabitation, 198; and lyricism, 202; and materiality, 199; realist style, 203; and utopia, 194, 199; and visuality, 85, 185, 192, 195–96, 199, 203
Harlem Renaissance, 43, 46, 81

Harlow, Jean, 31, 33
Harper, Frances, 62
Hartman, Saidiya, 38, 48–49, 243n106
Hawks, Howard, 132, 153, 171, 172–73
Hays Code censorship and prohibitions, 102–3, 253n41
Hays Office, and moral code for films, 50
Heaney, Emma, 256n95
heartbreak, 13, 39–40, 70, 87–93, 122–24, 153, 167, 225
Heath, Stephen, 151, 153, 156, 202, 267n46
hegemony: and classical narrative cinema, 10; and interpellation, 36; and pale formation, 63; white, 32, 63
Heidegger, Martin, 13, 164, 261n97
Helton, Laura, 243n105
Hemingway, Ernest, 6, 263n140
Hemmings, Clare, 30, 202–3
Hemmings, David, 127
Henning, Michelle, 55
Henstra, Sarah, 98
Hepburn, Katharine, and lesbian cinephilia, as icon of, 248–49n80
hermeneutics, 13–15, 35–36, 62, 65, 90, 94, 112, 120–25, 141–45, 151, 154–56, 170, 181, 186, 248n66, 268n59; anti-, 120
Herring, Phillip, 91
Herring, Scott, 90, 95, 120, 123–24, 243n109, 251n4
heterogeneity, 27, 198. *See also* homogeneity
heteronormativity, 5, 26, 90–91, 118, 120, 122, 135–36, 206–7; anti-, 251n4
heterosexuality, 8, 14, 19, 40, 116; compulsory, 89–90, 118
Hidden Way, The (de Grasse film), 132
Hilton, James, 245–46n24
historical chronology, 47–48
historiographical criticism, 47–49; and critical superimposition, 48
historiography: and extant, 49; and informed conjecture, 49; and literary modernism, 14; racialized processes of exclusion in, 48
history: dynamic contradictions of, 21; of human thought, 31; of modern subject, 51; and social relations, 21; of still life painting, 239n51; and time, 14, 17, 218
Hitchcock, Alfred, 101, 103
Holland, Sharon Patricia, 241n92
Hollywood. *See* classical Hollywood cinema
homogeneity, 156, 205, 267n46. *See also* heterogeneity
hooks, bell, 31, 241n92
Hoyt, Harry O., 132
humanism: anti-, 241n92; liberal, 224, 226; post-, 241n92
humanness, 220, 225
Hurston, Zora Neale, 6
Hutchinson, George, 49, 81, 243n104
Huyssen, Andreas, 26–27

ideology, 4–5, 8, 11–12, 14, 27–29, 41, 62–64, 78, 103, 134–35, 145, 157–58, 175, 205, 258n27; of autonomy, 261n89; classical Hollywood cinema, 33; colonial, 21; and culture, 228; of modernism, 2–3, 261n89; normative, 137; social, 139; violent, of Old South, 157
illusion: aesthetic, 175; of characters, 24; of cinema/film, 82, 109, 141, 180; of fictional worlds, 11, 200–201; of formal totality, 11; of image, 144; of love, 180; of material abundance, 56; mimetic, 106–7; of narrative continuity, 103; of physicality and exactness of human beings, 56; of physicality and exactness of things, 196; power of, 109; of presence, 141; of realism/reality, 11, 175; of social belonging and psychic unity, 47; of spatial depth, 188, 196; and trompe l'oeil, 109; victory as, 146; of volume, 49
Imes, Elmer, 43, 81–82

Imitation of Life (Stahl film), 75
immateriality, 54, 56, 106, 125. *See also* materiality
imperialism: aristocratic patriarchal, 185; and capitalism, 183, 203–4; liberal, 222, 226; and patriarchal violence, 182; and violence, 181–82, 226–27; Western, 203–4. *See also* colonialism
Improper Modernism: The Bewildering Corpus of Djuna Barnes (Caselli), 251n5
inconsequence: and anonymity, 203; arts of, 1–42; of classical Hollywood cinema, 29; and desire, tautological formalisms of, 41; and differentiations in life, 186; and disturbance, 216; films as, 29; formal meditation on, 47; and historical change, 219; and inexistence, 219; and irrelevancy, 73; and material reality, prohibitions of, 175; and modern fiction, 19–20; and modernism, 17–18; and plot, 82, 202, 218; and prohibitions of material reality, 175; and tautological formalisms of desire, 41; and women, 202. *See also* consequence
incrimination: and judgment, 150–53; self-, 229–30
individualism, liberal. *See* liberal individualism
inequities, 154
inexistence, 216; and emptiness, 190–91; and inconsequential/inconsequentiality, 219
infidelity, 180
injustice, and dispossession, 154
intangibility, corporeal, 57
interdependence, 2, 51, 217
interiority, 51, 61, 206–7
interpellation, 32, 34, 36
intimacy, 217, 233
"Introduction to 'Cultures of Argument'" (Dabashi), 243n108, 243n110

Inwood, Charlotte (fictional character), 101
Iola Leroy (Harper), 62
irrelevance: and glamour, 129; and significance, 129
irrelevancy, 47, 78, 127–29; and inconsequential/inconsequentiality, 73
irreverence, 119, 122, 136
isolation, 9, 31, 83, 134
It's a Wonderful Life, 205

Jaffe, Sam, 104
James, Henry, 3–4, 6–7, 14, 35, 90, 236n13, 261n95
Jameson, Fredric, 45, 60, 145, 158, 161, 178, 228, 237n21, 263n1
Jane Eyre (Brontë), 18, 58
Jannings, Emil, 111
Jesenská, Milena, 36
Jews, and inequities, 154
Jolly, Amy (fictional character), 111–16, *112*, *113*, *115*
Joseph, Ralina L., 62
Joyce, James, 19
judgment, and incrimination, 150–53
Just a Gigolo (Hemmings film), 127–30, *129*

Kafka, Franz, 6, 17, 21, 231, 243n103
Kahn, Madeline, 101
Kaiserling, Helga von (fictional character), 127
Kant, Immanuel, 235n5
Kaplan, Kyle, 37
Karenina, Anna (fictional character), 16, 23, 64, 239n55
Kauser, Alice, 246n24
Kazan, Elia, 75
Keathley, Christian, 37
Keller, Sarah, 34
Kelly, Nancy, 172
Kendry, Clare (fictional character), 62–65, 72, 82, 85–87, *86*, 249n94
Kennedy, John F., assassination, film of, 141
Kermode, Frank, 13, 35, 145

Kiss, The (Feyder film), 24, 64–69, 66, 67
Kittler, Friedrich, 237n21, 261n91
Knights, L. C., 239n55
Koch, Gertrud, 264n8, 265–66n33
Koepnick, Lutz, 111
Kollorsz, Richard, 105–6
Kornbluh, Anna, 5, 29, 34
Kovács, András Bálint, 264n3
Kracauer, Siegfried, 36, 141
Kuhlenkampf, Robert (fictional character), 186
Kuhn, Annette, 37
Kurosawa, Akira, 177
Kuzniar, Alice A., 116

Lady of the Camellias, The (Dumas), 25, 44, 49–50, 73–82, 222, 226
Land of the Pharaohs (Hawks film), 171
Lang, Fritz, 59, 250n98
language: and action, 159; and aesthetics, 189; and love, 217
Lant, Antonia, 56, 195–96
Larsen, Nella, 96, 250n1; and aesthetics, 22; and affective history, 49; characters of, 136–37, 178; and consequence, solace of, 178; and darkness, 83; death of, 83; desire in fiction of, 247n56; epistolary activity, 49; fiction and movies, 39, 44, 92; and Garbo, films of, 12, 34–36, 38–40, 43–83, 135, 137, 170–71, 189, 243n104; and Guggenheim fellowship, 43; and Harlem's cultural elite, 49; and hermeneutic poverty of present, 35–36; husband, 43, 81–82; on inefficacy of possession, 51; and interpellation and hegemony, 36; and literary fame, 43; and literary modernism, 21; and literary tradition, critical rejection of, 82; and marginalization, 81–82; and minoritarian subjectivity, 39; as modernist, 8, 14, 21–22, 170–71; and moviegoing, 12–14, 34–36, 39– 40, 43–44, 47–49, 81, 243n104; and narrative unity, 14; novels of, 39; as nurse, 82–83; and passing, fictions of, 49; plagiarism scandal, 39, 43; and plot, 5–8, 26, 39, 44–45, 82, 135; and popular film, 12; rediscovery of, 53; and resonant universe, 49; as seamstress, 66; and social marginalization, 81–82; textual tableaux of, 26; as understudied, 92. *See also Quicksand* (Larsen novel)
Lawrence, Amy, 255n62
Lawrence, D. H., 6
Léger, Fernard, 102, 177
lesbian cinephilia, 248–49n80, 255–56n75
Letter from an Unknown Woman (Ophuls film), 79, 203, 214
Letter from an Unknown Woman (Zweig novella), 223–24
Levine, Nancy, 92, 252n12
Lewis, Cara L., 9, 239n51
Lewis, William, 257n10
liberal humanism, 224, 226
liberal individualism, 8, 41, 52, 79, 181–82, 219–20
Liebelei (Ophuls film), 183
Lighthouse by the Sea (St. Clair film), 132
Light in August (Faulkner), 170
lighting, 29, 40, 67, 80–82, 93, 99, 105–6, 111, 124–25, 143, 200
Lilac Time (Fitzmaurice film), 153, 156, 175
Limits of Critique, The (Felski), 268n59
Lindsay, Vachel, 10
literary criticism, 2, 13, 22–23, 29, 45, 48, 109, 204–5, 239n52, 267n52. *See also* aesthetic criticism
literary modernism. *See* modernism, literary
literary studies, 23, 26–27, 40, 137; historicist/contextualist paradigm, 48
literary theory, 13
literary tradition, 60, 82, 220

literature, and cinema/film, 13, 48–49, 239n58, 263n1. *See also* modernism, literary
Lola Montes (Ophuls final film), 179, 207, 266n34
longing, 5, 8, 22, 36, 41, 47, 81–82, 85, 89, 123, 136, 177, 182, 192–93, 228–29
Loretz, Pare, 101
Lost Illusions (Balzac), 24, 161
Lost World, The (Hoyt film), 132
love: aesthetics of, 204, 268n61; and causality/causation, 125, 183; complexities of, 206–7, 267–68n53; and death, 204; and depth, 204, 208–30; and desire, 204–8, 268n61; elusiveness of, 204; and fidelity, 91; and finitude, 41, 177–230; and formalism, 268n62; formative force of, 41; and hate, 31; history of, 204; illusion of, 180; and intimacy expectations, 268n62; and language, 217; mannered, 217; and pain, 182; passionate, 216–18, 223–28; physical, 217; postcritical study of, 267–68n53, 268n59; queer, 85; and queer marginality/subjectivity, 89–90; reality of, 221; romantic, 31, 39, 173–75, 206; and self-becoming, 39; and sex, 89–90; study of, 267–68n53, 268n59, 268n62; and terror, 173; vanity, 217. *See also* romance dramas
Love (film), 64
Love, Heather, 93, 136, 181
Lover's Discourse, A (Barthes), 204, 216–17
love stories, 20–21, 26, 40–41, 78, 89–98, 115–25, 156, 173–75, 177–230. *See also* melodramas; romance dramas
Lubitch, Ernst, 64–65, 256n79
Lukács, Georg, 2–3, 7, 21–22, 96, 219, 235–36n8
Lumière brothers (Auguste and Louis), 140–41, 147–49
Lurie, Peter, 170, 257n6
Lynch, Deidre, 19, 34, 239n52, 267n52, 268n62

lyricism: of objects and sounds, 202; of objects resistant to narrative frames of reference, 193; stylistic, 93

MacDowell, James, 14, 115, 250n98
Madame Bovary (Flaubert), 265n30
Magic Flute, The (Mozart), 57–58
Magnani, Anna, 173, 209
Magnificent Obsession (Stahl film), 78
Making of Americans, The (Stein), 6
Mamoulian, Rouben, 101
Manfredi, Giorgio (fictional character), 173
Manhattan Madness (McDermott film), 132
Mankiewicz, Joseph L., 128–29
Mann, Frau (fictional character), 95, 98, 121
Mann, Heinrich, 111
Man with a Movie Camera (Vertov), 102
Man without Qualities, The (Musil), 6–7
Mao, Douglas, 30, 240–41n73
Marcus, Jane, 92, 251n4, 253n39
Marcus, Laura, 48
marginalization, 48, 81–82, 89–90, 136, 178, 180, 229
Marinetti, Filippo Tommaso, 3
Marion, Frances, 245–46n24
Marks, Laura U., 195
Marlene (Schell documentary film), 129–30
Marshall, Herbert, 116–17, 256n79
martyrdom, victimization, 139
Marx, Karl, 17, 218–19, 229–30
Marxism, 2, 218–19
Mason, Bertha (fictional character), 18
Mason, James, 199
mass culture, 26–27, 206, 240–41n73
"Mass Production of the Senses, The: Classical Cinema as Vernacular Modernism" (Hansen essay), 27
Mata Hari (Fitzmaurice film), 64, 67–76, *68*, *69*, *71*, *73*, *74*, 80–81, 129, 249n91

materiality, 7, 56, 106–7, 170, 181, 199, 220. *See also* immateriality
Matras, Christian, 187
Matthews, John T., 139, 154, 169, 233, 260n67, 261n89
Maupassant, Guy de, 179, 181
Mayne, Judith, 10, 14, 29, 47
McCrea, Joel, 172
McDermott, John, 132
McDowell, Deborah, 62
McIntire, Gabrielle, 61, 248n66
McKible, Adam, 46
McLuhan, Marshall, 237n21
media: archaeology, and film history, 10; modern, 9; new technological, 237n21
media ecology, 9, 237n21
Meeting of Two Queens (Barriga film), 255n75
Melford, George, 132
Mellard, James M., 258n27
melodramas, 14, 29, 47, 49–50, 75, 132, 175, 179–81, 200, 229. *See also* love stories; romance dramas
Melville, Herman, 90, 231
Menjou, Adolphe, 111–12
Mercer, Kobena, 36–37
Merzbach, Baron von (fictional character), 101
metaphor, 23–24, 91, 159, 189, 226
metaphysics, 165–66, 169, 182, 224–25, 235n5
metonymic, 57, 123, 205
metonyms, 191–92
Metropolis (Lang film), 59
Metz, Christian, 11–12, 29, 56, 103, 141, 197
MGM (Metro-Goldwyn-Mayer) Studios, 40, 43, 63, 65, 67, 91, 111, 171–72, 245–46n24, 255n66
Michelson, Annette, 238n44, 264n3
middle class, 10, 27–28, 52, 206. *See also* bourgeois; working class
Middlemarch (Eliot), 19, 177
Miller, D. A., 4, 90, 236n17
Miller, Tyrus, 251n5

mimetic, 23, 45, 52, 56, 60, 98, 102, 106–7, 182, 187
minoritarian: academic fields, 38; culture, 36, 38; groups, 48; modernism, 36; subjectivity, 39, 46
Miranda, Isa, 180, 186
mise-en-scène, 9, 104, 189, 199–200, 266n34
misogyny, 3
misrecognition, 75–76, 169, 268n62
modalities, 9, 268n59
"Modern Fiction" (Woolf essay), 3, 34
modernism, 46, 124; anti-, 264nn2–3; and art, 46; bad, 240–41n73; and bad infinity, 7; cinematic, 26–28, 30, 39, 48, 177–78, 263–64nn1–3; dialectical quality of, 18; falsifying, 261n89; genealogy of Euro-American, 17–18; good, 241n73; high, 1–2, 90, 120, 133, 171–72, 205; and intermediality, 9; and mass culture, 26–27; and plot, 5–6, 9, 19, 42, 51, 134, 137, 244n4; plural, 177; post-, 241n92, 251n5; and psychic challenges, 36; studies, 4, 26–27, 45–46, 177, 207, 244n4; vernacular, 27–28. *See also* aesthetics: and modernism
modernism, literary, 2, 6, 9, 13–14, 19–21, 26–27, 36, 45–48, 52, 89, 138, 158, 171–72, 177, 183, 205, 237n21, 239n52, 239n58, 240n59, 263n1; and consequential/inconsequential, 21; history of, 38. *See also* fiction: modern/modernist; novels: modern/modernist
Modernism/modernity journal, 46, 232
modernist characters, 21
modernists: and arts of inconsequence, 26–30; bad, 7, 26–30, 94, 121, 240–41n73; Black, 46; and detachment, 229; dialectics of, 18; good, 93, 109–20, 125; white male, 50
modernist studies, 4, 26–27, 45–46, 177, 207, 244n4
Modernist Studies Association, 46

modern literature. *See* fiction: modern/modernist; modernism, literary; novels: modern/modernist
Modern Screen magazine, 252n10
Moi, Toril, 27, 29, 45, 109, 182, 204–5, 223, 239n55, 239nn52–53
monarchies and monarchism, 20, 54, 73, 75, 78–79, 219–20
monogamy, 40, 89, 91, 118, 122, 243n109
monstration, 142
montage, 13, 59, 145; avant-garde, 28; literary, 28
Montgomery, Robert, 109
Moore, Colleen, 153, 156
Moreau, Frédéric, 219–20
Moretti, Franco, 51, 57, 226
Morgan, Daniel, 187, 189, 208, 217, 238n44, 264nn2–3, 265n26
Morocco (von Sternberg film), 40, 91–93, 110–16, *112, 113, 114, 115*, 118, 255nn66–67
Morrison, Toni, 1, 29–37, 44, 62, 241n92
mortality, 41, 165–67, 178, 182, 236n13. *See also* finitude
motherhood, 58
Mothlight (Brakhage), 177
Motion Picture magazine, 91, 252n10
motion pictures, 10, 133, 171, 181. *See also* cinema; film; moving pictures
motivation, 134, 143, 153–54, 172, 191, 258n13
mourning, 21–22, 51, 166
moviegoing practices, 12–14, 29–36, 39–44, 47–49, 81, 91–93, 113, 123, 132; and binge-watching, 36
Movie Mirror magazine, 110
movies. *See* cinema; film
moving pictures, 53, 110, 131, 140. *See also* cinema; film; motion pictures
Mozart, Wolfgang Amadeus, 57–58
Mrs. Dalloway (Woolf), 4, 6
Mulvey, Laura, 87, 180–81, 202, 215, 264n8, 264n11, 270n89
Muñoz, José Esteban, 32–33, 36, 46
Murnau, F. W., 249n97
Murphet, Julian, 237n21

music, 98–99, 101, 110–11, 128–29; extradiegetic, 267n45; film, 249n91, 267n45
My Brother Bill (Faulkner biography), 132
Mysterious Lady, The (Niblo silent film), 63, 64

Nabokov, Vladimir, 181
Nancy, Jean-Luc, 223
Napoleon Bonaparte, 215, 219, 226–27
Napolin, Julie Beth, 48
Narration in the Fiction Film (Bordwell), 198
narrative: action, 102–3; aesthetics, 153, 230; architecture, 4, 82, 119–20, 161; and characters, 164, 170, 269n78; classical, 9–10, 14, 224; and classical style, 198; coherence, 134, 235n5; complexities, 240n65; consequences, 41, 58, 73; contortions, 172, 184; desire, 12, 15, 28, 96, 216; development, 103–4, 143, 153; disorder, 156; disruptions, 229; and emotion, 181; enunciation, 161, 261n101; immersion, 2, 11, 36, 155, 179–80; instability of, 269n78; instrumentalism, 18; integration, 131, 134, 144, 215; intelligibility, 19, 104; meaning, 15, 61, 94, 96, 105, 140, 145–47, 156–57; non-plot-based progression, 237n19; omniscient, 32–33, 164–65, 261n101, 262n109; order, 94, 123, 134, 154; palliative, 169; of personal development, 45; and plot, 13–14, 123, 235n5; rejection of, 102; retrospective, 33, 59, 135, 158, 162–63, 261n101; socio-, 89; sophistication, 11, 131; surrogacy, 162; trajectories, 94, 121, 164; transformation, 151; transparency, 197–98; turning points, 57. *See also* causality: narrative
narrative cinema and film, 9–16, 22, 27, 29, 39, 104, 107, 131–34, 143–47, 150, 153–55, 189, 224, 237n25, 240n59, 259n62

narrative continuity, 11, 27, 96, 103–4, 138, 143, 169–70, 187, 198
Narrative Discourse (Genette), 16
narrative discourse, singular in, 16
narrative sense, 18, 78, 134, 138, 141, 157, 173, 192, 216
narrative unity, 2, 13–14, 40, 133, 138, 153, 156, 172–74, 235n5. *See also* psychic unity
narratology, French, 15–16
nationalism, 127, 228
nation-building, 244n4
nation-state, 90, 218–19
naturalism, 2–3, 258n27
Nazis, 227–29
negation, 18, 30, 51, 60, 90–91, 120, 135, 157, 190
negativity, 26, 30, 42, 45, 181, 244n2; of desire, 205; fetishization of, 40, 242n92; queer, 40, 91, 93, 136
Negga, Ruth, 85
neurosis, 46
New York Times, 54
Ngai, Sianne, 30, 36
Niblo, Fred, 63–64
Nicholls, Peter, 17, 238n43
Nietzsche, Friedrich, 10
Nightwood (Barnes novel), 1, 5, 13, 15, 22, 87, 89–125, 128, 135–37, 167–68, 172, 185, 206, 251nn4–5, 252n6, 261n101; as antihermeneutical, 120; as autobiographical, 89; as elegiac novel, 87; as queer modernist project, 40–41, 90. *See also* Barnes, Djuna
nihilism, 104, 137; political, 21
Ninotchka (Lubitch), 64–65
noir. *See* film noir
normalcy, 36, 205
normativity, 4–5, 8–10, 14–15, 18, 21–22, 28–30, 36, 52, 90–93, 96, 118–22, 137, 146, 150, 152, 182, 236n17, 256n95; anti-, 30, 41, 91, 122, 206; antihetero-, 90, 251n4; hetero-, 5, 26, 90–91, 118, 120, 122, 135–36, 206–7, 251n4; non-, 205

North, Joseph, 48
Novak, Kim, 127
Novarro, Ramon, 70
Novel after Film, The (Foltz), 245n17
novels: and acquisition, 51, 52–53; and cinema, 12; and classical Hollywood cinema, 208; eighteenth-century, 220–21; and film, 9, 39, 44, 49, 92, 208; history of, 51, 122; modern/modernist, 5–9, 14–15, 17, 21–22, 26, 28, 36, 41–42, 51, 89, 95, 133, 145, 157, 167; nineteenth-century, 2–4, 9–10, 12, 18–19, 51, 82, 90, 98, 120, 208, 220–22, 236n17; and plot, 12; readers of, 52–53; rise of, 239n52; and subjects, 51; and technologies of representation, 9; theorizations of, 51. *See also* fiction; modernism, literary; fiction: modern/modernist
Nünning, Angsar, 57
Nussbaum, Martha, 268n62

obsession: amorous and unrequited, 216; gendered, 266n40; and incrimination, 150; and narrative epistemophilia, 198, 266n40; with virginity, 260n67
occlusion, 101–2, 104
O'Connor, Matthew (fictional character), 15, 89, 94–97, 99, 101, 119–21, 123–25, 167
O'Hara, Scarlett (fictional character), 43, 82
Ohlrig, Smith (fictional character), 199
Oliver Twist (Dickens), 19
ontology, 23, 25, 196
Ophuls, Marcel [son], 227
Ophuls, Max, 79, 264n11; admirers of, 264n6; affects produced by films of, 39; as analytical, 181; and anonymity, 203; and antipsychological bias, 179; as avant garde, 179; and baroque architecture, 192; characters of, 178; as consummate filmmaker of artifice, 191–92; critiques of, 178–79; denouncement of, 264n6; duels,

Ophuls, Max (*continued*)
as narrative hallmark of, 184, 223, 226, 228, 270n89; and female image in classical cinema, 265n12; final film, 179, 207, 266n34; and formalism, 178–80; French period, 177; and gendered terms of cinematic suture, 265n12; Hollywood films of, 264n11; and inconsequentiality, 203; ironic distance in, 179, 264n8; late French period, 39; and lengthy tracking shots, 103; and love in films, 41, 175, 177–230; and marginalization, 180, 229; and materiality of cinematic medium, 220; as modernist, 178–80, 229; name changes, 229; and plot, 179, 183–89; and reality in films, 265–66nn33–34; and romantic love, 175; and shallow depths, 189–92; and source material, adaptations and repeated distortions of, 270n89; and suffocating interiors, 192, 199–200; and tight weave of compositions, 192; tracking shots, 178; as women's director, 178
optical unconscious, 141
Ordet (Dreyer film), 80
otherness, 45, 202
Oudart, Jean-Pierre, 11
Oxford, Mississippi, 12, 41, 132–33, 140, 172–73, 257nn9–10

Pagliero, Marcello, 173
Painted Veil, The (Boleslawski film), 24, 64
painting, still life, 239n51
Pallette, Eugene, 103
palliation: desire for, 22; psychic, and realism, 14
palliative etiologies, 26, 41, 168
Panofsky, Erwin, 109
Paramount Pictures Studio, 91, 102, 255n66
paratactical: causality, 169; experience, 22; language, 160; meditation,

228; relations, 20–21; structures, 8; theoretical infinitude of, 20
parataxis, 7–8, 20, 228
Paris Review, 141
Pasolini, Pier Paolo, 13, 141–42, 145, 236n13
Passing (Hall film), 85–87, *86*
Passing (Larsen novel), 49, 62, 65, 72, 85, 248n66
passing, cultural and racial, 44, 49, 62–65, 69–72, 75–76, 78–79, 85–87, 92, 248n66, 249n91
passion(s), 1–2, 11, 59–60, 119, 183, 192, 205, 216–19, 223–28, 267n52
patriarchal capitalism, 183, 203–4, 264–65n12
patriarchy, 69, 137–39, 156–57, 169, 182–83, 185, 202–3
Payne, Robert, 248n72
peeping tom genre, 260–61n85
Peirce, Charles Sanders, 140
perception, 161–62, 195, 225. *See also* apperception, spontaneous
Père Goriot (Balzac), 17, 24
persecution, 134, 154–56
Peterson, Dorothy, 43
Phelan, James, 15, 23, 45, 98, 262n111
Phillips, James, 99, 101
photographs and photography, 9, 141, 144, 182, 224–25
photoplay, 10
Photoplay magazine, 93, 252n10
physicality, 54, 56, 196
Pinky (Kazan film), 75
Piper, Adrian, 62
Pirandello, Luigi, 258n25
Plaisir, Le (Ophuls film), 179, 189, 199, 207
Plantinga, Carl, 228
"Playgoer's Almanac" (Barnes column), 92, 110, 253n13
plot: abandonment of, 2, 7; and aesthetics, 47, 191, 210, 216; affective investment in, 47; and arts of inconsequence, 15–22; and change, tracking of, 16; closural, 134; and

curation, 6–7; defined, 15–22; as demystification, 21; denunciation of, 157; and design, 6–7; as *discours*, 15–16; as dynamic force, 16; epic, 6; formal boundaries of, 46, 93–94; formal confines of, 202; formal constraints of, 93, 109, 134–35; as formal operations, 4–5, 134, 179–80; formal securities of, 36, 51; formal solace of, 89; functions and affordances of, 44–45; institutional development of, 150; kinetic, interpretive, and normative conception of, 15; life bereft of, 236n13; like life, 4; linear, 89, 128; mannered, 218; and modern media, 9; and movement, 15; and narratives of personal development, 45; normative limitations of, 93; and novels, 12; and order, 6–7; overtly synthetic quality of, 180; as paranoid form of sensemaking, 41; points, 96, 118; and polemical certainty, 5; political constraints of, 93–94; primacy of, 47; and progression, 15; refuge of, 122; retreat from, 5, 9, 19, 134, 137; retrospective ordering operation of, 53; and social climbing, 256n88; social constraints of, 93–94; spatial valences of, 18–19; and staccato jolts, 143; and thought, 42; and three-dimensional space, 48; tyranny of, 7, 90, 158, 244n4. *See also* emplotment
Plum Bun (Fauset), 62
Poetics (Aristotle), 15
Poetics of Prose, The (Todorov), 16
Political Unconscious, The (Jameson), 228
politics, 36–37, 90; aestheticization of, 20, 229; and ambivalence, 30; French, 219; gender, 133
Pollack, Mimi, 63, 248n72
polyphony, 221
Pomerance, Murray, 263–64n2
Porter, Cole, 101
Porton, Richard, 264n6

postcolonial studies, 46. *See also* colonialism
posthumanism, and antihumanism, 241n92
Postman, Neil, 237n21
postmodernism, 241n92, 251n5
Pound, Ezra, 46, 160
precarities, 45, 60, 136
presence, 24–26, 38, 65, 97, 113, 129, 134–41, 151, 155–62, 182, 227
present/presentness, 17–18, 41, 122, 238n44; limits of, 131–75
present tense, 135, 159–61, 163, 168–70, 173–74, 262n111
preterit (simple past tense), 60, 138, 157–58, 161–65, 167–68
Pride and Prejudice (Austen), 23
proairetic code, and action, 15, 120, 141–42, 186
productivity, Tayloristic measure of, 17
Professor Unrat (Mann novella), 111
Proust, Marcel, 6, 216
Przygodski, Paul von (fictional character), 127, 129
psychic unity, 47. *See also* narrative unity
Psycho (Hitchcock film), 103
psychoanalytic, 15, 29, 205
psychology, and causality, 6
pulp fiction, 132
purpose, one's sense of, 230

Queen Christina (film), 54, 64–65
queer: antinormativity, 40–41, 122; cinephilia, 255n75; love, 85; marginality, 89–90, 136; modernism, 40–41, 90; monogamy, 243n109; studies, 40, 45; subculture, 92; subject/subjectivity, 89–90, 120, 135
queer desire, 62, 65, 90, 119, 205
Queering the Underworld (Herring), 251n4
queer negativity, 40, 91, 93, 136
queerness, 90
queer theory, 40, 46, 205, 207, 241–42n92, 251n4

Quicksand (Larsen novel), 15, 20, 40, 46–53, 57–61, 76, 81–82, 89, 91, 96, 135–37, 172, 185, 247n56; as formal meditation on inconsequence, 47; and inability of experience to generate selfhood, 51; and inefficacy of possession, 51; as semiautobiographical bildungsroman, 44; serial narrative ruptures of, 82. *See also* Larsen, Nella

Quinada, Larry (fictional character), 199

Qur'an, vi

race, 63, 70, 72, 170
racial: exposure, 70, 72, 75; formation, 46; identification/identity, 40, 62, 66, 72; performances, 49, 70
racial passing, 62, 65, 69–70, 248n66, 249n91
racism, 31, 33, 99, 134
Rancière, Jacques, 7, 19–20, 158, 167, 239n47
Rashomon (Kurosawa), 177
Rastignac, Eugène de (fictional character), 4, 17, 24, 53, 121
rationality, 19–20
Ray, Robert B., 269n69
Reading for the Plot (Brooks), 15
realism: aesthetic, 8–9, 157, 175, 193, 212, 258n27, 263n140; and aesthetic illusion, 175; anti-, 138, 165, 168; Balzacian, 161; bourgeois, 8–9; causality, 168–70; cinematic, 212; classical film narrative, 14; classic literary, 14; dialectic of, 175; and fallacy, 109; and film, theory of, 269n69; form, 8; formal, 60, 160–61; French, 174, 178, 209; hapticity, 203; linear sequentiality of, 261n101; and linkage, 171; literary, 14, 24, 98, 221; narrative/narration, 7, 19, 33, 158, 160–61, 244n4; nineteenth-century, 14, 120; neo-, 173–75, 184, 192, 208–9, 263n140; novels, 28, 120, 246n29; paradigmatic formal, 161; plot, 7–8, 261n101; poetic, 174, 178, 209; and psychic palliation, 14; social, 209; and spatial form, 261n101; vestigial, 157
reality: and aesthetics, 261n89, 265–66n33; automatic capture of, 174; of characters, 25, 239n52; indexical impression of, 141; of love, 221; and modernism, 174; and narrative sense, 141; social, 146
Reckless Moment, A (Ophuls film), 264n11, 266n34
reclusion, 24, 39, 43, 48, 81–82, 110
Redfield, Irene (fictional character), 62, 72, 85–87
Regester, Charlene, 31
Reigl, Aloïs, 195
relationality, 9, 225, 242n92
Renoir, Jean, 174, 178, 209, 211–12
representation: and aesthetics, 20–22; cinematic/filmic, 25, 205; literary, 25–26; and logics of instrumental reason and conquest, 227–28; and modern discourse network, 162; and modernism, 258n27; and naturalism, 258n27; novelistic, 90, 94; queer, 136–37; and realism, 258n27; synecdochic, 130; and women, 264–65n12
Resnais, Alain, 46
rhizomatic configurations, 205
Rich, Adrienne, 89
Richardson, Brian, 237n19
Ricoeur, Paul, 13
risk: aesthetics of, 135; and uncertainty, 186
Rivette, Jacques, 207
Road to Glory, The (Hawks film), 171
Robbins, Bruce, 267n53
Robertson, John S., 132
Roderick Hudson (James), 3
romance dramas, 14, 26, 29, 65, 89, 120, 132, 175, 180, 182. *See also* love: romantic; love stories; melodramas
Rome, Open City (Rossellini film), neo-

realist World War II drama, 173–75, *174*, 209
Rome, Sydne, 127
Ronde, La (Ophuls film), 179, 186, 207–8, 220, 265n30
Roos, Bonnie, 120
Rossellini, Roberto, 173–75, 209
Roth, Joseph, 6
Roue, La (Gance film), 59
Rough Riders, The (Fleming film), 132
Rubempré, Lucien de (fictional character), 121, 161
Rules of the Game (Renoir), 212
Ruti, Mari, 40, 206–7, 241–42n92
Ryan, Robert, 199

Said, Edward, 46
"Sanctuary" (Larsen short story), 43
Sarris, Andrew, 264n8
Sartre, Jean-Paul, 13, 182
Sayeau, Michael, 19
Say It with Songs (film), 59
Scandinavians, 63, 92, 207
Scarlet Empress, The (von Sternberg film), 91–92, 102–9, *105*, *107*, *108*, 117
Schatz, Thomas, 171
Schell, Maximilian, 129–30
Schnitzler, Arthur, 179, 181, 183, 220
Schomburg, Arturo Alfonso, 243n105
Schoonover, Karl, 264n11, 266n34
screenplays, 39; as collaborative structure, 171; as corporate art, 171; as genre, 171
secrecy, 65, 75
security: material, 115; one's sense of, 230; of plot, 36; psychic, 36. *See also* torment, security of
self, attenuation of, 36, 182, 226–27
self-consciousness, 1–2, 24, 135, 178, 239n52, 247n56
self-destruction, 64, 134, 156, 162
self-effacement, 11, 26, 57, 171
selfhood, 18, 22, 26, 47, 51, 53, 59, 82, 219–20, 226, 242n92
self-possessed/possessing, 49, 57, 79, 81, 136, 206, 220–21

self-reflection, 5, 37, 172, 178
self-soothing, 12, 33, 47
semantics, 15, 58, 122, 141–42, 191
Semering, Baroness von (fictional character), 127, 129
semic codes, 120
semiology, 12, 140
semiotics, 131
Sentimental Education (Flaubert), 17
sentimentalism, 242n98
Sergeant York (Hawks film), 153, 260n76
sexism, 134
sexual violence, 46
Shakespeare criticism, 239n55
shame, gendered, 192, 202
Shanghai Express (von Sternberg film), 40, 91–92, 99–100, *100*, 103–4, 120
shattering, 28, 34, 45–47, 121
Sheik, The (Melford film), 132
Sherrard-Johnson, Cherene, 53, 249n94
shot-reverse shot editing, 11–12, 112–13
Shtupp, Lily von (fictional character), 101
Sicks, Kai Marcel, 57
Sieber, Rudolf, 110
Sight and Sound magazine, 178–79
significance: and causality, 16–17, 19; and consequence, 16–17, 128; deferred, 15, 61, 186; and irrelevance, 129; narrative, 134, 193–94, 196
Signora di tutti, La (Gotta novel), 179
Signora di tutti, La (Ophuls film), 179–81, 192–203, *194*, *195*, *197*, *201*, 208, 216, 218, 220, 267n45, 267nn50–51
silent films, 63, 111. *See also* sound film (talkies)
Silverman, Kaja, 264n8, 265n12
Sinclair, Joshua, 129–30
singularity/singulative, 18, 238–39n47; events, 16–17, 186; in narrative discourse, 16
Sirk, Douglas, 75
Sitney, P. Adams, 264n3
sjuzhet, 15–16
Skarsgård, Alexander, 85

Skin of the Film, The (Marks), 195
Slave Ship (Garnett film), 171
Smith, Bessie, 32
Sobchack, Vivian, 23–24, 223, 225
socioeconomics, 51, 74–76, 78, 81, 142
Song of Songs (Mamoulian film), 101
songs. *See* music
Sorel, Julien (fictional character), 16, 53
Sorrow and the Pity, The (Ophuls [son] film), 227
Soul Mates (Conway film), 132
sound. *See* aurality; diegetic sound; sound film (talkies); sound studies
Sound and the Fury, The (Faulkner), 15, 41, 133–38, 144, 153, 156–58, 165, 170, 172, 185, 218, 257n9, 261n95; formal experiments of, 131
sound film (talkies), 27, 63–64, 111. *See also* silent films
sound studies, and film music, 267n45
Souriau, Étienne, 267n45
spatial form, 2, 90, 95, 251n4, 261n101
spatiality/spatialization, 59, 143, 161, 187, 195–96, 261n101; and depths, 41, 56, 183, 188–92, 196, 202–3, 206, 208, 211–12
spectatorship, 13, 26, 28, 30–31, 36, 47, 49, 62, 143–44, 203, 241n80, 260–61n85
spectrality, 102
spontaneous apperception, 144–45
Stage Fright (Hitchcock film), 101
Stahl, John M., 75, 78
Staiger, Janet, 27, 242n100
Stanwyck, Barbara, 172
Star is Born, A (Cukor film), 128–29
St. Clair, Malcolm, 132
Stein, Gertrude, 6, 17–19, 29, 46, 122, 135, 141, 167, 238n44
Stein, Jean, 141
Stendhal, 16, 179, 181, 184, 216–19, 228, 269n74
Stewart, Garrett, 239n58
Stewart, Jacqueline Najuma, 31, 33, 48–49, 243n106

Stiller, Mauritz, 63, 248n72, 249n97
still life painting, 239n51
storytelling, 3, 5, 10, 28–29, 53, 102, 134, 146–47, 154, 156, 178, 240n59
straightness. *See* heterosexuality
Strange Likeness (Zhang), 21
Strawson, Galen, 13
structuralism, Barthesian, 15
Studlar, Gaylyn, 253–54n41, 254n61
stylistic lyricism, 93
subaltern studies, 38
subjectivity, 22, 46–50, 78–79, 203, 226; biracial female, 82, 135; contrapuntal, 46; and fragmentation, 46; majoritarian, 39; minoritarian, 39, 46; of modernist narrator, 161; political, 208; queer, 89–90, 120, 135; and relationality, 242n92; and unreliability, of modernist narrator, 161
subjugation, 46, 230
Submarine Patrol (Ford film), 172
substance abuse, 12, 43, 48, 81. *See also* alcoholism
suffering, 26, 34, 45, 60, 81, 93, 121, 124, 136–37, 168–69, 220, 224–25, 269n78
suicide, 59, 70, 136, 142, 151–52, 180, 199, 203, 226
Sundquist, Eric, 262n109
Sunset Boulevard (Wilder film), 128
Sutpen, Judith (fictional character), 129, 170
Swann's Way (Proust), 216
Swenson, Karen, 248nn71–72
synecdochic, 18, 180

talkies. *See* sound film (talkies)
Tanner, Laura E., 57
Tansley, Charles (fictional character), 20–21
Tate, Claudia, 248n66
tautology, 41, 168, 216. *See also* teleology
Tavlin, Zachary, 164, 261n97
Taylor, Frederick, 17
Taylor, Julie, 90, 97–98
Taylor, Robert: in *Camille*, 44, 77, 77–

78, 80; as man with perfect profile, 77, 78
technology, 9, 12, 79, 181, 196, 203, 252n12
teleology, 5, 8, 10, 17, 28–29, 58, 61, 90, 95, 111, 164, 205, 219. *See also* tautology
television studies, 36
telos, 18, 90, 93, 118–19, 123
temporality, 17, 58–59, 138, 143, 157–58, 160–61, 215
Temptress, The (Niblo silent film), 63, 64
Ten Commandments, The (Demille film), 132
Tenth Muse, The (Marcus), 48
Teskey, Gordon, 120
textuality, 20, 22–25, 40, 120–21, 124, 239n52; extra-, 24–25
Theatre Guild Magazine, 92
Theses on the Philosophy of History (Benjamin), 228
Thompson, Kristin, 27, 205
Thompson, Tessa, 85, *86*
Three Lives (Stein), 17–18
Timber Wolf, The (Van Dyke film), 132
Today We Live (Hawks film), 171, 172
Todorov, Tzvetan, 16, 72, 184–85
To Have and Have Not (Hawks film), 132, 171, 172
Tolstoy, Leo, 16
Toole, F. L., 133
Toomer, Jean, 6
topographies, 195, 201, 206, 261n101
Topsy (elephant), 146–50, *149*, 152–53
torment, security of, 40, 87, 89–125
Torrent, The (film), 63–64
To the Lighthouse (Woolf), 6, 20–21, 53; stillness in, 239n51
tour de force, 164, 183
Townsend, Nick (fictional character), 98, 117
traumatic dissociation, and neurosis, 45
Trentin, Filippo, 40, 91
Trial, The (Kafka), 17

trompe l'oeil, 109
tropes, grandiose, 146–47, 151
tropology, 61, 65, 167
Trotter, David, 13, 48, 239–40nn58–59
Truffaut, François, 207
turbulence, 43, 137–38
"Turnabout, The" (Faulkner short story), 172
Turvey, Malcolm, 240n62, 264n3
Tuskegee Institute (Tuskegee, Alabama), 51–52
Twentieth-Century Fox Studio, 171
Two-Faced Woman (film), 64

Ullback, Sylvia, 70
Ulysses (Joyce), 6, 261n101
uncertainty: aesthetics of, 90, 251n5; and risk, 186. *See also* certainty
Un chien andalou (Buñuel), 177
unconscious: optical, 141; spectral, 70
Understanding Media (McLuhan), 237n21
unfreedom, 5, 30, 182–83, 216
unity. *See* narrative unity; psychic unity
Univers filmique, L' (Souriau), 267n45
Unnameable, The (Beckett), 6
Ustinov, Peter, 266n34
Utell, Janine, 268n61
utopia, 192–94, 196–97, 199, 226–27, 228

vamp films, 64, 72
vampires, 70, 249n94
Van Dyke, W. S., 132
Vanity Fair magazine, 101
Van Vechten, Carl, 43
Variety, 112
Vayle, James (fictional character), 59
Verfremdungseffect (alienation effect), 2
Vertov, Dziga, 29, 102
Vichy-Nazi collusion, 227–29
victimhood/victimization: and dispossession, 156–57; and martyrdom, 139; narrative of, 153; narratives of, 41; and persecution, 134

Vidor, King, 113, 255n70
Vilmorin, Louise de, 183, 215, 219, 270n89
violence, 73, 156, 173, 230; colonial, 178; imperial, 181–82, 226–27; and narrative, 267n46; of Old South, 157; patriarchal, 182; and plot, 134, 175, 203; political, 178, 182–83; racialized, 226; racist, 134; sexist, 134
viscosity, 102
visibility, display of, 155
visual essentialism, 184
visuality, 192, 195–96; audio-, 198; narrative, 203
visualizing, 96–98
visual verisimilitude, 49, 189
Volck, George, 246n24
volition, 4, 101, 236n14
Volkbein, Felix (fictional character), 89, 94–95, 127–28, 135–36
Volkbein, Guido (fictional character), 94
von Sternberg, Josef, 40, 91–93, 99, 101–7, 109–11, 116, 120, 178, 220, 249n91, 255n66
Vote, Robin (fictional character), 40–41, 87, 89, 92–101, 106, 116, 118–24, 135–36, 167–68, 206, 253n39
voyeurism, 102–3, 107, 198
vulnerability, 34–35, 54, 75, 128, 163–64, 194, 221–23

Wademant, Annette, 270n89
Waid, Candace, 262n116
Waldron, Charles, 173
Walker, Kara, 43, 82
Walker, Rafael, 136, 246n34, 247n56, 250n1
Walkowitz, Rebecca, 30, 240–41n73
Warner, Michael, 8
Warner Brothers (Bros.) Studios, 171
Washington, Booker T., 51
Waste Land, The (Eliot), 261n101
Watt, Ian, 16
Weinstein, Philip, 135, 161, 168
well-being, 60

Western film genre, 132–33
Whatever Happened to Baby Jane? (Aldrich film), 128–29
White, Patricia, 114, 248–49n80, 255–56n75
White, Susan M., 180, 264–65nn11–12, 266n33
white beauty, 62–63, 82
whiteness, 10, 27–28, 31–32, 40, 50, 52, 62–64, 70–76, 79, 82, 111, 248n68; Anglo-Saxon, 62; hyper-, 63
white supremacy, 135, 138–39, 156–57
wholeness, 11, 26, 30, 35, 45, 52, 53, 175, 178
Wiene, Robert, 177
Wilder, Billy, 128
Wild Orchids (film), 64
Williams, Allan Larson, 266n33
Williams, J. D., 257n9
Williams, Raymond, 28, 237n21
Williams, R. X., 133
Wilson, Edmund, 2
Winkiel, Laura, 92
Winters, Ben, 267n45
Wittgenstein, Ludwig, 263n130
Woloch, Alex, 25–26, 239n55
women: biracial, 40, 60, 62, 82, 135–36; condition of, 180; dependence of, 154; and desire for freedom, 199; directors for and of, 178; exploited for commercial gain, 202; in history, 106; image in classical cinema, 265n12; as inconsequential, 202; and inequities, 154; lives of, 180; and marginality, 178; noir, 264n11; and patriarchal capitalism, 264–65n12; psychic destruction and othering of, 202; stories about, 178
Wong, Anna May, 103
Wood, Thelma, 13, 40, 87–93, 122–23
Woolf, Virginia, 3–4, 6–7, 20–21, 34, 38, 53, 90, 158, 167–68, 172, 236n13
working class, 10, 51, 63. *See also* middle class
"Work of Art" (Benjamin essay), 11, 229
World War I, 6, 67, 153

World War II, 173, 209
Wynter, Sylvia, 226, 241n92

Xiang, Zairong, 40, 91

Yu, Sun, 249n95

Zapruder, Abraham, 141
Zhang, Dora, 21, 98
Zichler, Hanns, 243n103
Zola, Émile, 2–3
Zucker, Carole, 105
Zweig, Stefan, 223–24